D1637291

AUTHOR'S EDITION

Albert Einstein noted that "the true value of a human being can be found in the desire to which he has attained liberation from self." Each of us defines our self by our values and associates. As Moliere noted, "Things only have the value that we give them." So in giving your interest to these concepts I can only say:

Life is a choice between conscience and convenience.

Thank you for being a leader who understands that the language of conscience is not words but the motivation of the heart, and for your part in creating a culture of character for today and tomorrow.

Gracias por ser un líder que entiende que la conciencia no se expresa con palabras pero con la motivación del corazón, y por su contribución en la creación de una cultura de carácter para hoy y mañana.

અંતરમાંથી આવતી અવાજ ફક્ત શબ્દો જ નથી પરંતુ હૃદયમાંથી આવતી પ્રેરણા છે એવું સમજવા માટે અને આજ અને ભવિષ્યનું ચારિત્ર્યનું ઘડતર કરવા માટે જે ફાળો તમે આપ્યો છે, એવા આગેવાન બનવા માટે આપનો આભાર.

תודה על היותך מנהיג שמבין כי שפת המצפון איננה מילים, אלא הנעה של הלב. ועל חלקך ביצירת תרבות האופי של היום ושל מחר.

अंतःकरण से आती आवाज़ केवल शब्द नहीं है, परंतु हृदय से उत्पन्न होती प्रेरणा है। ऐसी बोध शक्ति वाले नेता होने के लिए और, आज और कल के चारित्र्यबंधारण में योगदान के लिए आपका धन्यवाद।

شـــكرا لـــك لأنـــك قائد يعي أن لغة الضمير ليست كلمات ولكنها تحفيز القلوب، ولدورك في بناء ثقافة متميزة للحاضر وللمستقبل.

作为一位社区领袖，您深谙道德的理念不仅仅是宣传，更重要的是身体力行。我十分欣赏您对此问题的深刻理解，同时也十分感谢您为当代与未来创造一个具备鲜明特征的文化所做出的贡献。

"*The Wisdom of Generations* spotlights the moral hazards we all face in life as individuals and addresses the greatest global problems of the world. Skipper shows how both require great resistance to the lures of greed, irresponsibility, corruption, and the need to always stand on the rock of ethical responsibility for the greatest good."

—Bill Ide, Former President of the American Bar Association, Chairman of the Conference Board Governance Center

"*The Wisdom of Generations* is the defense of family values, integrity, and the necessity of institutions and corporations to adapt higher levels of governance, standards of competence, and responsible compassion if they are to protect market systems and what they can produce."

—Carlos Slim Helu, Honorary Chairman Carso Group, Mexico City, Mexico

"Consumers drive business, just as values drive society. Skipper Dippel has exposed a massive wound in our culture—a values-shift from conscience to convenience. He shows how, just as our economies have struggled from this shift, so will our cultural foundation. This book, *The Wisdom of Generations* presents a crystal clear message that should be consumed by every corporate leader who understands the impact and potential impact we can and should have in the community, in business, and throughout the world. This book exposes not only the lessons we learned in the past, but the path to economic, political, and cultural success in the future."

—Bill Fields, Chairman of Four Corners Sourcing and Board Chair of Lexmark International, Inc., Former President and CEO: Wal-Mart Stores, Inc, Blockbuster Entertainment Group - a division of Viacom, Factory 2-U Stores, Inc. and Hudson's Bay Company

The full length endorsements can be found on pages 423-432.

"This book, conceptually, empowers our future. *The Wisdom of Generations* forces us to think differently and more inclusively—honoring the cultures and histories of our past, and preparing for our future."

—Donna Deberry, Former Executive Vice President of Global Diversity & Corporate Affairs at Wyndham International and first Vice President of Global Diversity for Nike

"*The Wisdom of Generations* looks at the enduring significance of the values our nation was founded on – freedom, liberty and democracy. Skipper explores how those values have shaped our nation, and how critical they will be for our future. Skipper examines the rights and responsibilities created by the Founding Fathers in American economics, politics, and culture. His insightful findings will certainly have an immediate impact on the policy debates ongoing during this critical time for our nation."

—U.S. Congressman Pete Sessions (R-TX-32); Vice Chairman, House Rules Committee; Chairman, National Republican Congressional Committee

"The people rather than the political leaders determine our future by their actions or inactions. *The Wisdom of Generations* helps them understand the issues and challenges that face us as they make their decisions."

—Congressman John R. Carter, 31st District of Texas House Republican Conference Secretary House Appropriations Committee

"*The Wisdom of Generations* reminds us that character in a people is the ultimate strength of a society that makes it exceptional."

—Tom Neumann, Executive Director Jewish Institute of National Security Affairs

The full length endorsements can be found on pages 423-432.

"Ethics in legal and financial systems have been held under a microscope since the financial crisis. This book lifts the veil and reveals the impact our culture has on the perception of ethics, and the actions that follow. This is a framework and roadmap for any individual seriously-minded about such issues. And, ironically, in today's climate of corruption and greed, we all should be seriously-minded individuals about such issues."

—Dr. Gaytri Kachroo, Founder of the International Center for Corporate and Financial Ethics and Responsibility, Vice-Chair of the Global Alliance on the Madoff Case, International Financial Court appointee, and Principal of Kachroo Legal Services in Cambridge, MA

"The bridges built through Skipper's writings on conscience and common cultural values serve as a powerful advocacy of Western values to many of the critical nations of the future such as in China and Latin America."

—Representative Michael McCaul, House Homeland Security Committee, Chairman Subcommittee on Investigations and Oversight

"*The Wisdom of Generations* is bigger than a book. It's obvious to all that the world is in a state of transition. This book creates a foundation of thought that transcends boundaries, cultures, and politics. Tieman H. Dippel is the voice our world, our communities, and our perceptions need to initiate legitimate progress. He provides a framework of how to think, instead of what to think—a refreshing approach when so many powerful voices are intended on swaying thought or creating 'buy-in.' This book is for the serious minded individual, and the person who can truly understand that we are one world and one people."

—John Guerra, CEO, Aztec Worldwide Group, LTD. and the United Consumer Coalition, Former Managing Director, AT&T Caribbean & Latin America

The full length endorsements can be found on pages 423-432.

"Alfred Chandler, Jr. taught us the wisdom of studying business history as a management tool for progress and improvements. Thus, we must also understand that one day we will be standing on the decisions that we are making today. *The Wisdom of Generations* reveals how family values form the core of our culture. This book explains how those values guide our decisions—or should guide our decisions. We also learn what happens when those values are excluded from the decision-making process. Any serious-minded business, political, military or community leader should read this book. It is a must-read for anyone seeking to become a leader with a legacy—rather than just a boss."

—Ronald L. Loveless, Retired Walmart Executive/Founding CEO, Sam's Clubs, Business Consultant

"We cannot stop time. We can only manage it. Skipper Dippel brilliantly illustrates how time has told and will tell our story. Right now, this book is a reminder of our time. The generations to come will either reap the rewards of our conscience, or they'll be paralyzed by our convenience. *The Wisdom of Generations* is quite possibly the most timely today, and always will be."

—Ken May, Former CEO, FedEx Kinkos, Former Chairman of the Board of Trustees, March of Dimes Foundation

"America is better today because of Cesar Chavez; America will also be a better country because of the effects of Skipper's writings. We will always be friends because we know the depth of each other's motivation for our children's future, and motivation comes from the depths of the heart and mind."

—Dolores Huerta, Co-Founder, United Farm Workers Union

"Today, more than ever, we need to build a shared, borderless appreciation for the obligations between men and women to deal ethically as these obligations may be difficult or impossible to legally enforce."

—Charles I. Underhill, Former President of the Better Business Bureau of Western New York, retired Senior Vice President and COO of the Council of Better Business Bureaus, Senior Consultant, Council of Better Business Bureaus

The full length endorsements can be found on pages 423–432.

"A timely book that has inspired a new international dialog. Understanding the Language of Conscience provides not only an essential platform for examining the influence of comparative culture but even more a runway for rediscovering and relaunching the time tested ideas that reveal wisdom over folly and failure. Collective reflection and a culture of discernment is the key. In his most recent book *The Wisdom of Generations*, Tieman 'Skipper' Dippel, Jr. has insightfully provided a vital discourse equally applicable to human relations, law, education, business, government, economics, and international diplomacy in the pursuit of a more universal understanding of our common need for transcendent but practical ideals that are rooted in reality rather than the fantasy of failed political philosophies. Santayana warns that 'Those who forget the past are condemned to repeat it.' Dippel urges us to rediscover the past and chart a course for the future. It is no surprise that *The Wisdom of Generations* is influencing a new discussion between global leaders."

—Gordon Riddle Pennington, Managing Director of Burning Media Group, New York City, Former Director of Marketing at Tommy Hilfiger, advisor to the United States Council on Economic Development, board member @ charity: water and the Jonathan Edwards Center at Yale University

"Transparency is key to every great story. *The Wisdom of Generations* gives us a framework of values-based thought that is necessary in today's world—not so that we can tell a great story to future generations, but we can reveal a great truth."

—Richard Levick, President and CEO of Levick Strategic Solutions

"As a nation of laws, it's critical to understand that the values of our culture must be our guiding force. *The Wisdom of Generations* clearly shows us the realities of what happens when we let convenience over-ride conscience. This message has the power to change the world—but only if we act upon it."

—John Brown, Former Deputy Administrator of the Drug Enforcement Administration.

The full length endorsements can be found on pages 423-432.

"Technology is allowing us a glimpse at 'one world'. And, Skipper Dippel is giving us a roadmap to enter that world with a conscience. *The Wisdom of Generations* is a serious work. And, it will play a serious role in globalization."

**—Jay Elliot, Founder and CEO of Nuvel, Inc.,
Former Senior Vice President of Apple Computers,
Author of *The Steve Jobs Way*,
iLeadership for a New Generation and
author of an upcoming book *Leading Apple with Steve Jobs:
Management Lessons from a Controversial Leadership Genius***

"In *The Wisdom of Generations*, Skipper Dippel provides a compelling narrative of the diverse challenges of modern life. I highly recommend it to you, and to everyone who wishes to be enlightened."

—Dr. M. Ray Perryman, President and CEO, The Perryman Group Institute Distinguished Professor of Economic Theory and Method, International Institute for Advanced Studies

"In *The Wisdom of Generations*, Tieman Dippel, Jr. continues and advances the tradition of the great thinkers fathered by the ancient Greeks who have sought answers to these questions. In today's interrelated world of disparate cultures, how we address these issues has never been more relevant."

**—Paul O. Koether, Former Chairman
Pure World, Inc. and Kent Financial Services, Inc.**

"How do you build a strong corporate culture that lasts? The same way you build strong nations, vibrant communities, and healthy families. *The Wisdom of Generations* pinpoints a way of thinking that is often lost in the corporate world today—that when values are our guiding principles, we all win."

—Arte Nathan, Former Chief People Officer Wynn Hotels

The full length endorsements can be found on pages 423–432.

"Skipper Dippel's thoughtful focus on values as the basis of understanding our own and other cultures not only marks *The Wisdom of Generations* as humanistic in the best sense of the word but also provides direction for those who want to help create a world that is more harmonious, equitably competitive, and perhaps even wiser."

—Dennis M. Kratz, Dean, School of Arts and Humanities, University of Texas at Dallas

"The education of our children at any level, but particularly at the college level, must in some manner impart a sense of ethical behavior into their curriculum. *The Wisdom of the Generations* provides strong guidance into how this can be accomplished."

—Dr. Charles R. Matthews, Chancellor Emeritus, Texas State University System, and Former Chairman, Texas Railroad Commission

"I would recommend *The Wisdom of Generations* to all families who want their children not only to be successful, but to have a value-based satisfying life."

—Tony Chase, CEO, Chase-Source LP

"Skipper Dippel is an acknowledged leader and someone whose views are respected not only by those in the board rooms, but also in the public arena because with his depth of knowledge, he often challenges normal ways of thinking. Skipper has built a sound reputation among his peers and a great deal can be learned from *The Wisdom of Generations*."

—Milton Carroll, Chairman, CenterPoint Energy, Inc., and Chairman, Health Care Service Corporation

The full length endorsements can be found on pages 423-432.

"Skipper, "The Texas prophet of conscience," wisely realizes that Hispanics will not allow politicians to identify who we are. *The Wisdom of Generations* eloquently articulates our values—God, family, and serving others."

—Little Joe y la Familia

"This book is a MUST read for anyone who cares about America's future in the global world, our relationship with China and other countries. Skipper Dippel is a man of integrity, who exemplifies how respect and understanding of each other's history, culture and conscience is integral to peace, prosperity and success."

—Camille D. Miller, President/CEO, Texas Health Institute

"This book is valuable as a new way of thinking through the wisdom of values in the world, but, more importantly, it is a welcome cultural bridge in the modern world and the all important China-US relationship."

—Geoff Connor, Former Secretary of State of Texas

"This is the inspiration of the truly gifted! We are so fortunate to have Skipper's voice to hear and read."

—James Dick, Concert Pianist, Founder, Round Top Festival Institute

The full length endorsements can be found on pages 423-432.

Bill Ide
Former President of the American Bar Association
Chairman of the Conference
Board Governance Center

Lawyers have a significant appreciation of the fact that how you think about issues determines what you think about them. In this modern, rapidly changing world a perspective that organizes the significant amount of knowledge into usable decision making is critical—for your own life and for understanding how to teach the next generation. *The Wisdom of Generations* is equally appropriate to judging moral hazards we all face in life as individuals as it is in addressing the greatest global problems of the world—since both require great resistance to the lures of greed, irresponsibility, corruption, and the need to always stand on the rock of ethical responsibility for the greatest good.

The Wisdom of Generations focuses on the fact that economics and politics involve self-interests, while only culture involves values and as such should be the foundation of a society. Those values start with the family. Children are taught values—individual responsibility and how to think about issues, both equally important—by their parents and historically by their communities.

Skipper presents a set of ideas that have been called "Enlightened Conservatism" by political newsletters. These ideas have also been studied by groups as diverse as the Central Party School of the Communist Party. His point is that if individuals learn to appreciate the efficiencies of a free market system, but also the need to assure self-regulation driven by safeguards requiring ethical norms insisting that the greater good of the community be served, an innovative, investment driven, and competitive economy is created, assuring economic prosperity for all. The failure of business to have trust from the society that allows it to operate will lead to government regulation and less efficiencies. Trust is essential to building productive societies. As Skipper notes, politics and economics will only have productive outcomes if the right values and culture are in place to assure collective trust. It shows values and integrity to be strengths, not weakness. Such values are the ultimate defense of conscience over convenience.

THE WISDOM OF GENERATIONS

USING THE LESSONS OF HISTORY TO CREATE A VALUE-BASED FUTURE

SIXTH BOOK OF THE LANGUAGE OF CONSCIENCE EVOLUTION

TIEMAN H. DIPPEL, JR.

TEXAS PEACEMAKER PUBLICATIONS, L.L.C.

Copyright © 2012 by Tieman H. Dippel, Jr.

Published by Texas Peacemaker Publications, L.L.C.
Brenham, Texas

Distributed by Bookmasters, 30 Amberwood Parkway, Ashland, Ohio 44805
(800-537-6727)

Library of Congress Control Number: 2012941323

ISBN: 978-0-9829354-8-4

Printed in the United States of America

DEDICATION

Prominent in the U.S. Capitol is this clock with the statue of the Greek muse and Goddess of History, Clio. It is a thoughtful sculpture to those that understand it. Those who pass her threshold going about their daily actions tend to look at them through the scope of the current time. Daily items are the focus of news of the moment and seem significant now, but judged in the flow of history will they be? Clio instead is writing the history of the time from a perspective in the much more distant future that will have a very different opinion of what was important and what was not. Whether payroll taxes should be extended for two months or a year may seem significant now, but judged in the flow of history will it be?

The Wisdom of Generations learns from history, and it teaches you to think from a very different perspective about what is truly important. The great issues of our time will be whether we can find fiscal balances for the solvency of our nation, whether we can build the bridges necessary within the world, particularly with China, and most of all what culture we develop to address our many challenges. In my interpretation of the lessons of history, leaders and politics are very much secondary to the power of the people as they reflect it. How it is reflected in their sentiments depends on the culture and the way of thinking of the times. Are the commercial and political interests so dominant that the cultural values that served as the wisdom and conscience of society are minimized to the point that there is no longer the strength of character that sustains the nation and society? *The Wisdom of Generations*, in a nutshell, is that the success of any society or nation is directly related to its character, its will, and its educational wisdom based on core values. As they change or deteriorate, the fate of a nation may slowly deteriorate with them. If they are rebuilt and re-invigorated, the strength returns. Knowledge is different from the wisdom of how to use knowledge.

But that culture does not come as much from institutions as it does the way of thinking that the family teaches. If a culture is to change, it will in many ways happen only over time, and the place where values are most thoroughly transmitted is within the family. It is to history this book is dedicated, and secondarily to those who write that history by creating the cultural values that are important in preserving them. Each of us knows the sports heroes and media stars of our time, but they are not necessarily significant to the subsequent generations. What does survive us is how our children and grandchildren think because, like our DNA, our values are transmitted in the way we teach them to think and what we teach them to value. We must dedicate our focus to those that shaped our lives and to those lives we will shape if we wish to have an ultimate impact upon our society.

The success of their lives will also be determined by the public culture that surrounds them and the leaders that either inspire or limit them. To fully support them we must become the uncommon men who build a positive culture for dignity and opportunity.

A few years ago, I had a nine-generational chart of our ancestry prepared on both sides of our family. My parents had accumulated materials, as had my wife Kitty's parents. And it seemed appropriate that they be brought together in one consolidated book so, for the future, a great amount of information would not be lost. The resulting chart has significant impact if one studies it. You had two parents, but you had four grandparents, eight great grandparents, sixteen great, great grandparents, and thirty-two great, great, great grandparents. For your children, it is doubled because two lines are merged. In biology we look at the great diversity of DNA that produced our physical self. But it becomes equally important to realize that our inner values and our cultural being were also shaped by them. What each of them passed on to their children then eventually became part of the habits and values that we were taught by our direct parents.

What we owe to our ancestors is not just our existence, but also our perspective of life—even though we may not fully realize how our subconscious, our temperaments, our prejudgments, and many other factors are affected by our upbringing and theirs. Our satisfaction with life might be generally referred to as our concept of personal dignity and what is necessary to fulfill it. That view of what is a successful life and an acceptable level of personal dignity shapes a national character. Economics and politics matter, but ideals and values are ultimately the most important issues. These are what families teach. When they do, society orders itself with less government and more economic opportunity. When the family does not teach fundamental values, eventually the society weakens and the lack of personal dignity as defined by internal universal values emerges. God and nature, not government or economics, give us our ultimate sense of satisfaction and need. The fundamental lesson of history is that the culture shapes the law and government; the government does not create the culture, but tries to control it.

Our contemporaries in our generation shape our lives for they live life with us and experience the same levels of technology and concerns we do. Our lives are most affected by wives' and husbands' effect on each other. Yet the friends from childhood, from college, from business, and from social encounters all give us richer and broader lives and a more thorough understanding of each one of us that is quite different within the world. Many friends become like family because of common values, and you find that it is not just blood, but often perspectives of life that build a broader family of cultural values quite similar to the physical relationships. Your situation of close friends depends on your values and sense of dignity. They may be friends of conscience or acquaintances of convenience. In a world that is now global, these family cultural relationships are increasingly being built on a grander stage.

We must work with our contemporary generation to accept the responsibility and the cost that should be our burden to leave the world a better place for our children. The next generation is our responsibility. We cannot live their lives for them, but we must teach them to adapt to ever-changing and more difficult times. We must teach the values that are the mortar that holds their principles together and thus shape their approach to life. They need to understand that happiness in life may not be as material as is satisfaction. That satisfaction comes often not from what others think, but from how satisfied we are with ourselves in achieving our goals. We define dignity or satisfaction. Hopefully, both this generation and the next will focus on their children and their future as the most important legacy by which a life could be judged. For the second important lesson of history is to look at our times critically and not become lost in the moment. As we manage life, we need to remember the advice of Peter F. Drucker, "Management is doing things right, leadership is doing the right things."

A Personal Motivation

This book was written primarily for my children and grandchildren so that as my time in life diminishes, a more proper record could best be conveyed—like a nine-generational chart of values my ancestors passed forward to me. What have I learned in life that I can pass on to promote the ideals that I believe?

It is written in respect to my parents and ancestors who gave and shaped my life, and gave it meaning

To my contemporaries, I have also tried to reflect thoughts and ideas so that my cultural family, focusing on character instillation, can see the efforts that others have made. Because most of all, we have to provide our children with a contextual way of thinking that helps prioritize life for their success and their ability to work with others.

This book is a final installment of a series of works called *The Language of Conscience Evolution*. If there is a heart to the books, it rests in the fact that the advancement of civilization comes as parents teach their children not only what to do, but more importantly, how to do it well—and most significant of all, their motivation for doing it. The latter often determines the culture in which they live and how fulfilled they are in life. But they must understand the nature of the world and shape it or it will shape them.

Understanding Historical Power: The Core of Family Generations

The reality of the nature of politics is that it focuses on the short term because of the prospect of elections or popular stability. The reality of economics is that it ultimately focuses on long-term profitability trends that are given net present value but react to the policy that creates the trends. The reality of culture is that it is the power that balances the other two. If the culture accepts sacrifice rather than immediate gratification, long-term economic opportunity normally results in a strong middle class, but this requires that conscience dominate convenience—and the family is the key.

If you care about your children's future more than you do yourself, you will sacrifice with a strong will. However, the great problem of civilization is that people lose focus of the importance of conscience and do not pass it on to affect the balance of politics. This creates more destructive policies that do not address sustainability and add moral hazard. Good intentions for compassion that bring unintended bad results normally are the product of a failure to balance conscience's two-parts—compassion and obligation. Obligation is more complex, and its interpretation has to be fully understood.

The cultural ethics of a country will ultimately determine its viability, and today global competition will expedite forces. Cultural ethics means family values. The family is the bottom up training ground, but the top down influence of government impacts it. Individual responsibility has always been the key. The family teaches it as a showing of obligation and sets a tone of how to address risk and opportunity. The larger the government, the more risks it absorbs. But the more opportunity is sacrificed through the broader society as dependency replaces individual responsibility and lowers personal dignity, personal control is lost. The family adjusts to the environment of its time and remains the vehicle of relationship and responsibility. What needs be understood is that its values shape culture, which shapes government. When family cedes influence, broader society and government by not teaching values, responsibility, and character or demanding the same of society, family power fades and society loses strength.

The family is the Bridge Builder to the future and requires a concept of leadership to be in place. The family teaches conscience in that it is the closest of relationships. The essence of that conscience is the concept of the Bridge Builder, which passes the core of responsibility to the next generations. If Clio were to pick a proper recipient of the core passion that brings forward the best in history, I think she would suggest the proper dedication would be to the concept of the Budget. At no time in history has this been more important than in the current world.

THE CULTURE OF THE BRIDGE BUILDERS

In life we do some things because the law forces others and us to because, according to the Golden and Silver Rules, we owe it to each other. But our highest culture and development is when we, and our children, do things without expectations of gain, but because it is right—the culture of conscience.

This culture is best expressed by the concept of a Bridge Builder similar to Will Allen Dromgoole's poem by the same name. It tells the story of an older man who, even though it was of no personal benefit to him, took the time to build a bridge over a treacherous stream to benefit a less experienced youth that would follow. He had crossed the chasm but took the risk in his old age because he saw life beyond himself.

In every society or country there are men of conscience and convenience. The Bridge Builders are those who mentor and teach those that follow, not for personal gain but because it is right. They realize they do not lead to build a personal following for their achievements, but to inspire and build similar transformational leaders. This book is dedicated at its core to them, and has its length to teach them the experiences of many, far more experienced than I, in building the strongest of bridges that have to overcome the current raging torrents of convenience and its greed, envy, and hate. They often risk the reputation of a lifetime to leave an often unsure legacy.

Many times they find that their battle for conscience over convenience can work with others to transform society if they join forces to work on the same bridge and have the same thoughts on how it should be built. It is in them that the family values are strengthened in society. Because in all nations wise men understand:

The most durable and best cultural bridges are built, not upon the words and actions of men, but upon the honor and wisdom of their ancestors and the concern for the future of their children. For wise men understand that the lessons of history are also the strategic forces shaping destiny.

—Tieman H. Dippel, Jr.
Central Party School, Beijing, PRC
September 9, 2007

CONTENTS

FOREWORD

CONGRESSMAN KEVIN BRADY, 8TH DISTRICT OF TEXAS

The Wisdom of Generations is a very unique book in that while it is a father's final thoughts to his children and grandchildren, it also helps address the most significant issues we face today. *It does not tell you what to think, but it teaches you how to think contextually. It puts the world in a unique context for understanding and then defines the individual's place and obligations within it.* It acknowledges that there are two great forces—the force of change and the force of the status quo that is often the result of the power of history brought forth through culture. The balance between this change and the current status is one's concept of their personal dignity. Whether this sense of dignity is adjusted through elections or revolutions, it is how people perceive their control of life and their future—not only for themselves but also for their children and grandchildren.

One of my greatest concerns is to make sure that public policy looks at the big issues that make a significant difference to the nation's future, how to prioritize them and put them in context. The nation's current difficult financial situation is increasingly recognized and the necessity of avoiding moral hazard in policy is now more necessary than ever before as hard choices are made. The margin that America previously had is diminished by our financial challenges and the impact of future international competition. Not only do our domestic challenges create complexity but Europe's unstable financial balance, the Middle East's political instability, and the challenges of China's internal pressures on its growth model all create an environment that requires a very different set of organizing principles and method of thought than have currently been practiced in Washington.

Our current focus is the importance of Federalism and the limitation of the federal government in the lives of individuals with more control placed locally. Federalism is not only the recognition of State power but more importantly the reorganization of a limited government which keeps the individual and their dignity as the core of our Constitutional Republic. Domestically a distinction between the Midwest industrial model upon which much of the historical approach to our Federal government expansion (in the nature of the European state) has been based is compared to an alternative, the Texas Model. The former model looks more heavily to government expansion and to tax policy to fund growing government involvement in social programs and regulations. The Texas Model is based on a culture of growth with lower taxes, free trade, limited regulation, and a private sector business friendly environment. The bridge between these two concepts is difficult in partisan Washington. *The Wisdom of Generations* describes the Texas Model not economically, but culturally, which I feel is correct. Avoiding the political risks of moral hazard, so that government functions and is sustainable, requires an economic model for growth with innovation and ethical governance. Both require a value-based middle class with strong family values of responsibility and character. Skipper has been a scribe, thought catalyst, and driven proponent for the evolution of this Texas Model for over thirty years by arguing the necessity of its values and ethics-based core. It provides a new paradigm for how to look at our seemingly interrelated economic and political interest, by adding an ethics-based cultural decision base.

In doing so, this book bridges the values of the family and public policy for society. It teaches you how to raise successful children and in doing so how to formulate the culture of responsibility in a nation. He emphasizes that exceptionalism comes from existing values not past history. It must be recharged, and he explains how. The three great powers—economics, politics, and culture—all play a part and fit together in context. The future is about stimulating growth, maintaining sustainability of compassion, and making sacrifice acceptable by making it equitable in such a way that individual responsibility is enhanced and the Golden Rule better appreciated.

The greatest problem faced not only in Washington, but in much of the world, is how to bring people together, even if they disagree, to think through issues and try to find common ground. As Skipper points out not only in *The Wisdom of Generations,* but in the five previous books of *The*

Language of Conscience Evolution, economics and politics are often defined by self-interests, but culture involves values. It is far easier to unify people on trust and common values than it is to have people bargain for their individual goals. One is transformational while the other is transactional. Not only do we have to find the ability in America to unify and to work together if we are to succeed in our national interests, but we must also find common ground on which to work with our competitors in the rising undeveloped nations. These nations, particularly China and those in Latin America, will have a tremendous impact on our economy and our international political position. The modern world will be one where America will have to rely more and more on the power of its ideals and institutions of economics and culture which will be tempered by fundamental ethical principles that bring inclusion and fairness. The great issues of our time are the strategic ones, not necessarily the operational or technical ideas that are often the focus of our media and politics. This is a rare book that takes a family and its values of honor, respect, obligation, and sacrificial love as the base power of conscience and in turn develops a unifying set of concepts that change how we view the world. *The Wisdom of Generations* combines the best of a totally unique evolution of books that are the culmination of Skipper's wealth of wisdom and accomplishments.

The most unique recommendation of this book comes not from Skipper's many awards for philosophy, but the fact that Skipper's premier book, *The Language of Conscience,* was translated and published by the Press of the Central Party School of the Communist Party of China. It is unprecedented that a Western book be given the insignia of its Press. Since the Central Party School is the executive training institute of the leadership of the Party where ideology and strategy are discussed, this was a very unique distinction. Skipper's writings have been the pillars of a foundation of engagement with China based on common cultural values that will make economic and political discussions occur in a more positive environment. The book was described by the School as a bridge on ethics, morality, and cultural values.

It is important to understand why opposites are attracted by his ideas— Skipper is not a person of few principles who adjusts them to please diverse audiences, on the contrary his ideas are very well defined, and he has lived them throughout his life. He attracts the rich and the poor of economics, the right and the left of politics, because he is a magnet for those among them that choose conscience over convenience and who are driven to make a difference. He is a person a Congressman or a leader calls when the toughest decisions have to be made and they want an honest opinion of how a problem or issue needs to be analyzed. It is why two Speakers of the Texas House, strong adversaries, both joined in a Resolution to name him Texas Prophet of Conscience, why the Cesar Chavez Legacy and Educational Foundation would give its newly created Conscience Builder Award to a former President of the Texas State Chamber of Commerce and conservative author, and why China's most powerful institution would build a bridge through one of the West's most dedicated national defense hawks and defender of market systems. Skipper stands unquestionably for conscience and its components of obligation and compassion, and he is a magnet to similar strong leaders. One does not achieve such an image by displaying weakness or playing politics but by standing on character. It is a family history of extremes—his father is best remembered as one of the most influential Sheriffs of Texas by the Texas Peacemaker Award given by the Sheriffs' Association of Texas to the law enforcement officer who showed intensity and support of the community. His Mother is remembered by a fund giving Bibles and support to those incarcerated.

People do not identify with Skipper out of common interests, but join with him in a transformational effort that character is strength not weakness, values are a key to leadership, and unity comes from rising above self. Some call these the Texas Third Coast of Thought from his work with the Lyceum, others call them the principles of Enlightened Conservatism from his books, many of us who have worked with Skipper for many years on these efforts, agree with him that they are our individual and joint responsibilities to move civilization forward in a better form than we received it. He is clear they are not his ideas alone, but those of history and our generation for which he is an organizational scribe.

The Wisdom of Generations was primarily written as a guide to his children. As can be seen, the Dippel family has been guided by a set of principles passed down which are "reloaded" in each generation. It is thus a book that is of great value in raising your own children wherever you may live, because it teaches you the necessity of honor, of appreciating dignity and granting it, of a respect for family, and a commitment to the civic obligations that are a necessity for a functioning society. The book has two parts and an overriding purpose. The first section is a moral compass based on family values and responsibility to guide a life of purpose, the second section is a map to give perspective of how the world fits together to let you successfully navigate the past and understand our times—ultimately understanding the context of the use of the compass and map you seek and appreciate the magnetism of the pole of conscience while appreciating the competitive power of the pole of convenience.

It is a book that takes a great amount of knowledge and assembles it into a body of wisdom helping provide a perspective of how to think. You will never be the same after having read *The Wisdom of Generations* and you will find it has helped bring out the best in you and your children.

Note: Representative Brady is Vice Chairman of the Joint Economic Committee, Republican Deputy Whip, and Member of the House Ways and Means Committee (Chairman of Trade Subcommittee).

PREFACE

At 10:00 am on December 21, 2012, GMT the famed Mayan long count calendar will end at 13.0.0.0.0. There is re-alignment within the universe that is predictable to astronomers. Many modern interpretations make predictions about this date, but it may be accurate in that there will be a significant change in a cycle. At the end of 2012, the Chinese have selected new leadership, the American election will have been completed, Europe will have come to its decision point on unity, the Middle East revolutions will be changing centuries of tradition, and a host of other factors will have changed the existing world as it looks with more reality at circumstances and relationships. There will be great questions about the sustainability of many of the world's current systems and the recognition of an era of significant change that is about to occur. The Mayan history may be as good a place as any to look at the change since rather than the end of the world, their work reflects an appreciation of history and the ability to predict natural cycles. The world will not end, but the world as it has been structured will be significantly changing.

I had the opportunity to spend time in Mexico City's great Museum of Anthropology and appreciate the depth of the Mesoamerican Cultures. The great Mayan calendar was incredibly accurate using a focus on Venus and Mars. While much of their belief was metaphoric in nature and blended myth and history, they used cycles as ways to stop and re-evaluate the present and the future.

Cycles mark a beginning and an end with an organized progression within them. They may be short cycles within long cycles. The key is that they occur and at the end of one and the beginning of another, a society must rethink where it is, where it has been, and where it is going. It is the "New Year's Resolution" on a grand scale.

Our society has seen great change during the 5,125 year Mayan Long Count calendar that is now ending. Furthermore, in our last sixty years, the power of economics, politics, and culture have become much stronger in society. We saw a cycle of politics in the 1960s as market economics battled centralized planning with leaders like Kennedy, Johnson, Khrushchev, Brezhnev, and Mao.

The emergence of Western technology, computers, and communication—gave an advantage to markets and gave precedence to the power cycle of economics with Reagan, Thatcher, Gorbachev, and Deng remaking their societies. Milton Friedman's work and the Chicago School of Economics provided much of the intellectual vision of free markets. The recent cycle has been the movement from economics to the power of culture, while terrorism, lack of responsibility, fraud, greed, and other vices have led, with the leverage of finance, to our worst recession since the Depression.

But today, at the start of 2012, we see the critical mortar of our current global system beginning to crack. Europe is shattering from the unsustainability of its welfare programs as well as sovereign and private debt. America is suffering a huge imbalance due to its credit driven economy and debt, which restricts its position as the consumer of last resort. In the West the 60 plus year debt super cycle is coming to an end with austerity becoming necessary. China has grown by production and export and that model is not sustainable so it must develop more internal consumption since Europe and America are retrenching. The Middle East and its impact on oil reserves, which affects all three of the above, is changing and modernizing the leadership and cultural model but will go through difficult stages. The past is history, but the three great powers of economics, politics, and culture are entering a new global stage reshuffling. No outcome is known, only the risks and opportunities. There can be deterioration or rebirth, and many of these issues rest in our collective hands.

If 2012 is appropriately a time of cultural rethinking and cyclical rebirth, we would do well to study history and remember Scottish historian, Sir Alex Tyler's observations on Democracies in *On Athens* circa 1787:

From Bondage to Spiritual Faith
From Spiritual Faith to Great Courage
From Courage to Liberty

From Liberty to Abundance
From Abundance to Selfishness
From Selfishness to Complacency
From Complacency to Apathy
From Apathy to Dependence
From Dependence back to Bondage

Each stage marked a change in how a society viewed its collective "personal dignity." Today, each nation finds itself in a different situation but interconnected as a global world as never before. As the United States recedes from the global support it has given to rebuild its own resources, whether or not civilization unifies on values will determine whether the world finds common conscience and wills or deteriorates into a much more dangerous place dominated by individual conveniences.

Rome gives us the same lessons as Athens, and while many different causes of decline are described, the one I feel is most accurate was best described by historian Lewis Mumford in *The Condition of Man*. Thomas Friedman quoted this description in a column as one that gave him a shiver down his spine:

> *Everyone aimed at security; no one accepted responsibility. What was plainly lacking, long before the barbarian invasions had done their work, long before economic deteriorations became serious, was an inner go. Rome's life was now an imitation of life, a mere hanging on. It was the watch work—as if life knew any other stability than through constant change or any form of security except through a constant willingness to take risks.*

What America, as well as much of the rest of the world is rapidly losing is what I commonly call *The Language of Conscience*, an organizing principle and source of common discipline that acts beyond the law. Its components are more known by the inner self of conscience as:

Character / Humility
Individual Responsibility and Honor
Morality (Concern for Others and the Future)

Obedience to the Golden Rule / Fairness

Appreciation of the Common Good

Respect for Individual Dignity

Respect for the Rule of Law / Justice

Recognition of Obligation

Recognition of Charity / Compassion

The Emotions of Love, Trust, and Faith

While the words are in some ways synonymous, they cumulatively describe a way of life that is less material and more reasoned—thereby, for most, more satisfying. They are the components of the "Personal Dignity" of conscience.

The Language of Conscience has been replaced slowly but surely by a Language of Convenience, which has a powerful and reactive set of forces:

Intense Personal Self-Interest

Concern only for the Immediate

Materialism / Greed

Arrogance / Pursuit of Power

Use of Law for Personal Gain

The Emotions of Envy and Hate

Far more attributes could be added to either, but the points are defined. Moral hazard is the replacement of conscience with often hidden convenience in our modern society.

To change direction, you do not just switch political parties or leaders; you have to define a transformational set of ideas and have them fit in context, support each other, and serve as a way of thinking about how society should operate. Having lists and sets of rules matters little if you do not think properly. Most of history is usually revisionist as biased parties model facts to their interest. A transformational method of thinking cannot set all values because we are far too different. It can, however, set some basic values of how we judge fairness and how we see the critical goals of growing a bigger slice of life's pie for all rather than arguing over how a shrinking pie is divided.

Politicians do not change that; the culture of a people determines their future. America's future will be critically discussed in the proverbial 2012 when the Presidential election will set our nation on one of several possible paths. China, the other rising power, will have to make similar decisions at approximately the same time as its leadership is passed forward. Europe will redefine its vision of itself.

We have a world in rapid change but with structures in place, which represent the status quo from history that culture has moved to the current period. Therefore, we have to think carefully about how we restore the "driving force" of a civilization before it is lost—a civilization that is not just national but has international implications as well.

Several years past, the U.S. Naval War College had a superb presentation that originated as a "Conversation with the Country" as an explanation of American Maritime strategy. It shows the need for global cooperation, as does the work of China's Central Party School in developing an understanding for a conceptual "World Harmonious Society." Both countries, and most of the world, recognize not just global interrelationship, but shrinking resources and common problems. Current vehicles are stressed and will be more so as time and global imbalances progress.

But politics, with its nationalism, and economics, with its national self-economic interest are difficult to bridge. So to find organizational principles, the key has to be the values of culture and the choice or battle between conscience and convenience. Each society will have those within it who operate either for the common good and the future or for personal benefit now. Which one succeeds depends on whether the society values the future family enough to sacrifice. If so, the political result is that every generation pays its own way. The economics change—we have to limit materialism to save for the future and place a different value on our lives and possessions. Then culture changes to reflect a rebirth of the values of obligation and compassion within a society, and our worldview changes from each of us as the center of our own world to how we fit into society as a whole. Yes, we could use convenience to just benefit our family, but what type family would it ultimately be?

The French Revolution had the principles of equality, fraternity, and liberty. Liberty was a balance of the individualism of equality and the common good of fraternity. But the balance takes place in the values of the culture. Frederick Bastiat noted in his fine book *The Law,* that it is not the law that gives the culture, but the culture that gives the law. Edmund Burke in his observations of the French Revolution also noted that society is not a mechanism that could easily be changed independently, but was instead more like an organism where many things were interrelated. So, how you think about change matters. The thought process is crucial for leaders, but the values must be simple and clear so that those who follow them are not misled in a world of tortured facts.

This is the sixth book in *The Language of Conscience Evolution*. It chronicles the logic and history of the development, through many people and venues, of a method of thought that supports ethics, individual dignity, and the common good. It concentrates on forces and powers in societies and how to focus them to support cultural conscience and appreciate its value. *The New Legacy,* the first in the evolution, was written in 1986 as a result of the experiences in the formation of The Texas Lyceum. Other books, *The Language of Conscience, Instilling Values in Transcending Generations, Understanding Enlightened Conservatism: Granting Others the Same Dignities and Rights You Expect Personally*, and finally, *The Essentials of The Language of Conscience,* as a reference, have developed the basic concept. The history is available at www.thelanguageofconscience.com. The evolution has involved an evolution of thought from what is truly important to the concepts of understanding the force and power of morality and how it can best be expanded as a transformational force. History shows that little sacrifice occurs unless there is crisis, but having thoughtful options available in crisis is invaluable. The friction between change and the status quo of history is kept in balance by one's view of his *personal dignity*—what he thinks about his state in the world. Enlightened Conservatism is the family values approach to this concept of dignity or purpose and place in life.

This book simply takes the fundamental truth of conscience—The Golden Rule as taught by family values—and uses it as the basic leverage point in suggesting how discussions of change need to be focused. Conscience basically comes from a concern for others and the future, usually because of love of family, so it is where the evolution begins and ends. These will be my last words of guidance for my family as I pass on what I have learned in life. However, I think they resonate with many cultures where conscience is valued. In developing a method of thought, it is important to distinguish between telling others what to think, as opposed to how to think well. The purpose of this book is clarity of thought, but it includes your family values and how you think determines what you think. René Descartes in his 1637, Discours de la Methods said it best, "My aim is not to teach the method that everyone ought to follow in order to conduct his reason well, but solely to reveal how I have tried to conduct my own." Enlightened Conservatism is a contextual reasoning process using the fundamental values of The Language of Conscience. Some will fault it because it relies on a value-based system of organized thought, but it should be appreciated for the strength of bringing a conscience-oriented compassion to current convenience dominated theories. You can decide both how you wish to think and how well, but here is our family thought process.

I will begin with a few quotes as preparatory thoughts for examining life to help our children—mine and yours—gain perspective. Each has the merit of a great thought; the numbers show how many individual thoughts and issues exist. Our challenge is to find the best method to organize them all for effect. These lessons of history are like shotgun pellets with limited distance in the modern world unless we find a way to convert them to a rifle bullet and learn how to aim the rifle.

> *When I was a boy of fourteen, my father was so ignorant I could barely stand to have the old man around. But when I got to be twenty-one, I was astonished how much the old man had learned in seven years.*
>
> —Mark Twain

> *Life is an instinct for growth, for survival, for the accumulation of forces, for power.*
>
> —Friedrich W. Nietzsche

> *A living being seeks, above all, to discharge its strength. Life is will to power.*
>
> —Friedrich W. Nietzsche

> *Life is really simple, but men insist on making it complicated.*
>
> —Confucius

> *The best sermons are lived, not preached.*
>
> —Some country farmer

> *The tragedy of life is not that it ends so soon, but that we wait so long to begin it.*
>
> —Anonymous

How many cares one loses when one decides not to be something but to be someone.

—Coco Chanel

If each of us can be helped by science to live a hundred years, what will it profit us if our hates and fears, our loneliness and our remorse will not permit us to enjoy them.

—David Neiswanger

If there must be trouble, let it be in my day, that my child may have peace.

—Thomas Paine

The superior man . . . does not set his mind either for anything, or against anything; what is right will follow.

—Confucius

Wisdom begins in wonder.

—Socrates

He who asks of life nothing but the improvement of his own nature . . . is less liable than anyone else to miss and waste life.

—Henri Frederic Amiel

It was Thomas Edison who brought us electricity, not the Sierra Club. It was the Wright brothers who got us off the ground, not the Federal Aviation Administration. It was Henry Ford who ended the isolation of millions of Americans by making the automobile affordable, not Ralph Nader. Those who have helped the poor the most have not been those who have gone around loudly expressing "compassion" for the poor, but those who found ways to make industry more productive and distribution more efficient, so that the poor of today can afford things that the affluent of yesterday could only dream about.

—Thomas Sowell

Life is given to us; we earn it by giving it.

—Rabindranath Tagore

Our life is what our thoughts make it.

—Marcus Aurelius Antoninus

A good name is more desirable than great riches; to be esteemed is better than silver or gold.

—Proverbs 22:1 The Holy Bible (NIV)

Among a people generally corrupt, liberty cannot long exist.

—Edmund Burke

Freedom is a fragile thing and is never more than one generation away from extinction. It is not ours by inheritance; it must be fought for and defended constantly by each generation, for it comes only once to a people.

—Governor Ronald Reagan January 5, 1967

Timing is less important than geographical advantage, and geographical advantage is less important than human unity.

—Mencius

The history of mankind is a perennial tragedy; for the highest ideals which the individual may project are ideals which he can never realize in social and collective terms.

—Reinhold Niebuhr

Watch out! Be on your guard against all kinds of greed; a man's life does not consist in the abundance of his possessions.

—Luke 12:15

The greatest use of a life is to spend it on something that will outlast it.

—William James

The ultimate test of a moral society is the kind of world it leaves to its children.

—Dietrich Bonhoeffer

Kites rise highest against the wind – not with it.

—Winston Churchill

History also has its lessons that reappear. The great philosophies and religions began thousands of years past in what is termed the Axial Age. They were not only moral codes but also organizational guidelines to more structured societies. In a more simple time they asked the question—what is the most important organizing principle of societies toward which we must work? They dealt largely with culture, realizing that economics and politics would follow. Most like Christianity and the Analects of Confucius focused on the reciprocity of the "Golden" and "Silver" Rules as a core. One of the questions of history and the Enlightenment was the degree that value systems ought to be a part. Some like Aristotle, and I think Confucius in that he phrased the superior man as conversant with righteousness, logically began with the belief you had to have virtues to guide you. In more modern times the belief that the existence of knowledge and reason should make thought systems more neutral so individuals had a freedom to choose for themselves. I believe Emmanuel Kent argued this best. He looked at values as traditions and modern reasoning gave power to the individual. This is the question of "whose values to teach" if any at all. The Language of Conscience concept starts with a recognition of the need for values, but tries to apply how reason should both appreciate and judge them. It understands Jeremy Bertham's and John Stewart Mill's utilitarian approach to maximize the greatest benefit for the greatest number—what we would call "The Common Good." But today reason is increasingly based in the modern world on the self-interests of politics and economics; only culture systems with values can unify people. So these concepts plead guilty to being value-based. But the common goal is found in unity and unified actions and only values set a framework sufficient to civilize society. Ambition of politics and self-interests of economics are individualized.

If today we want a society where each of us grants to others a cultural system with the same rights and personal dignity we wish for ourselves, then we will also want an economic system with maximum opportunity for our children and a political system of efficiency and justice. These are found by family values dictating to government, not from the over-powering government dictating to family. We must find unity in a diverse world that is transformational, often of non-sustainable compromises. That requires a movement over long periods of time—not a sudden moment. But a conversion to reality is often provided by the crises of reality. This book is my explanation to my children and grandchildren of how to prepare for and think about the issues that will affect them. The quotations all have truth, some appreciated only as you travel life's journey. The secret is for parents to give a skeleton of wisdom onto which ideas and experiences can be placed in an accurate manner. It serves the child and the future family well, but also changes society. If you agree with the method, I hope it helps you. If you find merit in it, adapt it to your own values. If you find little value, then write your own method. But society is at a stage where it hungers for new ideas to establish opportunity and stability, rather than criticize, and to create a dialectic that may improve both. This is a system of reason that is dynamic and requires the challenging of ideas to bring unity to action. It is not presented as a rigid set of beliefs but a value-based way of thinking that shows dignity to other concepts but endeavors to create a stout defense of its own. That regrettably leads to length and complexity, for which I apologize in advance, but if you have chosen this book, yours is a serious mind and you are owed no less.

INTRODUCTION

It was a very cold morning as Kitty and I drove the fifty miles to the Medical Center in College Station, Texas, to be a part of the arrival of our fifth grandchild. It was an interesting occurrence because it happened on my Mother's birthday and almost exactly one hundred years from my father's birth. The name our grandson was given was Tieman H. Dippel, IV that followed a progression of four generations almost exactly within one hundred years. It was a rare symmetry brought into focus by the fact that I had just passed into my 64th year and now as the patriarch of the family and perhaps the next in line to depart, as a new generation came forth. My father died at 61, his father at approximately the same age, and my other grandfather at 42. Hopefully, not smoking, focus on nutrition although great quantities of food, and at least limited exercise will extend me awhile longer. But the loss of friends and close relatives brings a unique focus to life both at its end and beginning. What you learn on its journey and the choices you make define you.

I could not help but think back less than a month before when I attended the funeral of our friend Rosie Graves. Rosie had described herself as our housekeeper and maid, but we looked upon her as a vital part of our family. She had come thirty-five years earlier, immediately after the birth of our first child, Meg, and had been a part of everything that we had done over that period of time. Her loss seemed the closing of an era. Things would never be quite the same again.

Because of the closeness of our relationship with her and with her family and children, we were included at her funeral as part of the family in every aspect—from viewing to grieving. The bulletin at the funeral had an Anglo hand and an African-American hand put together in prayer and was kind enough to include a picture of our family with a note to us that said, "I am still here."

Her funeral was a more typical African-American celebration of life with a broader participation from all of the children and a number of Ministers. Her son Benny had put together a most appropriate service for her that gave not only the specifics but captured her personality, which was unique. As the Minister said in the obituary, there was only one Rosie, she would tell you exactly as she felt it was. While our entire family sat there in a front pew, I could not help but think of the funerals of so many—my mother's and my father's so many years past, the Lee family in San Francisco. All the funerals were quite different. The Asian funeral of the Lee's was very solemn contemplating and showed a great degree of grief and loss. My parents' funerals had been the more formalized Methodist approach of saying farewell. In Mexico it was Catholic and more ritualistic. Each was from a different culture, but each showed the very depths of the power of family at its best. Because each brought an appreciation of what was truly important in life and as such helped strengthen those there as they moved forward. All humanity has some things in common and the emotion of certain crystallizing moments grasps the important things of life. A cycle of life had ended.

As Rosie's funeral proceeded, they told of different stories over the years and talked of all of her flowered hats. Rosie had been to our children's graduations and weddings. She had helped rear all of our children and even helped with our grandchildren. She was deeply loved by all members of the family and she truly loved all of us.

At the Lee family funeral in San Francisco, the grieving was also intense but reflected differently. A Chinese Han ceremony lasts over 49 days, with prayer services held every seven or ten days until the family burial. Family members and close friends are expected to participate in each. They are very quiet ceremonies where people give thanks for the contributions of the deceased and ask forgiveness for transgressions. Mourners are positioned around the coffin by rank in the family. It is a very serious and reflective time of meditation—for the most part, in silence. It shows the intense depth of the family relationships through the expression of grief. Some funerals have formality, but not the intensity I saw in this funeral. The core of the family and its values are often most obvious at these times. After a burial procession, a wake must be at least one day for the offering of prayer. All clothing worn by the mourners is burned after the funeral to avoid the bad luck associated with death. The mourning period symbolized by a piece of colored cloth worn on the sleeve lasts for another 100 days. It is a time of family reflection.

Although I have never attended a Jewish funeral, it has been proscribed rituals where mourning includes only the nearest relations. It has been described to me as an effort to bring together the family for a shared experience of mourning, support, consolation, love, sharing, and memory. For seven days the immediate family is together, and then the rituals force the family to begin looking beyond their immediate relations and home and return to normal, productive life. However, they continue to share the experience and obligation to honor the deceased through saying *Kaddish*—yet doing so in the context of the larger Jewish community. In essence, while the basic building unit of the Jewish people is the family unit, it is contextualized within the greater community—as we are all one family. The love and embrace of an immediate family is transferred after seven days to the larger family of synagogue and community. This seems to be common in all family units.

The interesting thing is that we were totally different in our back-grounds, in economic situations, and in the ways we looked at life. Whether the funeral is African-American, Asian, Mexican, Jewish, or Methodist, we are very much alike. We show grief and respect differently, but the intensity of strong family bonds and love is the same.

Rosie was a very independent person who chose her own employer, and she gave us a couple of weeks as a trial run in the beginning. When I tried to do additional things for her like health insurance, she had her own approach. She did not want charity and insisted on having the dignity of being certain that whatever was done was fair. Integrity, responsibility, and honor were what she taught her kids and in part, my kids. Our children often played together. We had many more similarities than circumstances might suggest when you looked at our core family values and how much family meant to us. Family is the bonding tie, the values passed forward if it is strong, and the core of any society or nation. As it is strengthened or weakened ultimately so goes the society. A strong family teaches the fairness of the Golden Rule and the fraternity of getting along with others—you have a place in the world, but the world does not revolve around you. For a strong family both are natural components. So is an understanding of the family's common good and what it means to all. This is what sets the stage for the common cultural values, which define our society.

The question in my mind that morning at the hospital after Tieman IV was born was, "What type life would he see, and what culture would be predominate as time moved forward?" At thirty-year intervals the generations had proceeded. Dad was born in 1910, a different era that saw World War I, World War II, and the Great Depression. He went by the nickname of "Dip." I came along in 1945 as Junior, and my sister Deanna nicknamed me "Skipper." My son, Tieman III, came along in 1976 and got the nickname "Tee," and Tieman IV was officially nicknamed "Ty." We appear to be a family of nickname aliases with "Kitty," "Buffy," "Meg," "Cutie," and a host of others. Even our dogs and cats didn't go by their original names. That is the culture of Texas.

With Ty another generation began. And already it was in a far different state because of the tremendous amount of technology, not just in the hospital room, but the baby monitors, Kindles, cell phones, and PDAs, many of which were announcing his birth. On the other hand, there were a great number of characteristics in what was occurring that would have been very much the same at my father's birth. Family matters and the values and cultures it passes down as a legacy become one of the most important components of an individual's life and subsequently how society functions. The national financial debt our generation has saddled him with would be a financial burden to his independence and opportunity even though it would be years before he directly felt and appreciated it. Family is not just about giving life; it is about the quality of the life they live in future generations. It is about whether you have convenience to do the most for yourself presently at the expense of the future or whether you have family conscience to take less and try to give more for their future.

Family is the unit through which the vast majority of values are passed more than the individual alone. As stated in the Preface, the French Revolution had three dominant themes: equality, fraternity, and liberty. The important point is that equality deals with the individual and fraternity deals with the group. They have to be in balance for you to truly have liberty, and the family is the component that builds and teaches fraternity. You individually are important, but not exclusively. The fact that you need help in your early years instills this reality, and that you must give help in the future is instilled depending on your family situation. You are part of something, and you must appreciate that. When you consider only yourself, your decisions become "selfishly convenient."

In considering the effect on others, you learn the sharing of obligations and compassion of conscience. Its lessons, values, and the strength with which the family stays together make a huge difference in the success of all of the component parts. Each generation has to teach the next a set of values both in word and by example if it wants to fulfill its obligation in moving civilization forward. No matter the culture, religion, economic status, gender, or race, family is a natural entity. But it is directly affected by whether or not each generation does its part. It gives the dignity of belonging to something greater than self. The ultimate goal of the family is to leave a world where personal dignity is assured, and to teach that it is the next generation's responsibility to provide as well. *The culture of the future is the power of history in what values it brings forward.*

The question as my time wanes and Ty's is just beginning is, "What guidance message should I pass on to him?" As a grandparent what I can give is my perspective over a longer period of time. What has been the legacy of the family values and how have they changed? The values well taught became habits and that can greatly benefit him by incorporating experience. The place to start would probably be to convey to Ty the last conversation I had with my father summarizing the principles he taught me in my early years, many of which came from his father, Henry W. Dippel.

As I was returning to the Unites States Navy after Christmas leave in 1971 with the War in Vietnam setting much of the tone of the year, he gave me a "summation" of what he and Mother had taught over the years. What his father had taught him. His last conversation with me, three weeks before he turned worse begins in Chapter I in One Father's Last Words on page 3.

PART ONE

The Family Must Set the Moral Compass

from whence our values and thus wisdom come.

1 | SETTING THE STAGE

ONE FATHER'S LAST WORDS

"Now, I don't want you to worry about me. I will get over this as I have survived everything else. But just in case something unexpected should happen to me, I want you to take charge. Don't let the family dwell upon it. Time and life go on. I have been fortunate to be able to live my life as a lion. Two weeks of that is worth a lifetime as a lamb.

"I chose to keep our family in Brenham and Texas, rather than going to other places and trying new opportunities. That might have been more profitable, but Brenham still holds the values that first brought your great grandfather to the state almost 100 years ago. Some of these values will change, but most will remain the same as they have throughout history. It is important to remember that no matter how they try in Congress, they cannot repeal the law of gravity. God's laws and natural laws are the ultimate power in this world. Some people may only discover them after a lifetime, but they do exist. Recognizing them is critical.

"The most important thing I can leave you is a good name, and I think I have done that. Your mother and I have worked and saved a long time to create this beginning for you and your sister. Home has always been the most important part of our lives and should be yours. We hope we have taught you the importance of our values and passed along our heritage. You have an education that will help you achieve what is really important in life—being a responsible citizen, loving husband, and sensitive father. There may be more to living, but these three areas can make your life deeply satisfying.

"What I feel I will be leaving you is an opportunity—a start from which you can make your own mark. The time that we spend on earth is relatively small in comparison with the great movement of history. All we can do within our life span is to make the world better than it was when we first arrived. All fortunes eventually are dispersed, but the ideas and values that you leave to society can live forever. I hope you and Kitty will have a wonderful family, just as your mother and I had with you and Deanna. Being a good father is your greatest challenge and The New Legacy responsibility. Teach your children the ideals you think are proper. Give them the best values that you can. And teach them how to judge what is best for their lives and nation. We must try to make every generation's character better than the one before it and build a higher standard of living through wise policies.

"Don't underestimate the power and value of ideas, politics, and money. But never let any of these be your God. Learn to acquire and use them, but make absolutely certain that you understand the purposes for which they are being used.

"Lots of things have changed in Texas since I was a young man, and they will continue to change even faster during the next 20 years as your generation assumes leadership. You will need to keep a clear sense of what's important. I remember hearing how my dad came to Texas from Germany. Whenever a family suffered a bad harvest or business disaster, their neighbors helped them out until they were able to get back on their feet again. Now it seems that everyone is out for his own piece of the pie regardless of who else starves. There is still charity, but people are sometimes too busy to hear their consciences. Too often even charity itself is commercialized; but if a dime out of each dollar reaches the needy, it is worth our efforts.

"Life is already different from a few years ago. I'm worried about the way politics is changing. People don't know their leaders personally. They don't seem to have the same respect as they did in my day for the ideas that made America strong. Texas can have great impact on our country. But as Texans, we can either mature and bring our ideas to other Americans or we can create a petty state that will be defeated by partisanship. If that happens, we will make little difference.

"I have hope that you and other young people can understand the changes occurring in politics and economics and how they affect you. Then you'll be able to handle them. In the process, you'll turn Texas and America in a more positive direction again.

"Remember to associate with people who care more about whether they go to Heaven or Hell than whether they become Governor of Texas or head of a company. Ambition can be your worst enemy. Often you are not a good leader until you have lost your ambition and come face to face with what is most important in life. Guard against both ambition and pride or in the long run you will be a loser, perhaps not in appearance, but in reality. You will have to deal with all types of people in life. Some will be genuine and others not. It will be hard to judge them until you have had experience with them. Do not hesitate to cultivate friendships because that is what makes life enjoyable. However, watch new acquaintances for a while before giving them your trust.

"One certainty in life is that you are not always on top. There are many people who try to avoid the falls by changing philosophies. These are people of convenience. They're often successful in the short term, while they are on earth. But I have always wondered whether they were successful in the sense of eternity. I feel following conscience is a far better guide.

"Remember to judge people on their merit and not by their possessions or jobs. People should be judged by how they use their success rather than by how much they acquire. There is a difference between self-respect and pride. Just as there always will be differences in abilities and destinies, there always will be economic distinctions. But we have a responsibility to allow people to keep their self-respect. Your grandfather taught this to me early in life when he took me to his wholesale grocery. The Depression made life in Texas very tough, and few people made money. Everyone helped his neighbors and enjoyed closeness and cooperation. Your grandfather and I would slit open sacks of flour and spend what seemed to be a lifetime trying to crack, not break, some eggs. I thought this was one of the most foolish things I had ever seen and could not understand why he would ruin good merchandise at a time when everyone was losing money.

"So he sat down with me, and we had a conversation that I always will remember. He said his employees had helped him build the business. They had gone through many hard years together to make the business a success. They all knew he couldn't afford to keep them on, but my dad felt he had a responsibility to help. Dad said, 'If you offer these people goods for doing nothing, some of them would not take it because they would lose their self-respect. Those who would accept the goods would suffer equally from a loss of inner strength.' So, I watched with admiration as my father offered damaged goods to his former employees in exchange for helping him move the merchandise.

"The older you become, the more you'll recognize the importance of finding a purpose in life. But first you need to learn about reality. Emotion, more than thought, rules your life when you are a child. Ambition and ego guide your conscience more than responsibility. As your maturity and understanding develop, you'll think about mortality. Your thoughts will reach a deeper level of understanding. You will discover that God gave you freedom of choice in how you live your life. The most important thing you can do is to find a sense of love and oneness with God and other people. I became a better person when I learned the lessons of stewardship and how to deal with others by reading the Bible. In that way, I found my own meaning for life. You will go through a similar process as you question why you were put on this earth.

"The rule of the world is not just to take from life, but to put something back. We all have responsibilities, although sometimes we would like to ignore them, especially the difficult ones. Some men can affect very little, but they still have the responsibility to do what they can in a positive way. I have tried to do that. On occasions I have been right, and on others I've been wrong. When I was wrong, I was able to admit it. At least God knew my motives. That makes the later times of life, like these, a lot more satisfying.

"There are many things you can learn from the Bible. The parable of the talents teaches you that all of us are judged by what we do with our resources. The more ability you are given, the more is expected of you. God has given you a number of abilities. Please don't waste them."

It was hard to accept that my father was dying.

Tieman H. Dippel, Sr.

Editorial — *Brenham Banner Press* — January 20, 1972

The death of Tieman H. Dippel Sr. has taken from the scene a tower of strength that nourished all that is good in Brenham and Washington County.

During his lifetime of service to the people here he earned the respect and a place of honor in the hearts of all who sought out his wise council in the years allotted him, which was all too short.

He lived by a set of values reflected in the high standards he set for himself and demanded from those with whom he worked. He would settle for nothing less than excellence achieved through integrity in any undertaking in which he was involved.

First and foremost, Mr. Dippel was a family man, who showed his love for his wife, daughter and son, through example and inculcation that leaves a legacy each can look to with pride.

Whether in the field of banking or as sheriff, that covered an illustrious career in each, he dealt with his fellow citizens on a fair and impartial basis enhanced with dignity and unmarred by petty prejudices or rancor of lesser men so prevalent in today's rush to the proverbial pot of gold at the end of the rainbow.

Mr. Dippel never abused the vast powers of his influence—that could reach the highest offices in the state and nation with a phone call for personal gain or as an escape from what he held as a sacred duty in the service of his country as seen by his record of service as a 2nd Lt. in the U.S. Army during World War II, and the example passed on to his son, Lt. Tieman (Skipper) Dippel Jr., now serving in the U.S. Navy.

When he made what was practically an overnight transition from Sheriff of Washington County to the presidency of the Farmers National Bank, an old friend cornered him at his new office on his first day at the bank, and after extending congratulations, asked, "Dip," as he was affectionately known, "just what do you know about banking?"—"No more than I did about being a sheriff, when you questioned me on my lack of knowledge of that job 20 years ago," Dippel answered with a sincere smile. "You're right, I did," continued his friend, "and if you become just half as good a banker as you were a sheriff, I know my money will always be safe in your bank, so write up a receipt for my deposit."

His friend, like the thousands of customers he dealt with, never had reason to fear for their savings or his ability as a banker, for Mr. Dippel accepted the challenge with the same determination based on sound principles that made him one of the most respected sheriffs in Texas and soon he gained for himself the reputation as a progressive builder in the intricate field of finance.

Through his leadership the Farmers National Bank has enjoyed a rapid growth to become one of the soundest financial institutions in the state.

Mr. Dippel understood the meaning of compassion, as evidenced in his dealings with people in all walks of life.

As sheriff he commanded respect for the law without favoritism, but always tempered justice with mercy where warranted that resulted in restoring many an erring citizen to a useful place in the community and brought tranquility to those homes torn asunder by unresolved domestic problems.

In his role as banker, Mr. Dippel set many a family and business back on a sound financial footing, not always with all the collateral to support the loan, but because of his profound faith in people and his keen sense of judging character.

He held titles of leadership and responsibility in many businesses, civic organizations and fraternal orders. And in each, he left a record of achievements that speak for themselves and stand as a tribute to a man who utilized his God-given talents with a dedication that brought happiness to many and made Brenham and Washington County, which he loved so much, a much better place.

In his quiet unassuming way and without fanfare, Tieman H. Dippel gave unselfishly of himself to God, country and those less fortunate. It is with profound sorrow and sympathy to his bereaved family as we share the burden of his loss, and in all humility, we can only say, "Farewell" to a great citizen as he rests in that peace of God's eternal promise, to whom we can only offer a prayer of thanks for the short time he was allotted to be among us.

———————

When I wondered where Dad gained his values, I could see that they came from his mother and father. Grandfather Henry had been a very good businessman. Even though he was short in stature, he was a bundle of energy. He helped build a major wholesale grocery and spoke a number of languages because the era in which he lived was one of immigrants. As Dad pointed out, he understood the importance of the dignity of man. If Dad had one belief that he got from his father, it was the importance of human dignity and that you should give to every other person that level of dignity that you feel they ought to give to you.

The Golden Rule of reciprocity or of equality was evident in how Grandfather looked at life. Dad became a sheriff primarily because of a sense of justice that came from some of the fears he experienced when he was a younger man in the 1920s. There was great unrest at that time in the local area and in much of Texas. Following the war, minorities and immigrants were treated quite poorly and different groups formed—some politically to intimidate for their own interests and power creating a climate of great uncertainty. Grandfather defended the rights of the minority and immigrants because of his belief in dignity and was often threatened with being tarred and feathered or beaten.

As I would read back in some of the newspapers of the latter years of that period, I could appreciate the difficulty of taking a stand as he did. And also why when Dad was told as a child by others that soon his father would be run out of town on a rail or tarred and feathered, I could understand how the era would shape him. Grandfather Henry loved his family, his business opportunities, his matched team of horses, and his shotguns. (With his reputation for no nonsense, this probably kept him from being tarred and feathered.) Dad also picked up his strategy as sheriff from him—meet everyone with a handshake and smile and with sincerity to help, but wearing a gun never hurt.

His was a very close family that had been successful but then battled the Great Depression and took pride in the fact that they paid back every penny they had ever borrowed and had honored every obligation. It shaped Dad, and because it shaped him and the respect I had for him and Mother, it shaped me.

Dad always taught us that it was a far better strategy to lead than to condemn if you wanted to actually accomplish anything. He emphasized that humility was not only a necessary virtue for life, but also an extremely good strategy. He stressed patience over quick action, unless it was absolutely necessary, because it gave you a better opportunity to see the cards dealt and read them so they could be played to advantage. But most of all he emphasized that when we chose our friends, they should have both integrity and competence—with integrity being the primary consideration because without it the competence was doubly dangerous.

Mother's family had been a family of very successful doctors. Her father, while an excellent investor and a renowned doctor in his forty-two years, volunteered often to help with the fever epidemics and to honor his medical oath. He would make house calls for fifty cents as my sister Deanna showed me in one of his registers. Just before his death he had been working for almost forty-eight hours straight because of the fever epidemics. And the long hours plus a weakened heart, which had come from pneumonia during his participation in World War I, had its toll in his death. Grandmother Elsie, his wife, died two years later and Mother, at sixteen, took over the responsibility for her two younger brothers.

Life for Mother and Dad had never been easy, but they had accomplished a great deal, and Deanna and I became the absolute focus of their attention. To them education was everything, and as a result we understood early that education was a responsibility to carry on and advance the next generation of the family. They cared about individual responsibility and understood the importance of charity and helping others who truly needed it. But family values started with teaching self-reliance and leaving what you could to the next generation so they could get a good start. The new generation had to make their own way, but you gave them the values to succeed and tried to help rather than burden them financially. And if you did business with others, you made money *with* them not *off* them. Business success was from long trusted relationships in their style.

They instilled habits in Deanna and me that set the paths of our lives. Mother and Dad certainly loved us but believed in disciplined worlds and strong habits. Play was after the obligation of study. Piano and accordions had to be learned as well. (There was never a belief I would be a pianist but Mother wanted the discipline of having to focus to become a part of me.) In Boy Scouts anything less than Eagle with all the Palms was not so much a disappointment for her as a lack of potential for me—it conveyed values I needed to learn. An "A-" was not greeted by praise or disappointment as much as a "what did we miss?" since she often tutored me when I was young. They expected me to do my best. They understood in athletics that I was not Dad who was a superb athlete, but they never let me underachieve because it would become a fatal habit. The same went for manners, courtesy, and respect for age and others. Once I was often the highest grade average, they did not have to push me. I pushed myself because setting my own goals became important to me. They may not have given me the knowledge teachers did or the perspective the world did, but they set the way I valued things. The need for discipline and obligation, and the prioritization of how I organized my time and thought guided me in what was important in life—how I determined my sense of "personal dignity."

As I look back on my values today, they were focused by them. During my first week of school at Alamo Elementary, my first grade teacher told Mother I would probably be a "B" student from her observations. I do not know if Mother was irritated, embarrassed or challenged but that was not going to be. She focused on English and reading and Dad on math and science. Consequently, I was Valedictorian in high school and at the

University of Texas Business School. I remember at the UT Graduation Ceremony when I got the symbolic Delta Sigma Pi Key. Dad, in one of the few emotional moments I ever saw, told me privately he hoped I was not embarrassed that he had never had a chance to graduate from college and how uncomfortable he felt being there. He had great humility and did not fully appreciate himself. After his death I learned to appreciate the vast influence he held because of his dedication to values. I realized how much wisdom he and Mother had taught me and how it, joined with the more elite knowledge of formalized education, was a necessary part of what made a complete person. Anything I had become was in large part due to the time and focus he and Mother had given me.

Theirs was the "greatest generation" that was shaped by the Depression and World War II and the ascension of America and its unusual characteristics in the mid 20th century. My generation was that of the '60s and Vietnam. It was a very different generation that split on how you looked at issues, how you thought about obligation and compassion, and on how you viewed responsibility. Over the last almost forty years, we have seen America move very gradually from the time of my father's death to a very different society. Part of it has had to do with our much greater affluence after World War II and part rests in how the American vision of it has changed.

In modern times there seems to be great envy, class warfare, and despondency on the part of many if others have success. I remember my mother's viewpoint on others' success that was shaped by growing up in the depression. If success came to others from ethical sources, she was always happy for them, never resentful. She taught us that time spent on self-pity or envy was time wasted from constructive traits and lacked character. Their generation was appreciative of what life gave to their efforts and did not adopt pessimism due to lack. Individual responsibility, debt, and the character of paying all obligations for honor were sacrosanct. It set a perspective for us and built temperament and habits that supported it. We visited older relatives to show respect, were taught all the rules of courtesy, and realized we had many obligations to society.

I think that modern society might have been described best by a lifelong friend whom I met through the Texas Lyceum who has been as actively involved in politics, economics, and culture as I have been. However, he comes from a more liberal persuasion where I would be generally considered more conservative, but we would agree almost completely on a set of observations that he made at a recent presentation honoring him by the Center for Public Policy Priorities in Austin. Former State Representative and insurance executive, Lyndon Olson, was also the United States Ambassador to Sweden. But most importantly he has spent a lifetime addressing the needs of others and trying to build a better and a more positive society. His words rang home to me and to the audience that was of a more moderate to liberal Democratic persuasion as they all stood applauding in tribute. The same sentiments are in my books that have been distributed by other more conservative foundations and think tanks and usually receive an equal level of support. Values can unify if defined properly; the concept of warriors however, can unite even extremes if they believe in conscience and have common ground.

How is it then that I explain to Ty where our country is when most all groups seem to hold some similar cultural values but disagree so significantly in the political realm? For his future is not going to be just as a Texan or just as an American, it is going to be as a member of a more universal interdependence. Terrorism, the fear of plagues and health issues, and the environmental issues that will affect us all, are not just in one location but instead require cooperation that does not presently effectively exist. How do you put the world in context in such a way that not only you but others can see the family teachings of the Golden Rule, Common Good, and Conscience's joint requirements of Honoring Obligation and Compassion in such a way as to bring order out of chaos? The first step is to understand the chaos, which Lyndon's presentation describes better than I might and is from a perspective that is independent. It is presented in the next section with his permission.

Then we can look to the fact that each family has its own disagreements, often intense, but usually there is a common ground that helps people pull together. What may well matter, if civilization is to be supported, is how the next generations can begin to assimilate and understand the wisdom that is necessary beyond the technology, education, and knowledge that exists. The problem is how we look at things when we evaluate them. **How** *you think about something determines* **what** *you think about it.* We need to think with our conscience of the obligations of fraternity, not just the compassion of the individual.

The family is the core of that because it ultimately teaches us how to think by giving us an organizing perspective of life and what we should value.

If I can teach Ty anything, it will be to give him the perspective of how he ought to think about issues not in conservative or liberal terms for those words have now become nouns rather than the adjectives they once were. But to perceive in an organized system of balancing interests understanding the interrelationship of the most critical issues that affect us all—economics, politics, and culture. Culture will ultimately determine how strong civilization emerges because it is the power of history. It determines what values move forward. *Context of thought is key* and to begin on context you must define your problems as Lyndon very well defined them in the following presentation.

Lyndon is a member of the Council on Foreign Relations, the Council of American Ambassadors, and the Commission on Public Diplomacy. He also served on the International Board of Advisors for the Institute for Social and Economic Policy in the Middle East at Harvard University's John F. Kennedy School of Government.

He has served Texas in a variety of ways, most notably as a former member of the Texas House of Representatives and as Chairman of the State Board of Insurance. He serves on the Boards of the Lyndon B. Johnson Foundation, Scott & White Hospital, and he chairs the Board for the Texas Scottish Rite Hospital for Children in Dallas.

He understands the necessity of context between politics, economics, and culture. These are not separate issues; they each define our society by their combination. We served together as the Honorary Co-Chairmen for the Thirtieth Anniversary of The Texas Lyceum, an organization dedicated to integrity, wisdom, and thoughtful analysis of public policy.

REMARKS OF AMBASSADOR LYNDON OLSON
UPON ACCEPTING THE TEXAS LEGACY AWARD
FROM THE CENTER FOR PUBLIC POLICY PRIORITIES
AT THE EIGHTH ANNUAL TEXAS LEGACY LUNCHEON
NOVEMBER 12, 2009, AUSTIN, TEXAS

Thank you very much for this honor. I appreciate the kind remarks of my friend, Congressman Edwards. I also appreciate the opportunity today to talk to this distinguished group about a concern of mine. I want to talk with you about civility, both in society in general and in our politics in particular.

I encourage you to think back, for some of us way back to those report cards we got in first grade. Most everyone had different type cards and categories, but they were pretty much variations on the same basic theme. I'm not talking about your arithmetic or reading or penmanship grades. I'm talking about the comportment column, with things such as "exercises self-control," "respects the rights of others," "shows kindness and consideration for others," "indicates willingness to cooperate," "uses handkerchief," (important even before the H1N1 virus) . . . and, my favorite was usually right up at the top of that 6-week report card and it's of particular significance to our discussion, "plays well with others."

We were being taught about and graded on one of the most fundamental skills of our civilization: how to get along with others. There is a reason that "plays well with others" was one of the first things we were taught and evaluated on. And folks, I don't think we're getting a very good grade on "plays well with others" these days. Many of us don't even want to play with someone we don't like or agree with.

Where did all of this come from? In the majority of my life this hasn't been the case. Those of us in this room over 40 or 50 didn't grow up in anything like this environment. We didn't live like this. Not in our communities . . . not in our politics. We lived in a political world with strong feelings and positions, yes. And we took swings at each other politically. But it didn't come down to the moral equivalent of street brawls and knife fights. Politics has always been a contact sport, but the conflict didn't permeate every aspect of our society and rise to today's level of social and verbal hostility. It is very unhealthy. And I'm not sure what to do about it. But I know it when I see it and hear it. And I know it is time we focus as much attention on our civil behavior as we do on achieving our personal and partisan agendas. How we do that, I don't know. But I want to raise the issue, ask the questions, and encourage you all to give it your consideration as well.

We live in an era of rudeness, in society in general, in the popular culture, and in our political life. Our culture today, in fact, rewards incivility, crudeness, and cynicism. You can get on TV, get your own talk show or reality series if you out-shout and offend the other guy. Everyone screams, but no one listens. We produce a lot of heat but little light. The proclivity is to demonize our opponent. People don't just disagree . . . the challenge to the other is a battle to the death. Character assassination, verbal abuse, obnoxious behavior, and an overbearing attention on scandal and titillation—all that isn't just reserved to day-time TV anymore—it's the currency of prime-time, of late night, of cable news, of the Internet, and of society in general.

What happened to us? Should this be a sign of alarm? Is the problem selfishness—we won't be denied, we must be immediately gratified? We want every-thing we've ever seen in the movies? How do we live and get along like our parents and their generation? They had to sacrifice. They didn't get what they wanted when they wanted it. Is today's need for instant gratification a problem?

We are more inclusive today and that is a good thing—but has that good made for increased tensions?

Is it the 24-hour news cycle? The 24-hour news cycle demands instantaneous news, which feeds off of controversy, scandal, and easy answers to difficult questions. There is scant time for reflection or reasoned analysis. Market forces demand instantaneous information and jarring entertainment values not sober analysis or wisdom. The news media are more prone to focus on the loudest, the most outrageous, and the most partisan actors. And given the rise of the political consultant class, candidates and campaigns are louder, more outrageous, and meta-partisan. Political consultants have helped create a permanent campaign where politics takes precedence over governance. The political consultants egg on all this for profit, creating controversy where little or none exists so the message, the theme of the day, is played out on TV and the media. They're paid handsomely to cause strife and create conflict in order to raise hackles, money, and attention, fomenting issues to suit their agenda. It's all about the message, not the solution, not the negotiation, the debate, the compromise to move forward. It's about who is controlling the message . . . who is defining the message, who is creating the message, who is keeping the conflict alive often where none existed before the consultant decided one was needed. Is this what keeps us at each other's throats?

Is it talk radio, attack TV? Is it the talk shows, the shout festivals where absolute hyperbole is the only currency? Mean-spirited hyperbole and hyper parti-sanship breed cynicism. Citizens are increasingly cynical about politics and about their government's ability to work. The damage to the ship of state, to the fabric of the nation begs repair. Whose job is it to change course and affect the necessary repairs? I'm not sure I have the answer to that, but I propose that in a room full of policy makers and politicians, men and women who talk to the media, who work in the public arena, who hire consultants, who set agendas, maybe we have a role to play in making things better. You know, I can say that there are some people in this room, people I consider dear friends, who understand this problem and I believe share my concern. To those friends I say, you and I both know that we disagree very fundamentally on some very big issues but the truth is that we could care less about our disagreements and are more concerned about where we can find consensus and reasons to work and live together to construct a better future. I consider this kind of commitment to trust and open dialogue crucial to maintaining a sustainable society.

And indeed, isn't it about building a better future for our community, for our country, for our children? I say that even on the most intractable of issues, there is room for constructive debate, for consensus building, for the search for some common ground. President Johnson once said to his Democratic colleague, Gov. George Wal-lace of Alabama, during the crisis of civil rights in the South: "What do you want left behind? You want a great, big marble monument that says, 'George Wallace: He built.' Or do you want a little piece of scrawny pine lying there that says, 'George Wallace: He hated?'"

The people I know in this room are builders. But we are confronting a world today where hate seems to be a predominant factor in the crisis of incivility confronting our politics. Where are the rules that govern conduct? What happens eventually after this continuous rancor tears the fabric of our society completely asunder? Can we survive with this tenor . . . taking no prisoners, giving no quarter?

I'm asking these questions because you folks here are blessed with skills, talent, experience, and a commitment to a positive public policy. You understand the importance of maintaining and protecting our commonwealth where we strive to serve our clients, our community, our country, and our state. If civil discourse self-destructs, we cannot move on the issues that matter. Think of this as an environmental crisis . . . the environment being our civil society and our very ability to live and work and prosper together.

I don't want to sound pious or preachy here, but if we are to prevail as a free, self-governing people, we must work together. We shouldn't try to destroy our opponents just because we disagree. We have to govern our tongues. The Proverbs tell us, chapter 18, verse 12, "Death and life are in the power of the tongue." How we choose to use words—for good or for wrong—is clearly our choice. The health of our democracy depends upon a robust public discourse.

Recognize that I am not saying that conflict in our political life is to be avoided. Hardly so. It is not only proper but necessary for candidates to vigorously debate the issues of our day and examine their opponents' records. Don't let people confuse civility with goody two-shoes niceness and mere etiquette. Civility is a robust, tough, substantive civic virtue, critical to both civil society and the future of our republic. Civility entails speaking directly, passionately, and responsibly about who we are and what we believe. Divisions based on principles are healthy for the nation. Vigorous and passionate debate helps us to define issues and to sharpen positions.

Conflict cannot, should not be avoided in our public lives any more than we can avoid conflict with the people we love. But just as members of a household, as a family learn ways of settling their differences without inflicting real damage on each other, so we, in our politics, must find constructive ways of resolving disputes and differences.

Our work is here. We build from the base. We will foster change first by our example . . . by working together, respecting one another, and negotiating our differences in good faith and with mutual respect. Civility is neither a small nor inconsequential issue. The word comes from the French civilité, which is often translated as "politeness." But it means much more. It suggests an approach to life . . . living in a way that is civilized. The words "civilized," "civilité," and "city" share a common etymology with a word meaning "member of the household." To be civilized is to understand that we live in a society as in a household. There are certain rules that allow family members to live peacefully within a household. So, too, are there rules of civility that allow us *to live peacefully within a society. As we all learned in 1st grade a long time ago, we owe certain responsibilities to one another. Perhaps we spend a lifetime learning how to play well with others. So be it. It is a crucial goal for a civil society. Thank you.*

Lyndon's points are obvious to all sides. Civility is a key point. Emotion often drives action today rather than thoughtful wisdom. But **how** you think about something determines **what** you think about it. If like the analogy of Rome, we as a society are hollowing out our civility and values that band us together, how do we find a method of thought, a perspective that revives the necessary values that family teaches but have become diminished? How do we get our schools and universities to help show the obligations we have and the consequences of their loss?

Ethics and conscience are directly related to analytics and the way you think because unless you have the right facts and the right process for evaluating them they are only as good as a computer with bad data and a faulty program. So while we need the principles of ethics to guide us, we must also concentrate on a process of thought.

The critical thing is not to teach "rules." But the key point to a solution is that how you think about something is adaptable. To do this we need to understand some characteristics that affect how we think.

How we think is greatly impacted by the environment of thought surrounding us, and it is often set by the government to which we give our collective support. Governments have philosophies or organizing principles, by which they govern, and these, over time, have impact on our temperament and perspective. When you have partisan gridlock, there is no organizational process that provides wisdom to policy. But the people determine the government and are manipulated and divided by partisan politics. We as a people need to think clearly and with depth. We do not have to argue, but we need to respect an honest discourse to work to the right answers. We have become disconnected in our public discussions from the critical real issues. Part of the reason is that technology is growing so rapidly. We have so much information it is difficult to organize logically for reference and priority. This makes it far easier for emotion rather than logic to be our default system.

The riots of Greece and London in 2011 showed the mindset of many youth who had been raised with the intrusion of government on the family values and responsibilities of the past. While many looked at them as reckless things, I think the better analysis came from my friend Jim Windham's insightful "The Texas Pilgrim" (Volume 13, No. 9, of September 2011) where he quoted the explanation of London Rabbi Jonathan Saks:

> *"They are the victims of the tsunami of wishful thinking that washed across the West saying that you can have sex without responsibility of marriage, children without the responsibility of parenthood, social order without the responsibility of citizenship, liberty without the responsibility of morality, and self-esteem without the responsibility of work and earned achievement."*

I do not think values can be expressed more clearly than that. To reclaim these values we need to assess how we and our children think because it defines what we believe. There are no simple "plans;" there is only dedication to cultural values that must be re-implanted both in us and our government, which is our collective self. The essence of the individual and government relationship is our temperament for risk and how much we require of government.

II | KEY ISSUES DRIVING DECISIONS

TEMPERAMENT AND INTELLIGENCE

Often the effort is to increase knowledge and wisdom to better use intelligence, but the reaction to most problems is governed not so much by intelligence, which tends to enhance the strategies undertaken, but by temperament, which plays a very significant part in evaluating the strategic options that are available. While each of us has a temperament that considers levels of risk and directs us accordingly, one of the unique interactions of this temperament is when it is affected by conscience. Character is really about how much affect conscience has in overriding temperament because normally character situations are those where you have to act against your normal interests of convenience. Each of us is tested, some in very significant ways like Sir Thomas More. Others are tested on a more gradual basis as to the type of life that we choose to lead through our daily choices. Whether it be in the fears of politics or economics that affect temperament negatively or the greed and arrogance that tempt us to act, conscience is a regulator of actions from the value perspective that has some degree of control.

How much we give in to it to control our emotions/temperament depends on our inner values. It is in the more extreme cases that we are truly tested, not the minor ones, and at those points we know ourselves in depth even if others do not perceive. It is to these moments that we must condition ourselves in wisdom because they set the tone and strength of our lives and define us. To control fear in economics and politics in making decisions is not easy and often has consequences in doing the right thing, but our inner motivation defines our true being.

Character is temperament that has been formed much like the pressure on carbon forms a diamond. The easy choice is simple; making the hard choice comes from the character of doing right and also the wisdom of why doing right is the correct choice. Learning character is an appreciation of the values of concepts like the Golden Rule, the Common Good, and the Universal Values of Conscience. These change the evaluation of the choices of temperament.

Temperament is a very critical component in the success of business because risk is often evaluated by how a person looks at options. If a person has a significant degree of experience and a high level of intelligence, they may well recognize the risk as far greater than one who does not fully recognize the perils. Experience focuses on reality rather than perception and needs rather than wants.

The appreciation of risk is a necessity because it comes in many forms. We understand it more clearly in taking various levels of economic risk—a personal investment in a certificate of deposit as opposed to a small issue Initial Public Offering of a tech stock. However, on a more public side whether or not we want national health care, social security, or any major government program is determined by what risks we accept and the size of government it requires. The less risk, the more security is offset or balanced by less potential opportunity elsewhere because of the cost. It is a choice and needs to be a knowledgeable one.

Another aspect of temperament is often self-interest. If a person sees he can gain while others may lose by risking their money, the temperament of undertaking an endeavor, if not guided by conscience, has significant impact. While it may not have as direct an impact on him individually, it most certainly has an impact on the ultimate success of the firm (its owners, employees, and customers) that has to absorb any losses. This is the lesson from our current economic crisis. Thus, understanding temperament is critical, both in how risk is most effectively evaluated and in setting a moral tone that ultimately protects the entity and related individuals. It is the core issue of corporate governance.

Temperament is very much affected by context. The less you know about a situation the more naturally you tend to fear it. The more experience you have, the more you understand the interrelationship of the various parts, the better your temperament is developed to evaluate the reality of the risk. All business is the management of risk, particularly financial risk. Thus, the success of a business is determined by properly managing risk, not by its aversion. Life and business should not be a roulette game of chance, but one of poker affected by the ultimate management of resources. This concept of risk evaluation consists of the three major powers that inevitably affect most decisions—economics, politics, and culture. Each can have an impact on the others, particularly in a growing multicultural world.

While the individualized pieces of knowledge may help enhance decisions, the process of putting them together and seeing the potential risks of the interrelationship and prioritization of the major issues is critical. For that reason a thought process has to be created to organize information. The process is a contextual presentation with a categorization of issues developing key points. It is necessary to put an ethical component into decision making if you wish to look at the long-term best interest as opposed to a short-term convenient benefit. Leadership is not just pushing for activity, but pushing for thoughtful correct activity. Heavily pushing the wrong concepts does more damage than not promoting good ones.

It is important to remember that our mind uses only a very small part of its capacity in considering thought. A far larger portion is the subconscious reflex of prejudgment based on experience that gives instant readings, such as "instant danger," etc. Family values help create these responses that form habits and guide us in life. We do not overcome bad instincts or prejudgments easily unless we command our conscious mind to do so. Thus, learning how to think affects several levels.

The difficulty today is how to separate the levels of issues that enter our conscious mind. As the military looks at strategy, operations, tactics, and techniques, you have a pyramid of very different levels of importance. Thinking through the prioritizations necessary and understanding the concept of change is absolutely essential. The existing status quo is the culmination of historical precedent that put a society or company in its current environment. The change has to be evaluated against history lessons and must be relevant to today's environment. Looking at that balance becomes critically important because organizations or institutions are simply the sum of the talent that is within them. They ultimately have a current value of the anticipated net present value of the staff's future contributions.

The institution's culture, unity, and common thought processes truly matter. Envisioning a world model and the company's place, as well as the individual's place within it, begins with the organizational idea "what is most important and what principles will organize the strategy or vision." These are concepts that are thought first in general terms but as they are refined become the common ground for the ultimate success.

TEMPERAMENT, RISK, AND TRUST

Risk dramatically affects temperament and ultimately the use of intelligence, and is partially driven by trust. If you are making a business deal with people you have dealt for thirty years, the level of risk will be perceived far less than if it was a first time transaction with a relatively unknown entity. In political leadership, if it is a new leader who has expressed what you believe, you may be willing to support him. But when he or she asks for sacrifice, it depends much more on whether or not you trust their sincerity. How well a leader manages risk is a crucial judgment. Risk management usually includes four parts—identifying risks, measuring them, monitoring those you cannot control, and controlling those you can.

Thus, trust affects politics, economics, and certainly culture because you tend to assimilate with those of similar beliefs. Your opinions and how you view the world are partially shaped by those you trust. It is the essence of why family, from the beginning, has such a tremendous impact on how we learn to think and how we address the problems that face us. Family, normally, is the core of cooperative effort, provided that its values are of conscience and not convenience. Many a family has been pulled apart by an inheritance and the zero-sum game of materialism that overwhelmed strong ties.

Conscience is vital when looking at trust and as such must be fully appreciated in how it drives systems. To truly trust someone means that you see within them a sense of honor, individual responsibility, character, and competence. The level of trust varies based on past experience with the person or group and how one thinks through the situation and the risks involved.

The relationship of these entities—temperament, affected by risk and level of trust, and judged by the broad context of conscience—shapes all decisions and really originates in the family, what it teaches, and what experiences it grants. In the family you learn that each individual is unique and has different strengths and weaknesses so you refine the trust you have in their competence in areas, but you also judge motivations such as love and caring. What holds the family together is often the heart not the mind. It begins to define the differences between personal interests and common values.

THE IMPORTANCE OF EXPERIENCE

When I first visited with my father near his death, I thought that I understood the world clearly enough after an extensive education and that I perhaps had a broader vision of life than he did. But an education is often only the "hunting license"—you have to learn a great deal about the nature of the world. Much as in fishing, you learn that you care less about where the fish are and more about where their food supply is. Crawfish come out in the evening and return home in the morning. The fish know where to go and learn to follow the bait. What I realized is that oftentimes knowledge and wisdom have to be placed with the benefit of context. It is the ability to sense how different things fit together, and often it is not perceived as clearly as it should be. Perhaps the best way to explain context might be the example of football coaches. To someone looking at the field, the players seem to be winning or losing on physical ability.

That may be truer in high school, but as you move to college and then the professional ranks, the defensive and offensive strategies, knowledge, and adjustments determine the outcome. The higher level you play, the more you must understand your own abilities and what is happening on the other side to prevent you from succeeding.

Understanding how different factors fit together and how you may adjust them to your advantage becomes essential to ultimate success in life. It requires you to have knowledge of facts and wisdom of values as well as experience of how cycles and factors fit together. That context often comes with age—having seen short-term and long-term cycles of history, and how they shape the environment in which we operate. It is much harder to use on a broad scale in a time of 24-hour news and sensationalism, which pull your attention to the current but often irrelevant in the long cycles of economics, politics, and culture. However, systems are developed to help sort massive data into simpler issues, and instinct helps us do much of this based on trust and our appraisal of how others think. This is the essence of experience.

THE VALUE OF PERSPECTIVE

There is perhaps nothing more important than how you look at life and what you value. This ultimately determines your satisfaction and happiness. It has as much an impact on your physical condition as it does your health because it affects your stress level and how you see yourself. Lao Tzu, the great Chinese philosopher, often spoke of enlightened as "knowing self."

> *He who knows others is wise;*
> *He who knows himself is enlightened.*
> *Mastering others is strength;*
> *Mastering yourself is true power.*

Perspective begins with what values you hold. They organize your principles and how you view options. Not the least of which are your personal ethics, which often come in youth from a family. The great balance of one's inner self is the constant battle between conscience and convenience. In each of us there is the self interest in some of the natural instincts to do what is only best for us, while there is also a far better more cultured part that realizes we are here for more than ourselves and have an obligation to others and the future. This side realizes the common good and benefit of the Golden Rule. This same wiser self-interest realizes that self-interest to extreme is greed, which carries a lack of sustainability and the loss of benefits such as relationships and trust. It also can lead to excessive risk.

This relationship between men in the covenant of the mutual obligations of positive conduct is morality. If society affects us so dramatically in our lives, then we would hope that it would be a fair a society with an honorable set of rules. The fairness of the Golden Rule and the unity it provides is the foundation for any successful society (and thus it is the basis of most religions). If you are a person of conscience at the core, then it affects your future because you will choose your friends, as those of conscience or you will be uncomfortable with them. If you seek more convenience, then you will be drawn to those of similar principles.

The early arguments for convenience are many. Doing things that only benefit one's self often helps achieve success on an individual basis for those who have less self-applied ethical guidelines than others. But the strength of conscience is that it tends to be transformational in that you can join with other allies who care about the future as you do and have a far greater force than just individuals of convenience.

However, that transformational force of conscience must have a nucleus of uncommon men and inevitably a set of ideas and ideals to which they all adhere. It does not just happen, and the experience and the talent to develop and retain those concepts in society have to be reinvented continually through the nonprofit service organizations, churches, and humanitarian efforts that train these uncommon men. You have to participate in the common square of service and discussion to increase your contextual wisdom, understanding of other men, and leadership ability. Seeing others under pressure shows you who you can trust.

Your life perspective for conscience versus convenience determines your goals in life. Conscience looks to honor and compassion, while convenience often looks to materialism and pride. Quite frankly, it is easier to satisfy the former than the latter. When you care only about material things is there ever truly enough? Yet when you value honor and compassion, whatever you do has a satisfaction.

The concept of environments, beyond the family shaping values, is key to our children. No matter what we teach them at home, if they enter an environment where their peers are negative or work in a corporation where total convenience and greed dominates, then their perspectives are reset.

Schools and universities often take little responsibility for true character development beyond image and that has been a cause of our current problems. Teaching character and ethics is superficial because of the times of modern political correctness and whose values. Superficiality of knowledge does not form conviction or lead to challenging ideas. Galileo Galilei, the Italian physicist noted it best: "You cannot teach a man anything, you can only help him to discover it in himself." Contemplation brings depth. The issue is not "ethics or conscience" individually, but common cultural ethics and conscience that develops and reinforces values.

Our media has equal responsibility for our cultural change. Many of our most popular shows entertain by showing the failure of others and demeaning them. No great culture tries to rise in its own esteem by lowering the dignity of others. Culture may use political correctness to appear concerned, but we must judge reality by looking more at the core values deeper in society.

THE CONCEPT OF HARMONY AND CONTEXT

Another way to appreciate the "context" that the Golden Rule family teaches is to look at Asia, particularly China. Their culture believes as an organizing principle that all people are connected. The depth and quality of relationships is significant. Harmony is valued, so consensus is a necessity. Decisions require input from the leadership and from the lower levels so there is acceptance. "The Harmonious Society," which is their current goal, moves toward this and is not fully understood by the West because we look at a Western Democratic Republic where each vote is counted. So we take a more individualized perception of directly, and often aggressively, pushing our individual view with more of a "winner take all" result.

How you judge a government under such systems may be different. In the U.S. the winner pushes their policies, often on one political side or another against opposition. The U.S. is in a sense a political system pushing right versus left. Cultural based systems requiring consensus operate differently. The most successful leaders are those that unite and are competent in getting things accomplished. Each approach has strengths and weaknesses, but understanding these differences may help develop a system that gives more dignity and competence by combining a culture of law, intensity, and public service into a political system that helps make decisions with broad input. Family values are the key to the combinations. They provide an "ethics of sharing and obligation."

The East and the West can learn from each other, but they need to understand each other far more than they presently do. In the West we use a political approach based on individual rights and it is defined by civil rights and civil obligations, which the government more and more enforces as peer pressure of self governance recedes and more regulation and laws take its place.

China has a legal system but is more dominated by a cultural system where legal civil liberties are not the focus as much as cultural personal dignity. Eastern culture cares much more about courtesy, formality such as apologies, and the concept of shame or "face." Many of the same values exist but are perceived from a different viewpoint. If you bring up an issue to a Chinese leader complaining of civil rights politically, it is often done in a way that is an affront and meets resentment and a lack of success. The same would be true on similar issues to an American leader. Politics makes nationalism and it makes people defensive. Ask a similar question in the context of how would Confucius and your historic culture look upon the dignity with which this individual was treated, do it tactfully, and if there is a misjudgment there is embarrassment and correction.

Knowing how people think matters. We are linear in the West in our language. We use about 4,000 common words in sentences, paragraphs and pages. The Chinese have over 30,000 characters and think more in concepts. We may speak of paragraph nineteen of a contract and wonder what they do not understand about it when in reality they are trying to understand how it fits with the other eighteen.

A cultural system looks more to fraternity and where the individual fits into the whole. A democracy is more a political system that emphasizes the individual who can gain a perspective of being the center of the world individually. Both have benefits and problems, but comparing them in dialectic lets us see these much more clearly. Personal dignity may be seen differently by the systems. The essence of dignity is probably control or some sense of security over one's life. This involves more than political rights—economics, security, and cultural dignity. Whether you look at that from an individualized perspective or from a group effort changes how you accept control, or the level of control, before it offends dignity.

The size of government affects both of the criteria. The modern world is challenging the individual's ability to control his destiny, and thereby threatening his concept of dignity. Control of destiny is a central part of dignity, and harmony is necessary for cultural strength. While the context of economics, politics, and culture requires the balance that brings them to work together positively rather than threatening uncertainty. Harmony and context are the same.

Context and Political Systems

A problem today is that Market Systems are no longer truly markets but hybrids, and socialist systems are no longer basically Communist but are hybrids as well. Discussions use the term markets and socialism theoretically when neither exists in pure form, so in the context of "Harmony" we need to understand theory and reality.

Socialism emerged from the natural desire for fairness and balance, but the reality is that it usually results in an elite minority deciding what is fair. They may be very distant from the actual problems of the poor who need opportunity more than dependency based on government largesse. Individual responsibility or control of one's destiny necessitates a sustainable life with a positive vision of the future. Extremes of socialism lead to dependency.

Market systems argue not equality of result but of opportunity. They note that to redistribute wealth you have to create wealth. If you have a system that punishes the successful, it undermines dignity or the ability to control destiny.

Theoretically one system reduces risk by having government replace individual responsibility; the other accepts greater risk to have more dignity and opportunity. Context or balance would note that fairness is a cultural value. And when it becomes a political tool, it is often counterproductive because of its uncertain consequences. It often brings class warfare when cooperation is needed. The goal should be the dignity and opportunity for a large middle class, which is key to a balanced, value-based culture more focused on the common good.

Capitalism may create wealth better than socialism, but its key question for harmony is for whom is the wealth created. Capitalism can favor big business over small business by heavy regulation that deprives opportunity. Its extreme is "crony capitalism" or monopoly, and it gives the same elite control and distorts market competition and ethics (or fairness) with disastrous results. America has seen its financial crisis that was driven by cultural failures at high levels of business and government, particularly in the housing arena.

Context, which is the integration of the parts to create the fairness dignity needs, requires the market system of wealth creation, but also the structural competition, ethics, and innovation. In that context American Ethical Capitalism and "Socialism with Chinese Characteristics" may be closer on context than might be thought. As both seek the necessary forms of corporate governance, this will become more apparent.

Foresight and Context

When we speak of organizing information streams into knowledge and adding a value base to create wisdom, we speak in terms of analytical thought. We then refine those basic analytics by understanding prioritization and measurement of results. Those provide the base for content's most valuable tool to be refined and that is the understanding of trends shown projected forward or objective foresight. Whether a trend is sustainable or not requires thought more like a video than a snapshot. So thinking has to incorporate whether the key points make a trend likely to continue or likely to go to extremes that reverse it. Some of our largest problems such as demographics, subprime loans, and government deficits all require an appreciation of balanced thought.

Time moves so fast that short-term knowledge does not assist you, but trends let you anticipate, time, and adapt actions. As Darwin noted, it is not the strongest or most intelligent that survive but those most able to adapt. Foresight gives opportunity in business or life by anticipating change and opportunity in government or the economy by showing sustainability of trends and how to change or incentivize to direct them. Culturally they can tell you the future tone and equity in society. Thus at a simple level and a refined one, it is the key determinant of how one looks at this personal dignity and opportunity in the battle between change and the status quo of history.

Context and Economic Justice

The modern American family is being impacted by a gradual weakening of the middle class that gives Democracy its strength and its cultural perspective. In The Great Generation, work and dedication had a close relationship to reward. Unfairness in life existed but one's personal dignity accepted the fact that if you worked hard you eventually succeeded. It gave a sense of control over life. But as society became more affluent and commercialism overcame the teachings of thrift, political systems focused on buying support with money their generation did not have.

Technology and global satisfaction pressured the middle class and intensified political solutions. And in recent times they have accelerated taking from those that worked diligently, who are often in the middle, and bailing out those who put forth no effort to produce or favoring the wealthy on the opposite end of the spectrum. The political parties move toward the extremes we previously mentioned, but the economic and political middle class now must choose from ever more extreme options of policy and constituencies. *What the center has in common is a sense of justice that there should be a close relationship between the talent and effort and the reward given.*

This is what we might call the Golden Rule of Economics. If you wish to avoid moral hazard, the Golden Rule of Politics that parallels it is to incentivize individual responsibility over dependency. The Golden Rule of Culture is to recognize the obligation and compassion of conscience in sustainable balance over the natural inclination of convenience. Context will show how economic justice, individual responsibility, and conscience fit appropriately together as do economic unfairness, convenience, and the weakness of dependency (or lack of control of life) are often interrelated.

The right question regarding the taxation of the wealthy is not how much money they have, but how they made it. Did they make it "with people" by creating jobs, wealth, and supplying a need? Or "off people" by charlatan tricks of finance, fraud, and misrepresentations? This makes the issue not one of economic taxation but of political regulation and cultural justice. If you tax all builders to the point of inactivity in the "free-rider" concept, there is no economic growth. The balance must recognize the true value of work, but also allow honest and ethical opportunity so that work can grow and benefit all. The creation of opportunity is critical to economic justice having the close relationship between talent and effort with the reward given. But economic systems as a whole affect the opportunity. Unless this becomes the organizational issue, the extremes prevail and the middle class continues to weaken.

There is a great difference between economic justice and the current political agenda of class warfare. The bottom line issue is redistribution of income beyond true need for political purpose. It replaces individual responsibility with dependency in culture, but in policy it makes the political judgment toward equality of result rather than equality of opportunity. That has significant economic implications because those actions promoting equality of result normally damage equality of opportunity and gradually change the economic, political, and cultural system.

One of the great problems of class warfare arguments of rich versus poor is that they are simplistic in certain facts and trends. There is a significant series of work on the movement of people within classes and a lot has to do with age and experience. Some of the best is done by the Federal Reserve Bank of Dallas and is covered in previous books of *The Language of Conscience Evolution*. A perfect example is that persons who are 65 have saved much of their lives and have talents, experience, and contacts that make their savings and salaries much greater than someone just out of school. That difference itself is not an example of income inequality. But when you talk of 1% versus 99%, it is often not discussed. The issue is more to have the same opportunity, which is economic justice. Our current entitlement system favors the elderly greatly over the young. It will get worse as fewer retire early. The discussions need to be on how to provide opportunity to reestablish a middle class opportunity and look at a thought process that identifies the truth from facts more than generalities.

It is very important to make a distinction between the concept of economic justice and class warfare. Class warfare is a political and an emotional concept based primarily on envy to divide and align for political gain. Although seemingly similar in argument, this provides a very different policy result than economic justice, which looks to growing the economic system by supporting and promoting the creation of a middle class. To divide people rich versus poor as class warfare does not consider the critical component of how wealth is created. No one gains from diminishing the creative power of a market system.

Economic justice looks at the fairness issue of rewarding labor and the method by which wealth is obtained is often a key component in judging fairness. Fraudulent approaches that take advantage of people require regulation. What drives both arguments has been the median wage stagnation that has infected the middle class. The bottom 90% of families has had almost stagnant growth with a slight rise over the last forty years. The top percent's income has almost tripled. What has been even more telling is the multiple of earnings of CEO's over average workers. It has risen from about 25% to almost 300%. Part of this is a new valuation of talent, but there are many other factors. How to bring more balance can either reduce the top or increase the bottom or both, but how to think about it is key. Much of this change is in global economics and technology; it is an issue of productivity amplified by competition. Emotional speeches do not change this reality, thoughtful planning does.

The reason for the great distinction between class warfare and economic justice and their results on the system is their significantly different approaches to bringing fairness. Politically based class warfare looks primarily at a political redistribution of wealth regardless of how it is achieved fairly or unfairly— simply to take from the productive sector and give to a nonproductive or needy sector. This is why tax reform, which eliminates subsidies and favoritism by deductions, is more effective than raising rates.

Great and growing income inequality is a major threat to stability and the sense of unity and cultural dignity. Most everyone is opposed to it, but the key question seldom focused on is how to lower the inequality. Emotionally, it is easy to attack the wealthy by tax or other spread the wealth approaches. The wisdom of the issue must go to the question of how you raise everyone's standard of living more than how you lower someone else's standard to be closer to the average for fairness. Fairness alone does not feed hungry kids or care for the sick. Fairness should be the goal but must intelligently be created in a way that gives growth and opportunity. The "fairness" of redistribution is very different from the "fairness" of granting opportunity. Yet pursuing the first without contextual thinking harms the latter. Personal dignity in a superficial sense is soothed by the first emotionally, but ultimate personal dignity is given by self-sufficiency and the opportunity for it in a system that encourages it. Of even more importance is the higher growth rate for wealth creation in the system. There are many ways to bring more fairness, and it should be sought for economic justice, not emotional political short-term gain. The moral hazard of decisions must be recognized, if wealth is not created to be shared, it shrinks and problems are far worse. Systemic impact as well as the creation of fairness needs to be considered to find the best way to lower inequality and raise, rather than lower, all parts of society. You cannot separate fairness from the system to be used.

Market capitalism can be adjusted by tax policy for more equality, but the issue is whether the tax policy really creates socialism. That is the true issue. Moral hazard analysis tells us whether it is an issue of fairness or systemic change. If it is systemic change that seeks equality of result more than equality of opportunity, we need to debate that specific issue.

Economic justice removes the effects of crony capitalism's lobby-induced benefits. Income redistribution for fairness removes the incentives of the system to produce. They are two very different concepts with very different long-term results that are easily confused, often intentionally.

The key in understanding income inequality is its base cause. Causes can be different. All incomes could be rising, some less than others, but a positive trend, or high incomes rising quickly while lower incomes stagnate or fall. In the first there might be some envy, but the personal dignity is not offended as greatly because things are getting better. The second, middle class stagnation often caused by globalization and technology, is the more common modern threat and does impact the fairness judgment of personal dignity. There will always be some inequality in a nation that uses a market economy because talents are valued differently. The public policy question comes from how active the government should be in regulating the economic, and to a degree, cultural issue of equality because its actions shape the economic model.

Throughout the world this is an issue that has quite varying, but in many ways measurable differences, which give insights to the nature of the governing system. Too much power in the hands of the rich who use their wealth to increase the disparity can be a significant threat to them and the society if it affects markets adversely and hurts opportunity. The question is best understood by looking at policies as to how they affect the economy. Redistribution of income is an option many academics favor, but the ultimate goal needs to be empowering people with opportunity and dignity rather than increasing dependence, which is not sustainable demographically.

The key is reform that boosts growth for as many as possible, with strategic focus on limiting excessive benefit that goes beyond self-interest to greed, corruption, and crony capitalism. Competition that builds markets does not function well with these negatives. Most of the sources are found in exceptions in the tax code where wealth builds in special inequalities through the political process. This will still be a divisive political issue as greed or "the one percent" is debated, but the one percent is far less significant than how money is made and what is contributed to society. The economic justice argument requires an understanding of what affects growth and opportunity in the economy. The political issue in income equality comes from another approach. Ultimately the cultural issue of dignity will play a deciding hand, but how well understood the difference between the two becomes will be critical.

Economic justice focuses much more on the system to bring balance. If CEO salaries are substantially out of balance to those of workers, the most appropriate vehicles are enhancements of market systems to attempt to bring balance by exposure of the inequities. That is not done effectively in our current environment because in America the concept of "crony capitalism" very much protects and develops such imbalances. The issue is not the capitalism that is often destroyed politically in a class warfare concept, but is the cronyism that is the unique linkage between the political and economic systems that do not allow the proper performance of markets. It is the greed issue in its purest form.

Sustainable growth and the expansion of the middle class require a market system with economic justice and a balance for workers where compensation is more fairly based and opportunity provided. This is an extremely difficult theoretical goal to meet in the current world, but it still is far more beneficial than redistribution alone, which greatly changes the incentives of wealth creation and presses for the export of investment and jobs. The distinctions between political, economic, and cultural solutions are often hidden in the rhetoric of the day, but understanding those distinctions is vital to finding the most optimum approaches to be taken.

Class warfare versus economic justice further requires an understanding of the concepts of redistribution versus charity/needs driven government support. There is no doubt that there are those within a society that are incapable of addressing their circumstances alone. A culture that believes in service to others and doing for others with support, which does not necessarily have to be reciprocated, automatically recognizes and even prioritizes support of those people both through government and through private charity in service organizations.

Any system with such needs has a choice between creating increasing dependency and ineffective distribution through political taxation to equalize incomes, or organizing such political systems to governmentally support the truly needy and substantially enhance private sector charitable efforts to aid and assist beyond the government's ability. But a policy to disallow charitable deductions for tax purposes would be a policy action that had impact—government action impact. When the country was prosperous beyond all others it had the luxury of broad-based redistribution. In today's competitive world, choices of policy must be much more carefully determined. When policies emotionally look to class warfare, they want to means test wealth and income. That may be necessary with our deficits and choices, but those affected have a valid argument that efficiency be in government first.

Few times do you see actual implementation of the rhetoric politically determining the need for funding dependency. If the system does not have the morality within itself to only address those truly in need, it has great affect on the cultural power of how children and families view their position in life. Liberty is lost when one's self-image or personal dignity and life control is relegated to government support when it is effectively bought by programs. The great challenge will be when any country, finally reaches a point that the individual responsibility is no longer viewed as the right concept to teach children. Instead the family survives by gaming benefits from the system whether poor, middle class, or rich. Politics has trumped culture. This is the cronyness of capitalism at its core.

The ultimate test of the system is how government looks at handling the money that it takes in. Small governments have to even more effectively identify true risk and help those most in need that are not helped by the system. The nonprofit sectors in America driven largely by value-based organizations have done this well because the charity of man is the ultimate goal needing to be developed. Unfortunately even they are now being trained in many cases to look to governmental support to deliver the funds. No system will be perfect. The question is whether the concept behind the system is one that builds opportunity and individual responsibility or one that gradually removes it.

Growth and a bigger economy solve many of the problems. Most people that have limited resources have a natural desire to want to achieve more for their children, just as their children want to achieve a vision of a successful life. Creating that opportunity solves many of the problems redistribution of income is ultimately attempting, when in good conscience, to do. It is in many cases a well-intentioned effort for the right goals, but very much misses the ultimate cost of the type of solutions that are presented because it fails to recognize the longer-term moral hazards. These are distinctions of utmost importance when you look at the cultural aspect of ultimate personal dignity and the unity of policy it provides, which inevitably play a vital part in the political structure and economic structure of any nation.

Understanding these moral hazard concepts is imperative for the younger generations. Moral hazard takes place over time and is not as immediately recognized, but has extremely serious impacts on shaping cultures because it is a cultural value issue often affected by short-term economic and political interests. The current younger generations will see the effects of this far more than the existing generation, which has benefited greatly from it. It effectively pushes the costs of current benefits down to the coming generations.

Every generation ought to take care of its own. It should define itself by a high level of charity and by recognition of the value of others. One's personal dignity is looked at in both political and economic terms, as well as cultural respect. That respect, however, is gained by people doing all they can to take care of themselves and the government and charity only filling in those areas where they are no longer capable. Few people object to this charity, and society needs to be trained to appreciate that people define themselves by how they view helping others. The rich often see the need to give to charity and feel this is an obligation; they feel the opposite about income redistribution, which penalizes effort and is often poorly spent.

Unrealistic support that is only redistribution for the sake of gaining votes significantly disrupts moral hazard under the premise of need. These are not easy decisions and will often be debated intensely. One person's concept of need will be substantially different from another's depending on perspective. However, full understanding of the decision making process and its implications needs to be brought forth to create a sensitivity to its actual impacts, and additions to policies need to be made to assure effectiveness, trustworthiness, and control risk methodology. Policy needs to be refined in the sense of management of risk. Identify the risk effectively, quantify the likelihood and severity of impact, and then build in systems that either control or monitor the risks so as not to create policies beyond expectations.

The Scholarly Pursuits and Context

Besides family, what are the most important influences that instill values and create our common culture? Education is certainly a leading one, particularly with families having less time together. Education is a key to knowledge in the science and management it teaches. But it also has to shape values like the Golden Rule, conscience, and the common good, giving the wisdom to understand the ultimate benefit of honorable and moral relationships with others rather than the convenience of greed. One of the most important things in life is a good education. But the quality of the education depends on how well it prepares you for life and what you learned. Just knowledge of the facts of the world alone does little good if you do not put them into the streams of reasoning that involve wisdom in using those facts. Context leads to creative thinking.

Throughout my life I have had the benefit of learning through unique experiences. I greatly regretted that when I was in college to pursue finance and law that I had to study very specialized courses. In later life the more I have read the philosophers, the more I understand how the world evolved historically in thought but also how the times greatly influenced ideas and how the ideas of one stage of history impact the next. The reality of life is that the culture passed down from one generation to the next is what it values the most, and is the power of history to shape the future.

The reality of politics is that natural law balances out bad public policy by crisis. And the reality of economics is that market systems give the most opportunity and benefit provided they are ethical and long term, and self-interest, not greed, guides them. But these observations came from the experiences that give context. When education specializes and becomes dogmatic, it loses context and is of lesser value. It looks at individual facts and loses broad realism.

It is very important to understand the scholarly pursuits of research and writing and to give due respect to those scholars who study the intricacies of their fields. But it is also critically important to recognize that we have become so specialized in our modern world that the ability to see the prioritization of those ideas and how they fit into a far greater environment for forces and powers is not necessarily the same. Even if you invent a better engine, it has to fit in the final car. Teaching must pull together all the parts of the assembly line of education.

As I previously mentioned, one of the unique things in how the military views the world is a very effective system of analyzing and planning problems by four levels—strategy, operations, tactics, and techniques. In the form of a pyramid, the strategies are an overview of what you want to accomplish—for example, why you go to war, and if so how to rally your people and allies, and also with whom you must fight. Operations divide that problem into smaller parts that are manageable. For example, in World War II do you go into North Africa, was D-Day too early, do you go into Italy? Tactics tend to be the use of resources. What resources must be put together for each of the operations?

Techniques are much more detailed concepts like the coverage rules for a convoy so that its guns and the guns of every ship coordinate to protect the whole. These separate ideas into levels of importance. They are a method of prioritization, but prioritization alone is just one of the many factors that go into developing context. However, prioritization of the most critical goes a long way to a successful result.

Too often scholars look to the point, as we lawyers tend to do, that everything must be proven by precedent. They emphasize that footnotes and past history are significant. They say that bibliographies determine great books. Reality of life is somewhat different. Few of the great books of history had significant bibliographies. They were catalysts of ideas that were very understandable by the common men of their time, and they relied upon the common sense of the people that read them. They did not look at facts having to be proven by history, but by the very nature of man's life giving value to the observations that were shown. They were often the works of philosophers or sages who were not quite the same as scholars.

Milton Friedman used to make a critical distinction between those who had been educated and those who have simply been in schools. What you learn and its value to society is not the same as where you learned it. While elite universities provide networks and perspective, it is still quite possible to be well educated and underemployed. And if resentment is taught as the attitude of some education, it makes emotion not thought the driving factor. This to me is the anti-education since I feel education's purpose is to learn how to think with a civilized perspective, and have a broad range of ideas to consider. Many institutions are now not in sync with the realities of the modern world because they have become insular in their own world's vision of their importance.

In my perception, philosophers or sages are people who have had new and original ideas formulating a synthesis of concepts more appropriately affecting the times. They could grow to be an organizing principle that shaped the movement of ideas going forward in such a way that they had the power to draw a sustaining following. Many times the scholars and the philosophers of the day did not mix well. Christ was crucified. Confucius was pushed from office. Socrates was forced to commit suicide. And the same is true of the acceptance or rejection of many other ideas. The ideas that originate can be good or bad in how they shape the future. *But they should never be discounted if they strike the more populous nature of society and are able to enter the core of the individual's trust in their validity **from their own experience***.

There are three Chinese "curses" that show how life is often a balance of competing forces that deserve contemplation:

First, "May you live in interesting times."

Second, "May you come to the attention of those in authority."

Third, "May you find what you are looking for."

Every generation has its opportunities and dangers—it is how you react to them that truly matters. You do not know yourself or others until you or they are tested. Government can help you or frustrate you, but you are ultimately the government—as a voter in a Democracy or a participant of conscience or a lack thereof in a "harmonious society." And finding what you are seeking is determined by what you value and how you define personal dignity.

Chinese culture from which these came has seen the cycles of civilization and appreciates the "enlightenment" of beginning with the most important facts of life—your inner vision of what you value most. That vision is shaped by the family and its values. The method of adaptability depends on the way you see obligations in life as to how you prioritize organizing principles. Those obligations that are valued the most are passed on through teaching. But there is often a big difference between what is taught and what the student learns or retains. Focus and interest matter greatly and how structured the presentation is as well as the importance that values play in the key parts.

However, the most important factor is how you are taught to think. Our universities should develop the mind's organization to give it perspective. Although the reality of education, philosophy, or life is that *how you think about something determines what you think about it,* you often have culturally implanted biases that usually originated in history and were passed forward. They may be inaccurate for the times, but they exist. We might call them "prejudices," which are automatically made. They vary in different cultures and religions, but they exist because they are a part of how people think.

Recognizing them is important, but also recognizing that scholars shape their preconceptions is essential—particularly values, which are the most critical part of how the stream of information is put together. Scholars often say values are formed by the family by the time you reach college. But colleges are teaching the parents of the next generation and shaping how they think. Prejudices are not all bad, if you have a prejudice for honor, character, and seek responsibility, it is positive.

One of the unique problems faced in many of our highest universities is trying to balance science with religion. Historically, the two have often been in conflict, and unfortunately intellectuals often look at religion from a perspective of provability. Religion accepts much more on faith. In reality, science and religion are looking for the same thing—ultimate truth. However, they go about it in very different ways. Science uses doubt to disprove theories, but in doubting you may miss other truths. Religion uses faith and believing, but you can believe things that are not true.

Scientists have a hard time explaining relationships and concepts like honor because they are not easily reason based but faith based. Universities many times fail to realize science and religion are both critical parts of life and that students need grounding in a broadened philosophy of the great classics as well as the technology of the day if they are to have a truly educated mind.

One of the best examples of how ideas are shaped, and why how you think about something matters, is a story that circulates on the Internet. A university professor challenges his students with the question, "Did God create everything that exists?" A student replies that He did. The professor then notes that, "If God created everything then God created evil since evil exists, and according to the principle that our works define who we are, then God is evil." The professor then takes this logic and expands it by discussing the physics of sensing God through physical senses, and the answer is no. This is followed by another young student standing. He disagrees with the professor's logic noting that in reality cold does not exist, but according to laws of physics, cold is really the absence of heat. Heat is what causes a body or matter to have or transmit energy; absolute zero (-460° Fahrenheit) is a total absence of heat. The student then asked whether darkness exists, and the professor then noted that of course it did. Then the student replies that in both cases cold does not exist, nor does darkness exist. Darkness is in reality the absence of light because light you can study, but darkness you cannot. Thus, the student came to the logic of the professor's question, "Does evil exist?" The student noted that evil does not exist unto itself. Evil is the absence of God just like darkness is the absence of light and cold is the absence of heat. God did not create evil, it is the result of what happens when man does not have God's love present in his heart.

The story well conveys two very different ways a similar set of facts could be interpreted. How you think about these issues from a classroom will affect how you think about them in life because most students do not have the time, background, or thought to challenge a professor. How and what professors present, as well as who presents it shapes our cultural ethics. Albert Einstein best commented on the balance between science and religion in a paper he published in *Nature* in 1940. He wrote: "a person who was religiously enlightened appears to me to be one who has, to the best of his ability, liberated himself from the fetters of his selfish desires and is pre-occupied with thoughts, feelings, and aspirations to which he clings because of their super-personal values . . . regardless of whether any attempt is made to unite this concept with the Divine Being for otherwise it would not be possible to count Buddha and Espinoza as religious personalities."

The point that should be taken is that science and religion (and the value systems it represents) in many ways fit together. Einstein did not believe that a divine will exists as an independent cause of nature, but he also understood that it could not be refuted and that there are many areas science has not been able to yet understand. The significance is that he does not start with a belief that science and values cannot be coordinated because the conflicts between science and religion often came from error. It is not one or the other, but a more thoughtful approach to understanding that is necessary.

Yet today, often when speaking with my friends at universities about the importance of value-based education, I am told that I should concentrate on leadership rather than values as an approach. My reply is that Stalin and Hitler were leaders, but not necessarily in the direction I would prefer. What you believe and why is probably the core organizing principle of an individual—in context rather than just with intelligence and knowledge. Another quote from Einstein perhaps conveys the common foundation best when he noted in "Religion and Science," *New York Times Magazine,* 9 November 1930:

> *A man's ethical behavior should be based effectively on sympathy, education, and social ties and needs; no religious base is necessary, man would indeed be in a poor way if he had to be restrained by fear of punishment and the hope of reward after death.*

Science requires ethics and conscience just as much as the morality of religion. Thus, the way we think about the world should emphasize conscience as a primary organizing principle, not convenience too often taught in the modern world as the core of success. For those wishing to be more devout in religion, focusing on the relationship between God and man, it should be their prerogative. But there also needs to be a strongly taught morality of man's relationship to man where family values are not mitigated or refuted by educational systems relying only on what can be proven through an arrogance of man's wisdom extending beyond its current reaches.

Science as well as religion requires morality. It is necessary—even for those who are less religious. So it is a false argument to avoid talking about the necessity of morality by challenging religion. The issue is whose morality and whose values. Morality or conscience relates back to our historical upbringing and cultures often have similarities from their basic units. The point is that context or thought is shaped by the family, by the educational processes that teach how to think, and by the economic and political environment in which we live. Understanding each of these components is critical if we are to effectively understand how wisdom is placed into a process and how to judge our present manner of thinking.

How we think matters economically because education has a direct relationship to innovative and competitive advantages a country has in providing its standard of living. But what is often missed is that a full education is not just the facts and analytics you learn, but also how well you can communicate that knowledge to others. And building upon that, how well you work with others to achieve common goals. In a complicated world, a "master mind" of combined intelligence and talents is necessary for working together in harmony. That requires wisdom, not just knowledge, and is the area in which American education has been failing our society and affecting our competitiveness.

In the discussions of the generations, we have seen that the technological advances over the last hundred years in our family's generation have brought a significant change in where we get our information. We have seen how educational changes have impacted focus. It is helpful to return to Lyndon's observations of how we reached the current point of civility and then project how the generations following us will be impacted by value transmission.

UNDERSTANDING CHANGE BY DISTINGUISHING KNOWLEDGE AND WISDOM

Knowledge is expanding constantly at an incredible rate in the modern world. Like the example of a penny that is doubled: two cents, four cents, eight cents, sixteen cents, thirty-two cents, sixty-four cents, etc., in an ongoing progression. It multiplies dramatically. We know more today in grade school than the wisest men of previous ages were able to decipher from the knowledge of their times. Wisdom, however, is very different. As Confucius said, "Wisdom is recognizing what you know and what you don't." None of us may be as wise as Solomon who made decisions based on a much more thoughtful approach in a more simple time. Knowledge can build nuclear energy, but having the wisdom to use it properly is an entirely different matter.

Whenever we discuss change in a modern world, we have a number of opinions that are quickly given in support or rebuttal. It is in part because the nature of our social change has led to individuality in America. But it is also because the last several generations have lived through a very unique time of technological advancement and the enhancement of knowledge. We have moved to individuality in a way that adjusts for the aggressiveness of the times and brings immediate, almost defensive reaction to our views and diminishes the context. Technology helps drive this preselection and filters our ideas by giving us the opportunity to listen to those who are of our opinion, reinforcing it.

In part, that has led to an interesting dichotomy in how many of us view truth. It is not always exactly the same. As we just noted, there is a part of society where truth is limited by human understanding and what we can prove and understand. That is to say that we look to science and a rationalization of explanation in what some of us will accept. There is another group to whom truth exists beyond what is provable or able to be rationalized. Truth in the realm of faith, also understanding that we are not capable of a full rationalization of the world and have to believe that there is truth beyond the known.

This battle between approaches—reliance on science versus faith has been exaggerated by being distinguished as a battle between religion and science. But in reality it may be easier to see it as a battle between what is known and what is not known.

A second complication from that conundrum is the fact that information has become more specialized, and thus we have developed a much more elite class having significant knowledge in individual fields. The intellectuals of today are very knowledgeable in specific areas and believe that their wisdom should thus guide the direction of society. This becomes very apparent in our universities, political structure, and in some cases our bureaucracies and media. The problems are enhanced by the fact that many of these same people visit with each other often in a form of peer review that simply reinforces their perspective of the world. However, the world is much broader and more realistic than oftentimes the theories can support.

We may understand in science the macro of Einstein's Theory of Relativity, and we may understand the rules of the small particles of Quantum Mechanics. But we are seeking to define the linkage that provides more of a universal theory. We understand the concept of the "Big Bang," but there are some real questions of how the "Big Bang" itself emerged. The truth goes beyond just human rationalization and knowledge and involves much broader information and interrelationships physically and socially that often work different from theory.

One of the best approaches to addressing the problem emerged from the "Copenhagen Observation" of the great physicist Neils Bohr. He looked at every man's mind as being but a model of the world and how it could be enhanced by bringing people with different experiences and different knowledge together, so that the model was much more realistic. Today, that takes place far too often in the peer review or the gatherings of a limited number of people rather than the broad discussions of a greater number of the masses. Peer review is fine in specialization if it is fair and ethical, but macro issues have less certainty and less comparable peers. Economics is a perfect example if you judge the accuracy of predictions over time.

An additional problem is learning the true lessons of history. History has always had revisionism. Winners often write history. But in modern times—particularly with the Internet—opinion, facts, and truth get intermixed. There is an old saying that figures can be tortured to say or prove anything. One of our primary needs is as unbiased a source as we can find that is amplified by a proven thought, assisting in filtering abnormalities of logic. Another is assuring that history is taught. History is the ancestor of culture and problems of conscience—the Holocaust, slavery, and the exploitation of workers as well as financial panics. The wars and the lessons of history are critical to context. History teaches people that knowledge on public policy is far better than just being angry.

This is where the family and the wisdom it provided in the social context of civility of the Golden Rule and then historical presentations of how the world has tended to work became so very important in providing understanding and wisdom to the new generations. When we rely only on science and the most modern theories alone, we often disregard the more mundane knowledge that is critical in interpreting and prioritizing the more elite ideas. It is wise to have skepticism of the intellectual elite as they present their opinion and theory. They may be based on significant knowledge and thought process but may lack the wisdom of asking the right question.

I was reminded of the old Internet story titled "Old Spot." A bridge club was hosted by each lady in the group alternatively, and each tried to be competitively better. The lady of the house now hosting decided mushroom steak would be ideal but was shocked at the cost of the mushrooms. Her husband noted there were many wild mushrooms out back. She wondered though if some could be poisonous. He said, "All types of critters are eating them and they know what to eat and not eat." She thought about it, picked some, cleaned them, and as a test gave them to their dog, Spot, to see if he would eat them. He gulped them down, and satisfied she cooked and served them over the steak. After the meal, which all complimented, the maid came in and said, "Madam, I hate to tell you but old Spot is dead." Shocked and in panic she called the doctor who came with an ambulance and one by one gave enemas and pumped the stomach of each guest. Finally, all looked peeked and sat listlessly when the maid came in to clean up and said, "You know Madam, the sad thing is the man who ran over Spot never stopped." Wisdom is knowing when to ask the right question. There are right answers that may not matter.

Intellectuals tend to disregard those with whom they do not agree and in modern times have become extremely defensive of their own theories. This is unfortunate because discussion on a broader scale would be of value to everyone in completing a thoughtful common mind approach. This is truer in the individualistic societies of the West than in the consensus driven harmonious societies of the East. The West needs more harmony, and the East needs more individual innovations. There is a balance to be sought.

These observations preface a discussion on the change I think caused the evolution in our generation from a civil society to a much more litigious and aggressive one. The scholars will deal more with each of the individual generations, the Baby Boomers of which I was a part, the Greatest Generation that preceded me, Generation X and Generation Y, the Millennials that followed. They are all unique with different characteristics and much has been written about them.

But the reality of where we are now and what has happened to our civility is not really any one generation because all of these generations live together. All of them have differing core tendencies based on the technology, change, ideas, and cultural values put forth to them. They all affect each other.

The economic opportunities for the younger generation are limited in part by the needs of the older generation. Work retention is an example. With focus on individual issues, you get more litigation and laws that take the place of morality and culture that had peer pressure, lowering individual responsibility. The legalism of politics is replacing the justice of culture as society becomes more a salad bowl of generations and less a melting pot of common values. This leads to less force and support of the infrastructure of nonprofits, charities, and public service. The common good is less appreciated.

Mark Hattas, a friend who has studied generations and their characteristics, noted this as well. While the fiscal situation has changed, the "mood" of the country is also changing recognizing the needs of the crisis mode—a mindset that propels society's leaders to be more decisive, and a time when society is willing to make bigger sacrifices for the benefit of future generations. He notes that leadership is increasingly made up of Baby Boomers that grew up during the post WWII era. Society was at a new beginning—expanding, rebuilding, and repairing broken institutions. Now aging and longing for their youth, they will take aggressive, decisive actions to fix things and recapture the national high, youthful "mood" for future generations. That comment is consistent with the majority of our country feeling we are going in the wrong direction. But it makes a clear, critical issue of how to unify different visions of the future allowing for change.

Our challenge is much like that bucket of crabs. If they keep pulling the one in front down, they never get out. If they would use logic and build a common ladder helping those left, they would all gain their freedom. Getting out of holes requires a desire and a plan. Mark believes that we are living in a time that will go down as the greatest era for accelerating innovation in the history of humankind, but with mounting crises and broken institutional trust, it is also a dangerous time. To me the innovation is the result of scientific knowledge, but we need the wisdom to maintain a stable society of values to cultivate it. Do the crabs in the "hole" get out by the wisdom of conscience, or keep fighting and pulling each other down for personal convenience?

It becomes important to look to the trends that have evolved over the last several generations as a composite. Then begin to look at what the next generation needs to understand to bring back the civility and unity that will be critical. If the trend continues with the current generation's pressure for the dependency of society in old age upon the youth and tax burdens constantly progressing through debt, we will inevitably end up with great friction between generations, and a self-dividing pie that falters in competitiveness with the rest of the world. *Every society must have an organizing principle that is the premier effort of how it moves forward.* If it ever begins to recede, it normally falls quickly. The best example has always been the growing pie where everyone has a slice. And if everyone works together, the pie gets larger and their piece increases. In the corollary example of a pie in which all effort is focused upon division and not growth, the pie normally shrinks, and there is a battle between the parts as to who gets a greater piece.

The American middle class has been in this struggle as technology has replaced the jobs that built it. Americans see the Chinese taking jobs, but before China it was Mexico and other countries. Computers replaced manual accounting jobs, low cost labor necessary for a company's competitiveness replaced manufacturing jobs, and the ever growing regulatory tax, health, and environmental costs have impacted the competitiveness of all business as the world "levels or flattens." However, America started from a very strong base. With 4% of the world's population, it had achieved a quarter of the world's income and a third of its net worth in some estimates. Compared to average income figures for the world as a whole, Americans do extremely well. Ours has been the premier wealth generating system. That allowed the improvements in quality of life that regulation and laws provided. But we have gotten into a negative mindset that passing laws and creating money solve problems, and we do not think in a logical process of consensus but from extremes. Consensus building is a political detriment in a highly polarized political society.

Growth is essential for rising standards of living. Policies must recognize this. There is a huge strategic difference if the policy is primarily focused on dividing wealth rather than creating it. One key thing that has not been taught is the responsibilities of citizenship beyond just voting. It requires a knowledgeable vote for a continuing Democracy.

Politics overshadow the need for cultural unity and economic policies of growth. *Natural laws bring into balance bad public policies that ignore moral hazard by crisis. Conscience requires both compassion and obligation, but obligation of responsibility, individual and public, are necessary for sustainability. Conscience is defined by individual responsibility to self and others. Public responsibility requires focusing on the incentives within legislation to avoid longer-term moral hazard.*

Government and society owe support to those that cannot help themselves by both government programs and charity. But that is greatly different from unsustainable efforts that undercut competitiveness and growth having long-term consequences in leaving the needy when programs are no longer sustainable. *Having compassion is not the issue, but how to develop a system with consensus enough to do it well that brings a unity for sacrifice. That begins with the "Golden Rule" taught first by family.*

The issues must be discussed asking the right questions more than seeking the right answers, and this comes from thinking in context. Most ethics issues are not choices of good versus bad, but of competing goods. On taxation, the question is whether the rich pay their "fair share." What is a fair share when 10% pay a great percentage of the taxes and 50% pay little? When funds run out for Social Security and Medicare, some say means test and pay little to those that can afford it. But is it fair to take from those who have saved to care for themselves in retirement to pay for others who have not? Government does not create wealth—it only redistributes it.

These are questions balancing obligations and compassion and deal not only with sustainability of programs but the very nature of the culture. If your public programs and legal system penalize individual responsibility, you will ultimately get a dependent society that is not sustainable in a modern competitive world. We have to use different thought processes with reason beyond political emotions if we are to change courses. 2012 will be a critical point for these choices. Many feel the average population can never understand the full issues. That may be true, but they have an instinct for truth and trust to choose between leaders if they have a basic understanding of the critical issues. Restoration of cultural conscience is the key to this.

In every nation there are those of conscience and of convenience. There are those in each generation that hold the characteristics more important. To me, the issue is not so much the change of technology but the fact that families take the time to pass the values forward and interact with the children. Or it is that their time with the children is significantly limited, and the children are much more focused on getting their information from other sources, be it the modern social media or friends. Family is thus consistent with the teaching of conscience.

III | The Impact of Change on the Family Transmission of Values

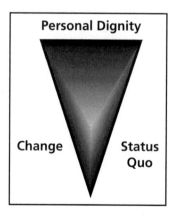

Perhaps the best way to look at the transmission of values from the family is to see its evolution and the technological change that is impacted over these generations. Looking at the above triangle, the side on the left is change. The opposite side is the status quo of the existing culture as developed by history (and the values it has moved forward shaping the culture). The third or bridging side is what might best be called "personal dignity." Personal dignity in this sense is how an individual sees one's purpose and satisfaction in life, and vision for the future. Is their organizing principle one of conscience in which their goals look beyond themselves and the present or is it really one of convenience determined largely by their current situation and how they see their best opportunities at improving it? There are costs involved in each choice. Personal dignity is also a reflection of how one views their control over their life. The more they sense they are in control, whatever their purpose, the higher they sense their dignity.

My father's generation was appropriately called the "Greatest Generation." He was a veteran who fought in World War II and was born in 1910. His family suffered through the Great Depression, and he was shaped by that very climactic period. His family was a very close unit. He focused on hunting and family involvement, and there were very few things that pulled him very far from home until he was eighteen. He put together a car, and with his father's encouragement to learn about the world, drove off to California with some friends. He carried with him letters from his father to various entities along the route with which Brenham Wholesale (a company Grandfather Henry helped found) did business asking them to help Dad should he need it as he traveled.

Grandfather told my father about all the different people he had met in business over the years and how distant friendships had become close because of trust and common values. He learned a great deal from his father because there was time for personal interaction with the core family values since life did not have that many distractions. Television was not prominent, and the Simon Theater, the local picture show with its newsreels, was one of the few sources of information besides newsletters and local papers. The interaction with other family members and friends was particularly critical. Sources of information were limited and much of what you learned was from what the family taught you from their experience. Courtesy to all, particularly elders, was expected. Mother's rule of never creating enemies and Dad's rule of giving all men respect as a basis of merit were enforced with daily reminders. Today people are easily offended and "disrespected" as if respect were an entitlement. In their day you got courtesy but you earned respect.

Politics shaped a great deal of the Texas environment at that time because leaders were often identified with certain sets of thoughts. Just as in Rome, where normally you had a leader identified with the elite and another identified with the people as a whole. Politics had such images throughout history and societies, and our political parties today do the same.

Discussions were critical. The area may have been rural, but it was the original location of several great universities. Local civic groups were very strong and discussed the available news. These groups brought people of different political persuasion together, and friendships and discussions honed civility. You did not have all the knowledge or material that 24/7 news provides, but the critical issues were understood in more depth. You did not hear the news from a "commentator" but from a wide variety of opinions at the Saturday night Courthouse Square Band performance, the Chamber of Commerce, the Library Board, the church, the Gun and Rod Club, or all the service organizations where you mixed with people of a common purpose that was not political. So more blended thought with joint understanding emerged. Racial equality was not present but sensitivity to it was. This was still Alexis de Tocqueville's American vision.

The Baby Boom Generation began at the end of World War II dominated by a significant rise in birth rates related to the impact of the war. Our generation, particularly in my college years, was a very split generation due to the counter culture of the 1960s and the Vietnam War's impact on it. Values effectively divided on a prioritization that has significantly impacted those years to the present.

Interestingly, as I learned at that time, conscience has two components. One part of conscience is the sense that you have obligations to fulfill to others and give them the personal dignity that is necessary and that individual responsibility recognizes and prioritizes this. These two often easily fit together in most parts of life, but there are times when they do not fit so smoothly and choices have to be made between versions of them. I am always amazed in ethics that the issue is not black and white—for example, whether or not to report the boss's son for theft—but the issues that make you choose between two potentially good and important issues that emerge.

The arguments in healthcare are a good example. Those who favor the concept of social justice and charity or having all covered by a program have one perspective. But the other perspective involves the obligation to those covered that any program be sustainable. And sustainability may well require limitation to the fact that those with individual responsibility do so, and only true private charity with focused governmental help gives a real compassion that can continue over time. Neither of these violates conscience, but the method by which decisions are ultimately made becomes critical depending on the system. You will get very different ultimate outcomes as cost becomes a determining factor. You also make a choice between a society of dependency or one of individual responsibility. Letting the issues divide you as a society inevitably ends with today's problems of not looking at issues that bring us together for discussion but at issues that only fan the flame of disagreement.

HOW WE GOT HERE

Many of the seeds of current conditions, even with all the intervening generations impacted by their parents, go back to the Baby Boomer's counter culture of the 1960s. In that period such social issues like gender and racial equality, and environmentalism were rising in social consciousness. To those taking such positions, the existing status quo was viewed as an institutional impediment to the counter culture portion of the generation that became active in opposition to institutions. On the other side of the coin were those that were not necessarily opposed to the issues brought forth by the counter culture, but who more deeply valued the concepts historically formed in the status quo regarding obligation, how to manage change, and to an appreciation of the importance that historical institutions provided as the civil process. It was also greatly impacted and enhanced by the Vietnam War. Families who participated actively in World War I and II had shaped many of the participants who looked at what would be called the "obligation" approach of the generation in their values. There was a sense of pride and responsibility in an obligation owed to the country. On college campuses, social justice and opposition to the war were combined as issues by one side while those who believed in the obligations to country and a protection of the civil process fell into the other. My family came from a background of law enforcement, military, and small business that had codes of honor or ethics that required a sense of obligation.

At the University of Texas in 1970 this became increasingly apparent as I ran for Student Body President. There were a number of candidates, but I was primarily the conservative in a field of very significant liberal and radical factions. In some ways the radicals and the conservatives understood each other better than the liberals understood either. The radicals very much wanted immediate change and attacked the status quo while the conservatives believed in the existing process and slower change. The reality dealt more with how people saw the world and what they valued. The conservatives like me felt you owed a sense of honor and obligation to the nation because of its history—nationalism out of respect for what it had given you through the sacrifice of previous generations.

In some ways my position on the issues was shaped by the fact that my family had volunteered for military service going back to the Civil War. My grandfather probably died at an early age because of contracting pneumonia during World War I. To volunteer for service in World War II, my father resigned as sheriff because he could not be drafted from that position. At the time I was running, I was an officer in the Naval Reserve and was going on active duty shortly. And years later my son Tee volunteered after 9/11 without us even discussing it because he felt it was an obligation from the past. These values came from close-knit sacrifices of the past and a value system of obligation to defend it that was passed forward.

The radicals did not seem to come from quite the same values but had a far more individualistic approach and viewing the issues in light of what they called social justice, and in opposition to the war, poor policy. Neither side really understood the other. I tried to explain to some of the radical leaders, heading to Canada when their exemptions were up, that I was probably less enthusiastic about the war than they since I would be going into it. However, I did see the values within the war as far as protecting Democracy as a theme presented. And I saw my obligation to the country primarily and the need for honoring it. To them, this fact carried little weight but seemed to be an indictment of my values. If they did not at least give me my personal dignity or security needs, then there seemed to be hypocrisy in the process. I am sure the defenders of the conservative traditions looked like the status quo and reactionary to the radicals. They so personalized the social justice concepts and valued achieving them much more than any destruction to the system that occurred.

In retrospect, the Vietnam War was escalated in large part because a civil war was expanded by misunderstanding the actions of the nations involved. This is an example of the benefits of closer, more accurate understanding of all parties. You have to stand when critical principle is involved, but because of the costs, you have an obligation to fully understand the context of serious actions to appreciate the consequences. It is a lesson history re-teaches often. But many times the public does not see the real battle in a strategic sense, only a tactical one.

An example might be a fort I once visited in Maine. A third level fort built in 1814 and primarily restored in the Civil War, it fired on only one ship. Many people said it was such a waste of money, but in truth, its purpose was not to fight battles but to prevent them by occupying critical ground to prevent attacks. Sometimes you fight battles like Pork Chop Hill in Korea for seemingly worthless terrain to show the strength of commitment. World War II did not start with Germany going into Poland, but with Japan going unopposed into Manchuria because it sent the message of weakness when no one intervened. The point is that leaders must make very careful decisions when they engage because they have significant consequences. However, there may also be consequences of non-engagement. Today leaders are second-guessed quickly with modern media, but the risks and the judgment of our determination remain. The sense of obligation in the 1960s trusted leadership to do what it knew best with more information than we possessed.

As I argued at that time, there are unintended consequences whenever the rules of society are disregarded. It is very difficult to reestablish trust and confidence once it is broken. At this point I realized that words like conservative, liberal, and radical had changed from adjectives that described how people thought about issues to nouns that described their positioning on a battlefield and the rigidity entailed. That was a significant change in our generation. After that time there was less discussion and more absolute division disallowing many of the broader compromises of the past. One reason I participated actively in the inception of the Texas Lyceum, a combination of liberals, conservatives, Republicans, Democrats, and Independents, was that it was based on a sense of honor and civility that allowed public policy discussion as well as discussion of how these issues fit together in context so more wisdom could be implemented in the process.

Over the years some moderation of the divisions in the population as a whole was needed, but how people look at themselves within politics has not ameliorated greatly. This led to a disillusionment of the following generations on institutions and an increasing lack of interest in some important issues unless they were emphatically put forth by family members. People's positions are determined by where the issue directly affects them, a transactional method of evaluation, not how things could be rearranged for a greater win-win transformational approach. Therefore, when a transformational idea comes, there is little unity or ground for its seeds to grow. Consumerism with immediate gratification became a rule where savings and the recognition that debt is weakness were no longer important.

We have been in the shadows of the Baby Boomer Generation that effectively dominated the consumerism and focus of the last fifty years. Generation X, as it is often described, was a group primarily born from the mid 1960s to the middle to late 1970s. As a generation they were affected by change in communication due to the wide spread access to television and other technology during their younger years. Information was communicated in other ways and in many cases the family was not as much of a core as in previous generations. The economy often required both parents to work and this generation had many "latch-key kids." These changes helped develop individual self-reliance and broaden perspectives within society because of increased diversity. However, the ever-continuing political battles were also shaped by Watergate and the cost it had to faith in institutions.

The parallel to the family for adults were the civic and political non-profit organizations that pull people together from different backgrounds and both engender discussion and build leadership skills. The new sources of information also began to be taken back to the family.

Over the last several generations, the family has been an evolving term that perhaps can best be understood by traditional married couples. They were the main part of the American population just after World War II, but are less than half in the recent census. The number with children dropped substantially as well. There are many causes from economic pressures to acceptance of more liberal lifestyles, but the central authority that the family held began a slow decline in the U.S. greater financial problems and pressures on the middle class has made income inequality more significant and that has an economic effect on cultural/social patterns—some marry later, some do not marry, and divorce became much more common. This means the family has less stability and personal dignity (or security), so its influence diminished as generations progressed. Some families remained focused on values, perhaps even more so with the cultural changes. But society as a whole loosened values and the family's instillation of values diminished.

Generation X saw a difficult economy and the pressures placed upon families where both parents worked and could spend less time with children. The Generation X group thus became much more individualistic. They relied on information from many different sources since they became much more closely connected through computers, and technology and the transmission of values. They could see a great deal of information, and they had access to knowledge. But increasingly the wisdom that shaped the context and perspective in which those knowledge streams could be judged was diminishing.

While families still existed, their friends became a very key source of many of their values. Peer pressure on what was important led not only to consumerism and the normal youthful trends, but also to less of an appreciation for the responsibilities that each generation has within a society. They were a generation that tended to dislike authority and preferred a great deal of flexibility in their lives. Individualism became more of a trait. In the previous generation where often their parents had existed in corporate America, their parents had sought mentors that could give them the context and perspective on achieving success within the institution. This new generation did not see institutions as loyal to them due to America's restructuring. Instead they put their trust in friendships, relationships, and faith in their own ability and individual work talents that would let them adapt to other opportunities.

Simultaneously, their parents' generation continued to see change affecting their beliefs in loyalty to the corporation since they were seeing significantly more pressure in the times of economic stress. Pension plans changed to 401K's, downsizing became much more of a reality, and the efficiencies of technology and the movement of jobs overseas began a relentless impact on how people saw themselves and their future. Views of the world were being moderated in the older generation and shaped in the younger generation. Change was rapid and serious and the status quo shaped by their parents' generation was evolving. So they took work much less seriously because of their parents' experiences. They began to rely more on technology as a solution since their faith in the mentoring of parents seemed less appropriate to the times.

Into this mix was born Generation Y—often referred to as the Millennials. From the late 1970s to the mid or late 1990s, it is larger than Generation X. And because of continuing changes in technology and social structure has a very different approach to receiving information and values. Through this time period most of the generations have accepted diversity and integrated, but to this new more diverse generation it is an accepted issue. Also because of the differences in cultures, they have learned more acceptance of others. They are individualistic because of this self-reliance, and institutions are even less significant to them than to the preceding generation.

The Internet and their ability to multitask with technology have made them experts on knowledge but often with specialization. This makes it very difficult for them to look at things in context and see the relationship that wisdom often provides for how these different issues fit together. Friends have continued to become a much more important area sometimes more than family, due to social networking and social media. Their focus may be with the family in youth, but once they become involved socially, life is driven by friends. Family nurtures and some values are instilled, but it is not the same as it was in the past. The relentless change of technology and the diminishing of institutions have led to less concern with the common good and more with individual issues deemed important. It is a much more emotional than thoughtful process of data.

Internet development causes one to write in a different way than they would converse person to person. Comment sections, often done anonymously are sometimes bitter and cruel reinforcing an individual's points at the cost of civility and respect. Comments are treated equally whether signed or anonymous on most sites, and ideas that are reasonable are often treated equally with attacks. This environment only makes hatred and loss of respect grow more quickly. People are equal, but ideas are not. Some are of far more consequence and have to be prioritized for qualities, interest, and source. Hopefully, the Internet will find its own solutions by giving priority to the best of comments. If we are not willing to sign our name in America, should we really be sending a message? And, how much credit do we give to the comments of those who do not? Not to mention questioning the competence of the commentator when he is unknown. If the younger generation gets its information in this manner, it is critical that they learn to think in a way that allows them to process it. The new media are the blogs, but for every highly intelligent comment added, there are also cranks. That requires systems that help evaluate logic and credibility. If you know how to think, the data is sifted accordingly.

EXTERNAL IMPACTS

Regardless of the generation, there is a great difference in where and how children are brought up. Just because they are in generations and affected by significant changes does not mean that families do not have a major impact on shaping the children's perspectives. When the issue of the children's future is a primary part of the conscience of the family, then the children react to this significant focus on them and are far more receptive to the information shared. In many cases it is not an issue of what is taught, but what is learned. Learning is often by example and time spent rather than just by the conveyance of information. These points show the basis of the home schooling efforts of many families.

In some cases geography makes a difference, economic status makes a difference, the value structure of the parents make a very significant difference, as does the amount of focus on the children. These very same issues occur in Asia where the generations are referred to by number. Generation X in China is looked upon as being the 13th Generation in their system. But technology is having an ever-increasing impact even there. Of equal importance in China is the single birth policy of families that created a generation of "little emperors" in which parents and grandparents have focused tremendously on individual children. This in turn has had its own benefits and detriments. What the Chinese comparison shows is that family involvement is a critical component part of how children look at society. Values may be conveyed, but just because they are conveyed does not mean that children do not become spoiled. There is a balance that is necessary. The older Confucian teachings of obligations and respect are restrengthening in China. The way of thinking is exemplified in China where children are superb at learning and preparing for tests. But creative thinking, necessary in the age of social networks to maintain character, is weaker.

In many ways, however, these cycles tend to be self-correcting. Generation Y is noted to be less driven in the workplace but more likely to prioritize family over work. There are realities within life that are often rediscovered. Cycles are a reality.

The point is that technology has had an ever-increasing impact on change, and so has education which shapes a great number of values. The world has also begun leveling in many ways and affecting economies. This has impacted the opportunities of the young and middle class skill and talent requirements. The economic situation in many ways has changed the nature of the family, as it had to spend more time and effort on earning sufficient income creating more uncertainty in life. This has formed an individualistic and socially connected generation more reliant on technology for knowledge and less trusting of the general media developed to focus on "markets" of perception.

But what has been lost is the ability to convey a much more thoughtful organizing system of how to think about issues and how history provides information in developing that structure. That structure is experience and the context it gives.

The generations have moved from very limited technology to a very significant use of technology and the multitasking with it. Detrimentally you have not had to think through books requiring more time and discussion because you can simply Google the information you need quickly. You have much more information in the form of knowledge, but much less context in the wisdom of how it all truly fits together and ultimately affects your future. By social networking the focus becomes personal and not necessarily time spent developing broader social talents or understanding strategic prioritizations that might make the most difference in one's success. People become the center—not events or ideas.

The depth of relationships is significant. A thousand "friends" may say a lot about popularity, but trust and the happiness of relationships comes from common values and times spent in deeper discussion of what values mean. Experience is a key teacher, but you need actual personal experiences, not vicarious ones, to discover one's inner self. The tremendous impact of social networking comes from the growing desire for personal dignity and recognition of self in a world where the old criteria of respect for accomplishment and character is replaced by notoriety and celebrity. The younger generation seeks people to trust and institutions to respect, but is often disappointed. If you cannot find inspiration in heroes you try to copy celebrity and judge your personal dignity by the shallow standard of recognition. But reality is that conscience asks recognition for what? And it drives a restlessness and search for truth.

The upcoming generation has a lifestyle that is focusing on social networking and texting to the deprivation of focus on education and wisdom, and in many cases because they have not experienced it, they do not realize what is missing. All the multitasking takes focus from what is important in a very competitive world.

EDUCATIONAL EFFECTS

Rising nations are improving their educational systems and are keeping a culture of focusing on education for success. Low-level jobs are disappearing with rising technology. To become or stay middle class, you must have thinking skills that machines cannot easily duplicate. The right education is essential, and its value has to be appreciated by American culture now more than ever. We are dropping behind the rest of the world not just in how we teach but also in our children's desire and ambitions to learn and succeed. Our economic success and affluence have given us a sense of entitlement that is being passed on to our children. Performance in schools has to be enhanced and education made relative to economics, but the family must go back to instilling a vision, desire, and responsibility to succeed beyond just popularity on social networks. One's value is what one produces.

As I attended my children's college graduations for their Master's or Law Degrees, what amazed me was the number of students, particularly honor students that were from other countries. Most used to stay in the United States, but opportunities now take many back home. This is very telling for our future as a country that must be a leader in innovation to keep our lifestyle. The middle class that is our core cannot exist without upping its level of critical thinking. So we must change our education system to be more competent, but more importantly we must reignite ambition and desire for learning by having the family again focus on what it takes to provide a good life. We all have "wants" and "rathers," but "needs" and "necessities" have to be distinguished. Debt made life easy—the new reality requires a new vision.

These are issues that have not been solved in the schools, but in contrast have often been minimized. Educational systems may be teaching information, but are not conveying the most critical pieces of knowledge for success. The example might be similar to an auto manufacturing line. Each part has added to a car. In recent times education has worked to have each part improved and specialized, but no one is effectively seeing that the parts fit together well. The quality of each part may be better, but the final product may well not be. For all the money we have put in education, we still rank poorly internationally. We have focused on ultimate goals but individualized goals. In consensus societies, coordination received more attention. In a very competitive world as America is about to experience, these are significant failings.

Contextual Information Assembling

One of the greatest needs, which would probably be well sought by the younger generations, is a method by which context or the organization of much of this information could be more easily assembled. It is that knowledge on a broader scale of public policy that would help solve the issues of civility we are losing. *It is not that people do not understand teamwork or working with others per se; it is that on the issues of social and economic policy, they do not understand the process of how decisions need to be made for the ultimate best impact for all, particularly for their children.*

There is a difference between economic redistribution and charity, for example. One is a broad based transfer of wealth and resources that has significant other consequences, and the other is a responsibility for those of wealth to assist the less fortunate. The first is political and commanded, the second is cultural and value shaped. Results may seem similar, but motivations and systemic efforts are very different in the long term. The issue that may be more important than social discussion for the future is going to be the sustainability of the support and economics. If it is not sustainable then all of the good social purpose has been lost, and in fact much more danger of instability has been created. More people are dependent rather than self-reliant, so a crisis is greater.

These are the types of issues that have to be understood by the population as a whole if discussions are to be more civil, wise, and not driven by emotion and class warfare. They are ones that often are positively impacted individually by the political organizations that work for individual issues, but we need to enhance the civic organizations that bring people together so they can "play well together." Many policies sold with good intentions only create entitlements that are weakness. The media and politicians seem to feel if the government does not provide for a need—homelessness, medical care, etc., that generally most under privileged find private solutions. They want broader coverage as an entitlement, but dependency on governmental entitlement buys and holds votes and power, which adds value to them. Entitlement has to begin to be realized as dependency and weakness. And individual responsibility has to be respected culturally.

To do that, there needs to be a common theory for family, business, government, and political discussion, and for society as to how many of the existing powers in each society for every generation throughout history can be looked at for thoughtful discussion. One's perspective may be affected by one's values, but how you think through an issue to be sure of the facts and base decisions on the intended and unintended consequences is critical. *How you think about something determines what you think about something. How you think may be guided in part by your organizing principle of importance, but the structural approach of how you think about it for accuracy and wisdom is a different matter.* The reality of the world is hard to change. While crises add speed to change, big issues are like big ships, they require time and thoughtful action to turn. You have to start with an idea because only ideas replace existing ideas, and complex ones of depth and context require organized and structured thought. But to have success, you need to create enough support for influence and power. Without them all is theory and words. What *The Language of Conscience Evolution* of books focused on was the forces and powers of morality and how they could counter the removal of ethics from statecraft.

So the best way to look at gaining civility and making quality decisions that balance issues for the greatest good with the power to evoke sacrifice is to think through how we think. Critics will say the modern world is too superficial for enough to want to become more enlightened and that the divisions within society attack ideas that are not theirs. This evolution has a different purpose in that it is aimed at the needs of modern individuals who want the personal dignity, satisfaction, and control that they feel should exist and seek it. The ideas are not aimed at telling what to think as much as confirming their natural experience although giving facts bluntly that get attention may well seem to be expressing values because the alternatives are so obvious.

IV | CREATING A CONTEXTUAL METHOD OF THOUGHT

BASIC COMPONENTS OF CONTEXTUAL THOUGHT: THE COMBINATION OF TEMPERAMENT AND INTELLIGENCE

Around 100 B.C. the Chinese warrior and philosopher Sun Tzu noted that:

> *Those who are victorious plan effectively and change decisively. They are like a great river that maintains its course but adjusts its flow. . . . They are skilled in both planning and adapting and need not fear the result of a thousand battles, for they win in advance defeating those who have already lost.*

That very thoughtful piece of advice has been reviewed and used by businessmen and individuals throughout the last two thousand years. The problem is that such strategy and adaptability requires not only information but also understanding how that information fits together. Sun Tzu had a huge network of spies that gathered information for him, and a very unique wisdom in taking that knowledge and organizing it so he could plan for the future through constant adaptation. What was most valuable about his "Art of War" was how it structured thought in the context of the most significant issues, and how it emphasized the need for keeping the high ground in morality. The certainty of his planning gave confidence, built trust, and became a major competitive advantage.

The nature of life with its ever-demanding pressures is to lower all to a lesser common denominator driven by convenience. The nature of civilization is to appreciate the benefits of a system of values that raises the common denominator for the common good through conscience. The appreciation of the fact that the common good is a greater self-interest requires contextual thinking so there is a consciousness of the consequences of actions. Civilization advances as values are appreciated over interests. Contextual thinking is the increasing refinement of thought and understanding of why values and interests are related and that values must control interests for a stable and just society.

Today's world is vastly different from the terrain of the past. America remains a dominant economy in the world, but with a set of limitations created by debt and the sustainability of many of its existing practices. The rest of the world has competitively adapted to a more market driven economy and is rapidly becoming competitive. The next decade will see a number of adjustments—what is often called the "new normal" as different businesses maintain course but "adjust their flow." Great questions are how accurate are we at gaining our information and judging its prioritization and relevance and how effectively do we put it in the context of other factors, allowing us to plan our personal lives and our corporate visions. Europe will be changed by the reality of its demographically challenged social programs. Asia will have its problems but will unleash creative talents and markets of its own. If you have not recently traveled to Europe and China you cannot appreciate the changes by mere words. Policies enacted now matter greatly. The Internet adds connectivity to the world with social networking teaching people how to use it. Old theories of economics, politics, and culture have to be adapted.

America has fewer margins and must commit resources thoughtfully. What we incentivize for the future and how we commit our resources will shape our success in this environment, but how well do we understand it? How do we organize decisions? As a people we are like the Board of Directors of a company. There are several key considerations—who do we choose to lead the company and how do we motivate them, and how do we keep them focused on where the company's resources are invested for the future? Those are the strategic questions, most use operations, tactics, and techniques. How do they and we think about an issue?

What we need to talk about today is not just retraining the conveyance of knowledge, but the development of how we think appropriately to formulate wisdom. The jobs of the future require judgment. Robots and machines will do much, and cheaper labor abroad will be more competitive. This is important not only on a corporate level but on an individual level.

Perspective matters greatly, and once you have a perspective, you must use it to organize the other factors that impact you to understand the context of the most challenging issues you must address. This is a very complex subject. It is not easy to understand the current world or in many cases to understand one's self within it. But the process by which you learn and how you train yourself to think makes a tremendous difference in how ultimately successful you will be. If it is for a company, it becomes the culture and refines its organizing principle for decision making. The strong companies of the future will involve the similar concerns of employees and customers. Quality talent will be in less supply than unskilled talent. The factory workers of yesterday will become the data input specialists of today. Even routine jobs will require more refined talents because it requires decisions not routine work.

It is not whether or not we face difficult times. The more we want to succeed in the world the more we must be active and risk difficulty. The goal is not to avoid risk; it is to effectively manage it so you can achieve greater levels of success. You will inevitably run into difficulties if you accept such risk. True success is the strength and ability you have in managing problems once you encounter them. That is what gives you value in the world.

In learning how to think we must realize that our own ambitions and push for excellence help us set goals that truly matter. A friend of mine, former University of Texas Football Coach, Fred Akers, often told his athletes to remember, "Seldom, if ever, do we exceed our own expectations." He attributed it to a mentor who probably found it is a truth of life. We cannot be more than we wish ourselves to be, so we must envision our future.

As we discussed before, two things are involved in context. One is your temperament; the other is your intelligence. We have used those very generally. Temperament tells you your capacity for undertaking risk. If you do not have to take on risk to reach your level of satisfaction in life, then in many cases you will not because it only adds potential danger. If you do have to take on risk then it requires a different mindset. Some people by nature are risk adverse. Others do not tend to let it bother them and are willing or do not realize the potential dangers. Intelligence is different from temperament. It is how well you are able to think through and react to a situation once your temperament has placed you within it. Intelligence may be a part of temperament in allowing you to recognize the full level of the risk you are taking, but in this case it is important to look at the two separately.

Temperament often involves a judgment of prioritizations and context. It is how you judge levels of risk and how you process the information that lets you make decisions regarding them. Intelligence is how well you execute the plan. Combining them in a seamless method of thought is vital. Intelligence can find minimizations for risk and in doing so change temperament, but structure of thought to give confidence through experience matters. The method of thought also organizes your subconscious to benefit your more prejudged reflexes. Risk management involves four parts—correctly recognizing the level of risk, classifying it (measuring), controlling what is possible, and monitoring what you cannot control.

Risk and the concept of individual dignity are combined. Dignity requires individual responsibility or control that gives confidence and is a competitive advantage in taking risk where dependency brings fear and risk aversion.

Another key component of temperament is a humility/arrogance balance. At times of crises and stress leaders must have a very clear perspective on the decision between what is a true need versus a desire. Hubris distorts this matrix by putting more value than necessary on maintenance of what gives status but limited benefit. In a world where focus begins with an individual viewing it with him as the center, this hubris is often accentuated. The answer lies in separating personal feelings from principles or issues that are beyond the person. The latter are often critical to the culture of a successful effort; but the personal emotions often cloud judgment. This is the greatest problem for politicians who need to become statesmen and CEOs of companies in crisis. You have to face reality of how you fit into the real world rather than your importance in it. If the culture is realistic from the start, this perspective is a part of temperament and dictates early focused actions preventing problems.

The Looking Glass, The Judges, The Hole, The Sports Car, The Wolf, and The Bear

Perhaps the easiest way to discuss the process is to use six examples of the most important things that we want to understand in a simplified form.

The Looking Glass

The first of these, context, would be an example of a man holding up a mirror in the center of a room and people sitting in the middle of each of the walls of the room. On one side they would see the mirror and the reflection.

On the other side they would just see a small back of an object that was not distinctive, and from the other two sides they would only see the edge, which was not distinctive at all. Yet, if the person then rotated the mirror, each side would be able to see what it is and put it into context. So, the first major issue is not just having pieces of information, but looking at how you have a broad enough vision and enough information to make appropriate decisions. There is a body of information needed and oftentimes you do not get it just from the media or your normal sources. In modern times most information is opinionated or shortened.

We look at the sources with which we agree so it only confirms a preexisting bias. An example might be looking at a major city newspaper. There is often a perception of danger. If 100,000 men went to a bar the night before and one was killed, the front page cover story will say "Man Killed in Bar" not "99,999 Men Go Home From A Bar Last Evening." You have to get all the information necessary to build an accurate model of the world rather than just rely upon the impressions you get from a few sources that report abnormalities. This information must also be processed thoughtfully by its level of importance.

As we discussed previously, the information can be judged in four levels. It is often strategic such as, whether you go to war and against whom. It becomes operational breaking the strategy into achievable parts (such as, in World War II, North Africa, Russia, D-Day, etc.). It then evolves on tactics (the discussion of resources needed to accomplish the goal), and eventually techniques (cross-firing positioning of ships to protect from submarines or aircraft as an example).

All of these levels of information are important, but they have to be put into the correct category prioritizing their level of importance for the ultimate goals to be achieved. Information is critical in the modern world, but not as critical as how the streams of knowledge you receive are properly organized for accuracy, importance, and the effect they have on the context of your decisions. You must be analytical with quality information. You must prioritize and measure the significance. And you must get it into the current cycle or trends. If it is just a snapshot not a video, you may get the wrong impression of the direction of the plot. These need to be a part of your habitual thinking. Education should prepare you for this, but today's education is often too specialized on knowledge. You must add a breadth of thought.

The Judges

An interesting thing about thought is how it is affected by where you sit in a discussion. A trial judge is often amazed when overruled by an appellate judge. "What was he thinking?" is the usual response noting that he was not part of the trial, and he did not see the emotions, chaos, the immediate decision, and the flow of discussion, which affected credibility. The appellate judge, however, usually has two or three very critical issues of the trial that are well briefed and specific. It is a different presentation of the law, usually less emotional and more focused. A good trial lawyer is always thinking of this in their presentation. The two positions of thought fit together giving a bottom up to top down distinction to contextual thought. Both need to be remembered in any situation.

A great benefit of this concept, specifically focused analysis, is that it helps you determine whether problems are episodic or systemic. If they are unusual exceptions an individualized approach is appropriate, but if systemic it requires a great deal more contextual thought on related implications and unintended consequences.

The Holes

There is an old saying that when you are deep in a hole you ought to stop digging. Another one says when you are in a hole, see how you got there and reversing the process may not be the way out. This is particularly true in putting principles into context. Almost thirty years ago, in *The New Legacy*, I wrote of the problems of deficit spending, high taxes, and overregulation. I have not changed views, but with the country deep in a fiscal hole, the options are different. If we had followed sound principles, we would not be here. But the depth of the hole may limit options. Conservatism and liberalism are now nouns describing positions such as taxation. In the past and probably the future, they will again become adjectives of thought rather than absolutes. I deeply believe you have to follow principles, but they will have to be adapted to current problems, rather than standing absolute, when adaptation thinks of how the solutions fit the principle and adding to moral hazard is no longer an available option. Holes require adaptability because oftentimes the long-term solutions need a flexible beginning to position.

The best example of needing to understand not digging deeper is the way you analyze a hole and option. The government seldom uses zero-based budgeting that would make every item justify its existence and thus prove the effectiveness of its funding versus other options. Many times it generally reduces a percentage from a base line of proposed spending that is increasing. So if spending is cut 5% from a base line increasing 7%, you really have not cut expenditures at all only the rate of increase. Too often several different base lines are used that give impressions but not reality. You may still be digging the hole while proclaiming victory. You may have to do this short term, but for the longer-term reality and effectiveness of spending in the context of moral hazard consequences is necessary.

The Sports Car

The third example, after you have the quality information organized, is how do you think about it? What is your process of thought? What is your range of vision and comfort with alternative thought and what is your confidence in making suggestions out of the normal thought? We can call this expanding horizons or "adaptability." Individual responsibility requires creative thought and adds innovation. The best example here is an old question from an employment exam that noted that a man was driving his two-seat sports car past a bus stop where he saw an elderly lady desperately needing to go to a hospital immediately. His oldest and dearest friend who had saved his life desperately needed to get to a business appointment, and a woman he knew would be the love of his life as soon as he gazed upon her needed a ride as well. Since the bus would not be there for a period of time, what should he do?

The moralists would argue that the elderly woman had the greatest need and he should immediately take her to the hospital. Those who believe in obligation would see the need to honor his obligation to his friend and take him where he needed to go. Those who value self-interest more would say to take the woman he wished to meet where she wished to go. The best answer to the question was often not an intense debate between each of the arguments, but for him to give his car to his friend on the condition he immediately take the elderly lady to the hospital on his way to the business appointment, and the driver would remain on the bench (and ultimately take the bus) to visit with the love of his life.

This was an "out of the box" style of thinking, but one that really explains the importance of how you think in terms of "adapting" to the option alternatives given. If you are able to think in terms of ultimate goals, then you would organize the information streams of knowledge, morality, obligation, self-interest, not just in a definition and a weighing of the merits of each, but in a way that the needs could be put together more effectively and blend with each other. That is what we are going to call "thinking in context." It is strategic thinking separated from many of the constraints of common peer approaches. As General Eisenhower noted, if a problem is unsolvable you can make it bigger and change the dynamics.

The Wolf

The fourth example is the wolf. It represents perspective or your personal organizing principle. And it is best expressed by another Internet story. An old Indian Chief was teaching his grandson how to become a warrior. As part of the process the Chief told his grandson that in every man there are two wolves, a good wolf and a bad wolf. The wolves inevitably fight with each other and the destiny of the man is ultimately determined by which wolf wins. His grandson asked him the obvious question, "Grandfather, which wolf wins?" The old man answered appropriately, "The one that you feed the most."

Each of us has an ongoing battle between conscience and convenience. Self-interest may serve us well, but greed and arrogance can well lead to our fall. We decide whether to be a person with a code of ethics and a vision of what we want from life and set levels of satisfaction judged by one set of perspectives or instead become quite materialistic and judge how well we succeed solely by what we personally can gain.

A conscience involves caring about others and the future. Convenience is caring about self here and now. For that reason, conscience requires individual responsibility in actions with an ethical sensitivity. When each individual's conscience or convenience is placed together, it determines the culture of a family, society, and business. It is not individual ethics that often shape the world but the cultural ethics including peer pressure of all those involved. In looking at the great scandals of the last decade, in each we saw that the culture of institutions was warped dramatically by the incentives and style of management the corporation undertook. Government crises come from under-appreciating moral hazard. The limits that ethics requires many times became burdens when corporate and the pressure of convenience drove public cultures. Short-term gain often overcame longer-term sustainability. If you are a person of conscience, the nature of people with whom you associate is quite different from those chosen if you are a person of convenience. People of conscience come together with others of similar beliefs and value systems and thus look at a transformative type of leadership with a higher set of goals and loyalties. People of convenience look for alliances and simply make transactional tradeoffs. The cultures of institutions take on the nature of the reality of the leadership not just the applause given.

A company may well take on these characteristics in its culture. The great Chinese philosopher Lao Tzu's observation that knowing others is wisdom, but knowing self is enlightenment is crucial in bringing harmony. The core of the perspective with which you look at information (using the example of half full or half empty) and how you put together information rests on how you see your life and personal dignity (your expectations for yourself, family, company, society, nation, and eventually the world). This is because almost all six billion of us in the world will be in some way interrelated, through the transmission of disease, economic imbalances, common environment, disharmonies of politics, and competitiveness that will take place.

The Bear

The old story of two men running from a bear is the pure concept of relativity. It is not how fast one man is but whether he is faster than the second man. Many times situations depend on specific factors like this, but it is critical to appreciate relativity conditions and the interrelationship with other factors. These often involve unsustainable trends. When a trend is steep and rapid, usually it is not sustainable. Higher price may bring more development and competition. Situations change because of relativity. America's bond market interest rates are low in times when finances are the worst in history. However, American markets are relatively better than the rest of the world so funds come here because we are the proverbial best house in a bad neighborhood. Debt cannot increase forever because no one will lend. A key part of contextual thinking is to assess longer-term effects that bring change rather than accept that current trend is certain. What are factors that make a situation relative to other issues? This is most important when doomsday arguments are brought forward in the extreme. Normally, they never reach the final stages because during an earlier stage change is forced by crisis. For example companies are often in crisis for liquidity before they are insolvent because credit is limited. Anticipating the relativity of the situation let's you plan more defensively for the earlier crisis or change.

The most important thing in gaining context is to understand how you look at the process. As we go through these thoughts, the goal is not for you to retain great amounts of information. It is for you to judge the reality of what is presented by your personal ordinary life experiences. It will hopefully give tools for organizing and better use the knowledge that you have—developing a more disciplined method of thought and understanding of what issues matter the most in the formation and maintenance of a culture that will be the greatest competitive advantage or disadvantage you, your company, or nation may well face in a very unique and difficult time. Its purpose is also to sensitize you to the power of ethics and recognize the power of a culture. As previously noted, the power of history is reflected in the values passed on and recreated in the next generation. What is most important to you? What satisfies you? Sensitivity to conscience can change perspectives and you can grow in appreciation of the satisfaction of helping others.

It is said that wise men often see eye to eye when they look to the value a society should have, but begin to differ when interests are added. Reality has interests, but we can minimize their negatives if we add them to a thought process dominated by conscience rather than starting with them and interests to add conscience. Reality seldom allows the latter because commercialism and the arrogance of power are strong thought processes of their own.

The Language of Conscience

Acquiring of sufficient security, food, and shelter often requires prioritization. Abraham Maslow in his 1943 paper, *A Theory of Human Motivations,* synthesized these human needs based on two groupings, deficiency needs and growth needs, portrayed as a pyramid with four "deficiency needs" and a top "being need." The deficiency needs had to be met before you could move to higher levels. They included physiological concerns like hunger and thirst, moved to safety and security, then the concept of belonging and love or an affiliation with others allowing acceptance, and finally esteem, gaining approval and recognition of others and self. In moving to growth needs, there are important concepts—cognitive understanding, then aesthetic concerns of symmetry like symmetry and beauty, and finally the concept of self-actualization, finding self-fulfillment and recognition of potential, closely paralleling Enlightened Conservatism's concept of personal dignity. Maslow's final concept of self-transcendence, which connects beyond the ego, automatically includes helping others find fulfillment and realize their potential. To Maslow, human beings were motivated by unsatisfied needs, with an order. While his approach has its critics, it has a substance of reality. You can only maximize potential when you have a stable environment. Any approach to life has to recognize the world's inequality and suffering. The approach must work at all levels. It should be noted that even in the direst poverty often religion and hope are strong because people must find a support for their dignity. The unstable environment's cause must also be assessed and many times is the corruption of power. Yes, noble ideas usually come at the top of the pyramid, but reality also should note that noble ideas may be needed to get from the bottom of the pyramid to the higher levels.

Even at lower levels such as security and food, working together with others is often a more efficient and necessary way to proceed. Once you reach a level where thought prevails, you look to more materialism or more satisfaction with personal goals to apply your time and resources. When you have choices you deal with the before mentioned personal organizing principles of why you do the things you do.

Those focused on materialism, even if they give great amounts to charity for "social image," are different from those who get satisfaction not from "what they did" but "why they did it." Much of life is a revision or shaping of history for private purpose. Successful cultural ethics requires reorganizing true motivations.

If you see life as providing and increasing benefits for your family and advancing society to a more civilized level, the values of conscience probably set your basic perspective of fairness with the Golden Rule as the core. The cultural philosophy we refer to as "Enlightened Conservatism" captures an organizing principle by which "you grant to others the same dignity and rights you expect personally." The concept builds a modern decision matrix on ethics to avoid moral hazard in public policy and tries to create an educated citizen of responsibility. But it requires the development of a common culture and peer pressure to make it sustainable. Theories are easy to write, but if you do not have some vision of your destination, efforts are often futile and in the hands of chance. As often noted, hope is not an effective strategy.

We shall refer to this perspective for the creation of a culture as The Language of Conscience since it is a mechanism designed to help you process information and issues, and build unity consistent with respect. At its core is the Golden Rule of reciprocity. It goes beyond just civility and shared ethics to a unifying, transformational set of cultural values that prepare a person, company or society to weather its most trying times with the strength of unity and restrains the pressure of greed and arrogance in the good times so the enterprise is sustainable in crisis.

Change constantly battles the status quo created by history. The balancing factor is how the society, as a collection of individuals, views their dignity. Dignity is their evaluation of the acceptability of their control of their lives. If they reach a point of frustration they revolt. How do they see the future? Do they sacrifice or revolt to bring change? Different cultures have different temperaments and values. Some are individualistic and some are consumer driven. Others are consensus driven and think longer term. Context requires assessing how personal dignity is measured. How is the capacity for sacrifice in crisis developed? How others look at life affects the culture that affects the individual.

PERSONAL DIGNITY: INDIVIDUALISM MUST BE IN BALANCE WITH FRATERNITY

While individualism gives strength, it also can create a weakness if not tempered by involvement with others—family, friends, and society. Pure individualism may lead to a philosophy of convenience and a lack of participation in or appreciation of the civic and social process. This limits personal growth, mutes gaining leadership skills and traits, and deprives one of the true contexts of life that is the reality model of one's mind. The biggest problem the world now has is that we do not interact personally much anymore. Our technology removes some of reality and replaces it with perception, relativity, and inherent self-interest often pushing us to convenience. We look at the world as centered upon us and give ourselves undue influence on the reality of events. We need to move into a position of not thinking the world rotates around us but how we fit into the world. This is the concept of context.

T. S. Eliot in *Choruses from the Rock* noted, "Where is the wisdom we have lost in knowledge? Where is the knowledge we have lost in information?" That is exactly where we are today only more so with the benefit of technology. Perceptions are often different, but may ultimately change the reality of mind, but not natural law. The problem is that natural law is physics, chemistry, and biology. They are rules that remain regardless of what we will them to do. To remove that person from being the center of the universe and attaining the balance required is really the acquisition of humility, the Golden Rule so you can understand others, and effectively, conscience, which is a respect for others and an understanding that life is about how you interact with others. This is the core of most religions. If we start here, how the development of an appreciation of conscience changes ones perspective, all the rest fall logically into place in its management.

Our minds get conditioned by the circumstances around us, and we cannot see things that are more obvious. We begin with a perspective that things are complicated and then make them so. We are used to going to specialists and unfortunately when you go to a person that is already highly defined, diagnosis starts upward from the complicated arena. Judging context and how things are put together as well as prioritizations thus are quite significant. What we have to develop is a "theory" or approach to organizing information that embodies the principle and goals we have been discussing.

This brings us how the individual (culture) and the society/government (law) are brought into balance. Today we can see how little control we have over our lives. In traffic there is less courtesy and personal civility with anger an immediate response far more frequently. Government or law fills in gaps and becomes even larger and more dominant as we rely on it to fill the gaps that the peer pressures of society used to maintain through culture. We have to realize that to regain our individual control we have to replace governance with more self-governance through culture.

V | To the Children

A Father's Thoughts for Your Future

I have often thought about what advice I would leave to my children as I reached my father's age and my point in the line to move on to a different realm grew ever shorter. One looks back more thoughtfully to the various stages of life and the choices that were made or not made. You look at what advice might be applicable to help the family move forward when you realize the uncertainties of life. You want them to find satisfaction and happiness.

I have re-read the thoughts in my father's last conversation. I think back on how much the early family values that he and Mother taught affected how I looked at life and my success. They were eternal thoughts of wisdom that were very different from the change that he had noted over his life. The speed of change that he described has only been accelerated and will be even more so through our children's generation and perhaps in a totally different context for our grandchildren.

These are probably the observations that I feel would be most important to them at this point in time if I departed tomorrow.

I would suggest each Father's Day you re-read my last conversation with my father that included the advice that his father had given him in shaping life. The values within have guided our family for many generations and have provided not only successful, but more importantly, happier lives. Because we have valued relationships more than materialism and honor more than money, success has been judged by our understanding that at life's end it is nice to have acquired its monetary treasures. But real success is often less physical and more mental in reviewing your life, your experiences, the depth of the relationships you have built, and most importantly your satisfaction with whether you have taken the limited time on earth to accomplish those things for which God gave you talents. Your satisfaction, personally, by your own standards as to what you have done to serve others and to find yourself tells the most of the life that you have lived. For those who value money, they have their own way of keeping score, but acquiring fame and riches often has a cost. If you can achieve those goals while still valuing the most important of life's gifts, your success is more meaningful.

Keep in mind that the most important thing you will teach your children is character. It is not just education, but the willingness and strength to accomplish goals. What you teach them forms the habits for the rest of their lives. The most valuable trait a person can have is to know the right thing to do, to appreciate when it ought to be done, and then do it even if it is not easy. The knowing and the doing are both important. Many people know ethics and morality and they may not commit sins, but they omit a great number of things that ought to be done that make a long-term difference. It is when you fully understand the world and how it operates that you begin to truly have impact. This requires the context of thought that we have discussed.

Generally, life rewards what you sow, and whether you reap benefits or problems is often directly related to where you begin. So teach the kids as they sow actions to do it carefully, to realize the importance of living to their full potential because most people operate only at a fraction of their capacities. Get them to realize that criticism is not necessarily bad, but you need to analyze criticism for its accuracy. Many times you are criticized because you are having an effect—not necessarily because you are wrong. Opposition often only appears when you are successful and are becoming a changing dynamic. They must understand not to back away from principle in a fight but also avoid personal issues because they are seldom issues over which they should fight.

Never let them forget Dad's rule of always recognizing others' dignity. If in life you become a person of authority and have others working under you, never let them forget the true judgment of them as a person rests in how they treat those whom they supervise. As Dad used to say, quite accurately the old axiom, "You meet a lot of people going up, and you will probably meet the same people going down." Everyone has their good periods and bad periods, so humility is not just a valuable trait but an excellent strategy.

Never forget that family values are normally conservative because they originate in reality. From Aristotle on, the best thinkers have realized that to change a society you must not only understand it but also acknowledge its strengths and weaknesses so you can help in its evolution. Reality is the core of conservatism as opposed to abstract theories of an envisioned world, but an enlightenment of reality is necessary to adapt it to modern times. Values of conscience remain relatively constant, but current interests of convenience evolve.

Make certain that they understand that problems are not insurmountable. They often can be turned into opportunities, and the real benefit of leaders is being able to see problems in a way you not only analyze the difficulties properly, but you see where much more can be gained from turning the lemon into lemonade. How you look at problems has to be on the organized basis of thought that we have always discussed. It makes you attack them analytically rather than looking at them in frustration as too big a problem. Getting involved in efforts that require addressing problems is necessary for growth—like military experience and training prepares you by shaping the temperament you have to judge risk. It helps to divide them into individual problems and then either expanding or limiting them until you can make them fit together in another paradigm.

Teach the children, and remember yourself, that getting independent thoughts and creating a mastermind concept of a group of people that have different perspectives and viewpoints than you do is critically important. When you are a part of the action in a driving force, how you are perceived may be quite different. Having those outside perspectives gives you a better idea of how you fit into the whole rather than just your own idea of your importance. Be careful what you say, your words will often come back to you. Teach them not to fear mistakes. Experience comes from having made mistakes, generally resulting from bad judgments, but at least you are taking actions. The more you can learn from the mistakes of others, however, the less painful it becomes. Having mentors is a necessity to true learning.

Experience is not necessarily what happens to you, it is more about how you react and address the problems you face by an experienced process that acquires wisdom from others. You learn to react thoughtfully and calmly because your temperament reorganizes the options. They need to always continue their education. Even if you reach a point in life where you have satisfied your material goals, you never really are able to obtain a full appreciation of life if you do not continue learning and improving yourself.

Make certain they understand the power of trends and how they can completely reshape an environment. Ideas are very much like the wind in that they can bring about tremendous change very quickly. When an idea's time has come, it generates a tremendous force that you must understand. Standing against it can be a great problem, but using it effectively to push your own momentum is an ideal strategy.

Recognize fear and the impact it has. Most of the things that we imagine and stop us from taking action are relatively immaterial or never occur. What is lost is our willingness and initiative to undertake action—in it could be a tremendous cost that may be much worse than an overly perceived concern. Look to the worst case scenarios but also evaluate probability. Actions should be based on the matrix of the two with significant recognition to the possibility that unusual events can occur.

Make sure you keep in mind that life involves rising above ordinary concerns and when those concerns involve people, you have to think carefully about circumstances. People are seldom for or against you, but more focused on benefiting themselves. Remember this in how you approach issues. You have grown up in a small town just as I did, but you have had the opportunity to see life on a much more statewide, national, and international scale. When people are the issue rather than events or ideas, understand the characteristics of competition among people and how different groups look at goals. Again, it is the example of the problem that crabs have getting out of a bucket because each crab grabs onto the other and pulls him down trying to get out himself. Too often in competitive environments that is reality.

As you ascend a ladder of performance, there are fewer and fewer people (but far more competent people) that have made each higher rung. The way you get to the highest rungs requires you to know how the forces and powers operate at each level. Hopefully, you also will have some allies who have common values. You also will have increasing respect, even for your adversaries, for the ability to make it to those levels although you will often question their motivations. Never let the children forget they will achieve little if they don't have a vision of what they want to do and are willing to make a commitment to achieve it. Most important of all, never let them forget Winston Churchill's observation, "We make a living by what we get. We make a life by what we give." That probably sums up life as well as any observation I have seen except for the wooden plaque in the Commissary at Camp Mystic where you attended:

My mind is a garden. My thoughts are the seeds.
My harvest will be either flowers or weeds.

A WELL-ENVISIONED LIFE

As I told you in your youth, it is worthwhile to consider the goals and purpose of your life when you are young so that you more thoughtfully face its challenges. You must think in these terms, top down, so that you organize your daily lives on a path toward them. Day to day life is "bottom up" and will always have more than enough context items to distract you. You never exactly know your future, but you can choose directions. To some, in youth this is a life plan to achieve political power, economic success, fame, or other focused ultimate goals. They then put together a strategic dedicated plan, and their determination and fate often determine success. A portion of that ambition is necessary. And if you do not have a vision and ambition for success, you have little driving you. This is the strategic knowledge plan of life.

However, as your mother and I also noted, there is also a greater plan of wisdom that hopefully tempers it as you move through life. As Machiavelli noted, life is part fortune and part ability. Even if you have longer-term visions, short-term reality often intercedes to affect your course. So you must temper vision with value judgments that recognize costs and prioritizations. Early in your lives you are seeing that raising families and dedicating time to them pull greatly from your opportunities to achieve more in the "success arenas" of wealth, fame, and power. It is a difficult balance. Short-term material success is hurt by commitments of time to relationships and conscience of purpose.

My parents sacrificed by living in a garage apartment and raising cattle on the side when Dad was Sheriff to save money for Deanna's and my education and eventually to invest in the bank when he became its president. Those were not easy times but brought an understanding of the value of sacrifice and satisfaction. If children are given everything, they are deprived the opportunity to learn critical traits. Just as we saved for you, we gave you the money at 18 as your own to spend or waste, hoping the values we had imparted would make you conservative with that which was yours. It did so, and each of you learned from the responsibility and experience. From working cattle as a youth to being a bank teller part time to the Navy, every job taught me something new and shaped me. Growth comes from learning to play the hands you are dealt by fortune, regardless of what they are. Whether you play them with a strategy of conscience or convenience dictates your tactics through your methods of acquiring resources.

But having lived my life and been blessed with an array of options, I would not change my choices. In youth I envisioned, as most young leaders, being Governor or more. I envisioned writing great works and building a great business. In some ways I have succeeded enough to know the taste of success, but none makes me as happy as when people compliment me on each of you and the job I have done raising you. The fact that each of you and your spouses chose to get either your law degrees, Masters degrees, and additional education tells me you have learned the life knowledge of strategy and the use of resources, but your choice of dedication to your families and to civic endeavors demonstrates you put the wisdom of a well-valued life as a goal.

You will find that those who do succeed must have success in their own judgment to be happy and that is a critical life choice. All people want to be relevant and to leave a legacy. Most people may fear death itself less than the prospect of not being remembered. As you grow older, relevance becomes more relative as you have a fuller appreciation of life. But, in some ways pleasing others is less important or keeping their high opinion as your own in what matters. Some spend their lives trying to keep a place of power and image, adding lines to the tombstone as we used to call it "touring the state cemetery." Others take satisfaction that they have done their best and find more benefit in mentoring the rising stars. "Society" or the current opinion of peers loses out to the reality of the recognition of reality judgments that you will feel truly matter—will you be remembered for substance?

It helps to remember that with the recent discovery of ancient remains in South Africa relatively modern man has perhaps been around several million years. Recorded history, of some quality, perhaps four thousand years, and in reality only the last several centuries have taken us to our rapid change. In the time that each of us lives, there are many "heroes" or in more modern terms "celebrities." Their time of fame, however, is often a fleeting glimmer. A generation down the road, the Super Bowl or Final Four hero of today will not be very relevant. The most powerful politicians or the richest men, on those characteristics alone may be remembered as footnotes, but may not necessarily affect that much of the future unless they have injected the ideas that change society. As I noted, when you are young, ambition is highly natural. The ability to achieve and to dominate, Nietzsche's Will to Power in a sense, is a part of the natural desire to be a dominant player or personality. Where you start in life has a lot to do with your priorities and your opportunities, but there is also a great deal that can be accomplished in effectively playing the hand that you are dealt. When you choose your partners for life, it is usually a result of some common vision. A part of that vision is a public effort on your part to help shape the nature of the society of your time.

The societies that grant opportunity to rise through education and support so their most talented are able to rise on merit have the benefit of the strongest cores in leadership. At the very least, lead in ideas and issues whenever you can. You determine much more of your future than you think, and that is the core value families must instill—individual responsibility.

There are a few relationships that if understood will help you put this advice into context. The first three affect how you look at issues as an individual and the last three how you must look at the fraternity or society or state. Understanding the more complex issues that follow require a refinement of understanding of these factors and relationships. Regretfully, they are not the desired rifle bullet path to follow but more like shotgun pellets because while related they require more depth and do not flow directly together. But they need to be fully defined in the mind to understand the presentations that follow.

ISSUES TO RECOGNIZE
TECHNOLOGY SPEEDS CHANGE AND THOUGHT PROCESS

My father noted how things had changed in his lifetime and how different he felt the future would be watching that progression. He was most certainly right because in the forty years since his death I have seen the entire computer revolution and effectively a new way of gaining information and communicating. As one of the first Baby Boomers, I have enjoyed living in one of the greatest periods of American history with its unique place in the world. But I learned how to plan and execute that life based on a way of thinking that dealt largely with a focus on books, as it had been the historical method. Reading a book took time, and you had to understand the context. You understood more of the characters and how issues fit together. It wasn't a case of scanning but of thinking that in part developed your thought process. You may have thought with different values depending on your station in life or as Dad would say, where you stand often depends on where you sit. But the method of understanding and the education were slower, more deliberate, and I think more organized in context. You had to remember facts because they were not a computer stroke search away. These made you compartmentalize them, organize them, and think more in concepts. It made you rely more on other people as mentors and resources.

Today with the advent of computers, the Internet, search engines, and social networks we are in a very different environment. Studies tend to show that people scan looking at the first few lines of a page, the left hand column that has its structure, a reading of a few lines in the middle of the page, and a continuation by structure until they see something that they feel is appropriate. The search engines pull up specific references, even in legal cases, but it is not the same as reading the case in depth to understand more of the context. With email and social networks we multitask dramatically, which often has an impact on focus. All of this and the way it affects how we think about issues is the change that has been most dominant in my lifetime. The method of communications, the presentation of data, and the structured thought—all have evolved but not in the most organized of approaches.

The Millennials in the new generations learn in different ways. They sense things perhaps more than my generation did. It is not that the different ways of learning are inferior because often more knowledge can be picked up more quickly and far more directly. But it does make it increasingly difficult to organize all of those thoughts into a unified model of the world. Those very same characteristics, with a modern education system, often focus on making the individual critically important. As a result, most people today automatically begin to think of themselves as the center of the world. Those things around them are the most important, and their lives exist in their own environment. That is not greatly different from what it has always been because people live in a certain circle of friends and economic environment, and it shapes their perceptions of the world more than in the past. If I live in a certain town, the world geographically is seen in relation to it. But if I am on a computer, distance is immaterial. That bottom up versus top down modern reality is trying to connect for a more common theme. The common theme is to be found in values not parochialism or nationalism.

The difference is that the world is changing very rapidly outside of those individual cocoons. And it becomes increasingly important for us to have a thought process that not only focuses on us as the center of the world, but also includes a concept of how the world operates and our place in it. When that concept is blended, it will bring much more reality to our individual lives so we can change those thoughts in our individual cocoons. It also matters how we maintain a "well envisioned life" or a "thoughtful life." Short-term personal focus leads to convenience and narcissism with the power of immediate gratification or materialism dominating. Celebrity and power dominate in how we get wealth. A broader concept of how we fit in the world more harmoniously makes our goals more focused on how we become a part of a greater whole with more purpose in life directed by our relationship to others and society.

One of my favorite writings dealing with this issue from a public policy perspective was Edmond Burke's analysis of the French Revolution. He noted that society was much more like an organism than a mechanism. Parts could not be easily changed because everything was interconnected. He understood the need for men actively doing good so evil did not prevail. He well understood the three great values of the French Revolution and how they fit together. The three core beliefs again were equality, fraternity, and liberty. We all understand equality and the fact that it is very much an individual focus of value. Today, fraternity is often diminished in its cultural sense. It is how men harmoniously work together to make a greater whole by value-driven interconnection. *In modern times fraternity becomes a political rather than a cultural value in that the government acts as the whole seeming to try to bind us together as individuals. But that is a very improper approach. Fraternity is a value-based trait not a politically directed action. It is the morality and obligations that we have between each other as men not what government forces upon us. Liberty is the key point of balance between those two.* In my life I have seen the need for finding a balance as the most critical effort.

My father talked of moderation being essential, and I never fully appreciated it until I reached my sixties and am putting into context the cause of many of society's problems. Liberty occurs when there is a balance of the individualism of equality and the common good—or the ethical balance of fraternity. Today we too often go to extremes and lose the moderating factors. Compromise does not automatically lose values or principle if it is transformational seeking justice or balance fairness for a common good. How common good is judged becomes the issue. This is not to say that there are not conditions and times that more extreme measures for principles are necessary, but it means there has to be a thoughtful process that balances and analyzes all the impacts. We need to remember Sun Tzu's advice not to fight unnecessary wars.

The concept of ethics in the West is more about doing the right thing while the concept of ethics in the East is slightly different. It is more an ethical consideration of balancing the shared interests of all involved so you can have a greater level of harmony. The two concepts are blended in many ways, but it is important to understand what they may add to each other. It is also important that this is an issue of culture and adaptability to change with a balanced thoughtful approach. The self-interest of economics and divisiveness of politics often overwhelms this balance until the natural laws bring crises that rekindle it out of need. Working together is important because it builds common discussion. There is an old Texas political saying that "if you are not sitting at the table, you may well be on the menu."

Change is really knowledge being expanded on an ever-increasing and vaster scale. The new environment gives us so much knowledge that we have to have systems that help us specialize our search and expertise. A grade school science student knows more about the universe than Copernicus because of our discoveries. Pulling all of this knowledge together effectively so a society of over six billion people can find a few basic mechanisms through which to cooperate, creates the need for wisdom.

The philosophies and religion of the Axial Age still dominate today because man has the same inner compulsions. The issue is how he controls them by what he values. Today vast knowledge will crowd out wisdom if we are not careful.

The culture in which we all grew up did a lot to set the values. It was not just the church services we attended. It was the Sunday Schools, the camps, the Boy and Girl Scouts, the school systems, and the cultural history of this area's past that greatly shaped both my upbringing and yours. Texas values began near Washington County where Sam Houston was baptized at Independence, Chappell Hill where William Barrett Travis' wife was buried, and where Stephen F. Austin who founded Texas had his home at San Felipe. We often walked through the ruins of where Baylor University began and spent many an hour at Washington on the Brazos where the Texas Declaration of Independence was signed. Our lives have been steeped in history and values.

In later life I read Cicero who probably defined values and honor as philosophically as anyone. But my core values were shaped by what I learned in this small part of the world. Those were history lessons carried forward with the power of culture. Interestingly, after traveling much of the world, I find that culture and values may differ, but core values of family, conscience, and reciprocity are in every culture. How elevated depends on the current systems of economics, politics, and culture in that society. The future world is what your global generation makes it through action or inaction. But unlike the past, interconnectivity of globalization will not let you determine that future alone. This fact will be increasingly evident.

As part of your upbringing and as you expanded your education, I insisted that you experience as many of the great books of history as you could. There is nothing like the diverse thought of the concepts of honor of Cicero and others compared to the cost of honor in a book such as *All Quiet on the Western Front* that tells the true cost and horrors of war. There is a balance that must be gained from seeing many different perspectives and not believing by rote, but instead creating values that are worth sacrificing to uphold. As you complete your life, you begin to understand far more clearly how much opportunity there is in the world for you to see and learn. Even if you do not have the resources to travel, the stoic belief that a man controls his life in his mind is a very accurate one. You can experience the world and learn from a variety of sources no matter where you are. You just have to have the desire. It is far easier to experience the diversities of the world now than at any time in history.

I have had the opportunity to see much of the world, and to play active parts working with groups of leaders in Mexico, China, Central America, and Europe. And I increasingly realize that while things appear very different, the same concerns for family values and the interaction of people eventually build relationships that last a lifetime. Conscience requires a different set of values for success in life and usually pulls together a different group of friends who look more transformationally at a common goal. They are a family of choice rather than of birth. Convenience makes life much easier in individual circumstances because it puts fewer restrictions upon you. But it also makes you only have allies and seldom have the ability to trust others. How you live your life will determine the type of people with whom you associate and how you think about people.

Giving trust is often necessary in building it. It is difficult when you do not know a man's history to know exactly how much faith to put in him. It is not until you have shared a difficult situation with him and seen how he reacts that you can judge the level of trust you can give him. As a banker I have seen that even those with trust operate far differently if situations become significantly worse and their interests are threatened. There must always be an awareness of those with less ethics trying to use those with ethics to give them credibility. Nonetheless, with all of those concerns, there is great merit to the old saying that if you seek a friend you will find one, and if you look for an enemy, you will find one as well. How you treat others sets the tone of a relationship. You must learn to take some risk in beginning relationships but to also be sensitive and test them as they develop. This approach is used around the world although in some places, it takes generations to build true trust.

In the developing world, families are often the core of economics and political power because of the trust issue. The Chinese and Jews have large family networks beyond their borders that understand their culture and can work with them. The ability for families to connect is often unique, compared to the Fortune 500 doing business, which involves lawyers and a less personal approach. This will increasingly be an issue as undeveloped countries gain position and are more able to choose with whom they want to build relationships. They too work basically on family systems as law is being refined.

In an age of terrorism, fraud, and distrust there is great value in relationships of trust and organizations and efforts that place people together to understand each other and trust given and maintained. These relationships have great economic value for families for generations if trust can be maintained as they give the opportunity to grow together for profitable business. One of my family's great assets is the relationship it has with others generation to generation. In Asia, such family networks are a key resource because the history of the region made them necessary.

As you go through life, remember some key distinctions that help in strategic thought. Understand the impact of government and economics. Both are systems composed of coordinated or competing institutions. You must not only understand them, but also build networks within them to affect your future and society's direction. You have a responsibility to do so for your children's sake. To have a proper perspective, you need to understand the distinctions between influence and power; how to distinguish between cyclical change and structural change; and how travel broadens an understanding of systems and history if you choose to learn from it. You can see sights, but know the history of the area before you go and what the sites really tell you. Never waste travel opportunities by foregoing research.

Power Versus Influence

People often seek power—the ability to control an individual situation. But it is often far better to seek influence having the ability to impact power through a different style. True power is very difficult to maintain and often to exercise. Great commitment of resources is required and often this restricts where power can be applied. Power is much like the American game of chess where the goal is basically to eliminate many of the players on the board until you get to a position of victory. It commits and uses up resources. The equivalent Eastern games are played differently. Their goal is to cover as much space as possible with the least number of lost players. Hard power is in the nature of chess while soft power is more in the nature of Weiqi, in modern times known as Go.

Influence usually involves credibility. A prime example involves higher-level government where money matters less than information and credibility, which are often the currencies of its bureaucratic function. Information can have a limited life, but credibility can be a powerful force if it is used in the organization of information or in forming the process. Most high-level meetings either have to control dominant forces to get a full discussion of ideas or assure balance of discussion. Power is often in recognizing the necessity of a sound process to decision and appreciating the talent to conduct it. Leaders are only as good as their decision process.

One of the distinctions between power and influence is in the styles most often used. Power requires the necessity of forcing action, usually necessary in a shorter period of time. This is often conducive to convenience and its tools of intimidation, greed, and manipulation, which are quite powerful and often more effective in the real world than conscience when the two meet in real stress. Influence can include the fear of what convenience can bring but more often is converted to power by respect and usually, in the reality of the world, self-interest as the best choice. You cannot change the reality that results often come easiest from convenience unless you create a culture where conscience is appreciated and power is more from consensus. In the modern world concentrations of economic, political, and cultural power are constantly being built and dispersed by new technology. So the goal is to focus on creating the vision and goal of how conscience through the governance ethics of business, the moral conscience of culture, and the moral hazard concerns for the common good politically dominate the culture. These convert their influence in combination to change the power matrix and use the powers of convenience for the ends of conscience.

Adaptation to the circumstances is what truly matters. As Darwin noted, it is not the strongest or the most intelligent that survive, but those who are the most adaptable. That is as true today as ever. Change occurs quickly, and you must have an organized mind to be adaptable and understand its implications. It is the discussion of looking at all the variables and how they affect each other that prepares a common mind. Once you reach a battlefield, a military plan is almost obsolete since variables change it quickly. The tactical generals on the ground take over from the strategists, but they know the ultimate strategy to achieve and they adapt. In that same way your mind needs to have a model of the world so the model can be updated. But that model needs to be shaped by the wisdom of values not just by the knowledge of changing facts. Otherwise, it has no real permanence of organizing principle beyond just the convenience of the moment.

Wisdom is the use of values and knowledge to organize your mind on an immediate decision basis. Wisdom also helps you see the ultimate, often unappreciated costs. If you are guided by values, you have pre-conditioned responses to concerns that others neglect. This is described as ethics that define us, but also protect us. It is not easy to defraud a man who is not motivated by greed, to tempt with power a man who sees its ultimate costs to his soul, or to persuade a man to ignore the values of his parents. Honor, integrity, ethics, and individual responsibility are parts of a code that if developed in youth, prepare you for a satisfying life and also protect you from the convenience of others. When those prejudgments are not built into the family, members are much more vulnerable. They are the ultimate influences. They often lead to power because others fear power in those that do not have conscience. At points of instability and crisis this is important.

In reality there are always greater powers, no one person ever has full power or control because areas of power and influence migrate with change and time. But there are always great powers even if they are not obvious— even if you have removed sacred cows, divine bulls are usually present. Short term you must navigate those powers, but if you focus on the ultimate power, God's requirement of conscience, then the power of the high ground of morality usually lets you navigate a truer course. If you always go with the easy wind and do not on occasion move into it, you have an aimless path that seldom reaches a destination.

Economic Structural Change Versus Economic Cycles

Many of those times of instability came from economic crises. While culture has been dramatically affected by the change of technology and globalization, economics has been significantly changed as well. The various generations since the "Greatest Generation" of World War II have lived a progression of economic change that has been highly dramatic. America's values, political system, and economic system have rested on a strong, large, and dominant middle class that often needs to be cohesive to provide the peer pressure that gives power to values.

In my lifetime, I have seen the significant changes that have affected the middle class. Early in life I saw education was the key to success in many ways. But hard work in a country with significant manufacturing and advancing technology produced jobs that in relativity allowed wives to stay home with their children creating a very solid middle class life. Over the years the economic stresses that have forced women to work changed the nature of the family. The pensions and security of an earlier time have been significantly diminished, except in governmental areas, for much of society. The stagflation that has taken place in middle class incomes has brought increasing pressures limiting the opportunity to save for retirement, and simultaneously causing more reliance on debt and the equity enhancements of real estate to make ends meet. This has led to more dependency on our government.

The growth in the levels of debt from the end of World War II to today when our brightest minds look at how to create second and third mortgages rather than innovation makes us increasingly a nation misallocating its seed corn. As our affluence grew, so did our cultural change from saving to consumption. Ever larger percentages of GNP went to consumer spending as applied to manufacturing. This showed a maturing economy that was supported for years by our innovation and productivity growth aided by investment.

America as a nation often underestimates itself, but unfortunately the future is determined by the decisions that are being made now. There is a new reality that inevitably must be adopted in America because we have taken on debt in huge amounts and adapted tax policies that make us far less competitive than our international counterparts. While we recognize the importance of higher level education, we also need to realize the huge debts that students face are deterring more and more students as they realize the fairly limited numbers of quality jobs that may be available. Part of this strength has occurred because the dollar has been the world's reserve currency and protected us from many of the natural laws of economics affecting other countries. It has allowed the United States to avoid structural changes, but it has developed weaknesses due to our misallocations of funds.

The issue of globalization is significant and free trade is becoming more the villain to many writers, but the real issue is the people's standard of living. As we take on debt we have limited short-term benefit in many cases, but a very long-term drag on the future when that debt has to be repaid. One needs only to look at England and the changes in its standard of living when the pound sterling no longer was the reserve currency of the world. The dollar gives America great benefit in this regard and because of lack of a substitute may well remain so for the immediate future. But how well America manages that benefit is a highly significant consideration that seems ignored by many in leadership. A responsible maintenance of the currency value is the most critical issue. And while the Federal Reserve struggles to accomplish that goal, the increasing burdens it has been given for the economy will make it more and more difficult to achieve. What the future will hold is a new reality that I fear may be more like Latin America where you have a very unequal society in the division between the rich and the poor. This leads to significant political swings within government hindering the ability to plan.

Few people consider that value is often determined by scarcity or, in most cases, by taking the future revenues from an asset and giving it a net present value currently. That net present value requires a discount rate that looks very much at certainty of the factors involved. If there is uncertainty or if the future is negative, the discount rate is adjusted to lower the current value.

One reason for America's current difficulties is we have tremendous uncertainty that affects those discount rates. It is not just taxes, inflation, deflation, regulation or the host of individual events, but the fact that America is seeking to redefine itself. Will it be the nation where opportunity to advance in status in an economic worth between classes is determined by merit? Or will it increasingly be, as the trend has been currently, to have less opportunity to move from poor to wealthy? Will America be a nation of class warfare that pulls all down because of the political use of envy or a reinvigorated nation educated on what it takes to build a competitive economy? These are considerations that look into the soul of America and the values it has had compared to the challenges it now faces. It is important to remember that price and value are two different things. Prices change dramatically, values hold close to an alternate use. We have been deceiving ourselves on prices while losing sight of values. Contextual thinking helps keep that focus.

Our government's decisions over the last sixty or seventy years have set trends and readjusted them. We have added great new social programs, and we have on occasion looked at how to promote growth. These are extremely critical considerations at this point because we have used up much of the margin built by past generations. Your children will be facing these consequences and that is of concern to all who care about their families.

America is at a very unique crossroads in how it looks to compete for the future. While we talk of many individual issues, which are often emotional, we fail to discuss the context of how they fit together and what the long-term implications of each may be. *For government to give something to someone it has to take it from someone. And when it takes it from someone, there is an opportunity lost in growth. What that person might well have done with it could have been more constructive than the purpose for which it is used.*

While there is considerable criticism in that we have such negative payments abroad for goods and manufacturing and jobs move abroad, we must recognize that many of the companies moving the jobs are American companies who manufacture elsewhere to compete with companies internationally on costs. America has had the opportunity to make social improvements because of its wealth. That is neither inappropriate nor unusual. Almost all prospering nations tend to spend to their benefit both individually and in governments. The problem arises when you reach a certain trend that begins to change the nature of the creation of wealth to the consumption of wealth and a balance point is lost. This problem is not easy to see because its effects are very long term.

In your youth, your mother and I always made you learn the ten major sites of any city we visited. This helped you remember the history of the area, and to understand how history formed the values of Western ideas. You memorized them from New Orleans, Washington, New York, Boston, San Francisco, London, Runnymede, Paris, Rome, and many other places in between.

On those vacations, we tied together the quotation that was attributed Abraham Lincoln (possibly not said by him but reflected his observations of society) that I felt defined the most important issues to be preserved to maintain balance. This balance must be maintained so that everyone's piece of the pie grows a little instead of declines where everyone fights over the diminishing amount that is left. The observations are simple, critical principles, but absolutely essential for culture, economics, and politics.

You cannot bring about prosperity by discouraging thrift. You cannot strengthen the weak by weakening the strong. You cannot help the wage earner by pulling down the wage payer. You cannot further the brotherhood of man by encouraging class hatred. You cannot help the poor by destroying the rich. You cannot establish sound security on borrowed money. You cannot keep out of trouble by spending more than you earn. You cannot build character and

courage by taking away man's initiative and independence. You cannot help men
permanently by doing for them what they could and should do for themselves.

—Attributed to Abraham Lincoln

History has many observations that often take the position of either
moral or economic decline that caused a civilization's failure. However, the
point is, generally the failure occurred and the two went down together.
One great problem in modern times, particularly among pundits, is the
revisionism of history. Every circumstance is in some way shaped to fit the
arguments of whoever argues the point. People pull out one particular sta-
tistic and focus on it rather than looking at the complete picture and placing
it in context more like a moving picture. This form of analysis becomes
increasingly important. It is not the pedigree of the scholar or tone-level
of the argument, but instead the logic of its compliance with natural laws.
Incentives do work, and when public policy institutes them with the force
and funding of government, they often matter greatly.

But as you live guided by principles, it is easy to be drawn into the pettiness of life. Never forget what I have taught you about the high road. You
almost always regret the emotional response when you finally reach a point
of frustration in a personal issue. But you should not regret it if it is based
on your principles and not on your personal ego. Always carefully think
through why you are frustrated and the consequences of that frustration.
As my mother taught me, "Never say evil of another for you will probably
someday need them as a friend and they may judge you." Dad taught that
arrogance and personal pride were not only sin, but terrible strategy. It helps
to remember a thought that usually will help you ignore the pettiness:

Great minds discuss ideas, average minds discuss events, small minds discuss people.

—Admiral Hyman G. Rickover

Teach your children the importance of courtesy and respect for others'
dignity. Dad taught me to not only leave a tip, perhaps more than expected,
but also to sincerely thank those serving so they knew the attitude with
which it is given. If it does not delay others, let others in line before you
when driving, and show courtesy in elevators. It is amazing to me how rude
the world is becoming. But the antidote is to show courtesy by example, and
others will often respond. In foreign lands show a respect and an interest in

their culture. Too often Americans do not realize how they are perceived even if they do not intend to leave an image of arrogance. Creating sensitivity to these issues with a respect for true dignity, rather than more superficial political correctness, helps give strength to dignity. When foreigners are here, show them the courtesy and respect you seek there.

I taught you that temperament can be as important as intelligence in addressing life and that controlling and understanding your emotions is particularly critical. The less you personalize issues, the more effective and strategic you will be. And the more you can address principles and ideas, the more leadership you will show and the more respect you will gain. Keeping that temperament is not easy. Whenever you try to lead, particularly on complicated issues that require joint efforts and sacrifice of individuals, it is easy to become frustrated. Efforts for good often bring criticism from those of convenience.

Throughout history leaders have had this same frustration. The great men of history were often reviled and bitterly hated by other groups in their day because they were effective. History has a tendency to reflect greatness after the fact. One of the problems with modern history is that it is always revisionist in the shorter term. People rewrite much of what was reality for political gain. It is said that the victors write history, and there is much to be said of that point. However, if your focus is to do the right thing in God's eyes and your own, then that should not matter that greatly to you. Who is president of what organization or governor of what state or head of which company or president of which institution may matter little fifty years hence—unless they have implemented policies that are so strong they have been institutionalized and convert influence into power.

While courtesy and restraint are key on personal issues, never fear to be forceful on principle—just be sure it is principle. Everyone loses their temper on occasion, but how you react needs a habit of thought. If it is principle, take the strongest position you can. Dad's eyes were hazel, but they would turn almost steel grey on occasion as his temper rose. He often felt he failed in that he could only turn the other cheek a couple of times, then usually decided principle was involved and the personality and dynamics changed. Never be afraid to work to gain power and influence or to use it strongly for the right reasons.

One concern is that our generation has done an extremely poor job of preparing succeeding generations with the character necessary for the problems they will face. Our media today is focused on short-term emotional issues, which miss the great potential consequences that lack of action is causing. The nuclear threat of terrorism is going to be a very serious potential consequence that continues to be under appreciated. The effective devastation from terrorism has to be considered one of the most potentially troubling issues you and your children will face. Historically, looking at Japan and the impact of the devastation of the two nuclear bombs, you saw the significant change in a hardened population that was willing to fight at its very shores. You see in modern Mexico the tremendous impact of the drug wars and what it has done to the peace and tranquility of a country until it becomes almost dysfunctional.

The strength of any nation is in its character and its people. Call it nationalism or pride—it cannot just be emotional. It has to also be a thoughtful consideration of values for which people are willing to live or die. Toughness is necessary, as are decisive policies and actions. If not, the country has a weakness that will inevitably put it into bondage. Our schools, and particularly our higher educational systems, have failed in creating this most important inner trait because they have limited teaching history. Many have increasingly declined to use great books that teach people to think and appreciate honor and responsibility, and have diminished the codes of honor and integrity, the very cultural ethics of society with their emphasis on relativism rather than character. It has not often been a direct choice, but packing specialized alternative courses.

Your generation will need character in the face of these types of adversity because America has lost the margin it held during my generation. Oceans no longer give America or any nation protection.

People increasingly are beginning to recognize that loss of character, as evidenced in popularity polls, minimizes political leadership as an influence and instead give more credence to military, law enforcement, and small business. The first two are unique in that they are almost brotherhoods to a common cause. They have codes of honor that, however, increasingly are being diminished, but that look to a more transformational purpose and obligation. Small business has an almost peer enforced ethics because its customers have to rely on its integrity or the business has no future customers.

Strategically, America has to reestablish value-based systems. Toleration is important, but absolute toleration makes Jesus and Hitler, and their ideas, of equal value. We are a nation that must recognize multiculturalism because of the future interaction of the world. And we have to recognize diversity where people enter into groups of common interests because their individual dignity is not recognized. The issue is how you unify those individual groups into a much more harmonized and greater whole.

Martin Luther King, Gandhi, and many of the founding fathers saw that as character defined by conscience and individual responsibility. You created the proverbial melting pot of common interests among all people for a common good through a society of conscience based on the rule of law and not of men. The other alternative far more common today is the creation of a salad bowl that potentially keeps all those individual groupings from joining together by the political correctness of relativism and absolute toleration. Too often any idea that is brought up by another that is not parallel to one's thoughts is seen as bigoted, racist, or self-serving. These are very effective destructive tactics and "cut off the head of the snake" of the opposition if the rising leaders can be targeted. One of the most effective political approaches today, used by individuals in both parties is Saul Alinsky's strategy from his *Rules for Radicals* "pick the target, freeze it, and polarize it." Only when the population as a whole begins to understand the true issues can ideas rather than men emerge and transformational change occur.

The transformational change that must be strengthened in America to reenergize and progress has to be character, requiring values, morality, and a way of thinking about issues. It is quite true that one question always has to be "whose values," but Conscience, the Golden Rule, and the Common Good are instinctive to each of us. If our goal is to build a society based upon conscience and individual responsibility, then it can be perceived quite separately from a society of convenience and self-interest. Never let the argument digress below the higher issues and become personalized. If others disagree with you on those issues, your battle is engaged.

As you analyze politics and the future, keep in mind that there is a great difference between campaigns and running a government. Look for substance and sensitize others to it. Campaigns provide "a feel good" atmosphere where you feel happy supporting what you believe is an entire package of the best ideas. Once you get into government, you have to understand that politics change reality. There must be compromise, and the key is making sure the compromise moves at least to a very thoughtful set of organizing principles that make society better. America is no longer in a position where gridlock is beneficial. We have too many negative trends that must be addressed. The goal is to move in the best direction as much as possible.

The government needs to look at how it can foster growth because that brings both the jobs and the increased standard of living that benefits all people. Growth minimizes the impact of existing debt. It should focus on what has to be done, even if there are sacrifices, for the benefit of your children and the future. This is the most important organizing principle that government can have. You must have cultural values, but government should not by its size impose them. It should look to economic policy and the politics of the system to make adjustments between the other two powers. They will largely succeed or fail together as our economy competes globally.

Jobs will be a huge issue as the world moves forward. When times become more difficult, that often happens and policies are put in place to try to mitigate the pain of unemployment. However, remember that many of America's problems have taken place a little bit at a time like a cancer where the concept of avoiding moral hazard and the importance of individual responsibility have increasingly been declining. At some point, this decline reaches a crisis point and is much like a heart attack. The secret is to treat the cancer early so you never reach the heart attack because once it is reached, all the wrong solutions usually are put into place. If we do not address our problems, the market will eventually do it for us with much greater force. The middle class is increasingly vulnerable in this particular environment, and it is the core of society as we have known it in our lifetimes.

What matters most is to change its decline and provide a recovery that will help bring prosperity and with it the ability to finance national security. That is not done by emotional rhetoric, but must be thoughtfully strategized and understood by a much broader portion of the public. The founders saw the necessity of an educated populace making decisions for the republic. Our educational systems are critical to our future and serious immediate concentration has to be placed on how to return them to some of the best in the world as well as producing responsible, ethical, harmonious, and understanding citizens.

For our children's sake as well as the economy, this is an immediate issue. Increasingly the wealthy send their children to private schools, but that is much like teaching your child to be ethical and then putting them into a corporation in which you can only succeed by convenience. They are either corrupted or they fail. The issue is broader than the individual families and how they see their family's future. The issue is how we can unify all groups on common appreciation of family values and futures to build a competitive nation. Inevitably, this will require sacrifice now for the future generations.

The future of America may rest on how our people decide to think about the future. If we have the debt to GDP ratio of Greece, France, and other countries when austerity begins, we will develop into class warfare and all will lose. The rich must understand their need for a more equitable system of compassion, and the less wealthy must learn what brings economic growth and prosperity. This is a common understanding of how to build innovation and productivity and their relation to standards of living that give the most support to the balance provided by a middle class. The wealthy might not mind paying more taxes if they saw the money efficiently spent. Many have compassion, but compassion requires everyone having individual responsibility in policies and not governmental freeloading on the backs of others.

This focus has to be concentrated on governmental budgets at each level. A budget reflects the priorities society has and what specific things it tends to value most. If we want to make an organizing principle creating a better life for our children and grandchildren and absorbing the responsibility we should have for our generation, then we need to look at the effect of these budgets and tax policies. What they inevitably design tells us where we should focus our attention and at the same time which political leaders are realistic enough to deserve our support by focusing intelligently. Demographics will make a huge difference in how well the older generation succeeds. In many countries, such as China, the one child policy gives it only a limited amount of time to achieve its full economic potential before the negatives of the demographics burdens them.

America has had a growing society where Europe and Japan have not. These have a great effect on our future, and the trends are only ignored at our peril. Western Europe is a perfect example of our current strategy as we are moving to higher taxes, potentially lower birth rates and immigration, and limited economic growth. The creation of jobs and opportunity are absolutely essential. Concepts of increasing taxes only put more pressure on the middle class and eventually the number of children that can be afforded affecting demographics. The debt that we create inevitably will have major impact upon our future. To pay it back, when reality finally forces America to address the potential decline of the dollar as the dominant currency, makes the risks substantially higher. Our growth economically usually came in spurts as new technologies give a boost to productivity. But this required that America remain the source of much of the world's innovation. And this is much harder if we put burdens on business and funding limits research.

America during my lifetime was one of the two superpowers until the cold war ended and left it as a sole power. Its economic strength let it dominate military power and gave great flexibility in foreign policy. However, our years of undisciplined spending, an increasingly dysfunctional political system for addressing longer-term risks, the demographics of questionably sustainable public retirement and health systems, and a host of related decisions that led to our current economic crises—all have shaped the future as one where the United States will be a key player. This will only remain true to the degree that it is a force for international governance and stability. America has been able to fund both its needs and wants, but it will now have to retrench to just meet its needs.

Our economic engine must become our focus since it will no longer provide the margins for aggressive foreign policy. No other country will step in. China has its need for growth and internal stability, and Russia has its mineral base but little ability to project power. The world will become a more uncertain and dangerous place unless a common culture of cooperation is developed for an appreciated common good.

America will face a choice of whether or not it can learn to make hard decisions, through a functioning system of governance. The budget process must become realistic and Americans must become more educated on the country's options and costs. This is not a change a super leader makes unless a wave of understanding is created for the leader to ride. The issues have to be viewed in context, and your generation will have to find a way they can be broadly understood. Your children's world will be shaped by the strategies in certain specific areas.

America's economics will be driven by concerns on deficits, debt, taxes, and the stability of the dollar. And the culture of the times will include understanding the power of ideas to transform, dealing with that power and the uncertain effects of the Internet. Our politics will require minimizing the extremes of partisanship and producing policies for innovation and growth through education. These politics must also include a more harmonious and civilized world in which to compete and live involving the critical current importance of China to America and the impact of a "level" world to their future.

These all fit together and affect each other so they cannot logically be talked about independently. These are your children's legacy to endure, but yours to begin to address in preparation for them, teaching them through your efforts. Unless you understand the problems you face, you have little chance of solving them. Leadership comes from people having confidence to think, prioritize, and then act rather than talk. But whether they follow also requires trusting a leader's true motives. Sacrifice, which is what true leadership requires, only comes voluntarily when there is true belief. You will make your own future in many ways as you cannot stand and hope others will do it for you without taking much greater risk.

LAW VERSUS CULTURE

In *The Language of Conscience* there are three distinct cultures that each society has in differing degrees. The first is the rule of law and discipline in society; the second, the culture of obligation or morality; and the third, culture of compassion and service. The first is basic—the rule of law, specifically defined as the common rules by which we must all operate enforced with a discipline in society, hopefully with great fairness. This rule plays a larger or smaller part in society depending on the power of the other two cultures. *It is man's relation to society.*

Skip to the third—the culture of compassion or service is what we do for others that is not required of us, but we do it for our own ethics to be of service to others. This is often the core motivation of religions and a society that believes in individual responsibility, charity, and treating others with the same rights, dignities, and opportunities that we would expect for ourselves. This culture creates a personal integrity that looks beyond self and to the true greater good as an organizing principle of life, business, and society both on an individual and an institutional basis. *In many ways it is a man's relation to God and what he values.*

The middle culture—the culture of obligation or morality is what we expect of each other and involves neither what society imposes nor what we decide in our hearts to be our operating principle of life. It instead involves the reciprocity of obligation with expectations. Courtesy, self respect, justice, and a respect for the Golden Rule and the common good are very much components *of this part of man's relation to man.* It is the balancing factor between men because there remains the expectation, even though unofficial, that society abides by certain codes of honor and respect. The culture of compassion and service is more individualized to the forgiveness and compassion that one shares individually. It is the fraternity of all men that has to balance the equality of individuality helping us see where we fit in the world as opposed to the world centering on us individually. The decline of this culture expands government to its vacuum or its growth replaces government. Basically, it is the values taught within the family and the middle class that have been declining.

The balance of these cultures becomes critically important in life, business, and institutions, providing the context of how these operate together. Within a corporation you may have four different generations that all look at the corporate structure differently as we discussed previously. They all understand there are certain rules to be obeyed, certain mutual obligations of courtesy that ought to be honored. But they may each hold different individual perspectives—whether they look at their position as a part of the composition or as an individual simply being there. If you are to have a culture in an organization that has generations of differing perspectives, it must be one of common values that are jointly appreciated. These values create obligations that should be mutually accepted.

In approaching an effort to reform or strengthen the culture of an institution, it becomes important to look at all three of these separate cultures and how they interact to find the values of the institution. These are self-imposed or peer directed obligations not formalized rules. As Marcus Aurelius noted, a man should be upright, not be kept upright. The strength of the culture is the depth of its acceptance of values.

To also keep man upright, regulation is the codification of the law and the method by which it is enforced or the discipline within society that is the critical portion of it. If regulation expands then the portion of culture that is both the culture of obligation and the culture of compassion tend to shrink. If society as a whole becomes litigious and the law and regulation tell all people what to do, the freedom for individual cultures diminish accordingly as does the freedom that supports individual dignity. If the cultures of obligation and compassion want to play a much stronger part, they must in many ways serve as a method of self-regulation through their peer pressure and self-governance. If people settle arguments using the Golden Rule or mediation rather than suing each other in court, it is a less tense society focusing more on judgment. It has a peer pressure that moves society more in the method of family values, coming to more equitable solutions without bitterness, hatred or the malice that normally comes from confrontation. It also tends to create a society that expects more of those that govern to maintain that society.

The role of lawyers originally was to be private attorneys to right wrongs before juries of peers. These cases would be few because the peer pressure of society should make people accept individual responsibility. And the power of maintaining ones dignity was a cultural force to do right and let conscience dominate. However, when society loses this peer pressure litigation and regulation expands, if balance is lost, the first step of taking individual responsibility means taking liability—often undermining acceptance of responsibility in the culture. You look at compliance, not at what is just and intelligent. The more society punishes taking responsibility the less there is. This is an under appreciated moral hazard of a litigious system and why juries mattered more where they were the peer pressure.

This balance between law and culture is the tipping point of a society and is seldom recognized. It is the balance between the rights of the state versus the individual that is often hidden in the regulation or control of society. These two points must be fully understood to think clearly about the forces and powers that shape dignity. They are complex but critical to understand.

Regulation Versus a Culture of Conscience

Regulation in itself is a part of the society of law, and if expansive, frequently has very negative attributes. The more regulation and power placed in individuals the more opportunity for corruption, the more arrogance, and the more depletion of the dignity of those below. Power within bureaucracies feeds on itself and makes princes of those who have limited experience in the realities of many sectors of life. This slows innovation at a cost to growth. There are obviously good and bad regulators, but a regulatory system is normally administrative and often becomes limited in flexibility. Problems are often unique.

In effect, regulators normally alternate between two approaches. In better times, there is often more of a relationship of mutual respect and trust. It is in the industry's benefit to have this environment because it self-polices many of the problems. The industry members do not want increased regulation and focus from the regulators and normally only those institutions who violate that trust by their actions receive most of the focus. However, when you have economic shifts or ethical breakdowns within an industry, the regulators look into the abyss and as Nietzsche noted, "It looks into them," and their attitude changes. From a perspective of a culture of respect and supervision, you then revert to a culture of intimidation and absolutism from ratios that are quantitative rather than qualitative. The culture of the regulation is key. Does it have integrity and fairness throughout swings? Does it treat the small the same way it does the large? Do the Inspectors General of the agencies assess this culture or just look at techniques of regulation and miss strategy level concerns?

Regulators will argue that extreme times require extreme measures and that some actions have to be taken to deal with the size of the crisis. However, once you lose the culture of respect and trust, it is seldom very helpful. If the regulated believe they are nothing more than a set of numbers to be achieved and that there is no balance and fairness in qualitative decisions explaining their actions, they have little to gain in maintaining the appropriate relationship with the regulator. If the regulator is seen as a street policeman, not a balanced judge, it sets the context of the discussions and strategies. In many cases that leads to a significant reappraisal of actions. There can also be significant impacts to the broader economy. When banking goes into one of its regulatory intimidation periods, you have a chilling effect on jobs and lose many that would not need to be lost with more balance between a culture of respect and the imposing culture of intimidation. Because of crises, usually discretion loses out to force. In defense of regulators, one of the problems they face is the great change in the industries they regulate. It is hard to foresee the future, and being ahead of the well funded profit driven sector is hard with normally limited functions. We are expecting more of regulation than it can provide.

In the balance of regulatory cultures of coercion and respect, it is necessary to maintain a perspective of how the institution's management views the situation. If they feel it is in their interest to maintain the respect of the regulator, they will work that much harder in the difficult times to avoid a negative relationship that may bring even stronger supervision. However, if you cross the line that there is no effective judgment beyond just what numbers from a Washington office dictates and no real substance given to localized understanding of the wisdom of actions, the system loses a great amount of credibility. Respect and trust are powerful implements often discarded carelessly by regulators and in doing so injure the ability to rebuild the system because trust is not restored. The concept of personal dignity is critical in regulation. How things are done is as significant as what is done. There are different ways to accomplish the same end, and some may not have the political image but may minimize the ultimate damage.

Regulation generally is enacted to solve a significant problem—and partially does. But the regulation cumulatively grows in mass. Even though the now smaller problem can be handled as an unusual exception in the changed culture, the mass of regulation both hurts competitiveness by raising the bar for new businesses and limiting respect for law because it is so massive no one can know it all. Regulations need to be regularly proved and better peer systems used to create cultures that comply through market forces. The Better Business Bureau and many online performance-comment websites are perfect examples.

One of the best approaches is to promote self-regulation. The peer pressure of the unit, if self enforced, can readily replace regulation because the populace strains under it and reorganizes its burdens. However, self-enforcing culture to replace regulation must have a nucleus and has to develop over time to prove itself to be a viable option.

In the mid 1800s, *The Law* by Frederic Bastiat explained this most effectively. He noted very accurately that it is not the law that shapes the culture, but the culture that shapes the law. And correspondingly, the absence of a strong culture requires much more law and regulation. Alexis de Tocqueville's *Democracy in America* similarly shows that the power of America is in its people and comes from their unique nature of nonprofit and civic organizations, family interaction, and understanding of civic obligations. The comment that America is great because America is good is often attributed to him. If America ceases to be good, America will cease to be great. While this is not shown to be an exact quotation of his, I think it captures both his thoughts and the oft debated concepts of American Exceptionalism. It is not America itself that is exceptional, but its modern democracy and free enterprise and the unique ideas and institutions it gave the world. These have defined it. When these values no longer truly dominate its culture, America will lose its exceptionality, and that will happen when regulation replaces its values as a guiding light and its people lose self-reliance to dependency.

An example of recent note is how legislation can affect counter purposes. Looking at defense industry scandals, the concept of compliance within corporate America was significantly enhanced by legislation several decades ago when the Judicial Sentencing Act became a part of the punishments for violating corporations. It took into account the company and a voluntary compliance program and how effective that program was.

Almost every major corporation put in a program that might differ on effectiveness but at least gave it the chance at some benefit in crediting the penalties. Quite often this was under the legal department and the general counsel who often have a greater duty to protect the corporation and the senior officers. So many times, discretion moved to lesser compliance that might spawn potential problems. If systems were extremely forceful, which is necessary to focus employee attention, they also created more problems.

However, in more recent times the importance of culture within the institution was recognized as separate from compliance. You need a corporate compliance system that is effective in its ability to quickly focus on problems, but you also need to build a culture where the entire corporation serves as a watchdog by knowing exactly what is expected. If the FBI or other entities investigate a corporation, the usual way is not to take what is said at the higher levels where awards may be given for integrity, and there are some significant documents reflecting it. Instead interview lower level employees to see exactly what they know, how they would report any potential violations, and their level of confidence in the system to protect them if they did so. That is the reality of a system.

The concept of creating corporate culture was given a very significant boost in the Sarbanes Oxley legislation, which put more responsibility on senior officers. Many programs were greatly enhanced, and companies attempted to address fraud allegations internally by setting up confidential hotlines for employees to report violations. They also offered significant training programs to enhance the culture of the organization. These were good beginnings, but only in a few instances did they address the conversion of the culture of the corporation in how it did business. This is one reason why the fraud and greed in business strategies led to many of the problems. A lack of responsible vision overcame concerns of compliance and culture on a more internal level. Nonetheless, the progression of many academic and consulting firms was moving positively toward creating internal cultures with employees and providing hotlines and more extensive internal focus.

Recently the Dodd Frank legislation, in an effort to expose fraud, included a significant "Bounty Provision" that rewards employees for reporting violations to the government rather than internally. One recent whistleblower stands to gain $96 million for doing so. While this may stand out as an example of how to punish corporations, it runs in total contradiction and opposition to strengthening internal fraud detection efforts that try to create an internal culture of compliance. It is certainly not in "context" with the system needed to accomplish its goals.

This culture of compliance is far more important because it affects many more issues than the individual "bounty" and is a more appropriate way of dealing with problems. An employee now can choose between working and helping establish an ethical culture or trying to retire with a homerun in finding anything that might be a miscue. This is not to say that violations don't need to be effectively prosecuted and that the government has a responsibility in using methods to achieve these goals. It simply notes the inconsistent policy between the two pieces of legislation and its effect. Under the new approach of the "Bounty Provision," general counsels are going to be far less open and the cultural benefits of ethics will be significantly minimized. This changes the nature of the corporation and also the competitiveness of the company as it may give more fears to innovation and competitiveness where risks in these areas are much higher. The ultimate goal should be to create peer pressure and ethical cultures within corporations not only internally, but also in how they view their relationships with society and other stakeholders. Profitability is better with sustainability, but it requires consistency throughout the organization.

Much of the pressure on regulatory compliance has the potential to destroy the far more significant cultural ethics systems. It could be implemented so that peer pressure kept many men upright. If people know there is a greater chance of them being reported on a broad base, managers react to transparency. But that transparency requires a broad system and a sensitivity that only the cultural systems can provide. When a corporate whistleblower can take original evidence to the SEC or Commodity Futures Trading Commission and potentially get between 10% and 30% of a penalty that is over $1 million, they are going to use that system rather than taking the risk of reporting it internally to someone's dissatisfaction. But the internal system has to be built on integrity, and it is counterproductive to significantly impact those efforts.

The reality of regulation is that the discipline with the society or the method of enforcement, the intensity, has a very significant impact. As noted, fear and intimidation always used in times of crisis "to get attention" have a tremendous negative impact on trust. Many regulatory systems, particularly those involving the need for intelligence, require trust and the support of the people regulated to function most effectively. Any system that facilitates between these approaches seldom builds levels of confidence. Much like the beginning of the Lord's Prayer, the concept "Our Father" gives an indication as to how the words following should be read. The substitution of the words "Our Judge and Prosecutor" for the word "Father" completely changes the context of the words that follow. When there is uncertainty of intent, trust and cooperation lessens.

The chilling effect of regulation often comes from an excess of intimidation. On the other hand, too much leniency provides negative incentives. The bottom issue is the culture of the regulator, its integrity, balance, and professionalism. In days of lobbyists, legislative intervention, and uncertain philosophies, it is difficult for regulatory agencies to maintain the necessary style of independent culture. The use of ombudsmen, policy reviews, and other issues independent of the agency itself might well help bring balance to approaches that vary dramatically. This is not an American or Western problem as much as it is for all countries where bureaucracies become large with growing government. Any time you have power, it is corruptible, and the question is whether the power is in the people or the culture and whether that culture is dedicated to fairness in codes of honor.

One of the difficulties of regulation is that it has to be quantitative, driven largely by figures with little discretion, or qualitative, which requires much discretion on decisions. One is more top down and the other is more localized. The problem is when you try to combine the two you often get inconsistency, which leads to uncertainty and frustration of those regulated. If it is rigid top down, there is limited justice for individual exceptions. If it is discretionary, you have to have demanding, constant judgments on how it is approved; the rules and regulators are not even in dispensing good judgment. Some are excellent, others are lacking. Even though regulators try to bring in professionalism, it is the culture of the agency that is key to equal justice and that is usually lost in the administrative system. Corporate governance oversight policies could do a great deal to stabilize regulation if it were added to the existing more haphazard system of Congressional oversight and Inspectors General. Confidential surveys of those regulated on a regular basis by the GAO would be a good way to identify problems, as would a focus on the internal culture of regulators. When anyone has more direct oversight, it improves culture if oversight has integrity and professionalism, so GAO and Inspectors General need oversight as well. Interestingly that would have relatively limited cost in simply reengineering current systems, but probably a huge benefit to the economy if regulation was more reasonable and self-policing for ineffective rules.

Similarly, how the General Accounting Office and Agency Inspectors General operate matter greatly. They are the regulator's regulator, and Congress in requiring information sets the tone. They need to examine not only the problems in the industry, usually finding failures of the regulators, but whether solutions are balanced and fair when regulators are pressured. Today, often a problem leads to a Congressional hearing, Congress demands the investigation, and it is a search for blame with the regulators crunching down on both the bad and good. Congress needs to more carefully instruct the investigation to look to culture as well as compliance. They must police the culture of the regulators for fairness as well as efficiency and not just criticize. Congress is the representation of the people in this situation.

While today talking about corporate values is a cottage industry, it is far more serious than fine words. We have had an age of greed exposed by the decline, and people as well as corporations are looking more seriously at life and corporate responsibility's role in a business' ultimate success. Having a well-defined culture of values (beyond the normal posted list) helps you make a melting pot of diverse people that now make up an average business—age, gender, religion, background, and a host of others. Such a culture is the cement that stabilizes the gravel, sand, and water of concrete. Regardless of past culture and history—character, morality, and ethics can set a tone that attracts similar beliefs and repels convenience. If people buy into a culture, it helps set the "language" of the enterprise, which often reduces compliance needs, sensitizes to handling and recognizing problems early, and unifies employers and management on fairness that builds morale.

If we look at our culture in more modern times, we have seen that partisanship and politics have in many ways extinguished the concern for the common good under the banner of more extreme principles that are never fully balanced. In business, greed has replaced the self-interest of market economics with monopolies and crony capitalism in hand with government affected by lobbies and campaign contributions. These have diminished many of the forces of competition and self-regulating ethics that previously existed. As a result, the people as a whole have lost interest in institutions and leaders.

Commentators and consultants fill the airways primarily talking of the faults of others and excuses for diminishing performance. We focus on symptoms, not causes and that leads to focus on the wrong questions. The world is shifting and changing dramatically. The existing structures have been sorely tested by the changes that are primarily in the people as a whole reacting to technology and self-indulgence. A new paradigm will need to be developed that can begin to address how problems must be viewed.

This paradigm, in the United States, is presently being filled by ever-increasing regulation in an attempt to equalize and level society. However, regulation ultimately creates another set of winners. China went through much of this period in extreme during the times of the Great Leap Forward in the Cultural Revolution. The "free rider" concept of "those that no longer worked because they did not need to" emerged as a very significant concern. And it was only when China adjusted its perspectives to recognizing a greater benefit achieved from more appropriately valuing the quality and amount of work that their economic system began to take root. China has the problem of adapting a large system to a new set of principles from the direction of absolute intense regulation of central control that brought with it significant corruption. America is moving in the opposite direction trying to make increased regulation the solution to markets that have become extreme because self-interest and conscience turned to greed and short-term personal convenience. The middle class suffers in both, and society loses the "personal dignity" that gives it character. If the government regulates, it controls you but removes independence and responsibility in degrees.

The problem China faced was that a family's income depended on the performance of a significant number of other farmers in the collectives created. So how hard one would work was diminished for the individual since his additional efforts gained his family little. If you had a particularly large cooperative, the "free rider" problem became even greater because of the disincentives of the ever-larger group. America is moving this direction through tax policy, redistribution through entitlements, and intense regulation by government. The arguments for society are compassion, fairness, and need. These are legitimate arguments on many of these issues. But the approaches are often not balanced to maintain moral hazard and "free rider" concerns. They do not reflect the obligations to those who earn the money the government is taking, rather than creating, and the natural law of sustainability will eventually punish all in the society when the policies no longer grow everyone's slice of the pie.

The markets in America no longer became true markets when they lost their integrity to greed. Some balance of regulation was obviously needed but was removed or not enforced due to the political benefits of the time. It is important to look at market capitalism in a sense of reality. Most of the commentators today either extol its virtues in the extreme or castigate it for the tremendous inequities it can cause. The market system is a T-square that has both benefits and detriments. It has extremes because the nature of society is to operate through cycles of greed and fear. It requires a rule of law that keeps integrity in the markets and restrains the worst of forces. But that regulation is never going to be totally effective. If you do not have honest markets there is not honest competition, and without competition, true markets do not exist. That is true in China and in America.

What would have been far more satisfactory as a balance beyond heavy regulation would have been the Boards of Directors of many companies looking at the longer-term sustainability in judging their managements and serving their customers more than the immediate focus just on return. Corporate governance is a key because of the importance to our systems and its power. But the culture of boards is more in form than substance. This developing issue comes from the last effort to make executive pay realities based on performance. More than cash, stock options were used to tie interests of shareholders and management and short-term thinking through greed emerged. Our current problems resulted from bad public policy and greed that affected politics, economics, and culture.

In the last twenty years greed has become more of an individualized power through incentives in much of our society. The corporatism that has made huge institutions refined the crony capitalism of alliance with government and the new visions of elite executives not only forgot the middle class, but also continually increased its vision of entitlement and value. Systems and people built the value more than leadership and trading.

How we as a society looked at using the economic system determined to a great degree what happened to us. It was not just the fault of a few executives. They simply executed to our wishes greatly to their own benefit as well. We as a people created the environment in which they operated. We undertook ever-increasing debt without responsibility in many cases.

Our politicians created imbalances in the housing markets by where funds were granted in the subprime areas—through housing institutions creating free market opportunities and rewarding those that most aggressively took advantage of them, even though it may have resulted in ultimate ruin. The culture at each stage, the lack of concern for the future or in many cases integrity and the conscience of what happened to others was largely ignored. We elected these leaders; we ignored civic concerns.

In the same situation these same results would occur time and time again. The question is not whether there was a problem, but instead what was the most appropriate and effective way to solve it. Increased regulation alone does not address many of the issues and will only result in hiring more lobbyists and consultants to take care of an ever-increasing array of special interests. The secret is to build systems that more effectively show the benefit of a common interest to people as a whole and unify them. It is not going to be found in a new Consumer Protection Agency that assumes people, perhaps well intentioned, who have often never run a business, can regulate it without destroying innovation. Regulation may be necessary for a balanced playing field of fairness and consumer protection. But in excess it is used to create social behavior at the expense of markets and their creativity, which is necessary for a rising middle class that keeps family values.

A great society should be educated on its own affairs rather than herded as children into limited options. If people create fraud, jail them with hard sentences, claim back ill gotten gains, allow companies to fail in order to bring back responsible actions and concerns. But do not destroy the most powerful economic system in history in giving a standard of living on the premise of giving it value by redefining it through regulation and government power rather than rebuilding the culture of conscience and responsibility.

This assumes that regulators, often having not been in a business due to conflicts of interest, know better than you do what your opportunities should be. There is no question that abuses are in the system—the issue is the culture of the regulators in addressing them. Broad vision that they must control the industry for fear of evil, impacts the producers and investors who create opportunity and value as well as the rising convenience driven speculators and greedy. The focus needs to be on the latter, and whether that occurs, depends on how the agency sees its goal. Too often it is as a prosecutor rather than as a judge. That usually impacts small business, which creates the majority of the jobs, rather than big business, which hires lawyers to minimize the problems.

When it has the prosecutorial attitude, you do not rally those of convenience in the industry that would create peer support of regulation but a fear that stops the necessary innovation. The distinction is significant because producers and investors usually make money with people by providing benefits. Speculators and the convenience driven focus normally makes money off people and thus needs more regulation. Regulation can be tyranny or justice, so before it is supported or condemned, it needs to be defined. The wrong choice forces producers and developers to cease efforts and hurts the very people the regulation was to protect by forcing them to do without a service or go to more expensive and burdensome alternatives. A strong positive regulatory culture focuses on "convenience" and is strong in enforcement but recognizes justice, creating legitimate systems for the appeal of actions.

It is also wise, when national regulation is necessary, to remember the advice of Alexis de Tocqueville that local administration of laws, even national, has great merit because it adapts to the reality more effectively. The recent banking crisis has shown the normal condition that when a problem becomes severe, top down leadership often directs even more from the top to attempt to gain control. This control removes much of the discretion from local regulators and often removes both judgment and justice from individual situations. Quantitative ratios replace qualitative analysis, which often only enhances problems. The culture of regulators, the method of enforcement, the oversight of regulators, and similar concerns have a great deal to do with the ultimate effect of laws and the integrity of the system. Laws were in place to prevent much of the last crisis but were not enforced because the culture of the time did not pressure doing so and often prevented it. New laws will probably have the same result if the culture is not changed.

Change to responsibility is not going to happen easily. It is not going to happen just out of the universities. And it is not going to happen just in one country. Trade is essential to everyone's standard of living. Change will occur from crisis and frustration that will inevitably stem from the problems and gridlock that caused serious imbalances. When they happen, the question will be how to find appropriate solutions. Before reality ultimately faces such a choice, the question should be how to build the type of institution that can both soften that blow and provide alternatives at the time choices have to be made. The vast majority of problems are man-made and thus solvable by man. But to solve them we must have sacrifice, and sacrifice requires a different culture than one of self-interest.

In business, the strengthening of organizations of corporate governance ought to address this true cause of the problem, building stronger self-governance in industries and individual corporations if they wish to lessen regulation. Society will no longer allow the past, so what is the vision for the future?

Regulation is a political action that has automatic economic and cultural implications. By political will, it supplants free market economics by removing choices and demanding behavior. In cases where there are abuses, this may be quite beneficial. But if it has moral hazard implications, it needs to be seriously questioned because of the impact on the economics where it deprives opportunities and costs that are not fully appreciated. It also impacts as well the deprivation of personal dignity in that freedom is taken from the culture and the concept of individual responsibility is minimized. Regulation is often used as a substitute for legislative actions to exhibit control and shape both economies and individual opportunities. Sometimes it is an indirect way of accomplishing economic goals not unlike using taxation to punish or reward specific behaviors rather than just raise money. The larger the government that is a compilation of all of the regulations, the smaller is the independence and freedom of the culture. And opportunities and innovations become increasingly limited.

The State Versus the Individual

It is also very important for society to recognize that the government's budget is actually a contract of the government with its people. The size of the budget and where the money is spent tells a great deal about the society. The larger the government, the greater percentage of the gross national product it spends in providing services and regulating behavior. Quite often this has to be by taxation because the government basically removes money from one sector and gives it to another. It does not create money unless it is fiat currency. It does not create wealth. It does so with great inefficiency because it does not have the same cost constraints that a private sector effort requires. While significant needs for compassion and human dignity are necessary for those who truly need assistance, the increased size of budgets has significant implications to ultimate sustainability.

The greater the budget in size, the more is required from the private sector, and certain levels become tipping points that may differ in the changing conditions and technologies of time. While regulation is the enforcement mechanism of the budget, where money is spent and how society is taxed have significant implications. If money is spent in infrastructure and areas of substance that could be considered investment, then it provides an ultimate return to the society. If, however, it basically is short-term support, money creates a dependency that must be funded over the long term with limited benefits to growth. Thus, the nature of expenditure becomes an extremely important concept of the budget.

A governmental budget is very different from a private one in that many items are "off budget if they are unique costs." This makes it quite deceptive and removes the focus from them because they matter less. The concept of running Social Security tax collections through the budget in many cases masks the true nature of the deficits being created. Just as the Social Security reserve funds being used to purchase government bonds masks the problem that when the generational balance is such that money must be withdrawn, it places a double pressure on the liquidity of capital markets. This happens when both retirement must be funded and existing debt must be serviced when the bonds purchased by the Social Security fund have to be turned into cash. Both parties have played games with the budget, and America's prosperity has allowed it without significant consequence.

The experiences of Greece, the current efforts in the United Kingdom to bring balance to budgets, as well as many of the conditions throughout Europe show what occurs when democratic socialists' concepts reach sustainability problems and more draconian measures have to be taken. While America is not quite to that point, its trends lead it there, and the size of the problem is magnified much more quickly.

The budget is thus not just a contract economically—it is a contract culturally as to how obligations will be satisfied and choices made. To govern is to have to choose between policy options. When you delay, create uncertainty, and fail to choose, you do not govern. Very thoughtful organizing principles must be used throughout to share sacrifice and not create moral hazard within the culture simply by means testing, and thereby taking it from those who have saved and not created the problem. That only creates a culture with a lack of responsibility and no reason to not be a "free rider" in the coming generation. Crisis will change that, but only at great cost. Thus understanding the budget and the nature of regulation is a necessity for any government to appropriately make its changes.

We must also remember that regulation is in part a replacement of morality, conscience, and ethics. Once you begin relying heavily upon government or the law to enforce rules, the lawyers can find many ways around it. Normally, these rules only come with disclosure as an out. Heavy regulation is an admission that the culture of morality is not doing its job properly and that peer pressure is not working. It also has to be understood that regulation takes place a little bit over time but eventually becomes massive. It starts with a very good intention, often to remove specific ills that deserve attention, but it grows because it becomes part of a bureaucracy that increasingly desires power. It is the nature of nearly all bureaucracies. And only when you reach a certain stage is a significant impact of that regulation on opportunity realized.

Regulation is often presented as a benefit to the middle class and the less privileged as an effort to protect them. Often unconsidered is the consequences of omitting what might be opportunities—the unintended consequences of the regulation. Big business does not necessarily mind regulation nearly as much as small business and entrepreneurs. Regulations make starting businesses much more difficult because it requires greater expertise and funding. Competition is the ultimate protector of the middle class and opportunity.

Perhaps one of the best examples of these types of cycles occurred during President Jimmy Carter's administration. He appointed Alfred Kahn as Chairman of the Civil Aeronautics Board in recognition of the problems that exist in the industry. Kahn encouraged competition in an effort to make air travel more affordable. Today that deregulation may be the cause of some of the problems in air travel, but it made air travel a reality for the middle class rather than just the wealthy. There were few new airlines under heavy regulation, but the smaller airlines and the number of start-ups changed the nature of the industry and made cheaper prices possible.

In this cycle we begin again putting severe penalties on airlines for delays over three hours on the tarmac. The penalties are so severe it most certainly gets the attention of the airlines. But for that reason they will far more quickly cancel flights that might give them liability and take other actions that inconvenience passengers. All regulation has a consequence, and the analytics of understanding the unintended consequences are absolutely critical. But most important is that when regulation is seen as a replacement for morality, you are moving society in the wrong direction. You should be adapting moral hazard principles with competition and peer reputation through a culture of regulation that understands this impact and blends it so that only the most egregious violations are focused on while competition is enhanced.

Opportunity requires the freedom to take risk, not the limitation of it by economic dependency or controlling regulation. Management of risk is the key to innovation and opportunity. This allows the opportunity to create wealth and the temperament of a free society. Government, which removes most of the benefit of risk economically and uses regulation to remove opportunity for risk by its burdens, may create a dependent class that has limited risk but severely limits the creation of the wealth that sustains the system over time.

The Uncertain Effects of the Internet

Perhaps no issue is going to be more important in your lifetime than the tremendous transformation in how ideas, concepts, and information are transmitted. Media shapes culture. Each day brings a new application and a new approach to communication. The problem is that we have a tremendous amount of knowledge at our fingertips and very limited wisdom. We also have very limited trust in information on the Internet because the vast majority of people contributing information may have agendas and purposes we do not understand. Building credibility in sources of information is absolutely critical. One important thing to do is get information from a wide variety of sources that help you shape an independent perspective. But of even more importance is trying to find or be a part in developing sources of information that put material in context and help you understand what all of the changes actually mean. It is not a process of just finding a site that gives you information. It must be a process of finding a site or a system that helps prioritize and process that information on a logical basis that you trust. The Internet can be one of the greatest benefits to man and completely changes the way history operates. But it is also capable of producing many problems if it allows emotion to overcome thought and civility.

And how do we build systems of close relationships that can shape insights to others' credibility and integrity for mutual benefit? Trust, credibility, and competence are value components that require more protection and codes of conduct and honor.

One place to start is to judge a source by how it views critical issues. Economics gives indication whether a philosophy grows a pie for all or focuses on dividing it. If you think long-term harmony, you need to understand the concept of growth where prosperity is sufficient enough to be shared. Even if the U.S. has a much higher standard of living than China on a per capita basis, if U.S. standards are declining and Chinese rising, direction will have more impact on satisfaction than absolutes.

VI | A GRANDFATHER'S HOPES

For Evelyn, Wright, Margaret Grace, Victoria, Ty, Cuatro, Evan, and . . . . ?

While my children's generation will face many of the choices of how to reenergize America, I fear that my grandchildren will have the greatest challenges. For many of the most significant problems, if they are allowed to emerge, will take place in their generation's era. Futurists tend to look at the current trends and project them forward with some adjustments for sustainability. Historians tend to look back at history and revisit it, and often rewrite it from the perception of the times. Because of my involvement in finance I have tried over my lifetime to follow many economists and thinkers because trends generally show opportunities for investment and limitation of risk. I have not found many economists who were right consistently or many prognosticators, particularly pundits forced to make short-term comments on a daily basis. The world is a very complex organism and interrelations cause a great number of changes.

So even moving forward with the directions we presently have, and trying to look back from the historians' view of the future will judge this period of time. We see that America will emerge from the current recession in a new structural environment both because of its past reliance on debt that must now be addressed, and also the questionable sustainability of its social programs, the necessary reviving of productivity in competitiveness internationally, and most important, the determination of the organizing principle under which this will be done. It is not possible to predict the future with so many uncertainties determined by the level of will to accept sacrifice and the circumstances of fortune in a world that is far less insular for America and much more international.

The best advice that can be given to the coming generation is to understand some of the most key principles of how societies restructure themselves so their generation will appreciate the positive changes that our generation and their parents make. Or, if we make the wrong choices, they will have an ability to affect their future by understanding the fundamental truths of how economics, politics, and culture interplay. Leadership is one of the most desired commodities in the present world, and it requires you to coordinate people working together toward a common goal. True leadership is not just getting what you can personally out of your job or effort, but what you are able to do to bring about a more transformational concept. That does not happen with one man although it is often necessary to have one symbolizing the movement through his articulation of the ideas and confidence within him. The movement is a far broader group of people that are the uncommon men that I refer to in *The Language of Conscience Evolution*—the 5% to 10% of the people that become educated on issues and take an active role to have an impact on the marketplace of ideas, even if their ideas are inconsistent with others.

Again, what is necessary for their generation, and for ours, in anticipating this situation is an organizing principle of conscience over convenience putting moral hazard into public policy and moving it toward the common good. But it also needs to be a continuing effort for efficiency in governmental policy and a vision that has the most impact. The rights of all people as individuals should be equal as should their sense of obligation. There is no equality of ideas, some are far more important in the ultimate outcome than others. We have talked of strategic ideas, operational ideas, tactical ideas, and ideas for techniques. We must teach our grandchildren's generation to concentrate on strategic ideas that set the ultimate goal. Changes will not be made quickly, but they must move in a positive direction that can then be capitalized into a net present value easing the burdens on current and future generations by making them more acceptable over longer periods of time.

If people see money is not wasted and that there is fairness in the distribution of funds and not a "free rider" concept of redistribution, compromise can be more easily found since it is for the good of all. But these changes require an understanding through our children's education and a fundamental commitment to policies of integrity and growth. They also have to become the ideologies of politics more than redistribution or the hoarding of capital by a few. There is a great difference between investors and producers and those who operate out of convenience and greed. If they are thrown together and the producers and investors are injured or taken from the equation by even well-intentioned efforts to stop greed and convenience, the system is negatively affected. The simple issue that each of us in our own mind has to begin to clarify is which efforts are ones that make money for society by helping produce for all and which simply make money off of society with benefit to a very few. There is not that difficult a dividing line to assess as long as you do it in a thoughtful manner with integrity to a judgment rather than a rationalization. We seek the balance of the previously discussed economic justice.

Simply put, unless we teach our children the critical issues that most directly change their environment and unless we educate them in the ability to recognize the choices that they make rather than simply be led by the divisions of politics, there will be little common ground for sacrifice. The question that must be asked of our educational systems is not just what they teach but how they teach students to think about it. Whose values may be a legitimate question. But which values ultimately result in the greatest benefit to society as a whole are much clearer when people are given broad exposure to them and consider them from their own natural experience.

The grandchildren's generation will span fifty years of impact. How we prepare them now, teaching them to think will prepare or fail them in adapting and accepting policies at the most critical times. We must teach them the difference between conscience and convenience, but we must also teach them that conscience has two very important parts. The first is recognition of obligation, and the second is recognition of the acceptance of compassion. If we are of conscience, we must care about the future, and we must aggressively use the social institutions such as nonprofits, charities, and support groups that use not only our money but also our talents to help those in need. And we also must recognize that the obligations of conscience require sustainability and the necessities of the policies by which we enact redistribution or governmental compassion will have tremendous impact on the overall productivity and society's standard of living levels. In attempting to equalize society, we deprive our children of opportunity. If they are to give up their economic liberty, imposing debt and government upon them should be their decision not ours.

The next fifty years will shape their destiny in how early they learn and support what is truly in their best interest and the best interest of their children. These are the issues that we will be discussing in our generation during the next ten years, and they must have a thoughtful and careful knowledge of them. America has a margin that many other countries do not have, but we are wasting it quickly. We must find ways to come together and define what we consider to be convenience and remove it from our policies. But we will also have to outline carefully how we define charity and obligation.

Although there are many problems to be faced by the world's current generations, America still has very substantial resources and abilities that will help cushion its most serious problems for a decade or more. Too often the negativism of the needs do not appreciate the depths of our strengths. Our trends are significantly challenging and the question of immediate concern is what action is needed in this coming decade to adjust them. The timing of our most serious problems may well depend on the confidence in our government debt and our dollar. So our politicians will determine the policies and perception that may create reality. This perception will in large part be on the sustainability of programs and level of sacrifice over the longer term. Europe's problems fiscally with the effects on the Euro are an example.

The great questions are not just the challenges faced by the generation in its thirties and forties, but perhaps even more important their children and their children's children. Those legacies are in significant question. What is important today is to realize the impact our actions will have longer term. Smaller changes now, using the thought of chaos theory where small changes have tremendous impact over long periods of time, are very appropriate in our current planning. We have let situations fester so long that now it will require many more major changes. China, for example, is a nation that understands its weaknesses and uses those concerns to focus attention on the necessity for bringing solutions through sacrifice. America may underestimate its strengths but also fail to appropriately appreciate the seriousness of its growing problems. How do we build a set of philosophies that can be transformational? They will not come immediately but will start like an acorn and grow into a tree with refinements brought forth by necessity. Too often people look for the solution in individuals or in political parties, but our problems are ones that are only going to be solved by a very significant change in our way of thinking.

We would be far more successful looking less at personalities and slogans and spending far more time in understanding what has to form the character of any new movement to make that change.

History has moved the nature of our politics into intense partisanship, and to correct the problems we must begin to address that fundamental but absolutely critical issue. Partisanship is not bad if it discusses issues, but at extremes it defeats the purpose by gridlock of action. Change does not occur within politics itself but has to come from the reality of economics and the demands of a civilized culture. The nature of politics is to understand who you are and the role you need to play, whether it is as an individual, a party, or a nation. The great forces of politics are to find what it is that bonds men and women together. From the sense of politics and economics, which is our current organizing principle in America, we automatically divide our population into those receiving benefits and those paying for them under the tax code. Our media focuses on issues of "giving equity to those in need from those who have benefited" or "taking from those who earn and take responsibility to give to others." We tend to muddle along by moving back and forth like the man in the shower who keeps adjusting the water. The problem with that principle for the future is that we will move more to cutting benefits and also taxing more out of necessity. This will make both sides mad, and how we cut or tax will have a great impact on our growth and our competitiveness. America has to reengineer more than cut or tax. We are back to the contextual thinking of the sports car, bus, and three options. We have to think out of the box to minimize pain.

What reengineering means is the necessity of a new vision on how the economy moves forward from where it now stands. This is critical to the maintenance of a middle class through the creation of jobs. The past is gone. America lost many jobs to international competition, technology, and "business burdens." While some jobs can be brought back from abroad, that is limited if we want to keep our higher middle class standard of living. Americans do not wish to work for what some other nation's citizens will. The reality of international competition will not allow us to become protectionist and insular without great long-term cost to the nation and our children. However, technology investment in the U.S. can help create higher paying jobs and make up for low wage differences.

So the question is why does the investment go abroad? The answer is because of the business burdens from taxes, regulation, and business climate (the attitude of business is considered the problem not the solution). We have an economic policy driven by political alliances and by national goals. Environmental policy, energy policy, and health policy are a comparison of extremes with little discussion of ultimate reliability or reality. Business bears part of the blame since it had often failed in corporate responsibility. Government has failed to use the common good as an operating principle as it has become more partisan and has ignored moral hazard. And we as Americans have moved far more to materialism and self-interest, which has allowed our cultural change and a unique historic system of wealth creation and dignity to weaken.

We cannot bring back the past economic reality because we lost freedom in debt and equalizing international competition. But we can restore our competitive strength by reclaiming the values that made us exceptional and by strategically planning policy. The future will have its need for military power for protection, but the great battles will be for economic resources. And the battle for minds will be within cultures that will greatly affect what they export in ideas, and also affect whether they work jointly or competitively on economic issues.

For too long the elite did not understand the power of culture. They now realize that they have overestimated the differences between cultures and not the more universal desire for individual dignity, which is beyond just freedom and includes opportunity and respect.

Culture does not change easily or quickly; it takes time and a dedication that recognizes both that change is necessary and a belief in the future model. Politics and economics can change rapidly because they usually are a loss of confidence or change of interest, but culture is built from positive experiences in its strongest cases. It involves a way of thinking about issues, the ultimate contextual thinking of what is important. The Middle East will be an interesting example where the Arab Spring seems powerful, because of technology, to bring democracy. But the necessity for a change in cultural thinking will challenge it. China will be another example where the power of cultural change is better understood and appreciated. It will face similar challenges, but the framework for change exists and its benefits appreciated. Cultural change is not of the action of the movement but is a movement that requires thought as well as emotion.

To reengineer we need to start with a common understanding of the world that we will need to support as an organizing concept. That has to include trade and cooperative efforts or the world suffers. However, fairness of the Golden Rule needs to be a core of that philosophy. American business, indeed all business, needs to realize if they want a reduction in business burdens, they have to show responsibility and self-governance. Strong harsh penalties for truly serious violations are often far more effective than broad rules for social policy that can be lobbied to reduce penalty.

As government is forced to reduce the safety net, it must counter by giving opportunity. Policy changes will argue about the damage to the economy in the short term versus the necessity for long-term fiscal responsibility. These become false arguments when the real issue is the judgment of will not just of the government. But the society that elects it long term has to be serious about its future. Politicians arguing are far less important than the dedication of the people to be willing to sacrifice for their future and their children. How to reengineer is much simpler once politics do not distort it. The reengineering starts with America reclaiming the values that made it exceptional, competitive, and unified.

America is a centralist country overall, probably a little to the right. But our perceptions of issues are all different because we get more extreme emotional information. So we have to define where we want the country to go as we begin to engineer. We are never going to be a Harmonious Society, because unlike China we are a nation of many cultures. What we do have in common, in large part, is a cultural vision of a better life, particularly for our children. People came to America and remain here because of that.

If that is the case, it becomes clearer that we need to make our culture the blending point both on dignity and responsibility as learning how to reengineer it into new forms, rather than cutting alone. The taxpayers are not against giving more to worthy investments. But they do not wish to give funds to bureaucrats who say they know better how to spend their money or to people who could be responsible but desire not to be. Compassion is a necessity in any society, but it should come in part from a desire to be a good person and define yourself by what you do without having to do it. There is a fullness of life that comes from doing things for others for the right reasons. Government policies are often phrased in this good intent— the subprime crisis and the government push through legislation and Fannie Mae and Freddie Mac funding to increase minority ownership are a prime example. Even though well intentioned, the result was quite different. Many believe there is less home ownership now after all the foreclosures than at the inception of the program and much of the burden of the fall was to the minorities they were partially designed to help.

The welfare programs and incentives of the late '80s and '90s had some of the same results. Whether America can get the various groups that are now organized on a political/economic axis to reorganize on a cultural axis is the great question. It may be more likely than not. People characterize the Tea Party as just being against taxes, yet I see it being more for individual dignity and responsibility. Where will the leaders take it? On the left there are many minority groups that focus on conscience and have a lot in common with those wanting dignity. We in America will never all agree, but if we can agree on how to value what we want for the future and incentivize the responsibility to get there, compromise is more likely and probably less painful.

These fundamentals of obligation and compassion are not as far apart in reality as they are in the extreme of politics. And the question has to be how a society finds the right ways to reinvent and to refresh itself taking advantage of the strength of its unique position rather than squandering its seed corn. This is much easier to say than to do because the realities of politics, particularly in the modern world, are far more intense. However, society reaches certain points where the people determine their own future by how well they recognize their problems early and make the appropriate changes. There is a power of ideas if understood within society to transform. It is intensified when people realize what they have to lose if solutions are not found. It is the cultural power of adaptability. "The Language of Conscience" is simply a term that reflects the combination of characteristics that are usually required for any such effort to succeed. *It seeks an equitable balance from the necessary positive forces of obligation and compassion by focusing upon individual responsibility to give sustainability to the most efficient growth ratio for the common good.*

All of you grandchildren are less than ten years old, but your future is going to be determined by what your grandparents, your parents, and you decide to do in the next several years in making hard choices. Whatever choices are made, the intensity of the effects will increasingly be felt in the future as the rules of reality in crisis bite evermore sharply. So it is critical to understand the implications of how some of the largest forces will affect you. Culturally the Internet is going to have the effect that media has had in the past as it spread ideas and thoughts, but the question will be just how accurate and trustworthy the Internet will become. The cultural power of ideas to transform society is particularly powerful. And I think the Internet as well as globalization will contribute to that transformative power. In economics you are going to deal with the issues of deficits, debt, and taxes and the significant impact they have on the stability of the dollar, which will dramatically affect your status of living. Within politics you will have to minimize partisanship or all will be eventually lost because to succeed within the world for your children the political policies will have to be for innovation and growth to create a greater pie for each individual person's slice.

Of significant overall perspective will be the international global competition in a more level world that will affect you in a great variety of ways whether you interact with it or not. The search for a more harmonious and civilized world will occur automatically. It is the nature of life that conditions deteriorate if they are not positively enhanced and built. There must be an effort to work toward building far more harmony and cooperation between nations as the world's resources diminish and the joint effects on all of us are more critical.

China is the significant rising power that is far more important to the United States than is realized because of the economic relationship that has been built, the funding of American debt, and the purchase of Chinese goods. Our future and their future are much more entwined than might be thought. They must develop a domestic market, and we must revitalize our manufacturing. However, that is not a zero-sum game but one that must be developed into a win-win proposition. China and America do not understand each other well. Even though the rest of the world will have a great impact on America's future, we increasingly will need to understand how China thinks because many of the problems they face are similar to the ones we face in America and are often the mirror image of them. Their demographics will place great pressures upon them, just as our health demographics will place burdens upon us. Both America and China will be fighting against time in order for the U.S. to remain wealthy and for China to become wealthy enough to keep their prosperity sustainable.

China is perhaps the most important proxy for an international world, but Europe, Latin America, and the other developing nations are not far behind. We are no longer in an isolated world. Financial regulation is a perfect example. Finance is now international, and bankers can find the least difficult country in which to make their deals. So, whether we like it or not, we will have to build international institutions for stability—health, finance, environmental, and others. Whether these institutions have any influence in dealing with sovereign nations depends on the credibility they hold as opposed to legal powers. Cultural powers of respect will trump unenforceable legal powers for sustainable compromises and usually come from accepted agreements not legal enforcements.

That leaves the question of how the United States and China will see their independent and joint futures. Your generation will be greatly influenced by what their people decide they will be. Both nations are in major transition. Where they ultimately decide to go and how those visions relate to each other will have a major influence on other countries' perspectives and will shape their systems. This will be evolutionary over the next decade and will have a tremendous impact for the future. One key point is the level of equality or disparities in income levels. Will America's middle class re-establish its dominance? Will China build a dominant middle class? These are the ultimate questions that determine concepts of individual responsibility, society's acceptance of risk, level of innovation and growth, and the political and economic environment created.

The first and most important concern is to understand that there are positive things that can be done. To simply complain does very little good for hope is not an appropriate option to strategic thought, and strategic thought requires understanding similar points in history. The only way to know the future is to help create it.

PART TWO

CREATING A MAP
TO NAVIGATE
THE MODERN WORLD

*What knowledge we must have to apply
wisdom and gain vision.*

VII | THE THREE BIG ISSUES OF THE FUTURE IN CONTEXTUAL THOUGHT

Having built a base of how to think about issues, it becomes very important to strategically look at the biggest issues most impacting your future and your children's future from a broader context of the three great powers—economics, politics, and culture. *Those three big issues are not that difficult to determine strategically. In politics, it is a sustainable, fiscally responsible, functioning government. In economics, it is a growth driven market economy, which provides opportunity and incentivizes production over consumption. In culture it is a unified society that requires a strong and growing middle class, which promotes family values of individual responsibility and conscience.*

It is important to note that each of these fits in context with the others. A fiscally responsible government will also have to be one that depends on growth. That is a smaller government that intrudes and costs less and operates efficiently. With the many problems of our current debt, it is increasingly difficult to bring balance even with cutting expenses and raising revenues. The least painful and best solution is significant growth. Debt to GDP is a relative figure. The amount of debt is not as important as the leverage factor of how large a percentage the debt and deficits are of GDP. This is an extremely important concept because growth is one of the few positive solutions to sustainable fiscal responsibility, but the environment for that type of economic growth is particularly affected by the direction of governmental policies and their certainty. The cultural value of individual responsibility, which is symbolic of many of the family values and independent dignity taught in its structure requires a middle class that sets the rules of society rather than a very unequal society of a few rich and many poor. The latter often lacks stability and affects both the governmental structure and the economic system by dominance of a few or a dependence of many when market systems of opportunity are the best methods of wealth creation as opposed to income distribution.

These three issues and their interdependence need to be carefully understood. Conscience is an organizing principle of all three. Conscience would bring about the obligation to recognize moral risk in political policies and to recognize that compassion was granted but only where truly needed and not as a political tool of support. Market systems do not operate without morality that allows competition. So there must be moral regulation of economic activity to allow fairness and prevent fraud, but choosing winners and losers destroys the competition within the system and the major benefits of the market. The cultural benefit of conscience is clear. It is a different environment upon which both government and business occur and normally is based on the Golden Rule and the common good. These are values that society has to have and when they begin to lose them they are replaced by governmental edict and regulation or the legal system that pushes out cultural obligations. This latter issue of culture versus law/regulation is a critical one. It is a point that drives culture and indirectly both politics and economics.

In America this was probably best set in the Constitution by the 10th Amendment. The Tenth Amendment explicitly states the Constitution's principle of federalism by providing that powers not granted to the federal government nor prohibited to the states by the Constitution are reserved, respectively, to the states or the people. What this effectively did is limit government to certain specifics, and the people through their culture of responsibility and civic obligation, created the environment more than the government dictating it. As time progressed with technology and education, there has been the need for government taking on more powers to adjust for the times. However, there is a difference in the government taking on powers beyond those necessary which effectively remove the liberties of the citizens and their choices. The issue moving forward, in its most critical form, will be how Americans, and indeed the people of other countries, look at their relation to government from the sense of their individual dignity.

Budgets are simply the existing contract of the government and the people economically in how money is spent and raised, and politically in how their life is regulated and directed. Personal dignity is the assessment of satisfaction with that exiting system, and whether there is harmony or revolt. If you have dependency you do not have freedom, but if you have freedom you have risk. So the way that personal dignity is interpreted and understood depends a great deal on how educated the population becomes on the relationships between the powers and how significantly it affects them both in the short and longer term. These are history's lessons that are often not being taught and they are the economic lessons that become reality as you reach certain stages in a democracy's existence and crisis points are remembered. What becomes important is shaping these basic concerns in your mind and understanding them individually as well as understanding the nature of how culture, government, and the economy all interact. Consequences of actions in one area often have unintended consequences in the others.

Simply, the great issues will be whether America can find a fiscally sustainable government and an innovation driven resurgence in its economy, creating jobs and redeveloping a middle class. But most of all it will depend on whether or not a unity can be found in people with a common culture and vision for themselves and the future of their children. There are issues that you need to learn to recognize to fully develop the concepts of how these great themes fit together. The great Chinese philosopher, Mencius, who developed the thoughts of Confucius, pointed out that the most important issue in strategy was often not geography or timing but human unity. He was correct several thousand years ago and the accuracy of his observation will become increasingly important in the current world. We must recognize the lessons of the French Revolution that there is individualism and there is the fraternity of society. And true liberty or personal dignity only occurs when there is balance.

You need to start with what cultural values your families shaped to set the thought process on what your vision of satisfaction in life should be. Then you can learn the factors affecting a functioning government and an innovative growth economy. But these thoughts need to be put into the additional context of a changing demographic in America—particularly the impact of Hispanics and to a lesser degree Asians, and the dramatic impact China, as a proxy for a multicultural world, will have on the future. The past is no longer a prologue.

THE FIRST BIG ISSUE: A FUNCTIONING
SUSTAINABLE POLITICAL SYSTEM

Of the three great issues facing your generation, the greatest political challenge is going to be a functioning sustainable political system. Partisanship has made it increasingly difficult to govern because of the gridlock of more extreme positions on both sides as groups position for an election. Media and the Internet have democratized the public far more than in the past and consensus is far more difficult to gain.

Since governing is in effect the concept of making decisions, often by thoughtful and intelligent compromise, great thought is going to have to be given to how many of the original concepts of the Constitution can be regained. The problem with the partisan system is that it has become a war for power rather than a vehicle for collectively finding solutions. If discussion on the serious points of issues is never reached because of the preliminary positions, no effective decision occurs. Since primaries allow party activists to control the nomination process the prioritization of issues becomes very distorted from what was originally intended. Jefferson and many others wanted to avoid the arrogance of power by appreciating the motivations of serving and saw the benefits of term limits. Even with some of the problems of term limits, simply attacking incumbency where people have to lay out at least one election, serves to make the mindset of those in power less focused on personal careers.

Most legislators start with noble interests, but the system gradually shapes and warps them. We have to change the system. The system will inevitably have to address changes in how Congressional districts are gerrymandered by removing a portion of the power from state legislatures to go to more independent bodies that are selected without partisanship. They can base decisions on thoughtful criteria that give appropriate local character to districts beyond candidate selection and term length issues. Congress will have to address its committee structures, which have become large and unwieldy and allow far more politics and special interests determinations than in the old days. Now the subcommittees of subcommittees give a few people great power over certain sections of the industry. And this power is not lost on the independent lobbyists and special interest sectors that wish to control it.

Many of the problems with our economic system have been caused by the corruption of our decision making process through special interest legislation. We have not the normal free enterprise, but corporatism that gives a great many benefits through legislation. It is inappropriate to look at this just as benefiting large corporations for the corporations often end up lobbying against each other. It is instead corporatism that involves the interests of labor unions, public interest groups of every nature, as well as broad ranges of economic interests. They have found that because of the way Congress has evolved, they are almost required to be within the process. That logic, in large part because of the committee structures and how they are selected from chairmanships to committee memberships to the selection of staff to guide the committees—all fit within a system that operates to gain and maintain power. The structure is neither democracy as envisioned in the words of de Tocqueville or economics as envisioned by Adam Smith author of *The Wealth of Nations.* It is a system that has become its own master over a longer period of time without the full appreciation of the changes being realized by the American people. It has its own language that is changed to circumstances and short-term focus automatically creating moral hazard.

What both parties have in common is not only the desire for power, but in many ways the growth of government because the more government grows the more power those in office actually have. While recent movements have begun to show populous concern in many of these areas, true change within the system is not just in the political arena.

The ultimate question is government size and responsibility. Government has a purpose, but it is a more limited one to those areas that the private sector cannot accomplish and makes certain that the private sector abides by rules of fairness and integrity. As we will see in the sections on culture, the role of government (politics) and the role of the private sector (economics) are much like a seesaw. If one becomes extremely heavy then it becomes dominant. If you want a true democracy then the power of peer pressure and culture needs to settle the majority of decisions of the society as opposed to the government forcing such decisions through regulation and law.

As we previously discussed, it is important to understand that the rule of law includes its enforcement and has to include the broad regulatory power of government, which can overshadow the individual and the private sector within society. So when we discuss a functioning political system, if government is not going to be the dominant force, then what values, systems, and institutions will fill the vacuum where government does not? If legislation weakens the private sector and the individual, then government automatically grows.

Our present system is for the first time in many years being analyzed in this way. It has to be looked upon in depth not just as the three branches of government of the Constitution, but instead the more important analysis of discipline within society that looks at how that system implements law and what driving forces are behind it. The current budgetary and committee structures and partisan framework are very different from the past and are one reason that spending and budgets have gone far beyond past levels. The issue is not just in spending or revenues, but it is the nature of the evolution of the system that makes the decisions and how governing has evolved. This affects the efficiency of the budget if systems are not zero-based, but base line increase driven programs are not evaluated as to budget or value and remain forever.

It does not allow the collective decision-making on the basis of what is best for society if it is effectively a war for power. The rethinking of the process is particularly important and has to be blended with similar thoughts on our economic system and our cultural unity. Perhaps the most significant issue of the way government functions is the sustainability of its contract with the people. This is the budget that provides for spending on what choices are made by government. For money to be spent, it has to be taken from someone and thus deprives an alternative use that may have benefit as well. It leads to three significant issues: 1) The concept of deficits where a government does not balance its revenues and expenses, 2) the concept of debt, which is in effect a passing of the obligation onto another generation and has limits in its own right both as to size and significant impact on the economy when it reaches certain levels, and 3) the concept of taxes and spending. The possible monetization or money creation through fiat currency is simply taking it another way.

Each of these is interrelated and has very specific impact on the functioning of the economic system and the culture of individual dignity that has existed in America. Just like the appearance of government, the reality of the functioning of government may be different from the appearance. The impacts of these changes within government are felt in the other two great powers dramatically.

Recently, the big issue has been whether to increase the debt limit or "default." This was a superficial issue because the limit was not the principle at stake as much as it was the rapid increase in debt. It only started an inevitable conversation on sustainability. The national debt itself is the wrong issue at $14.5 trillion; it only represents the true fiscal dollars owed to creditors. The big issue is the fiscal gap that represents government's commitments for future revenue and spending. These are the true obligations and people are depending upon them. They are more solvable than people think if early solutions are found, but they are holes that are still digging and disguised by cloudy accounting, variable definitions, and time period qualifications. Changing the accuracy and integrity of the budgeting system requires a change in the will of the people to add or force character to Congress. We demand all of these things, and we must understand our choices more clearly.

Perhaps the best place to start to understand these relationships is in the form of the theories of economics being relied upon as the basis for economic policy. One of the best summaries I have seen as well as a well considered observation of how debt affects them is the work of Van Hoisington and Lacy Hunt (www.Hoisington.com). With their permission, I have excerpted and condensed part of their Second Quarter, 2011 Newsletter. This recession is different and the competitive world is changing. In the charts, note that private debt and federal debt are treated separately.

Three Competing Theories

The three competing theories for economic contractions are: 1) the Keynesian, 2) the Friedman, and 3) the Fisherian. The Keynesian view is that normal economic contractions are caused by an insufficiency of aggregate demand (or total spending). This problem is to be solved by deficit spending. The Friedman view, one shared by our current Federal Reserve Chairman, is that protracted economic slumps are also caused by an insufficiency of aggregate demand, but are preventable or ameliorated by increasing the money stock. Both economic theories are consistent with the widely-held view that the economy experiences three to seven years of growth, followed by one to two years of decline. The slumps are worrisome, but not too daunting since two years lapse fairly quickly and then the economy is off to the races again. This normal business cycle framework has been the standard since World War II until now.

The Fisherian theory is that an excessive buildup of debt relative to GDP is the key factor in causing major contractions, as opposed to the typical business cycle slumps (Chart 1). Only a time consuming and difficult process of deleveraging corrects this economic circumstance. Symptoms of the excessive indebtedness are: weakness in aggregate demand; slow money growth; falling velocity; sustained underperformance of the labor markets; low levels of confidence; and possibly even a decline in the birth rate and household formation. In other words, the normal business cycle models of the Keynesian and Friedmanite theories are overwhelmed in such extreme, over indebted situations. . .

In 1933, Fisher held out some hope that fiscal policy might be helpful in dealing with excessive debt, but within several years he had completely rejected the Keynesian view. By 1940, Fisher had firmly stated to FDR in several letters that government spending of borrowed funds was counter-productive to stimulating economic growth. Significantly, by 2011, Fisher's seven decade-old ideas have been supported by thorough, comprehensive, and robust econometric and empirical analysis. It is now evident that the actions of monetary and fiscal authorities since 2008 have made economic conditions worse, just as Fisher suggested. In other words, we are painfully re-learning a lesson that a truly great economist gave us a road map to avoid.

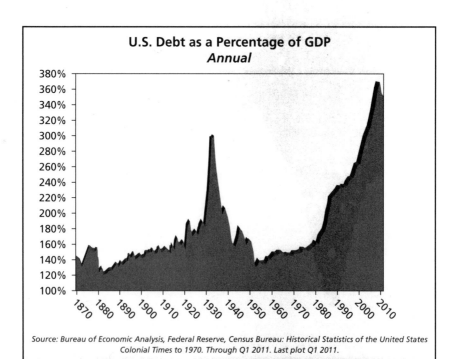

U.S. Debt as a Percentage of GDP
Annual

Source: Bureau of Economic Analysis, Federal Reserve, Census Bureau: Historical Statistics of the United States Colonial Times to 1970. Through Q1 2011. Last plot Q1 2011.

High Dollar Policy Failures

If governmental financial transactions, advocated by following Keynesian and Friedmanite policies, were the keys to prosperity, the U.S. should be in an unparalleled boom. For instance, on the monetary side, since 2007 excess reserves of depository institutions have increased from $1.8 billion to more than $1.5 trillion, an amazing gain of more than 83,000%. The fiscal response is equally unparalleled. Combining 2009, 2010, and 2011 the U.S. budget deficit will total 28.3% of GDP, the highest three year total since World War II, and up from 6.3% of GDP in the three years ending 2008 (Chart 2). Importantly, the massive advance in the deficit was primarily due to a surge in outlays that was more than double the fall in revenues. In the current three years, spending was an astounding $2.2 trillion more than in the three years ending 2008. The fiscal and monetary actions combined have had no meaningful impact on improving the standard of living of the average American family (Chart 3).

Why Has Fiscal Policy Failed?

First, the government expenditure multiplier is zero, and quite possibly slightly negative. Depending on the initial conditions, deficit spending can

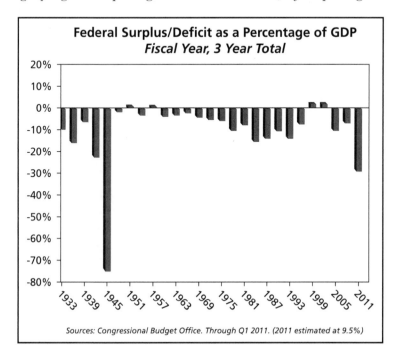

increase economic activity, but only for a mere three to five quarters. Within twelve quarters these early gains are fully reversed. . . .

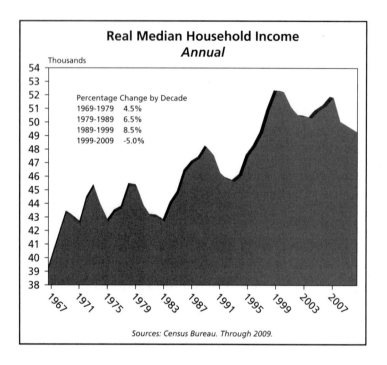

Real Median Household Income
Annual

Thousands

Percentage Change by Decade
1969-1979   4.5%
1979-1989   6.5%
1989-1999   8.5%
1999-2009   -5.0%

Sources: Census Bureau. Through 2009.

The problem is not the size or the timing of the actions, but the inherent flaws in the approach. . .

Second, temporary tax cuts enlarge budget deficits but they do not change behavior, providing no meaningful boost to economic activity. . . .

Third, when private sector tax rates are changed permanently behavior is altered, and, according to the best evidence available, the response of the private sector is quite large. For permanent tax changes, the tax multiplier is between minus 2 and minus 3. If higher taxes are used to redress the deficit because the seemingly rational need to have "shared sacrifice," growth will be impaired even further. . . .

Fourth, existing programs suggest that more of the federal budget will go for basic income maintenance and interest expense; therefore the government expenditure multiplier may become more negative. Positive multiplier expenditures such as military hardware, space exploration and infrastructure programs will all become a smaller part of future budgets. . . .

THE DEBT BOMB

The two major U.S. government debts to GDP statistics commonly referred to in budget discussions are shown in Chart 4. The first is the ratio of U.S. debt held by the public to GDP, which excludes federal debt held in various government entities such as Social Security and the Federal Reserve banks. The second is the ratio of gross U.S. debt to GDP. Historically, the debt held by the public ratio was the more useful, but now the gross debt ratio is more relevant. By 2015, according to the CBO, debt held by the public will jump to more than 75% of GDP, while gross debt will exceed 104% of GDP. The CBO figures may be too optimistic. The IMF estimates that gross debt will amount to 110% of GDP by 2015, and others have even higher numbers. The gross debt ratio, however, does not capture the magnitude of the approaching problem . . .

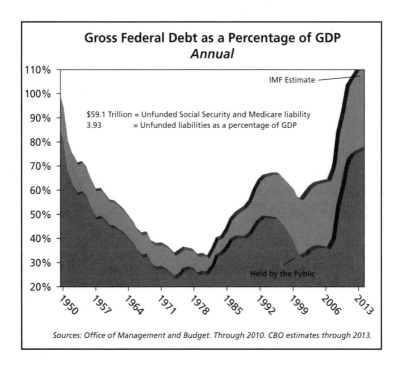

Gross Federal Debt as a Percentage of GDP
Annual

$59.1 Trillion = Unfunded Social Security and Medicare liability
3.93   = Unfunded liabilities as a percentage of GDP

IMF Estimate

Held by the Public

Sources: Office of Management and Budget. Through 2010. CBO estimates through 2013.

Finding the Tipping Point of Debt

To me, the Hoisington/Hunt analysis gives a clear picture that we are in an unusual situation and tipping points become critical. To understand the issue more clearly each part of the equation needs to be understood in more simple terms.

The critical point to understand is the deleveraging process. It is beginning in the private sector. Companies have been addressing this, now it is the household sector. Between 2008 and mid 2011, household debt of mortgages and consumer debt fell 4%, but 3% of that was from defaults. Government will have to begin its deleveraging shortly as is seen. The great concern is not just the size of debts. Whether or not time allows reductions depends on interest rates because while the ratio of debt to income may look bad, the servicing costs look more manageable because interest rates are low. If confidence is lost where rates rise without an increasing economic benefit, it is much more dangerous. This decreased servicing cost of low rates increases risk as they rise. The same is true of the government. The government has, surprisingly, borrowed longer at higher prices and to keep cost down borrowed shorter when recent rates are low. This decreased servicing costs but increases risk. It is critical to separate the issues of levels of debt and servicing costs of debt because the former is more of a solvency issue, the second can become a liquidity issue and strike much more quickly if rates change. Human nature requires us to learn these experiences in cycles.

Deficits, Debt, and Taxes

Having discussed much of the world's movement to debt and high leverage in the last decade, we must address what will be one of the current challenges that will have the greatest effect on the next two generations, both our children and our grandchildren. Some of the worst effects are a few years out but quantitatively certain unless growth and policies change. The policy question is whether we slow the car down gradually or crash at full speed.

Many things will affect your future but one of the simplest ways to identify them is what happens to your purchasing power. Debt and deficits can cause inflation or deflation. You also have the decline of the dollar. A basket of groceries my go up 5% with inflation from a variety of causes, but the dollar may have gone down 5% as well on an international purchasing equivalent as it weakened. Inflation and dollar devaluation are related, but have other causes as well. This could double the impact if the goods were imported. The point is that the changes are complex and often hard to calculate but need to be understood to truly address problems.

The obvious direct costs or taxes get the emotional political response, so hidden ones are used. An example is rising retirement ages or means testing for benefits, one is a 100% tax on the years not paid and the other is just a partial tax. The younger generation must learn to think in equivalents in its analysis if they are to use policies for growth and fairness. Means testing is perceived to just affect the rich but often it affects those that have sacrificed and saved over long periods such as families that have prepared for children's education and retirement. If the "means tested" came from the sacrifice of personal responsibility it is not just "taxing the rich."

Defining Ultimate Problems and Possible Solutions

The problems we face today cannot be solved quickly. The solvency of government on a sustainable basis with the issues of our current deficit, our unsustainable spending patterns, and limited resources and archaic tax code, constitutes our basic problems. But how those issues are considered impact and are impacted by our politics and culture. These problems were a very long time in developing, and they will take a very long time to solve. The first and most important requirement is to understand the nature of the problems and to be consistent with the policies that must have solutions. If intelligent men were to design an appropriate program with the best of theories, they would come up with a very different set of philosophies and goals than what presently will have to be done simply because of the very different situation in which America, and much of the Western world, finds itself.

The current fiscal crises of Iceland, Greece, Ireland, and the contagion that occurs are simply symptoms and early warnings of what happens when you reach the final extents of leverage and restructuring economies becomes imperative. Nations are in very different positions, but the trend is what becomes most important. People look at the immediate, but what guides judgment are the longer-term expectations of actions brought forward with a net present value calculation. And often this net present value is highly conservative since it values the final years very little in current discount terms and costs may be escalating greatly in the last years.

There are many different ways to look at the current situation in America. We talked previously about the significant rise in debt both privately and in government. Some countries in the world had their governments take on debt, which results in more of a credit crisis for the sovereign. In other cases where private companies took on debt, a currency crisis in many ways works into the same set of issues. Reality affects both the private sector and government. The value of the dollar, greatly affecting the American standard of living, will eventually be one of the most critical issues. As a reserve currency, it is operated quite differently from most other currencies and has often been a place of safety in the past.

The Federal Reserve has been charged a dual mandate of price stability and full employment. In political terms Congress looks at that as maintaining the dollar and promoting economic growth. Those two goals are now becoming difficult to reconcile. Many of the recent actions of the Federal Reserve were driven by its necessity to address immediate issues, but will place significant burdens on their ability to affect outcomes. Now, with their greatly enhanced balance sheet, they are almost entering a new business model for the institution. There is finally recognition after sixty years of increasing leverage that significant changes must be made. America compromises on its wants where both sides get something they desire, but they have failed to address compromise on needs, which involve both sides sacrificing something. That takes a different style of leadership and a different perspective from the citizen. We have to educate to higher levels civil responsibility.

Government Problems Work Down to Become Personal Problems

One of the concerns of shrinking the deficit will be the lack of support to the states for portions of their budgets and eventually, in some states, the state support of cities. In recent times of revenue sharing and stimulus, many local budgets are sustained by state or federal largesse. The Federal Government has to get serious about its funds, and it is highly likely that Dad's old axiom "people seldom care about you but about themselves" comes into play. They will reduce support down the line. The rest of the world has shown a willingness to buy Treasury Bills, so for a period it can sustain itself. But states will increasingly see weaknesses from funding social programs and limited revenue increases. They, and particularly some of the cities within certain states, will have a harder time standing on their own.

This is where the "Greece" awareness will begin to be felt in the United States. Reliance on debt has been on all levels of government, particularly with pensions and health care, and the smaller the entity, if it has not been prudent, will have more difficulty. Cutting the deficit will in many ways be more personal than many suspect as the services they are expecting may be curtailed.

Many today talk of cuts but avoid the biggest social programs because of the certain political cost. But if you do not seriously address them at the start, you have to concentrate on discretionary spending primarily, and the impact would be massive on both some wasteful programs and also on many specialized ones that fill key voids. The entire system does not need to just be cut but reengineered to a more efficient concept.

To bring about that realization, we must recognize the necessity of major change. Mathematical necessities for funding will ultimately drive actions rather than the usual battle of special interests. This is becoming the lesson of Greece and Europe as nations try to regain solvency, but the personal impact is great. Austerity is not only painful but impacts growth. Flexibility in the economy has to be restored for growth and that has personal costs or change overwhelms the economic status quo. The question is how to put restraints and process in the system to bring effective and fair choices to the forefront in the place of symbolism.

Addressing the Problem of Austerity and Sacrifice

The ultimate approach to a solution for the debt is not to phrase the question as just cutting spending or taxing the rich. These are solutions suggested without fully looking at the problem. They involve positioning on interests, which brings gridlock when we must have change because our direction is toward crisis while time is no longer on our side. The deciding principle needs to look to what level of support government should give based upon who really needs it so the sustainability of payments can reach those truly in need.

The rich do not want more taxes, but the biggest objection is the waste. You should not penalize the achievers to redistribute to others that are not in need. Similarly those with compassion need to oppose those without true need getting benefits because they must protect sustainability for those that do need it. There can be no "free riders." Spending can be sustained short term by pulling resources that are investment and growth related, which hurt long-term sustainability. In this global environment nations must become competitive for everyone's sake and that is not just taxes and spending, but reduction of regulation and creation of opportunity so the economy can innovate and respond.

While many in academia and pundits would find fault, the best way to explain our choices would be the story of a farmer. After World War II he cleared fertile land, irrigated it, used the best practices with fertilizer and rotation, used the best seed and equipment, and worked very hard. He had great crops and with profits built houses and infrastructure. All this was from the profits he made. Since he was doing well, he started using the water for swimming pools and fishing lakes, he bought cars rather than new equipment, he traveled and used profits for personal enjoyment.

As he got less profits due to competition, he spent less on good seeds, did little repair, less fertilizer. Now debts are due, crops are much less productive, and debt is a great burden. He has a cash flow problem, so does he use less fertilizer, cheaper seed, etc.? Or does he realize that his business model was and is a good one that he had to sacrifice, and go back to it. It makes sustainability more easily understood.

On all our political solutions, Dad used the old country approach to describe options as eagles, which soar into the difficult wind, turkeys that are relatively stupid in actions, and vultures that live off the distress of others. Today we have a lot of turkeys and vultures, but few eagles. We need to bring in more inspirational eagles and that comes from looking at ultimate motivations.

The Evolution of the American Budget Problems

The last several years, we have added trillions in debt, a huge percentage of our existing debt. Most of the cost drivers are in the social net that will eventually falter. They were designed generations in the past with good intent, but never anticipating demographic, cultural, and economic factors that now exist. Similarly our revenue system in the form of a bloated, special interest-driven tax code that had as much to do with social policy as revenue generation is equally in need of reform. The question is our level of will as a people. That depends both on education on the issue so its discussion will be enlightened and not emotional and if we can agree on an organizing principle or vision of our ultimate goal. This has to include fairness of sacrifice, a better world for our children, and the most efficient system possible that recognizes the power of incentives, growth, and opportunity and how they are linked.

Reengineering politics will take efforts to make the common good the organizing principle rather than political gerrymandering for preservation of control so that critical issues are discussed with logical rather than extreme solutions. *This will also ultimately bring about the understanding that the real issue is not best described as big or small government but efficient and strategic government.*

How America solves its fiscal crisis will satisfy no one if it is a balanced compromise. While smaller government gives more opportunity through the private sector, our past has saddled us with legacy programs and debt that have to be addressed. This was a key point in the first of the Language of Conscience books, *The New Legacy,* written twenty-five years ago. What has to be the only acceptable course is to reform the system and the spending and taxes that compose it on a concept of efficiency and competitive strategy so the burdens will be moderated and growth enhanced.

The youth of today will demand equity in any generational compromise as they learn from reality. We can wait a few years with token discretionary cuts, but eventually American debt will be additionally downgraded, foreign confidence will falter, and substitutes for the dollar will attempt to grow. *The delicate issue is not just a financial problem that is becoming a political problem. It is at inception, and in reality, a cultural problem of the acceptance of responsibility.*

We are a spendthrift family, which just discovered the bad side of debt, and the ultimate question is how we address it. The obligations of needs are conflicting with the compassion of wants, and the level of our character with the vision of our leadership will define our family destiny. How we think about the problem, hopefully for the common good and not just minor parts will have a huge impact. Unity is the strength that gets far more accomplished for all.

In addition, the moral hazard considerations of cultural responsibility have been minimized in our current solutions. Those responsible for many of the problems in the financial arena remain in effect, if all the CEOs and government leaders are still there with new compliance restrictions but little cultural change. In the political arena there have been some changes in people but little in the dysfunctional method of government. Transformational change needs reengineering under new ideas that must have cultural will, sacrifice, and support.

History shows these cycles, which are reviewed in the other books of the evolution, and the question is always whether society has deteriorated beyond redemption when crisis brings realization. We have to minimize the class economics argument of rich versus poor, and the political arguments of right (small government) versus left (large government) to reorienting all of us primarily by the conscience versus convenience of culture. It completely reshuffles current thought. Politics must push government to efficiency and strategic decisions for growth in an innovative economic system. Economic justice can be balanced more by private forces than government mandate. The ability to fail brings moral hazard, which is a sobering factor.

Enlightened conservatism is nothing more than a concept to define an approach to the definition of that process when crisis puts various ideas for change in competition by necessity.

To understand the situation in a simplified form, it is probably worthwhile to look at government as we would a company or an individual. That has never been a truly accurate analysis because the government's purposes are different from those of an individual. In difficult times it is usually counter-cyclical and has the necessity of stimulating at a time when revenues may be down. So, on a short-term basis, this is often not the most effective approach. But for a longer term it is essential since you need to understand the trends and the factors that affect these directions if you spend in times of need, you need to save with Rainy Day funds in prosperity.

For a comparison, the income statement equivalent would be the budget and the deficit problem, which is often best judged by a relationship of revenues and outlays as a percentage of the GDP. Rather than pure numbers, government must operate in relative calculations.

We talked about the importance of significant growth because growth, if higher than the increase in expenditures, eventually solves or mitigates the problem. You may not have to solve the problem immediately because it may be far too drastic, but you have to have the trends and directions moving properly. Government complicates this by operating on base lines that estimate needed spending. So often "cuts" are not in level of outlays but theoretical money not spent. This can become a game that hides reality. Families often use rationalization in the same way.

In the Language of Conscience Triangles, we talk about analytics, measurement and prioritization, and trends. It is extremely essential to find the right answers through this trend analysis, particularly because of the effect of demographics and other issues. But public policy requires conscience versus convenience distinctions to get people to focus less on immediate gratification through materialism and more on longer-term stability, solvency, and a legacy for their children.

Perhaps the easiest way to look at a political system is to recognize that there are two competing theories—one is that the government tends to be the most appropriate solution and the second is that the private sector is the most effective solution. These two sectors are competitive and intermixed. They are not separate entities since each affects the other. If one believes the solution is government-based then often the tax power of the government is used to acquire revenues from the private sector progressively from the wealthier members by efforts such as increasing tax rates or reducing deductions such as charitable deductions.

But a policy that sustains the governmental sector's concept of being the major solution by weakening the private sector charity changes balance and necessitates more government. Many current economists look to government spending as having a "0" ultimate multiplier. It may help in stimulus for the first three years, but there is no added benefit over the longer term. This concept will be the key issue of focus when the crisis requires efficiency. That policy sustains the governmental sector's concept of being the major solution by weakening the private sector because private sector charity is what is necessary to impact many of the problems of society that the market system does not address.

The draining of investment funds as opposed to consumption funds from society impacts the reinvestment in technology. Technology and change by new investment is absolutely essential. The jobs to be created for the future are not the same assembly line jobs of the past, but have to be new information center jobs for the future. These types of issues bring up the critical question of whether the government sector's approach can invest as effectively as the private sector in spotting the right places for investment and bringing in efficiency driven by competition.

Significant government programs do reduce risk for the individual, but often at a cost usually at a lesser rate of return on investment. Significant government programs do reduce risk for the individual, but often at a cost. Perhaps the return on the money of a government program might be 1% although guaranteed, compared to a 3% or 4% for a private sector investment of the same funds if it was retained within society. This may not seem significant or is often unappreciated generally, but it makes a very significant impact in longer-term competitiveness—where the United States now finds itself compared to other nations in the world. Europe has followed the governmental approach as an ever-growing sector and because of the continuing involvement in the economies has impacted them very significantly. The search for security can over the longer term cannibalize the real strength that gives ultimate security to a society.

Similarly, government involvement in the private sector such as the Fannie Mae and Freddie Mac dominance that occurred in residential home lending and the Community Reinvestment Act Regulations that effectively redirected credit can greatly distort the private market with limited recognition. While the subprime crisis was a significant part of the overleveraging of the economy, the low interest rates now required to help sustain risk assets and work out of the recession greatly impact savers and additionally distort investment markets. These two sectors of government and private markets have to be looked at in context because the more the government market supports consumption and reduction of risk the more it pulls from the private market and its investment in long-term job creation. The government is seldom a successful investor because it does not have the competitive forces that bring about accountability.

When the issue of sustainability of government finance is addressed is critical because when you change with strength, it gives you far more options than when weakness dominates choices. Reducing debt by policy takes time. And the longer the time frame, the less painful options will be— for crisis situations limit time. So *when* issues are addressed becomes the first critical issue.

The second is *how*—with what final vision that coordinates the many piecemeal decisions. Here it is critical to marry cultural values with political and economic interests. If that is not done, the moral hazard consequence of a public dependent upon the government is as damaging as the debt creation in its ultimate effect on competitiveness and sustainability. Extremes, particularly in cycles, need to be avoided because of the damage done as opposed to logical change that does not destroy a necessary confidence. This takes systemic change and national will.

The balance sheet of government shows the national debt. Government has the ability to tax and raise money; it owns a significant amount of assets in everything from the national parks to systems that provide services. But the national debt, as a percentage of GDP, gives a very good indication, by its trend, of where the country is heading.

If you have significant deficits that are not being covered by current expenditures, you add to debt. And if this is an unsustainable long-term trend, you lose confidence in the government, in the economy because taxes will have to be raised significantly, and in the currency which affects the standard of living. Beyond the debt alone, you have to consider unfunded obligations that are much larger, but can be reduced by policy changes over time. They also have to be part of the equation.

Global Impacts and Our Debt Problem

In America in recent times, some of these natural laws have not interacted as directly as they normally would because of China's purchase of American securities that has given strength to the dollar. This has been an unusual situation that is now beginning to reach a point where the American/ Chinese financial relationship will need far more sophistication as both countries attempt to solve internal problems while working together. China is not only America's largest creditor but was its purchaser of debt.

Chinese savings and American spending have been the financing mechanism for trade. But solutions are not nearly as easy as pundits and politicians prescribe. Raising the value of the Yuan by 15% would increase costs to Americans, lower the trade deficit, and create some jobs. But then employment in China would decline. And Americans would pay much more in costs for Chinese goods that are numerous, and no one is sure of the effect that would have on the system. Rash actions would benefit no one.

The best question to ask is where must both sides move to appreciate the needs and the recognition of mutual necessities. America's current financial situation is a big part of that decision and will be a core issue. China itself forces many challenges as domestic efforts reach limits such as construction spending and bank support of weak companies, while international demand for products is lowered by financial strains.

It is important to understand that the United States is not alone in its long-term structural problems of debt. Nearly all developed countries have these same problems because they result from basic demographic changes and the nature of politicians from many countries to promise more than they can deliver in the future for current support. These are all bubbles of some nature of debt or obligation that are being inflated. When a major crisis is such that it truly shakes confidence, the results could be quite devastating with the interconnections currently in the world.

The world today deals with only current deficits and ignores long-term structural problems. Once necessity requires the new focus long term for confidence, great care needs to be taken not to overreact. Confidence is a very necessary commodity and requires both trust in integrity and in competence, as well as an appreciation that a plan of action will accomplish a needed goal. The problems of the European Union and Greece show the realities of options.

The problem is the American dependence on foreign debt for it removes many freedoms of action and a great deal of our control. A debt crisis would probably have a sharp increase in interest rates, an increase in inflation, a significant impact on the dollar's value, and with unemployment probably increasing significantly, a rise of protectionism.

All these would have serious implications for the rest of the world, which would have their own problems and only reinforce ours in a negative spiral. So the world collectively needs a far more serious approach to understanding its need to not only address these issues but to also think of them in more global terms since the problems causing them are often global as well.

A Less Predictable World

What is not appreciated globally, particularly in the developed countries that have used predictive models for years, is that the world is far less predictable and thus more risky than understood. Many of our existing programs are unsustainable and will not be able to be continued in the future. So a future without them is very different from current calculations. Like chaos theory, little changes can be extrapolated to large impacts. This is even truer when you have a very indebted world where the leverage can quickly turn small impacts into major problems. No one knows the future, but you have to prepare options that let you think about consequences and hopefully adjust to them.

The speed of change may well be variable as we muddle our way through crisis, but avoiding locking into positions that cannot evolve is necessary. Adaptation will be the key strength and that requires a form of contextual thinking. Ideologies are important in their principles, but the road to getting to their ultimate goals usually has bends rather than straight lines. How you think about accomplishing the goals is more important than a strict set of rules, but you must never lose sight of where you need to go and how to bring others with you. Strategic generals know their plans are changed by the tactical generals to adapt almost at the battles' inception, but overall goal and vision still drive the action if it is well considered.

The solutions for many of these problems are going to require significant sacrifice, but if undertaken early enough, they could avoid many of the potential problems. Not that long ago America had surplus and not deficit policies. And goals matter and do bring change.

Understanding the Key Problems in More Detail

Key Immediate Problem – The Deficit

The first thing that needs to be understood is the U.S. federal deficit issue because we are not only in a deep hole, but digging deeper at a rapid pace. In brevity for the short term looking at the proposed fiscal year 2011 budget, revenues have fallen to about 15% of GDP due to the recession. Spending has been raised quite high to approximately 25% of GDP that was last at that level around World War II. While the President's budget was not adopted, the historical presentation probably has some of the most recent calculations for discussion of the problem. The attached graph shows the historical pattern of the last thirty years:

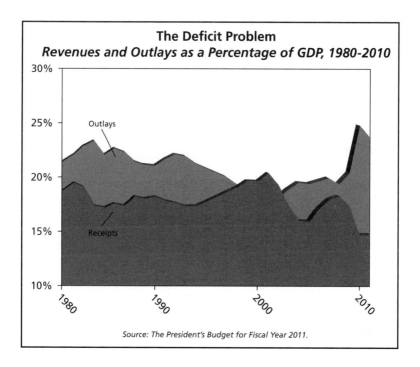

The Deficit Problem
Revenues and Outlays as a Percentage of GDP, 1980-2010

Source: The President's Budget for Fiscal Year 2011.

The question is how to take the receipts and increase them while reducing the outlays. Once the recession is over, it would be anticipated that faster growth would return the revenues toward the 20% range with the more solid recovery. However, whether that is possible or not, is subject to a great amount of conjecture since this has been a structural change with deleveraging, substantial cutbacks, and regulatory policies that are not helpful to growth. The Irving Fisher analysis previously discussed and the probable negative impacts of spending cuts and tax increases may hurt short-term growth even if necessary for long-term solutions.

Rate of growth is highly related to a nation's competitiveness and productivity gains. This competitiveness is not just the spending of money on a problem as the Federal Government often intimates. You can do a great deal with less money if it is spent well. Private spending, if encouraged, is often more targeted for productivity and finds innovation by reengineering. Standard of living increases come from value production not just spending programs. Cultural character matters in how hard a nation works, innovates, and produces.

The Importance of a Long-Term Perspective

So one critical component of any strategic planning is to study the issue of how solid long-term growth can be best shaped and aided. Getting the national economy at a higher growth rate to GNP is the least painful of the solutions. The other concept of cutting the outlays is in many cases painful because you have significant problems in the entitlements of Medicare, Social Security, Medicaid, and forthcoming in several years, the new Obama Care that will add significant costs and uncertainty.

To maintain those entitlements, you will have to significantly increase receipts by increasing taxes that may impact economic growth. The point not to be forgotten is that to give money to someone, it must be taken from someone else who would also have had a use for it that may well have been more productive. How budgets are balanced is not a lost art. States and companies do it all the time, but decisions are forced by necessity. In recent years the federal government has abdicated that will, and now will be forced to face it. Choices are made between needs and wants, but the principles of choice will say a great deal about America's future. A significant change in the budget process, which forces decisions and transparency of choices, is the key as well as less partisanship to reform.

The greatest problem is not Social Security, which will have its controversies in adjusting benefits probably by extending future retirement ages, means testing for some benefits, changing the annual inflation increase formula from wage inflation to core inflation, and increasing the level of earnings for payroll taxes. Some variation will be the likely solution. Benefits may be adjusted particularly if you have the concern of intergenerational fairness, but if begun early opportunities exist. The most challenging problems will be with the significant increases in health care entitlements. This is the great danger area where the issues of affordability, access, and quality will battle each other for funds.

Health Care Is a Critical Issue

This is many times more serious. One of the reasons is not just the increasing life spans but the metabolic syndrome whereby obesity and many of our health issues are being magnified. The metabolic syndrome of extra weight adds not only to diabetes, high blood pressure, and numerous other health problems, but also to the rapidly increasing numbers of people, and these demographics will affect the system dramatically. The problems are starting early in life with childhood obesity that will only magnify the impact. The cost to the economy is far more than the medical costs including absenteeism, loss of productivity, and many other economic factors affecting growth and competitiveness. Individual responsibility for wellness and prevention through nutrition, exercise, and access to quality care can have huge impacts. Genetics may play a smaller role than thought.

Control of environment and personal discipline are the keys to solving the cost issues. Health systems will need to address access, quality, and cost control for sustainability. In the future a cultural component will be crucial to meet the needs since all the wants will be unsustainable. Individual responsibility is again the key character trait needed rather than dependency on medicine.

Obama Care focused on insurance reform to a large extent with many smaller experiments. The need was to focus on health care reform not insurance reform, companies may have at most a 5% margin, many 1%. The 80% to 85% ratios for return of premium to consumer may adjust insurance spending, but the truly big issue is the 85% spent at medical care. How effectively is it spent? Comparisons of government efficiency in the process are misleading because providers are charging private carriers more to make up the difference and the system is distorted. When Medicare does not pay its costs, they up charge private plans and eventually it is not sustainable.

But there is significant waste in that we have a medical sector not a medical system and that hampers opportunity. For example, a financial system's credit cards are available to many users and recipients, telephone systems connect many diverse groups, but our medical system does not have the same interaction. The electronic medical record is the beginning of integration, but I fear the intervention of Obama Care will make it more difficult to let market competition reform the system. Cost will be the driver and the most controversial part of budgetary reform.

Tax Reform and the Budget

One of the other significant budget issues will have to be tax reform where some forms of common ground must be found. In the class warfare argument of taxing the rich, incomes vary with economic conditions affecting stability. Also if you have an expensive welfare state, there is not enough money there, and you eventually tax the middle class putting more pressure on them and reducing opportunity. Europe does this indirectly with value added taxes that are less obvious. The solution is controlled and prioritized spending aimed at efficiency, which seldom takes place in Washington where the "cut in budget" is usually a smaller overall increase.

Only in government is a billion dollar increase considered a billion dollar cut just because someone asked for an eight billion dollar increase. Congress exempts itself from many legal rules, but it also seems to be trying to exempt itself from the reality of the natural world and principles. Taxes are so critical to economic motivation and revenue generation that it is imperative to truly understand consequences of choices. It is the integrated whole of how a tax system works that matters the most. Individual small pieces are often political tokens. The reality is its driving vision, which will set the tone for economic decisions.

Tax reform is not just a revenue economic issue, but is also a political and cultural size of government issue. In the United States many government programs or efforts are indirectly funded by deduction and credits to the tax code rather than the more direct and obvious taxes and payments in European countries as examples. This indirect social funding began largely with the Roosevelt New Deal concepts but has grown largely from the benefit of its lack of direct transparency. In many ways this makes government in reality much larger than it seems on its direct budget expenditures. Our tax credits to business or individuals are really money just spent for the government programs indirectly since the tax money would have gone to the government spending if it were direct. This makes tax reform an effective but difficult process to balance the budget. Many of these provisions are special interest and usually weaker in merit or they would be in the transparent government programs, but they have much more impact on the economy than is perceived because when removed, in many cases the problems are real and would have to be addressed.

One key consideration in any tax reform is what organizational principle to follow—producing results with less unintended consequences and clarity so people can plan to mitigate the shock of the change. The current discussions focus on higher taxes on the top 1% of earners, growth, or indirect social planning. In today's competitive world, we need to focus on growth to address the deficit and debt for stability and competitiveness. Markets will judge the efficiency and theory of any plan as financial crises worsen. An amalgamation of compromises that may solve a few problems will not capture the momentum that a sound new and bold direction can in transforming thought. Timing is also important since austerity at the wrong time impedes growth. Failure to enact austerity early enough creates emergency situations and limits options. "Tax Reform" is key because it involves the considerations of budget cuts, tax policy, and timing of impacts in its determination if it is sound.

A discussion that will be an impediment to that transformative thought is the organizational principle to tax the rich for justice. Regardless of discussions of merit, that is a poor and ineffective principle for the base of a tax code. The key in decisions is to ask the right questions, not move to preordained answers.

The top one percent needs to be better understood. The elite of our society are not the college educated professionals versus the poor. It is probably not the one in a hundred that is elite but closer to one in a thousand. This often includes sports and entertainment stars, and corporate executives—particularly financial fund managers. Many of them make money and lose it. We may question how they make their money and feel they are overpaid. They likely are. But scarcity of their level of talent and the leverage mass distribution gives to earning potential create high values. If the concept of taxing the rich seems to include raising the capital gains rate, you may get some of the one tenth of a percent, but you hurt the entire growth system by limiting it and the creation of jobs and opportunity. This slows the ability for young people to rise. We need to push positive efforts rather than be driven by negative ones that distort positive incentives.

People may be born rich but die poor, or vice versa. Age usually adds wealth if people save and raise families. There are not just standard locked in groups of people in society, it is constantly changing. That is a key point, and the real issue is how much opportunity for change exists in the society. These risks run both ways and government plays a part by its policies.

The class warfare argument needs to be dissected as to symptom and cause. Nearly everyone dislikes the greed of some corporate executives and lawyers. They are slightly more tolerant of executives, athletes, and music stars that earn related to the scarcity of talent, but the real problem is that the middle class is slipping while these are rising, bringing envy and fear that is emotionally vented at the symptom.

The rich and poor move between quartiles, but today that migration is much less because opportunity is limited, in part by technology and globalization replacing jobs, but even more so by our national policies that have hurt growth domestically and built a culture of entitlement and debt use that has damaged our competitiveness. We have to focus on domestic economic growth in a clear bias and certainty of that as a policy, and realize that while the rich need to pay their share, taxing too greatly or using regulations for social ends may satisfy symptoms with less envy, but the cause has not been treated and will only get worse.

You do not get wealthy taking from the rich and giving to the poor when you reduce wealth creation. Government does not create wealth. Philosophies need to focus on opportunity, which develops wealth and raises all. Pundits will make many arguments, some with merit on the short term, but the logic of the need for wealth creation before any redistribution is historically clear. Economic growth should not be looked upon as a zero-sum game of rich versus poor. It is a win, win situation if designed properly, so the policies need to create that environment.

As we also look at who has benefited in the last decade while the middle class has suffered, we cannot forget the many beneficiaries of the crony capitalism that have emerged with the huge expansion of government that has benefited the connected of both parties from the large number of highly paid defense contractors to the green industry venture capitalists.

Too big to fail protected favored banks while pushing smaller institutions into a process of too small to succeed with overburdening regulation. Good policy needs to look beyond the generation of the media to much more specific facts.

Government itself has played a significant part in removing opportunity through burdensome taxes and regulations and inefficient allocation of resources. America has significant failings in infrastructure and less effective quality education but funds have gone to less successful projects that favored support groups. These groups have become wealthy or protected.

Concepts of Tax Reform

President Obama's Deficit Commission suggested cutting tax rates in return for closing various tax loopholes. In effect, their concept is that this would not only raise revenue, but also do so by increasing the efficiency of the tax code and make it more equitable. Lobbyists create many of these benefits for the affluent and the powerful, and, as was shown in the Reagan tax cuts, you can get lower tax rates that are helpful to economic growth by removing a number of specialized benefits that only help a few. The equity of each of those benefits is significant.

Tax reform will become critical. How it is done will establish much of the nation's future because it will determine our competitiveness and affect our cultural attitudes on individual versus government responsibility. Since Franklin Roosevelt, the tax code has become far more than a means to raise money. It has increasingly become a method of social policy by rewarding or punishing social and economic behaviors. It is a perfect example of contextual thinking and power.

Reform, as with President Reagan, and other reformers before him, removed deductions, credits, subsidies, and primarily lobby negotiated special interest benefits to give lower rates, and allow market systems to more rationally determine spending. The efficiency of the market and Schumpeter's concept of creative destruction build competitiveness. Failure is necessary in market systems to keep moral hazard and allow capitalism work. The current subsidy-filled tax code is no different than the selective benefits of crony capitalism in finance, but they are less obvious. A special interest gains a great deal from a small provision. Taxpayers pay little individually for the subsidy, but over time and many subsidies, great impact, and inefficiency in the allocation of resources, is created.

The great dilemma in reform is that the same lobby will ultimately drive it and the appearance of reform, yet true problems may not be resolved. The process will have to be judged on whether it brings true transformational change rather than negotiated transactional compromises that do not return market forces as the determinant success. That is the answer rather than a new round of different compromised subsidies.

This requires it to be convenient for lawmakers to have conscience because the people demand it. As noted, each individual has only a very small interest in a subsidy put in, but a few have a great deal and hire lobby support. Only when you have big transformations where the average person can see his interest does change take place.

Judging Purpose and Impact of Deductions

Taxing the rich by getting rid of deductions sounds populist, but the solution is not rich versus poor, it is the justice and logic of the deduction. Do you want an inefficient tax code that is a cancer over time to international competition, which is what determines jobs and a middle class or a social code of indirect social redistribution? That is the foundation we will ultimately face. You will never get a pure code one way or the other in a political world but the tilt makes a great difference.

When groups blame Mexico or China for taking jobs, and attack companies for taking them there, they miss the true point. We ought to be creating a need for companies to stay in America not by negative force but by incentive of market profit, not by bribery, but by subsidy. A positive climate also attracts foreign capital as well, which is now critical.

Since tax codes are part of the budget concept, and the budget is the contract of the government and the people. The Golden Rule ought to be the core of that contract, and if so social planning except support of the truly unfortunate ought to be minimized. The issue of how tax reform is accomplished will be as much an issue of how people look at the role of government as it will the specific items involved.

Many people feel that America will eventually end up with a value added or consumption tax that might well be the only way to increase the revenue substantially enough to match the outlays. If it is added in addition to the income tax, you will probably finish with a far greater tax burden that is not helpful to economic growth and counterproductive to the strategy with which you began. As usual, how you think through these issues will determine a great deal about what you think about them. There has to be an understanding of the purpose of what is done through several generations. Level of taxes is critical, nature of taxes significant, and understanding the relationships of taxes to economics essential.

It is not possible to succeed with constant shifts in policy similar to the example given of Milton Friedman's man in the shower constantly adjusting the temperature of the water but never leaving enough time for a final result to take place. Without agreement on a longer-term vision, we will accomplish little, and current partisanship will not allow that until crisis changes thought. The first question is—do we appreciate the crisis early enough to make it less dramatic? The second question is the timing of how we implement change—the right level of austerity with the economic growth, and the third question, do we have the will and confidence in the commitment made for the long term?

The Will to Accept Austerity

The faith that people have in government will greatly determine how much they are willing to sacrifice. The current riots in the streets of most European countries serve as a particular warning if the leadership has not given the people a true understanding of the crisis and the options that must be taken. The people have to understand those easy money policies, if inflationary or that lead to a decline in the value of the dollar, end up hurting the poor and the middle class worst. They have little in real assets that can adjust in value. So they have the most reason to keep a sound currency.

Retirees most certainly need this stability or inflation will erode a lifetime of responsibility and savings. Monetary policy that has to be driven for economic reasons, such as keeping interest rates low, has fairness issues with retirees and seniors who deserve a true economic market interest rather than a controlled one.

In the years that I have been involved in politics, I have learned to have an appreciation of the great difficulties that those in legislative positions face. When you go to town hall meetings and see very diverse groups, there are no easy answers. Those with resources that are having them taken away, object strenuously, and those who are in need argue a concept of compassion. The problem is to find a consistent approach that gives unity but also promotes growing the pie for all to have a larger piece.

The budget process and the legislative approaches in modern times were described by a friend of mine with every new set of elections as being "the same circus but bringing in a new set of clowns and a few more peacocks." Too often the cynicism of the public holds that view. The question that has to be asked is whether the circus brings in new acts that change the nature of what has been.

Many of the Western nations are now on high wire acts that require a great deal more seriousness and that will, hopefully, become the focus of attention. The European financial problems and the debt ceiling increase in the United States are turning points on awareness. There are no easy answers, and those who criticize would find a deeper appreciation of the problem if they were in the cauldron. *Change is not the ultimate issue, but change to what?* Emotional commentaries may be fine, but how do they fit into a system of governance with an organizational principle? The issue needs to be the organizational principle not the individual item, and moral hazard needs to be the first organizational consideration.

Integrity of Reform Process Is a Necessity

There is little question federal spending and revenues will be restructured. The reports of the several Commissions and groups studying these issues began the discussion, but to date action has reflected the political lack of will because of the painful reactions that were sure to follow. However, what is done, how it is done, and most importantly, the motivation with which it is done will determine whether America continues a current weakness or reignites its economic engine if it restructures correctly for growth. But the issues must be understood. It is not just the obvious deficit and debt figures at issue, not even the hidden off budget unfunded mandates, but the budget system itself that is not transparent or driven to make choices.

Significant benefits are given through guarantees. If you remove risk for your friends, it is the same as giving money and can be often given for positive purposes. But this distorts the proper allocation of resources as housing finance has shown. Any successful restructuring of government must be transparent and created with an organizing principle of fairness for enhanced economic growth. This requires a value-based concept that has been ignored in current solutions since it does not give the corporatist and lobby results the system desires if it continues to focus on competing special interests rather than a more common good approach that would add broad growth and reduce moral hazard. *Any nation's exceptionalism ultimately comes from having exceptional values that will let it take actions that are strategic for the common good.*

Our Currency as a Barometer of Our Success or Failure

The strength of our currency tells a great deal. To understand the importance of the dollar in the modern world requires understanding history. After World War II, America was the remaining major power militarily and financially. Its culture and laws made its financial markets deep and trusted over time. Any major currency must be liquid, retain its value, and be competitive. The deep markets financially in America have been critical to liquidity, and the Federal Reserve has formerly concentrated on maintaining value. But the greatest benefit has been that there have been few other competitors as the American economy dominated the world by its respective size. Well over 80% of worldwide foreign exchange transactions are done in dollars according to the Bank for International Settlements, so even transactions that are not involving the United States require them. This requires a significant supply of dollars internationally and gives significant benefits to American business and government in issuing debt. They can be financed cheaply and more easily.

American businesses did not have the inconveniences of doing business on another standard or the need to hedge as much as competitors. The need for dollars gave them extra value and has helped us finance our consumption and standard of living. Even when the United States went off the gold standard to a paper currency of confidence, this unique position was held. It has not always been so, historically many including Thomas Jefferson, worried that paper money became the ghost of real money if there is no confidence in it. Credibility matters a huge amount. The dollar's status as the world's reserve currency has lessened pressures, as far as reform of our systems and not required the austerity other countries would have naturally faced as quickly.

But as the previous information on deficits and national debt show, we are weakening our position at the same time others are strengthening theirs. The decline in the use of the dollar is not immediate, but periodic because it has had such dominance. There is no immediate substitute for the dollar, probably for another fifteen to twenty years, but alternatives and substitutes will grow.

While the financial crisis hurt the image of Wall Street and the United States in the confidence of the world, the safe haven of the dollar has been increasingly tested. As noted, the great benefit that the dollar has is that there have been few competitors. And for the immediate future, the Euro has recently been challenged by financial crisis in sovereign debts in Southern Europe. And the Yuan does not have the internal banking markets and systems to give it the liquidity as well as the need for the Chinese government to look to exports for growth which impact the free adjustment of the currency. The risk of defeat at the time Congress debated the debt ceiling increase did not seem to show that the world feared an immediate set of problems.

However, communications advances and the expansion of foreign exchange markets may make it much easier for sophistication to emerge that reduces the need for dollar transactions as smaller currencies can increasingly be matched. The point is that a sudden loss of confidence in the dollar could bring very bad consequences in a leveraged world. But the more likely scenario is a slower decline as other technologies and currencies increase share. This will cause adjustments that will be negative to the standard of living to Americans but more like a growing cancer than a heart attack. However, the United States ought to be concentrating on keeping as much strength as possible in the dollar as a strategic advantage, which requires more fiscal responsibility.

While the Federal Reserve is currently blamed for the monetary expansion, the ultimate cause is the unbalanced debt created by the government's spending that is fiscal policy. When you are going into debt and asking your banker to give you the equivalent of a loan, you ought to concentrate on your spending, not criticism of your banker, even if he is not necessarily wise in lending.

The next ten years will tell a great deal about how the American economy and society will address the future. The dollar is a canary in the mineshaft as an indicator of danger since it is the constant reflection of the world's opinion of us. What built the dollar in its strength originally was an economy built on solid principles of growth, stability, the rule of law, and the creation of confidence. These were cultural powers and strengths. What is weakening it is also cultural. The value of a currency is affected by many things, but the future of the economy is a very big key.

The future of any economy depends on its income stream and opportunities. Politics, economics, and culture are all interrelated, but the cultural thought that dominates will set the stage for the other two over time and that is brought forward in the same concept as a net present value of economics. The budget gives a direct insight, like the appellate judge focusing on a few big issues, as to where the major issues lie and their direction of growth.

Understanding the United States Budget

Again, the budget is the contract of a people and their government. How the money is raised and spent affects all forms of endeavor and creates significant economic incentives for social policy beyond just raising money. It is also a snapshot of how people view the relationship between them and the State. A small government has a small budget because of limited activities; it may focus more on functional activities and keeping integrity in the system by balancing. It will grow as the population grows, but big jumps mean the government has expanded. Many times this is because the population wants the government to reduce risk for them—retirement, health, subsidies, etc. But any expansion has to be paid eventually by taxes, fees, or debt (which is postponed taxes).

The other alternative is the monetization of debt where government inflates its way out of debt with fiat currency at significant cost to the nation. Fiat currencies or monetarily devalued ones created just by printing, emerge as the vehicle between the realities of economics and the unsustainable promises of politics. If you debase a currency, the people pay for the increasing entitlements and usually growing unemployment in a slower less painful and obvious fashion. But that requires keeping inflation to lower levels. But only national governments have this power.

So looking at a budget, you need to know when you are spending money and why, where you are getting the money, and the implications of the sources in opportunity cost to growth and the trend of both. If you have a deficit, you must know what the trends for it will be, how it is to be raised or financed, and if financed, will it be repaid by higher taxes later or monetized. These questions tell you a lot about your economy, the nature of your politics, and the reality of your culture.

As noted before, it is easy to compromise on wants where both sides get something desirable. But the real test of a political system and a culture is if it can compromise on needs that often require sacrifice and delayed gratification. The will of the nation is the determinant, and character is the base of that will. Parties and economics are driven over the long term by cultural values.

If you want to change your direction because of the pressures of a large percentage of debt to GDP affecting solvency or stimulating economic activity, you have to look at a sampling of where you are currently. Many theories are better than options, but they work well from a clean sheet of paper. And if you have existing status quo legacy systems, options become limited. Good theory has to be adapted to reality. So philosophers are very good to avoid getting into holes, but are not that helpful getting out of them.

The CBO fiscal year 2010 federal spending can be broken out generally into components that help understand the situation:

Health	24%
Social Security	20%
Defense	20%
Safety Net Programs	14%
Interest on Debt	6%
All Else	16%

That is simple as a snapshot, but what are critical are the trends. These are primarily transfer systems not wealth creation programs but redistribution systems. If one of those categories grows, then either it has to take resources from another or debt has to be increased or taxes or other revenues increased. How you spend your money, how you raise your money, and issues like debt and the stability of the value of the dollar all fit in a close related context.

Interest on the national debt, for example, is currently at the lowest rates for decades, and the term of debt being issued is very short. If rates rise because of lack of foreign interest, inflation, or a better economy, this factor can automatically grow substantially. So you face the problem of increase in interest that is sustainable. This makes no reduction in principal and with increasing debt, would only get larger and becomes a greater problem.

As you look at the rest of the budget, it becomes important to again realize that the size of government and how it spends money is directly related to the population's desire for security from risk. There is a significant cultural implication in budgets as to the acceptance of individual responsibility. The health component and social security, as well as the Safety Net Program, largely are domestic approaches by which society has determined it wants government to mitigate risk. They were designed as self-funding programs even if not in the true sense of personal investment.

But demographics and unrealistic political policy are making redesign a necessity. This redesign has both moral and economic implications. Compassion and recognition of obligation created by individual responsibility have to be balanced. Society must learn to see the costs as well as the benefits of the programs. Just as with healthcare—if someone else is perceived to pay the bill, cost control is less an issue.

Whenever you mitigate risk, you affect the nature of the economy because resources have to be taken from other sectors to accomplish that determined end. This usually has a negative impact on investment and growth if it goes beyond certain levels. There is without question a responsibility of the government to take care of those who cannot take care of themselves. The issue of importance is at which stage individual responsibility to prepare for one's own retirement, rainy days, and health should be a significant part of a moral hazard.

If government allows such trends that eventually are no longer sustainable, they create a much greater problem because they put everyone at risk since many of those with individual responsibility have increasingly been deprived of their opportunity to save responsibly by the reallocation of their resources. In recent times, convenience is a major vote getter when benefit is promised, but you have an ongoing moral hazard in policy that does not accurately question sustainability. Public pensions will soon make this extremely obvious and set the stage for decision.

One of the fundamentals of growth is planning so there is confidence that allows temperament to take more risk. That requires some certainty in key areas. If there is significant uncertainty plans are tactical and address immediate problems rather than strategically involving the longer range planning necessary for wealth creation and job expansion. One of the greatest problems America will face is this uncertainty because of the current political divide. Certainty needs a perspective in context with all three powers—political, economical, and cultural. So the basis of higher growth starts with determining an organizing system for society that can be projected with confidence in the future.

For the United States to recognize that it is about to face many of these problems will increasingly require an understanding of the consequences of different actions. The U.S. still has the opportunity to make many of these changes. While its debt, particularly what was added since 2007, is very substantial, it is not to the levels of many of the European nations where problems are taking place. And as the world's most powerful economy with the dollar as a reserve currency, it has some decided advantages beyond many of the current countries in trouble.

While there are different ways to estimate the ratio of U.S. debt to GDP, it is probably in the mid 60% range for "public debt" but goes rather quickly to about 100% if the IOU's that are owed to the Social Security Trust Fund are included as they should be. The issue, as has been mentioned, is the ultimate growth rate of the economy. That depends largely on the longer-term governmental policies to create a healthy business environment and whether America can help its innovation edge. America has many assets beyond the small countries in fiscal trouble, but unless we address root causes, we will eventually follow them.

Health care has been a major issue and is perhaps the one that is the greatest challenge of all with the budgetary future. While much discussion took place in the passing of the recent legislation, it missed the greatest single problem—cost control. Where estimates in potential savings were discussed, I fear that many of these will be unrealistic, and once the bill was signed into law, a very powerful constituency was formed that benefits from it, thereby making it very difficult to change. The three primary concerns of health care are access (facilities and the ability to deliver service), quality (the level of service that is given), and affordability (the cost and the resources provided). The bill concentrated on access by adding at least another 18 million, and it spoke in many areas of quality.

But the cost controls will be the greatest set of concerns. Insurance companies, as opposed to government, are often unpopular because they undertake the concept of controlling costs. That lack of freedom often puts them in conflict with their policyholders. But they serve an extremely vital function since the concept of insurance spreads the costs over a much larger population. Lower cost means more affordability and access. It also often demands quality because prevention is a necessity in modern times.

The government could probably handle writing checks in volume more efficiently, but the ability to control costs effectively has not, at least in my opinion, been shown very well in any of its agencies. Many of the most shown benefits that make companies keep children on longer, eliminate pre-existing conditions, etc., could have been put in one bill and forced upon insurance companies. They probably would have been happy to add them if their competitors did as well. All the conditions would do is increase the premiums we all pay by spreading the cost to us but allowing them to increase income by their margins over a bigger base.

Since Medicare and Medicaid are many times more a problem in their potential deficiencies than Social Security, many of the forthcoming problems are going to require dramatic solutions over the next ten years as the problems force different alternatives. By looking to funding medicine primarily as the solution more than the individual responsibility of wellness and prevention, we have diverse incentives. The only real solution for many of our health problems will be a return to individual responsibility where people are careful what they eat, exercise, and become increasingly aware of the factors that affect their health as well as becoming sensitive to costs. If they believe pills are a solution, at little cost, it is counterproductive.

Genetics is a much smaller part of what affects one's life than is often perceived. The living environment, nutrition, limited drinking and not smoking, the level of health care received, and a host of other considerations can have tremendous impact. This is an area where the Chinese traditional medicines and practices, as well as those of Latin America, may well be found to provide insights beyond just the clinical approaches of the West. Health care will emerge as the most difficult part of the budget because of the increasing lifespan, the demographic growth of the Metabolic Syndrome, and the significant pressures on the costs of the provision of health. Health is not just a financial issue but also a moral one, and that makes it especially complex. But this is a decision that should not be left to bureaucrats—a cultural determination of values needs to be passed.

Obviously because of increasing lifespan, the Social Security System will have to have adjustments made to maintain its solvency. Originally when Social Security was passed, the average life expectancy did not necessarily meet the 65 years age limit. You had many more workers within the system for those receiving Social Security, and the economics might have been appropriate to its age. Now, even Social Security notes that in determining retirement options a typical 65 year old today will live to age 83 and one in four will live to 90. So, the increasing demographics create ongoing necessities to adjust the system, and eventually reduced benefits, increased taxes, and some means testing will probably be implemented.

China, which focuses on treating causes more than symptoms, is looking at technology, but also the emphasis on individual responsibility for wellness. They understand better than the West that their population saves 40% for fear of health and other problems. That limits a consumption-based economy. Health care and economics are closely related. In the U.S. we give lip service to that but are placing increasing cost burdens for health care on our companies and economically driving jobs abroad, which only necessitates more transfer payments and bigger budgets. We also must address causes not symptoms.

Many of the components of the budget all have highly negative trends, and the adjustments that will be made can have tremendous impacts on the levels of growth, which is one strategy to ease problems versus redistribution of assets for current problems. The decisions on how to approach these issues have to be in a very coordinated and educated environment or the problems can easily be made worse rather than better.

The ultimate issue is risk. How much individual responsibility is undertaken within the population? The more reduction of risk that is given by government, the more resources have to be found and less pressure on people to take individual responsibility. There is a significant difference between charity and care for those unable to care for themselves and the concept of removing risk for a population that has the ability to remove a portion of the risk themselves. Government's incentives in building these policies are absolutely critical. The "free rider" concept within societies is at the core of how these issues have to be viewed for moral hazard.

U.S. Federal Government Receipts

Similarly, once you have understood where the money is spent, it becomes important to understand where the money arises. The fiscal year 2009 Federal Budget showed the main categories of U.S. Federal Receipts:

Individual Income Taxes	43%
Social Security and Social Insurance Taxes	42%
Corporate Income Taxes	7%
Other Sources	5%
Excise Taxes	3%

The key point the revenue sources chart makes is the dependence upon the economy. If it grows, they increase with individual income taxes, corporate taxes, and employment related taxes. If it falters or declines, the income streams drop, sometimes significantly, as in the recent recession. The size of debts and deficits will eventually bring about an examination and in all likelihood, because of the code's complexity, resulting inefficiency, and its impact on competitiveness, a new tax structure. How it is designed will be critical. The current system taxes and burdens the creation of income; a competitive system will tax consumption to promote investment and growth. Wealth creation and wealth distribution are competing concepts. Tax structure favors one at the expense of the other in most instances.

Tax reform has a positive that tax rates can be reduced if many special exemptions are removed. A number of these favor the "corporatist" benefits gotten from groups by the lobby. A more clear code would bring incentives to work just as the Reagan tax cuts generated benefits for a number of years. Reform solely for the sake of raising more money for spending without offsetting rate reductions would probably decrease incentive.

When the income is less than the expense, a deficit occurs that creates and adds to the national debt. The recent deficits, which often do not include off budget items like the Iraq and Afghanistan Wars, show the very significant increases. Part is due to the recession, but much is related to spending:

1999	125.6	Billion Dollar Surplus
2000	236.4	Billion Dollar Surplus
2001	127.3	Billion Dollar Surplus
2002	157.8	Billion Dollar Deficit
2003	374	Billion Dollar Deficit
2004	413	Billion Dollar Deficit
2005	319	Billion Dollar Deficit
2006	248	Billion Dollar Deficit
2007	162	Billion Dollar Deficit
2008	455	Billion Dollar Deficit
2009	1400	Billion Dollar Deficit
2010	1350	Billion Dollar Deficit

Balancing a budget is a test of will. You can require balance as most state budgets do, but it makes you cut, which is politically painful. You fund by finding new revenue for cutting somewhere else that is less important. If you fund wealth creation and growth, you usually have more to divide for the future. If government does not have the will, then freezes or automatic reductions can be put into law that may form decisions that many would wish to be avoided. These are not unsolvable issues, just difficult ones, requiring sacrifice that necessitates fairness. If people must pay more taxes, they want to know there is not waste, fraud, or "free riding."

The National Debt

These recent deficits make a rapid increase in the size of our national debt. The debt is often described in two ways—one is the debt held by the public, which is everything not held by U.S. Government institutions such as the Social Security Administration and Federal Reserve. The second and more accurate picture is called "Gross Debt" that includes intragovernment obligations. These are obligations that will have to be redeemed, liquefied, and paid to beneficiaries in most cases, so Gross Debt is probably the best comparison. For 2010, Public Debt was about 63% of GDP and Gross Debt about 94%. But they are increasing quickly. Historically, the following chart gives the trend:

Year	Gross Debt in Billions Undefeated	As % of GDP
2000	5,628.70	58
2001	5,769.90	57.4
2002	6,198.40	59.7
2003	6,760.00	62.6
2004	7,354.70	63.9
2005	7,905.30	64.6
2006	8,451.40	65
2007	8,950.70	65.6
2008	9,985.80	70.2
2009	12,311.40	86.1
2010 (13 Dec)	13,848.00	94.0 (3rd Q)

The other important fact to consider is that Medicare, Medicaid, and Social Security have mandatory committed payments. Payouts will currently exceed the revenues over the next 75 years, which will require funding from other sources such as additional taxes. The present value of these unfunded obligations has been estimated at about $46 trillion—a significant multiple of the current debt. Adjustments will have to be made for solvency but will be very difficult because of public policy that encourages reliance on the government rather than individual responsibility.

The problem with increasing percentage of debt to GDP is the likelihood of a substantially lower growth ratio for the economy, which hinders the main solution to the problem—faster growth. Debt adds heavy weight and reduces freedom of action. There is debate on the level of debt that is threshold for major impact. However, trends make this less important in the current analysis when you realize many guaranties of institutions like Fannie Mae and Freddie Mac are not included. Student loan guarantees and similar obligations are not clearly defined as liabilities. If the government were looked upon as an individual or a company, it would certainly not meet the transparency and substantial disclosure requirements.

The total debt is not only massive, but also increasing in many little understood ways off ledger because of the increasing scrutiny on the numbers. In 2012 we will be close to the 100% debt to GDP ratio that many take as a critical point. Many economists think that ever lesser figures retard growth and the debt will be increasingly responsible for our stagnation of growth.

The Stability of the Dollar

As noted, the middle class and the less privileged have significant risks from the debt if it causes inflation, increasing interest rates, or slower growth. They do not have assets that increase in value and have concerns about unemployment. This would occur through another currency, or likely a basket of currencies, replacing the dollar as the reserve currency internationally. If to reduce its debt the government simply monetizes it or prints it, there is devaluation, and government pays debts back in cheaper dollars. But the U.S. has to borrow to finance its government and trade deficit. And how long will foreign countries continue to loan if their dollar revenues keep declining in value?

The dollar will buy less, and the standard of living will go down comparatively. This will be a critical issue in both your generations. However, there is no immediate challenge to the dollar because of the size, stability, and liquidity of America. It is the trend, if unaddressed, by which we will determine our own future by our policies.

It is important to keep in mind that the debt to currency ratio can well be affected by other characteristics. Japan, for example, has one of the highest debts to GDP ratios of over 200%, much higher than Greece, Italy or the United States. However, Japanese investors primarily hold Japanese debt domestically, so the risk of currency impact is substantially less than those countries with a less GDP ratio where government debt is held by outside creditors who can more quickly undermine a currency by selling or not buying debt.

Domestic savings rates are critically important and that is one of the significant distinctions between the East and the West. The cultural impact is significant. Japan is certainly a developed country. This is why the Chinese relationship to the United States, as its major creditor is particularly significant.

Why all of this really matters and how it fits into our contextual thinking is because it is probably the hidden factors that will most affect ours and our children's future. While people talk of the United States defaulting on its debt, it is far more likely that if actions are not taken to bring sustainability to the budget and the biggest entitlement costs, the results will be negative but not fully appreciated. When governments in history have not been able to pay by either cutting costs or raising revenue, they often print money and control interest rates to minimize the immediate impact.

Ultimately this results in inflation, although bad business conditions may occur first with a little deflation. But then the rise in inflation is accompanied by unofficial currency depreciation as other countries currencies are worth more thereby causing inflation domestically and the problem of negative or low interest rates that distorts economic choices often from the productive resources needed. People see the problems as symptoms of what is wrong, but seldom understand negative interest rates, value deterioration, or even monetary causes of inflation. They blame politics but need to understand the causes. The problem is that the causes were a long time in building and are seldom easily solved—time is a necessity. It is true that a weak currency helps sell goods abroad and assist the balance of trade, but if weak currencies were the only consideration many African countries would be manufacturing giants. However, strong currencies show stability.

The effect of these policies are to take money from prudent savers who want to prepare for their futures by giving them little return and in devaluing the dollar to weaken it reducing what they can buy with it. What people do not understand is that the poor who are supposedly the ones that should benefit from the continuing costs of entitlement systems are eventually those most affected by these results. The poor or the middle class have limited assets that rise with inflation while the rich have money to invest in protective assets. Those that do, have the ability to move their money internationally. Inflation helps assets, but if you do not have assets, it only increases costs.

Much like corruption, it steals opportunity from the poor, so enlightened ethical leadership is not a naïve hope but a necessity. A strong economy investing on market principles for productivity is the only real solution and the more we move into policies that distort it through taxes and unsustainable programs, the more we commit ourselves and your generation into a down cycle that will only build upon itself.

Tipping points are being reached today that did not exist before. The lack of understanding the ultimate causes and consequences are a self-imposed burden because our media looks to people and events, not to ideas. We may discuss the hats at a Royal Wedding, but we have little concept of the costs of unofficial devaluation of our currency or its causes, which is what will ultimately determine our lifestyle and that of our children. Even if you have assets now, if you follow the history of many economies that become desperate, you will see that forced conversions or indirect taxation can reduce them quickly unless you have the capacity to work internationally. This is beyond the middle class and many of the wealthy. While America will have some heart attacks financially, the real problem is a slow cancer aided by a stroke that does not let us seem to comprehend the reality of our situation.

Structural Budget Reform

If the great political issue of the next generation is going to be a functioning and sustainable federal government, then two primary issues will have to be addressed. The first is an operational one that helps to put a structure within government for the budgetary process that requires decisions to be made and an intelligent and effective way of comparing alternatives. The second is going to be the need for the American public to fully understand the issues put forth so that a transformation can take place from the highly partisan and special interest driven system that currently exists. A knowledgeable friend of mine who had long fought alongside me for government transparency noted that while transparency served many benefits, one unfortunate side effect was that it revealed the nature of pre-existing special interest favoritism and in doing so significantly diminished the respect with which the populous sees the institution.

The best way to reform the system is to place structural goals aiding transparency by bringing issues to the forefront for discussion. The debate on the debt ceiling increase helped sharpen focus, but showed the need for a new process—and then we must find how to transform civic responsibility in bringing unity. This is by far the most difficult and, while discussed generally, is covered in much more detail in the cultural sections that follow.

One of the most significant Committees of Congress is not an operational one. It is instead a strategic information-driven committee composed of both Republicans and Democrats from the Senate and the House. It is the Joint Economic Committee of Congress, which works at generating ideas for governmental change as well as receiving a significant amount of information in testimony. One of the most interesting studies I have seen within government comes from the recommendations of a new bill formerly referred to as the MAP Act ("Maximizing America's Prosperity Act" H.R. 2319). Its author is Representative Kevin Brady, Vice Chairman and Ranking Republican on the Joint Economic Committee (as well as Chairman of the Trade Subcommittee of Ways and Means). The Act primarily follows a significant study by the Republican Section of the Joint Economic Committee.

The most significant finding of the original study, *Spend Less, Owe Less, Grow the Economy,* was that the foundation of effective fiscal consolidation programs was spending cuts. In looking at government spending reductions of global competitors they found such actions increased long-term growth, but also provided a larger boost to growth in the first three years. Normally, successful consolidation programs were composed of about 85% spending reductions and 15% revenue increases, a part of which were some privatizations or asset sales rather than tax increases. The conclusion was that reducing federal spending relative to the size of the economy was essential to maximizing America's prosperity.

What followed in the MAP Act largely focused on two avenues. The first was a definition of terms to be used. If you are going to have a baseline, what baseline would be appropriate, and the second dealt with a series of sequestrations, mandated budget compliance, with a series of issues:

1. Realistic sequestration
2. Mandated budget compliance with MAP caps
3. Prioritizing spending and honest budgeting
4. Legislative line item reductions for the President
5. Permanent continuing resolutions
6. The Sunset Commission
7. Transparency
8. Rainy Day Emergency Fund
9. The impact of bills on the federal debt

Each of these were guardrails, many of which were ones used by states like Texas to help their budget process. Undertakings such as the Sunset Commission have been particularly helpful in going to the equivalent of zero-based budgeting in that all agencies and programs will be terminated over a twelve year cycle unless Congress specifically votes to extend them. This requires an ongoing review of the size of government and adds efficiency to it.

A balanced budget amendment to the Constitution alone is unlikely to counteract the inherent bias toward higher spending unless it includes these type spending limitations. A simple balanced budget amendment could force job-destroying taxes to pay for an ever-rising level of federal spending unless spending itself is addressed in an organized manner. Government spending caps that are expressed as a percentage of GDP accurately measured have been successful.

What much of the research has shown is that metrics matter significantly. Choosing the right measurements will largely determine success. There is thus a significant distinction of the specific definitions of what is chosen that brings much more focus to equalize comparisons of alternatives.

While the MAP Act has far more detail and support, it becomes important to look at the summary presented for what it attempts to accomplish. In many cases it is not just a Republican version because the concepts such as the Sunset Commission in Texas were supported by Democratic concepts that also desired efficiency within government. It became a way for those within government to have conversations rather than avoid them and to force governance to make a choice in a transparent situation.

Keep in mind that much of the current budget deficit is driven by economic weakness, which may persist. And super committees alone that can operate with default mechanisms do not give the same choice between alternatives. The choice of not acting, or gridlock, is no longer one that the country is able to tolerate.

The rapidly increasing size of the debt created by the current deficit is the first problem. The looming cash deficits within the Social Security and Medicare systems are a much longer-term problem that has to be addressed but are really almost secondary to the immediate concerns. Integrating the two together becomes a part of the solution, but they must be seen as pieces of stages since the solution to each section is unique.

The materials supporting the MAP Act are voluminous but are captured in five graphs, which give credence to the recommendations. They are included to reemphasize previous points and bring them together continually.

They make these key points:

Most of our spending is mandatory, not discretionary, so the more we cut discretionary spending the more we cut into the "muscle" beyond "fat" in key areas.

The level of spending is creating a debt crisis, which necessitates change, and is not an option.

What drives the debt increases are primarily medical increases and Medicaid because of demographics, new benefits, and the consequence of the modern metabolic syndrome of life style.

The necessity of structural change is obvious when you see the comparative and unsustainable levels of debt and the resulting effects of the economy and sustainability of benefits.

Growth in government has an effect on the private sector through regulations and competition.

It should be appreciated that capitalism is not synonymous with crony capitalism or greed beyond self-interest. Today there is a belief that government needs to regulate business and capitalism and cannot be trusted. However, Europe was far more regulated financially and has far worse problems. The issue is how it is regulated, not by micromanagement by the inexperienced, but penalties of failure so that you do not socialize losses.

Many oppose the greed, economic injustice of much of Wall Street corporations like a disease, but the method of addressing the disease is different. Bloodlettings versus antibiotics are drastic differences in approach. Thought must be used to discuss the real issue—cultural failure of governance and ethics. It is what can solve capitalism, but some leaders of capitalism, particularly on Wall Street, and some governmental leaders have minimal interests in ethical change because they are part of the problem.

While growth is critical to the future, it is not enough to count on it alone. The problems are too significant and more immediate than perceived. As seen from the following graphs, the interest on debt is now at one of its lowest levels, and when it increases, the effects will be very dramatic and rates will rise as confidence in our credit falls with our inactions.

The market will become dominant and the effect will fall on the weakest among us. Defense, a critical issue, cannot be cut haphazardly without great risk, but it must be cut since our greatest threats are our huge economic challenges that indirectly have great effect on defense. We must learn to use soft power more effectively to counter threats by common interests. Our tax system must be reformed to make us competitive and lower burdens as well as revenue for easing transitions.

As the revenues and spending are brought into balance, European approaches may give an indication of direction. Entitlement spending has been maintained at the cost of defense to the point that most nations, including Great Britain have hallowed their military. The early compromises on the American budget with the "Super Committee" take the same approach but excuse it by a strategy of working more burden-sharing with allies. This has far more significant unrealized impacts to economics and political options than will be immediately appreciated in the choices and will make relations with China far more significant.

Most of all we must address health care as a cost. It is growing at very unattainable rates and costs much more than other countries, which provide better care. However, our recent changes add to the problem because they deal with accessibility and a degree on quality but are highly inefficient on cost control and sustainability. But our greatest problem is one of will. All these issues have been discussed, perhaps best in the Simpson/Bowles Report. Will is a cultural value not a political or economic interest and must be made a part of the discussion if a solution is to be found.

Civilizations or societies can decline relatively quickly, in a decade effectively, if confidence is lost in its governmental institutions and financial structure. However, the conditions causing the final decline are usually long lasting as the confidence and trust decline over time, so faith is shallow. It is far easier to treat the first cultural cancer than the financial heart attack, but you have to recognize the cancer and have the will to fight it rather than wish it away or ignore it.

Even though the graphs show unsustainable spending, the effect will be felt much earlier. Organizations or individuals face two financial break points—one is liquidity and one is solvency. While they are indirectly connected, it is important to understand both. Solvency, in this case, will be gradually lost at an accelerating pace if not addressed. However, liquidity or cash flow will be a problem far earlier. The bond markets will see the trend and risk and with temperament changes, the deficits will not occur because they will not be able to be funded.

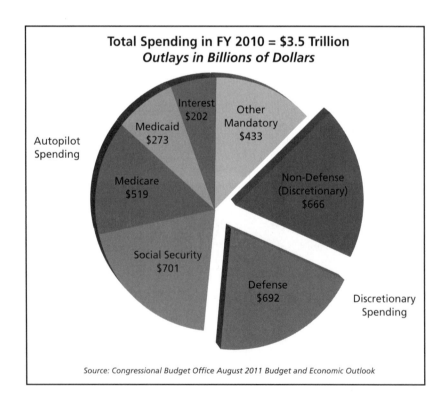

Source: Congressional Budget Office August 2011 Budget and Economic Outlook

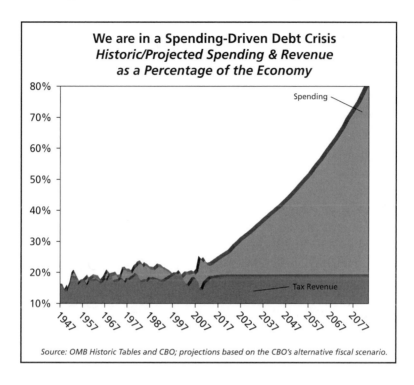

We are in a Spending-Driven Debt Crisis
Historic/Projected Spending & Revenue
as a Percentage of the Economy

Spending

Tax Revenue

Source: OMB Historic Tables and CBO; projections based on the CBO's alternative fiscal scenario.

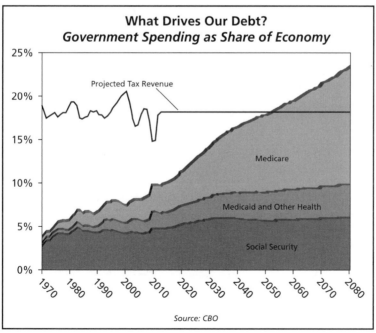

What Drives Our Debt?
Government Spending as Share of Economy

Projected Tax Revenue

Medicare

Medicaid and Other Health

Social Security

Source: CBO

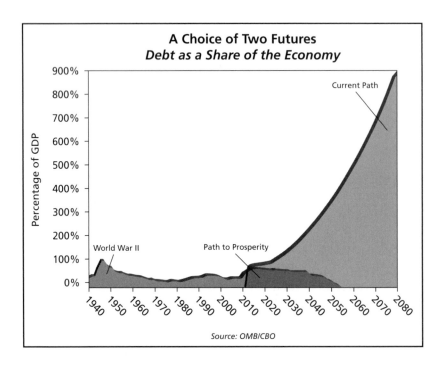

A Choice of Two Futures
Debt as a Share of the Economy

Source: OMB/CBO

THE MAP ACT

Kevin Brady's "Maximizing America's Prosperity Act" provides the map for the path to prosperity.

A Better Way To Control Spending

America has a spending disease and its symptoms of debt and a ballooning deficit are impossible to ignore.

Congress cannot control interest payments on the existing federal debt, but it can control discretionary and mandatory spending.

Other proposals to cap federal spending rely upon inappropriate metrics causing them to address the wrong problem or fail over time.

The MAP Act caps federal **non-interest spending** as a percentage of **full employment GDP** (also known as potential GDP) as its metrics.

- Focusing on federal non-interest spending attacks the problem – unsustainable growth in spending on federal programs, not the symptoms.

- Focusing on non-interest spending prevents political gimmicks (such as claiming that tax increases will also reduce spending through lower interest outlays).

- **Full employment GDP** is a more stable measurement for capping federal spending than actual GDP.

- Eliminates the pro-cyclical problems so spending can grow rapidly in the boom years under a GDP-based cap only to require large, political difficult cuts during recessions that have caused some states to bust their state spending caps.

- Reduces uncertainty by providing a more predictable path for spending over the next ten years.

New Guardrails To Restrain Spending
In The 21St Century

The MAP Act will help change the way that Washington does business in several ways:

1) **Realistic Sequestration:** Congress must live within its budgetary means. If Congress fails to keep spending below the caps, the **MAP ACT** provides for a sequestration that balances spending restraint with humanitarian concerns.

2) **Prioritization of Spending:** The President would be required to prioritize all spending programs in his budget submission in order from most essential to least essential.

3) **Legislative Line-Item Reductions for the President:** The President may submit up to 4 line-item reduction bills to Congress each year—considered with expedited procedure—to rescind funding for discretionary budget authority.

4) **Sunset Commission:** All agencies and programs would be terminated over a 12-year cycle unless Congress votes to extend them.

5) **Permanent Continuing Resolution:** A permanent CR would fund government at 90% of the appropriation for the previous fiscal year if Congress fails to pass necessary spending bills on time. Thus, "big spenders" could no longer threaten a government shutdown to push for more spending.

The critical point is that there are solutions to the problems. The MAP Act may be a very organized way to structurally make the system work and because it is already in consideration by the Joint Economic Committee has significant merit. The more important consideration will be how the public looks at government and how the partisanship can be minimized to make the discussions not so much on convenience of political and economic interests but of cultural values of conscience that look to balancing obligations and compassion. There must be compassion and assistance for those who truly need support and government does have a function and obligation. However, when governmental actions use resources beyond what is needed to redistribute broadly rather than by specific true need, the sustainability of the system is in doubt and the obligations to the people as a whole, as well as those that need continued funding, are greatly impacted. This distinction is essential as the heart of any choices while an effort like the MAP Act can be the hands and mind.

An Overview of Modern Political Direction

In political times direction will change because reality will force it to do so. But the speed will depend on whether it is an enlightened change of personal necessity by a more unified people or a bitter battle of interests until all are exhausted and accept reality. The adoption of a functional budget system puts issues more clearly before us, but the critical issue is the process we use to get them. Leadership matters here as does the cultural organizing principles that unify leadership.

A basic problem we must recognize in democracies is that the freedom given makes it much easier to change leadership than to solve the problems in society. Even though changes may go in the correct direction they may be temporary or the leadership loses support when calling for sacrifice. The core of a democracy has to be the responsibility of the people. That involves their values and how they think. You can have the difficulty of not understanding the depth and context of problems or you can reach the point of not having the will or caring. In the first, conscience and education can be a longer-term solution, in the second, personal convenience dominates. It is more difficult since the education has to show the personal benefit. It must be noted that both come from a decline in the acceptance of personal responsibility, which often lowers the need in their mind for high level civic responsibility and education. This is why the failure of educational institutions to effectively teach history, civic responsibility, and broad-based courses on classics that give alternative thoughts, forcing you to learn to think and choose is so damaging. Society must have a civilized core that understands its best interest.

The problem of current politics of media and polls is that entertainment and sensation value make it increasingly necessary for candidates to go with the flow of a campaign by letting the interests of the people determine their stance as they move to it rather than defining a position that is truly transformational. As long as the process defines the candidates and the nature of leadership is effectively minimized by the "kingmakers" of media and notoriety, then building a transformational base in the people is the key to change. The division of interests in economics and politics does not allow that, but cultural ethics, which is effectively the Common Good and Golden Rule, can unite activists if they adjust perspectives to the needs of the times.

The Founders understood that political parties were necessary to advance one's ideas. There is always division within any nation on the path taken, but as Jefferson noted, "Not every difference in opinion is a difference of principle." But today, 24-hour news and sharp opinion create a very different environment that does not seek common principles but lucrative opinion audiences. We need a longer range vision that is based on principles to which opinions are then shaped. A perspective of true needs over wants and recognition of the sacrifice are necessary. We must remember that a modern view of events may not be as important as how the historical view of the times will be in helping prioritize.

It is easy to campaign with promises and rhetoric. It is easy to write columns or books, host talk shows or radio, but governing is very different if you wish to do it well. Every decision brings controversy or the disappointment of unfulfilled expectations. Unless we have a more thoughtful culture, we will waste the critical time we still have to maintain and increase our strength as a nation.

Intense partisanship is being rejected by America if not by politicians. The Party System of modern times goes back to about 1860. It has shifted power. We have a significant independent voter base. This usually leads to about a 60-40 country that agrees on more than we disagree until you have critical divisive issues like the 1994, 2008, or 2010 elections when changes in attitude are shown. The old school of politics taught that in all things except in elections, you put country first and politics last. It certainly did not always happen that way, but concern for the nation was stronger. Today elections are the only thing of consequence to the governing elite in a constant war for power.

Our recent environment, largely due to money, arrogance, and media intensity, has made partisanship a constant. What is needed now in leadership is more of a Moses than political Messiahs. Old politics had politicians; now much of the debate is not on the floor but by the "unelected" pundits, intellectuals, celebrities, bloggers, and fundraisers. Most of them handle issues on emotion rather than any depth of study because of their need to hold an audience by being cutting edge to a certain population. And we Americans greatly reward this attitude.

The problem is not so much them as us because we desire it from our more base instincts. Our media caters to making us feel better by lowering others through their failure as much as elevating fear or celebrity more than reason and honor. Why should politics, which is formed by culture, be different? This is culture replacing family in the modern world and instilling its own values.

This is true of both parties. Because we are so preoccupied with other activities, a real problem has developed in our society that was once termed "idea illiteracy" or an inability to understand and handle concepts whether they are economic or political. So now there is more vulnerability to the programming and manipulation of minds by the media—a case Horace Busby made to me many years ago as a prediction. Horace, or "Bus" to his friends, was a preeminent commentator on American Politics who served for much of his life as a key advisor to President Lyndon Johnson. Johnson recruited him to make his presidential speeches more like Winston Churchill's. Busby became a thoughtful commentator on policy and on the American character and political transition.

The new way of thinking is not in the context of ideas but emotion and gratification. A truly revolutionary idea that would be shocking to the current Congress would be to force the members to not divide between partisan aisles, but to sit interspersed as a collective group not an arguing pair. In olden days there was a larger moderate overlap—some blue dog conservatives. Some Democrats were much more conservative than some moderate Republicans. Now there is little if any overlap after redistricting. The most liberal Republican is probably more conservative than the least liberal Democrat particularly with the presence of party voting. At least symbolically mixing them might bring less pressure and more civility. The Texas Legislature has always been interspersed.

Our present parties each have goals that represent interests and different perspectives, but policies are often inconsistent with platforms. If a third party forms, it will be from a new constituency. In my thinking a most likely one will be individual responsibility as an organizing principle because of the great pressures faced by deficits and the choices that have to be made. A new culture war will not be social but economic between those that have saved and provided for themselves and those receiving growing redistribution through entitlement benefits.

When systems are no longer sustainable, cutting will take place. But will the means testing that makes those that have worked and saved no longer get the benefits they feel they purchased? They will argue the philosophy of teaching people to fish rather than giving them a fish. But there will be many who are used to the delivery of the fish and will not desire to go fishing. This is the crisis we must avoid. Many wonder where the Tea Party will evolve. It has these instincts, but in its diversity does not currently have an organized philosophy of coordinated policy.

The Fundamental Thought of Politics

In *The Essentials of The Language of Conscience* we focused on the fact that there were two relationships that mattered greatly within a society. One was the relationship of men to each other by the moral codes that were self-enforced within the society (equality), and the other was the relationship of the society as a whole (often represented by the government) to the individual (fraternity). These are critical items of balance that every society addresses by action or inaction and often adjusts to the times. History, economics, level of development, and a host of items that change, interact with the existing status quo created by history and often expressed in modern culture, which represents historical values pushed forward.

Any combination or balance must recognize the change social networking media has made. No longer can a few send information to many since today cross sharing makes change certain. The key is to build the traditional values and morality as a vital part of that media. Men and women instinctively know the value of the Golden Rule and the Common Good.

How strong the moral culture of peer pressure between men exists greatly determines how strong and large the government has to be. The more that is done by the individual private sector in economics and in the support of others through charity, the self regulation of business practices, and the values that are enforced morally, the more these help in defining the nature of the culture. In those places where society fails, government enters the vacuum. In other cases where government is aggressive, it takes from the private sector and removes powers in its desire for additional control whether it is for good, benign, or negative reasons.

You must always look at society as a circle. The line that divides it into two sections between government power and private society is often changing. It is not necessarily down the middle as a theory might propose, but it fluctuates with the needs and wants of the population and the power structure of reality that emerges from it. The world has been filled with true democracies and absolute tyrants. Both have succeeded in controlling power, but the key to great civilizations are those that build a harmonious balance of people working together and maintaining a culture that accepts most of the responsibility and limits government and the courts to only the most serious of issues. It is that culture that often best succeeds—at least in the way I have seen from the reality examples we have given in *The Language of Conscience Evolution*.

The societies that are dominated by ideas, often supported strongly by religions, philosophies of the nature of man, and a respect for the historical lessons learned, add much greater balance to this cultural power. When men rule themselves they normally have a moral set of guidelines that instill the character and the peer pressure. The family teaches the values. When you have only relativity and total toleration, the issues are settled more by government or the courts because there is little self-government or invisible hand to make the correcting philosophies. The more government assumes power, the less the power of the individual and often the opportunity he has. *It becomes an issue of gaining power through government rather than gaining the support of the people through leadership.*

The issue to watch in the nature of societies is found in the word freedom. It means many different things to different people. If you have been ruled in a totalitarian country, just a few freedoms give you a new and different meaning to the word. Liberty is often the term most used in the West for political freedom, which is the recognition of the rights of individuals. We use terms like democracy, liberty, and a variety of others to describe differing circumstances. But it becomes very important to define exactly what freedom is and how freedom works in terms of an organizing principle contextually.

It is not a simple term, but one that each man judges himself in his current environment. Freedom depends on whether he sees himself as the center of the universe and all things circulating around him or sees himself as a part of a bigger whole and an intricate part in affecting it while recognizing that it has the intervening power of the involvement of many others.

Free will is critical in understanding true freedom. In my belief, God gave us this right to see how we would exercise it. So how we think philosophically about the issue of freedom, or free will, becomes important. If a man could do anything he wished in free will, then for all intents and purposes he would have absolute control and could direct others. So since others and their free will are involved, freedom is often adjusted by the rules defining the boundaries each of us will mutually accept as limitations of free will for our own good as well as that of others.

These are more commonly called the "Rule of Law." But in America, the "Rule of Law" starts with the United States Constitution and the Declaration of Independence. Both gave the philosophies and ideas under which rules would be established and gave balance to society that favored private efforts and encouraged a culture of self-governance more than strong governance. Other republics and democracies because of the cultural geographic and economic circumstances operate differently.

There is not one certain method but instead a balance that is found within society where there is agreement on how the government operates and what its balance with people should be. That balance may be accepted in a different form when the government is operating in unique circumstances such as a war or providing economic growth at times of difficulty and transition. It is not a constant balance, but the freedom perspective becomes important in maintaining it. This was the genius of the American system of the Constitution because in its checks and balances it limited government and forced the people to take more responsibility unless they abdicated. The people and states maintained the power not directly given to the federal government.

Historically, civilizations have been changed, and this balance changed if they were conquered. But more often in great civilizations, they somewhat committed suicide by lessening strength and gradually deteriorating. Their morality and economics faltered and their vital internal forces diminished.

A friend once described the circumstance by an old axiom that God takes from you those things that are most important but that you do not fully value. I agreed with him in one sense that the process of deterioration was often like a slow cancer because it did not have specific issues that were often worthy of great battles, and therefore, enthusiasm slowly drained. However, I disagreed with him on the quotation that God took these valuable things. It was the absence of the presence of God, or the dominant philosophy of conscience, that often built a great civilization and as that set of ideas retreated and were lost, the strength of the society went with them. One has but to read the great books of history, particularly the key observations in Alexis de Toqueville's *Democracy in America,* to appreciate how character brings goodness and how goodness reestablishes character.

The best way to explain this is that a strong society has a strategy of value-based concepts. If they deteriorate it changes the operational structure of the society, which loses the power of character that drives and guides it. The tactics become increasingly of convenience of how business gets done. Rather than strategic goals of recognizing moral hazard, you digress to techniques of compromise and corruption or political intimidation usually with more regulation to replace the peer pressure of integrity being lost in the culture.

Thus freedom is critical to understand in the context of political, economic, and cultural liberties. Slavery was the worst example of an abuse of human dignity that existed or exists for it is an absolute lack of freedom. We understand slavery in the concept of individuals. But we really do not appreciate slavery as effectively in the concept of economics. Debt, and the moral obligation it gives, is a form of slavery that is often not seen. Slavery is the absence of freedom in many ways and debt or restrictions on opportunity that are provided by a lack of the ability to succeed are oftentimes simply another form. To pass debt to our children or have their economic conditions shattered by default is putting them in economic bondage. There are reasons for debt, but they must be productive ones.

Economic imbalances within societies often result from the lack of capital available to the middle and lower economic classes. The ability to finance, or use debt, is absolutely essential for them to have the opportunity to move higher in life. The concepts of microfinance of Southeast Asia are a perfect example in modern times as well as the home equity loans that generated small business in the United States. But as we have seen as debt goes to the extreme, problems emerge.

This becomes vital in government. When we give more and more power to government and require it to borrow to support rather than paying our due for our generation, we put incredible burdens upon and deprive freedom from the generations that follow us. So freedom is not only a political concept.

Political correctness is not the power of culture but is the influence of "society" or those that believe they know better than others what should be done and why. The power of the elite within any society often deprives the cultural freedom of those below because the elite have the power to establish it. That may be good if the elite, as Confucius noted of government officials, operate with the morality seen as examples to the people as a whole. But that cultural power of celebrity is not beneficial nor does it give freedom of cultural opinion if it is used for the purpose of individual interest and not for the people as a whole. Character, integrity, the common good, and conscience are fairly good values markers that bring harmony and unify society. Much of current celebrity does not celebrate them but far different lifestyles.

Thus, the fundamental concept of politics is how you balance big government versus small government with the rights of the individual being the focus. I would venture to say that the proper concept for this is not necessarily many of the approaches we normally take, such as saying civil rights or legal standing is the determinant. Freedom is a far larger issue than that and with the individual I think it is more properly termed personal dignity. You can have rights, but if you are not respected and the culture looks down on you, they are of little real benefit.

This was apparent in the racial problems in the United States over the last century. Civil rights acts gave political rights, but this was a very different concept than the personal dignity that was needed. That is a cultural power not a political power. Personal dignity also reflects an economic component since men care about the quality of their lives and about the quality of their family's life and future.

In judging the level of personal dignity in a society, we must see how minorities are treated. But a key judgment, because of the core family's values setting the tone, is the position of women. The level of rights and respect they receive culturally is related to the opportunity they have economically and their rights politically.

So the three great powers of economics, politics, and culture—all are a critical part of the concept of freedom and personal dignity. The change that takes place in a society is balanced against the status quo created by its history and existing culture. How those changes affect the existing concepts of personal dignity often determine the stability of the society. If change is too dramatic, or not dramatic enough depending on the circumstances, you have revolution and a change in the system. So personal dignity and how one perceives freedom in that society at that time may well determine the individual's perception of acceptable "freedom."

These are personal decisions that often revert to our conscience and by that affect the action or inaction of the people as a whole. While Machiavelli wrote *The Prince* to try to regain influence with the Medici's, it should be noted that the Medici's, through Giovanni, one of the dynasty's early founders, understood that you must look to the power of people because they and their action or inaction ultimately determine what occurs.

One thing to always remember in life is that there will be failures and successes if you lead an active life with a leadership temperament. Take failures with regret, but always learn from them. The experience should refine you. John Locke noted, "All men are liable to error, and most men are, in many points, by passion or interest, under temptation." Realize no one is perfect. Learn to correct and minimize the failures. Recognize them in others, not as personalized, but as the greed, arrogance, envy, or evil that may be at the root of their actions. You will think more clearly and plan more strategically when you do so. Life is a temptation of convenience over conscience, and convenience is a powerful and shrewd adversary.

Remember that many blame whoever is in office for the problems and see the solution as voting them out or changing government. However, political leaders are symptoms, not causes of the problems. We normally vote on short-term convenient economic issues, political preferences, or prejudices as consultants divide us, or on very narrow focused cultural issues. We should be sensible enough to choose on longer-term issues of the future. We tell ourselves we are doing so, but our subconscious knows that even the compromised solutions that do move decisions forward are seldom that wise in the long run. We have lost our instincts, warning us of the moral hazard of "too good to be true" options and rejected leaders who spoke the truth to us—to the degree many do not run for office or if they do, fear speaking truth.

We will not find success in a political messiah for we are too divided among ourselves. We will only find a true path by examining ourselves and reinventing what is truly important within us as a society. That takes time to repair economic and political damage and to restore values, and full success will take a generation learning lessons that will only be taught by crisis. The MAP Equivalent for changing culture will be discussed in the later Tao of the Triangles of Enlightened Conservatism.

The need for a solution to both effective budgeting and national will cannot be explained more succinctly than this final draft that dramatically shows the huge rise in U.S. debt as a percentage of GDP. The federal deficit expansions are now simply replacing the private expansion of debt, and as they are limited, deleveraging will occur with very substantial economic consequences as was indicated in the Fisher theories.

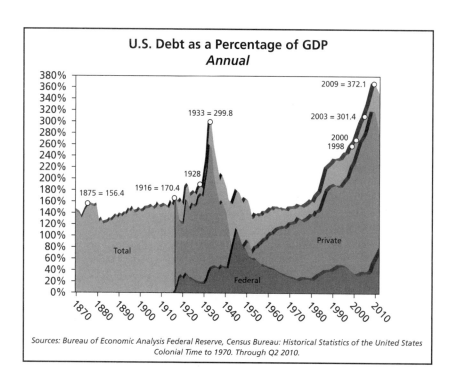

THE SECOND ISSUE:
A GROWTH-BASED ECONOMIC POLICY WITH INNOVATION

The problem government often has is that the political sector looks at immediate result due to the short election cycles while real change requires longer-term known and certain conditions to generate actions. Confidence is essential and uncertainty is its greatest enemy. There are innumerable concepts of Keynesian industrial policy or central economic planning. They have some benefits particularly in areas where the private sector is not appropriate. However, there is a great deal to be said for market capitalism provided appropriate safeguards are built in to keep integrity within the process. When motivations become solely greed with little concern for conscience regarding long-term strength of the company and country, then the system inevitably suffers. This is why governance is so absolutely critical in any expanding free enterprise system. The leadership has to maintain an appropriate level of integrity and responsibility. So the culture of institutions becomes the most critical part of their success over longer periods of time. If the cultures are such that responsibility is removed, then the entire decision process is warped.

(The Texas Model as a Case Study)

"The best description one might give the Texas Lyceum concept is that it is an idea in evolution about a state in transition. It is many things to many different people, but they are all attracted by a common tie: their belief that Texas is a unique place and that it has the opportunity at this particular moment to play a major role in the evolution of American society. Under the Lyceum umbrella, the leaders of each segment of our state's society have come together in an effort to look to the future, to learn from each other, and to work toward a greater Texas."

— Tieman H. Dippel, Jr.
Texas Lyceum Association
Chairman's Foreword, 1981

Over the last thirty-five years, I have had the opportunity to experience the dramatic change in Texas from a state dependent on oil and gas, cattle, and agriculture to one much more driven by technology, trade, and a creative business climate.

Richard Fisher, President of the Federal Reserve Bank of Dallas, gave an interview to *The Wall Street Journal* in June of 2011, focusing on what many magazines have called "The Texas Economic Miracle." He noted that some 37% of all new American jobs since the recovery began were created in Texas. Texas was also among the few states that are home to more jobs than when the recession began in December of 2007. The Texas economic model is quite different from the one in Washington and in many ways is very appropriate to the current economic situation.

All states operate under the same federal regulation and monetary conditions. This fact makes it worthwhile to understand why some states are performing far better in the current environment, which is more likely to be the environment of the future than others. As President Fisher pointed out, "Texas stands out for its free market and business friendly climate. Since human and investment capital is quite mobile, it migrates constantly to places where the opportunities are larger and the burdens are lower. The fact that Texas does not have a state income tax and its regulatory conditions are constrained is balanced with the fact it is fiscally responsible and its state government is relatively small. It is very open to trade and competition and competes as a right to work state."

Mr. Fisher also noted that one of Texas' significant competitive advantages was its ongoing reform of the tort system, as well as a conservative lending approach that required equity following the problems of the S&L debacle of years before. I believe that this Texas environment is a set of conditions that are driven by a culture that is quite different from the other major states.

While this observation comes from the economic perspective and others look at the Texas Model politically, I would venture that the true distinction in the Texas Cultural Model is its reliance of values that look to meritocracy, individual responsibility, desire for opportunity, and dignity that restrains government. Texas' lack of state support programs politically reinforces this self-reliance.

We have had political leaders who tried to reform the state to the Midwest Industrial Model of government support. The most effective advocate was my friend, Governor Ann Richards, with whom I often argued these points. She was a very capable and articulate advocate of change, but the character of Texas culture eventually dominated.

This is not to say the political leadership and legislators of Texas have not added greatly to this climate with their policy issues in areas such as tort reform, lessened regulation, and moral hazard concerns. But in part this ability to make such policy approaches and implement them comes from the support of the culture of the populous and its desire for responsibility. Vision is necessary to lead, but the will to support sacrifice and responsibility as well as accountability comes from the people as a whole.

One of the necessary formulas of capitalism is Schumpeter's theory of creative destruction. It demonstrates how companies innovate, grow rapidly, mature, and decline to be replaced by an innovation. Growth, innovation, jobs, and the middle class are well explained in that formula if you develop the connections.

During the agricultural revolution most everyone was a farmer—today 3% of Americans are. This era was replaced by the industrial revolution where innovation, or new value creation, produced a higher standard of living. We then moved to the post industrial revolution where today in America only perhaps 16% of our workforce is in manufacturing. We have now moved to the information revolution or the cyber era.

The financial decline has been severe but is partially the result of companies using it as a reason to force labor reductions that technology had been obsolescing for years. Many of the jobs lost were not cyclical but structural as we have noted and the resulting unemployment holds wages low and greatly impacts the middle class. Our economy is often valued in market pricing. A better way of looking at it is through the intrinsic worth of value creation, which leads to expansion and job creation, competitive wages, and a strengthened middle class. If there is wealth creation in an economy it requires service providers and that is where you find new jobs rather than trying to reclaim old ones that create no real value.

There are many ways of wealth creation, but the two most significant are normally the value of scale as businesses get bigger and more efficient, often with technology that is less favorable to job creation than innovation, which often can have smaller companies that create wealth and more jobs as they grow. Technology in innovation creates jobs by often creating efficiencies in larger operations that may in ways replace the need for certain jobs, so education at higher levels becomes increasingly important since it drives the level of the technology and innovation.

Government too often does not realize this distinction in its policies. Government runs its business by balance sheet accounting rather than cash flow maximization, which can reduce the need for capital and debt. It is lack of appreciation of the climate or environment necessary to incentivize innovation or wealth creation that drives it offshore and penalizes our middle class. Investment is necessary for innovation.

Strong economies have several driving characteristics. Innovation is like a racehorse with one set of characteristics—productivity increase is the workhorse. Productivity comes from more capital investment where machines reduce human burdens and increase output (often at the cost of jobs). This favors competition because it lowers costs. Standards of living often rise or fall with this growth in productivity. Education, innovation, and capital investment are all components of it. Recognizing it as a goal is a critical issue. We need to see productivity as a way to be more efficient and as a goal for creating new jobs. If we create a machine to replace a worker, do we generate a worker manufacturing the new machine to replace the former—with both making more because more is produced? What we have done recently is fashioned an investment climate that manufactures this new machine elsewhere.

Our ownership institutions have benefited with their limited employees—who have often done very well—but we have tried to help the displaced worker by subsidy, not by revamping the creative system. Our focus should be on using the principles of capitalism not forgetting them. The cause of our problem is not capitalism. It is a lack of control of the greed and fraud that have replaced self-interest, combined with a failure to see which actions support productivity in government policy and which worsen it. Often well-intentioned, compassionate acts have negative consequences in moral hazard if we do not use wisdom in crafting solutions.

The future will have many innovation arenas requiring much higher-level education, but also a service workforce to sell and adapt them. Apple is the ideal example from the iPod, to the iPhone, to the iPad. It is not the product that now creates jobs as much as sales and the creation of applications. There will be huge new fields in biotechnology and healthcare, including a greater understanding of how the brain thinks, which in itself will create marketing industries. Our venture capital company once invested in an early space technology company and the future opportunities for commercialization are immense. From nanotechnology, to the many new expansions of the cyber world and its virtual reality escapes, to the environmental necessities we must develop, the world had opportunities.

Just as energy in oil and gas was declining and the tracking method of increased production opened huge new opportunities and jobs, there will be advancement. The issue is where the necessary investment will be and by whom and how it is incentivized. Government has been a poor decision maker but can be a helpful catalyst for the private sector; the critical issue is the integrity of the effort. The Texas culture/economic/political model has its problems, but it is the most competitive model to accomplish these ends.

The Model has significant benefits, but also must address its problems. So it becomes lost in the argument of political extremes where truth is not found in the middle ground of discussion but is a casualty of the loss of wisdom of logical process. The Texas Cultural Model is, or was before modern transition, easier to define. With its proximity to the frontier and Texas Republic, the culture understood the necessity for deferred gratification and investment for growth as opposed to the demand creation driven materialism of consumption. This caused the political thought to be not entitlement from the government but independence from it since it was realized that debt of government was eventually personal debt indirectly. And debt is a burden on liberty, opportunity, and unity. Economically this both limited government interference and promoted investment in balance with consumption. The Golden Rule brought fairness even if subconscious in discussion.

To understand the Texas Model, it is best to look not just at its economic effects, but the underpinnings that create its politics and economics. Those cultural values are far more unifying for the future than the economic interest of rich versus poor or the political right versus left. The approach we must take is a new way of thinking about the economy and government that is more efficiency and ethically based to refine the Texas cultural model. The best way to describe the approach might be to give the example of financial statements and the normal ratios like debt coverage that are broadly used. We often accept them without thought because of the formality of presentation and the fact that they are often the best structured information available. But they have many flaws. Frequently assets are at cost not market, goodwill does not spend like cash, LIFO and other accounting methods effect valuations; patents, brands, and intellectual property may not be included.

The systems are adequate for some purposes and market valuations may fluctuate in relation to them. However, over the long term the market price is different from the core intrinsic value of an entity, and it is better in the long run to think in those terms when making decisions. If you take the same statements and recast their components to give free cash flow that can be withdrawn from the business, it often gives a very different appearance. Intrinsic value is the net present value of that cash flow. But that requires some certainty of future business, inflation, and taxes so the necessity of a broadly accepted view of the future is necessary. Government has to minimize uncertainty or no real action takes place on this method. It is why there is limited investment in the decline since this analysis is more common in investment decisions.

When innovation is applied to the economy in this way, research and development as well as the necessary education levels are key. The same new approaches must be used there. Education, even in university research, resembles a solution, but if it is not market driven but professor interest related, it is often wasted. There are many ways to get accountability in government and education. The issue is the will and the politics. It is why the concepts of ethical governance are where you have to start, not just in token compliance but also in transparent culture. Any new way of thinking needs its origin and grounding there.

Since competitiveness and innovation in a modern competitive world depend a great deal on education, reestablishing the middle class and providing opportunity are intricately related to successful and affordable education. America's educational systems are equal to the world's best at the very highest levels, but have deteriorated at lower levels significantly. Educational reform, particularly for efficiency and affordability, and curriculum for relevant economic talent skills is broadly recognized.

Almost thirty years ago, I chaired Texans For Quality Education, Inc., and a nonprofit that reviewed a series of Texas educational reforms. It was amazing how many interest groups and perspectives differed. One fundamental difference related to the battle between equity in spending and excellence. Affluent school districts or class one universities wanted focus on excellence whereas poorer districts and schools wanted support for more balance.

In *The Language of Conscience Evolution* we explored the necessity of having both to be economically competitive and that decisions ought to be based on transformational result analysis rather than political ideology. In the thirty years since that time little has fundamentally changed except changes on the edges even though reforms have been tried. The system often "reforms" reforms.

One of the most criticized issues of current education is that colleges need to tie curriculum to jobs. Many graduates do not have needed skills even though they have sophisticated degrees. Junior colleges and technical colleges have much to offer and need additional support in filling needs for the marketplace. Tom Pauken, the Chairman of the Texas Workforce Commission, has made one of his top priorities to help match jobs and education. With shrinking benefit this is difficult, but one of the most difficult jobs he has had is to get students to look at alternatives. For manufacturing to return to the U.S., skilled workers will have to be available.

The contextual cross currents of our present state of self-gratification and the pursuit of excellence are often missed. Excellence is the focus on detail and perfection that comes from discipline and practice. Innovation in a society is thus related to its pursuit of excellence. Immediate gratification whether by social networks, games, or our educational rationalization that all kids must be winners and thereby little benefit in striving for excellence, set a tone to the culture.

Our children and young adults have less patience for excellence. They become more self-centered because they lack the experience of working out difficult problems or relationships. Being told you are a genius does not make you one, and in the real world sports proves that bigger and faster are real, competitive terms. It also shows that being smarter often means understanding what to do and doing it—a practice that leads to excellence and exceptionalism. We do our children no benefit, nor our culture, in failing to recognize reality. There are intelligent and thoughtful ways to do so, and it begins with a commitment not to let our current culture shape their temperament through narcissism.

For the Texas Model, education is key because free enterprise does not work without it. Schumpeter's model of creative destruction makes the economy advance and to be a part of it you need to lead in the new models of growth—frequently technology or systems. In Texas one of several organizations that have been active with education is the Texas Association of Business. Its President, Bill Hammond, notes that by 2018, the Business Roundtable estimates that 63% of new or replacement jobs in the United States will require at least some college education, while 45% will require at least a bachelor's degree. He notes that today just over 30% of Texans aged 25 to 34 hold an Associate's degree or higher.

The Texas Association of Business holds forums (often in past years with the Texas Lyceum) on education issues. Their most recent one, as noted in their Texas Business Report (volume 26, Issue 10, October 2011), concentrates on the necessity of recognizing that school systems are incentivized based on the number of students in class, not on the success of those students. The graduation rates and time for completion are shocking, particularly for minorities.

There is much to reform, but the correct starting point is an objective analysis of outcomes with recognition this has great impact on our future economy affecting government funding. A shortage of workers will increase the need for immigration in the future because of demographics, but the need will be for skilled workers, so to build a middle class education is vital. However, it must be reformed not only to reduce cost and provide efficiency, but also for a greater external concentration of job creators to anticipate needed skills.

The greatest risk to any company or economy is strategic risk, particularly where technological obsolescence and globalization greatly maximize the talent risk, which results in the workforce becoming uncompetitive in the new environment. It involves at its essence the issue of temperament and how society views risk. If individual responsibility dominates the workforce itself and looks to improve talent to compete, government and private support may be necessary for temporary readjustment and compassion. But if it does nothing to incentivize increasing talent by training, it leads to dependency, which ultimately is negative for the individual opportunity and societal competitive. The Texas Model's flaw is that it needs to look at education and retraining in different ways. However, its fundamentals regard individual responsibility as the necessary driving factor. Strategic risk is ultimately systemic risk in this case.

Looking at the decline of our middle class, a good part of the stagnation is from technology and globalization. Similar to Europe, another big factor is the decline in social mobility and part of that comes from our welfare model. Families do not appreciate the necessity of thrift or self-reliance if they know government will take care of retirement, health, and other problems. The nature of character in society changes.

Texas as a culture began not by those fleeing to the edge of society, but by man wanting to create empires. That culture has absorbed and has been a magnet in its history for those wanting opportunity and willing to work for it. There is not a Texas Economic Miracle or a Texas Political Vision—there is the Texas Third Coast of Thought, which is a powerful cultural model that drives the other two from the bottom up.

In this, government has a place as a catalyst and educational visionary that needs to be present for support—not to dominate.

Part of Texas' growth in current times has to be credited to the fact that oil and gas has become more valuable and Texas has it as a major resource and significant employer. The fact that healthcare and trade with major cities like Houston benefiting from its Medical Center and Port have given it unique boosts as well. But what must be appreciated is that while there have been many natural considerations accounting for a part of Texas' unique situation (including the land retention when it joined the United States as an independent nation and thereby the benefits of the oil under the land for its educational systems) it has served to develop its resources. The oil and gas business is international.

The great service companies that have developed the techniques and pushed forth the technology are in many cases driving Texas. The openness to trade in the expansion of the Port and the commitment to research and development and education has helped build the medical centers. While it has the highest percentage of uninsured, if it can have the growth, those are problems that are more easily solved as part of a sustainable system. Any nation or state becomes a captive of its economic power because those resources limit its political opportunities. So economic growth, if it can be maintained, provides a base for solving many of the other problems.

The Language of Conscience Evolution covers that evolution over the last thirty years. One catalyst was Dr. George Kozmetsky's work and his institute, IC2 that brought innovative ideas with the importance of technology clusters to growth to Texas in the 1960s. The Texas Lyceum in 1980 has continued over thirty years with public conferences and quarterly meetings to look at public policy issues and how they relate particularly in economic development. The Chambers of Commerce heavily supported it, and one significant point occurred in 1986 at a beginning low point of the very severe Texas recession.

Texas depended largely upon Mexican trade, oil and gas, and agriculture as the three legs of an economic stool with real estate being a significant economic generator. In the late 1980s and early 1990s, the state looked evermore clearly at what had to be done to evolve. A very good foundation had been laid over the last years. Technology companies had been recruited in Texas particularly in Austin and Dallas. The Houston Area Research Council that served as one of the sponsors of the Lyceum united government, education, and private sectors.

In 1986 at the Sesquicentennial of the Battle of San Jacinto, I visited with Speaker Gib Lewis. We talked about how the state could help promote an economic recovery. Out of those conversations, the Speaker's Economic Development Committee was formed. We brought together a number of thinkers that resulted in several bills looking at strategic planning and the equivalent of the Texas Department of Commerce. While these efforts helped centralize activities and make them more efficient, one of the key observations since then is how relatively ineffective government efforts are compared to private sector efforts, and how critical it is for government to help prepare opportunities for the private sector.

If we learned lessons from the process, it is that government has a part to play, but it should be supportive in coordinating private sector growth more than trying to provide the growth itself. That cultural belief is what has dominated much of the Texas philosophy. Each of the considerations that President Fisher mentioned comes from a cultural observation that a smaller, well-defined government, protecting against excesses but encouraging growth and investment serves the state best in the long run.

The Texas Model is not the extremely successful one that some promote because it has additional benefits beyond some states, and it has some weaknesses where it has had omissions. However, it is a far more competitive model, and one that can more effectively assist the development of a middle class than other models competing with it. It is thus the best one to choose as America and other countries move forward in the world. But it needs to be improved by enlightening where targeted investments in education, health, research, and infrastructure can substantially enhance its competitive advantage. It is the best example of an economy driven by conservatism that could be enhanced further by a more enlightened conservatism, as it is more fully understood. It is important to understand why that model fits so well in the current international environment.

The Significance of Growth

In *The Language of Conscience,* there is a presentation that I made to the Texas Legislature on the importance of the Arts and their relation to economics. It primarily focused on the fact that quality of life needs to include the essence of the Arts, and quality of life is, in many cases, driven by whether one has a job and how good a job it is. To reach levels of sophistication most important to the elite of a society and for there to be sustainability according to Maslow's Hierarchy of Needs, you need to have growth within society that is relatively equally spread because of opportunity and merit. As we discussed in Horace Busby's perspective of how America changed, the middle class becomes increasingly important. It was the source that gave strength to the essence of our democracy because of its broader fairness and because it gave them the purchasing power that allowed stability to grow. Solid economics promotes marriage and family and affects culture.

In modern times, globalization is a reality and the leveling of the world economically has slowly but surely had an impact on the American middle class and on the three powers—culture, economics, and politics.

The impact of globalization really began with the United States' union with Canada and Mexico through NAFTA and many of the free trade agreements made individually with countries as well as the expansion of the World Trade Organization. This new globalization has had very difficult effects on much of the middle class because of the loss of manufacturing jobs in the U.S. It is in large part a necessity due to global competition. Most of the benefit of the arguments was lowering other countries tariffs to our goods since the U.S. has normally had a very open market. Ultimate growth occurs when the rest of the world gets to a level of income that produces many more consumers for everyone's products.

The concept of globalization and the issues involved are discussed in more detail in other books of *The Language of Conscience Evolution.* However, one key point always needs to be foremost in your mind. The specialization of labor and its ability to reduce costs is the core of why you have trade. Whether it is internal commerce or international trade, the same natural laws apply. For example, let's take the manufacturing of a belt. In olden days there was a leather artisan that spent a significant amount of time making a belt. It was much more costly at that time because he had to exist and could not make many belts because of the time involved. Once mass production became a reality, the mass production dramatically lowered the cost per belt. But what also happened is that once the price of the belt dropped from $20 to $5, more people could afford belts, and everyone's standard of living improved.

Perhaps the artisan who was no longer competitive lost, but overall more people had belts and could afford more things for their children than before. By building supply chains that concentrated on this cost principle, major companies like Walmart have significantly reduced the cost of goods. *This brings up a critical point. What actually determines your standard of living is not how much money you make in nominal dollar amounts, but instead what you can buy with the money that you make.*

To give an example—if you look at home prices in the United States particularly at the real estate peak, you will find average homes in San Francisco sold for around $800,000, in Boston for around $400,000, and in Houston for around $150,000. After the recession in San Francisco houses sold for around $400,000, in Boston for around $300,000, and in Houston for around $139,000. Regardless of the salary you make, the real question for the middle class is what they can buy with that money.

So, many of the current solutions, like forcing China to revalue the Yuan, which may also be in the best interest of the Chinese because of inflation, have consequences that need to be understood. If we make Chinese goods more expensive by forcing currency adjustments, we may make more positive opportunities for American jobs. At the same time, we may also increase the costs of those products because they will be more expensive and affect the standard of living of the middle class. If Walmart prices go up 15% as a consequence, one problem is eased but another created. This is when we must think out of the normal box. There are significant trade-offs that are not fully appreciated in short-term emotional solutions.

This fact makes it necessary to understand the difference between longer-term structural changes in an economic system and short-term adjustments for cycles. The current American recession is significant in bringing the concept of careful planning for future growth to the forefront. This has been the worst recession since the Great Depression. It has also been a very different recession because it was not caused by inventory adjustments or the Federal Reserve increasing interest rates to limit inflation.

It was caused by a significant "heart attack" within the financial system. That will make recovery slower and more difficult than anyone expects because while industry is the muscle, the financial system is the blood that carries its oxygen and energy. The business cycle will show normal improvement, but the lessening of the use of leverage will challenge business models and consumption. While there have been many programs to restore the financial industry, many of the causes of the decline have been ignored.

There are many explanations, but the points that I find most reasonable look at the natural effects of America's growing affluence and how the strong dollar as the premier international currency allowed us to a do a number of things that did not fit with natural financial and economic laws. We were much like a man jumping from a plane. He normally would go down very quickly. But if he had a parachute that assisted him, his decent was very gradual and did not seem dangerous.

America has been on an increasing leverage strategy through much of this period. It began very positively with what Horace Busby noted in the desires for every American to become a part of the capitalistic system by owning their home and other assets. The real success in life comes from having your net worth work for you, particularly in retirement, rather than constantly having to work for a paycheck. So whatever net worth and capital can be gained, even in small amounts, is usually very relative because of the differing levels of people's lifestyles.

In America we have increasingly looked to debt to help us establish growth and ever higher proportions thereof. This is a sound concept if the money is spent for the right reasons. If money goes to the expansion of a business, if it goes to the creation of infrastructure, or if it is spent in education that is effective in improving the talents and values of workers, then this leverage is an extremely important benefit. One reason that America's middle class has had such a high standard of living has been the amount of investment in technology allowing the mass production that could make goods more cheaply.

At one point at the inception of NAFTA there were different estimates, but an estimated disparity might have been $60,000 invested in the equipment to support an American job while it was perhaps $5,000 in Mexico and $3,000 in China. An American worker had the productivity of many Mexican or Chinese workers. While these figures may not be exact, what drove America was a very significant amount of investment in job creating infrastructure and technology. This investment let us move to a service economy and still be supported by manufacturing and agriculture. It also resulted from the U.S. being the most innovative country in the world in generating new products and jobs.

This technology, often helped by constructive debt, is what has replaced a number of middle class jobs. Now robots in assembly lines can do the work that used to be handled by experienced workmen and higher-level managers supervise the robots. So technology has eliminated a great number of jobs and that is both good and bad. It has had the effect of creating more higher-paying jobs for those well qualified, while limiting the opportunities for many that are not as qualified in the current environment. Large numbers of middle level management were no longer needed as computer programs let data concentrate management.

So, as we have seen from income tax payment data, these changes have resulted in a growing disparity in wealth. Even though there has been substantial growth, it has been unequal. And we also have to realize that it is a natural law that what you make is usually directly related to the value that you provide. An innovative economy is the best way to create value, and an innovative economy is one with more risk, which requires incentive.

While not as obvious in the short term, in the long run when you go through a difficult recession such as the one we have had, it makes these decisions of wants versus needs and of size and efficiencies much more focused. The results have been a substantial amount of the layoffs, and many of these jobs will not return due to structural changes and the obsolescence of expertise. We have done a poor job in our educational systems in focusing on the needs of a competitive economy instead of the wants of its social priorities. We have great research universities but the commercialization of that research to benefit the middle class has been lacking.

Conceptually, America should have always been growing and creating new jobs through its educational system and the opportunities provided each new generation, and in retraining existing generations giving them valuable skills that let them move up the chain. Instead, the educational system has in many ways failed to address reality and governmental policy.

In an effort to make adjustments, it has in many ways impacted corporate decisions for growth. Growth takes policies working in context with reality, and we have had significant policy failures. We tax our corporate income harshly and make repatriation of corporate foreign income onerous, so you could expect corporations to invest those funds abroad, costing our workers the technology investment advantage.

To take an example from interrelationships, we need only look where many mutual fund managers are beginning to find investment opportunity. The money to create jobs is now being invested globally. To not do so means that their performance would be less, and they would not be able to acquire the money of many Americans that invest in them because of this performance. In the past, the major places of investment were the United States and Canada, but movement today is more in areas like Hong Kong that have the impact on China's growth as well as other Asian and Pacific countries.

If you look at the funds going into Brazilian, Canadian, Indian, and other stocks, some countries are even attempting to limit the amount of investment therein. This is the money that creates jobs and that gives an advantage. Mexico's policies versus China's in the 1990s are a prime example. China wanted plants. Mexican companies just sold their stock. One was more productive than the other. Privatizations to only one buyer, as often happened, did not create competition. The secret is in production.

Software and services are more where America has moved in the higher chain of performance. But to rebuild middle class manufacturing competitiveness, you need significant investment to leverage human work. Much of the equivalent work will be data input, which requires thought for execution. When we no longer make America competitive on one side, it is not at all surprising that America's other side, its investment and ownership philosophies, move out of necessity.

Each era has a product or idea that stimulates growth—computers and the Internet are examples. The new one is thought to be Green Energy, but much of this is government subsidy driven, which will affect its sustainability in difficult budget times. We have to return to research and the commercialization of it. China has many times our number of engineers and physicists that are very good. America understands commercialization and markets. We need to find ways to benefit jointly more than compete.

Globalization had a significant effect in moving jobs abroad. Today China, as the dominant economy, is blamed. But quite frankly, China has simply picked up many of the jobs that were previously placed in Mexico or in

Eastern Europe. America was losing many of those jobs because of the cost of U.S. labor and the pressure on corporations to reduce their costs that in many cases forced relocations or business failures in much of the Midwest. It has to be remembered that even though most corporations are now international and corporatist, they are still driven by their bottom line. This bottom line looks at return on investment that includes tax policy, regulatory costs, benefit costs such as health care, and a host of other considerations. They move out of competitive necessity because their competition is often international.

At one point the major corporations of the world in value were heavily American and European. Current lists show a much broader range with major industrial leaders throughout the world. This makes an insular American policy inappropriate if we truly want to consider future generations and necessity growth. We can impact some of the effects on the American population in the short term by protectionism and changes in tax laws, but in doing so we are simply adding the parachute to a decline.

The much smarter move is to figure out how to stay in the plane and build it to go to much higher altitudes. That requires an entirely different way of looking at issues and how they ultimately will affect you. There is little doubt that eventually the United States will have tax reform, the question will be its design and the effectiveness of spending reforms.

The greatest problem is that in many ways we have become less competitive now because investment that used to be in America to help produce the leverage on work is now primarily going to other countries in the world—China, Mexico, Brazil, India, and Eastern Europe. Those investment dollars create much more economic opportunity there. Yet at the same time they allow American companies to be able to compete, and they do generate higher paying jobs and senior management positions in the United States.

Many of these companies are American-based and would prefer to have the jobs in the United States because it is simpler for them than trying to repatriate profits, but many of our policies over the years have been less capital friendly. This is not to say that we do not have a great amount of waste in what the government allows in special benefits to corporatist America. The problem is that the policies were often designed to help individual companies and in many ways give them benefits, but they were not necessarily focused on what did the most good for the overall American population, particularly the middle class.

The lobby and special interests in Washington have very carefully taken care of corporatist America, but policies that help big business need to also be policies that provide incentives for them to do business in America. Bills that want to tax them for taking their jobs abroad are quite counterproductive. The type of bill that should be focused on is how to encourage bringing money back to the United States to create the jobs here and incentivize them to do so. Corporate tax reform that removes subsidies and truly lowers rates would be a very positive solution. America has one of the highest corporate tax rates in the world to help fund many of its governmental programs. That alone is a disincentive.

Also of significant impact are the heavy levels of regulation that will be directly enhanced with many of the regulatory efforts in the new health care and financial legislation. The issue is American competitiveness because the world is one in which you must win not just hope, and that usually comes from a strategy when the rest of the world is focusing on growth.

China is seeing rising labor costs and huge dollar receipts, so it is increasing investments abroad. We need to encourage this repatriation of investment into the United States. Just like the imbalances after the oil increases of the 1970s, money needs to flow both ways. The Chinese will become very major investors in the U.S. in part because they want assets and not paper dollars. This can be a win–win for all concerned. In 2010 this process began to accelerate.

For many years, as President of the Texas State Chamber of Commerce and later as Chairman of the International Committee of the Texas Association of Business, I hosted trade delegations. In recent years I have worked with the Houston Partnership, which has a very well researched strategic plan that understands the significance of China and the new Panama Canal to Texas, as well as the County Judge of Bexar County who has been very innovative at bringing foreign investment and jobs to that region. The opportunities for expansive growth are there, what are lacking are catalysts that bridge cultural and economic differences with the government becoming more of a positive force.

The Importance of Investment:
Why It Is Needed and the Sources of Money

When I served as Texas Chamber of Commerce President, our main focus was economic development. We learned that you can recruit companies by paying them to come, or you can have economic development by creating an environment that has great education and training, fair laws and taxes, and thus a very strong culture. Companies that come for those values do not need to be greatly enticed, and also help preserve the culture.

This makes the current economic environment a cauldron of issues that have to be sorted out regarding what the organizing principle of America will be moving forward. But it is important to understand how the financial crisis evolved to appreciate the problems we face. It also explains why we will need foreign investment for expansion. As we discussed before, America up to the 1980s had used leverage and debt very effectively and government had the benefit of a substantially growing gross national product so that many of its actions were aided by the benefit of growth.

Once the squeeze began to hit the American family, you had a cultural change—rather than the wife staying at home with the children, the wives went to work to provide more income for the family. This had an effective cultural change seen in the perspectives of Generation X and Generation Y. It also encouraged the use of debt. The tighter economics of families affected the timing of marriage and thoughts on the number of children.

America generated its growth with ever larger leverage because small profits within the financial system could be leveraged by debt to much higher rates of return. The capital ratios of many of the largest financial institutions were far less than they had been historically. This was based on the concept that they understood risk in a much more sophisticated manner and the regulators' false concept that they would never operate with levels of risk that would endanger the company. The problem is that incentive structures rewarded management much more on performance judged in the short term. They considered far less the implications for the longer term and the levels of risk since it was often with other people's money—pension funds, insurance companies, and individuals. While these may seem institutional, they are really each of us since they serve us individually as investment vehicles.

These incentive programs with the legal system that removed much risk if you simply disclosed it are different from the more substantial systems of Europe that often required a more ethical full disclosure. And they allowed for a perfect storm to occur. Corporate governance focused more on technical compliance with "best practices" than on ethical cultural principles. It involved a decline in the concept of responsibility and accountability.

A good part of this financial storm came from a belief that you did not have to look at the normal creditworthiness of loans that our community bank has always used. To us, you looked first at an individual's character, which was the most critical component of his creditworthiness. You then looked at his cash flow to see that he would be able to maintain the payments that were necessary with a reasonable reduction. And finally you looked at the collateral, so that in the worst case you would be able to foreclose. You usually had a significant down payment as a cushion.

When many of the banks failed in Texas in the savings and loan crisis, you particularly realized the significance of cash flow and the impact with real estate as collateral. Real estate usually tends to increase, and as long as it is increasing even a small amount, tends to hold value. But once it begins decreasing and the image and psychology change, it will often fall dramatically.

The same is often true of the stock market. It is the perception of future value that is given a net present value, and so dramatic changes in perception affect the price, which is often higher than true value. This matters because the perception is now quite different. Its dangers are appreciated, the institutions that made it available are gone or chastised, and there is a new paradigm going into place. Credit will not be as easy as it was, so new sources of credit will be important. To appreciate this we need to fully understand the mechanics of what happened to appreciate the nature of change.

Much of Wall Street finance and international finance looked at many of the mathematical models for risk and left the creditworthiness approach of judging loans on some mass items to concepts that would best be called quantitative theory or, more appropriately, default ratio analysis. This concept is not unlike an insurance actuary looking at a pool of people and determining premiums based upon life expectancies and thus probable loss.

The housing market became the biggest beneficiary of this concept. Housing prices had increased steadily over the years, and there was an assumption with price appreciation, inflation, and lower interest rates that housing prices would continue to rise, and that thus the collateral part of the analysis might be of more importance than the character and cash flow. The analysis looked at large pools of mortgages, which could be estimated historically for default ratios. In a pool, perhaps 5% of the mortgages might be expected to default, and there would be riskier tiers of maybe the next 10% to 15%.

But the cash flows of the entire pool—particularly of the 80% that would be assumed to have no risk of default—would be substantial. As long as the cash flows went to the higher tiers of less risk, they were well covered. Just the bottom, riskier tiers that were paid last, were perceived to be problems. Since houses were perceived to always increase, risk was judged as minimal.

These pools were then divided into strata with the riskier 5% usually getting a higher rate of return, the next segment with more risk getting a little less return, but many of the remaining 80% that would get cash flows first rated very high, often AAA by rating agencies. This default ratio analysis worked well for a period, and because of its success and the fact that Wall Street quickly moves to winners, amounts were dramatically expanded. It was aided in great part by governmental policy that pushed Fannie Mae and Freddie Mac and other government agencies to help less privileged people get homes.

This is not unlike the original positive concept in the early part of the decade as Horace Busby mentioned. However, there were two flaws. To produce more loans, Wall Street required little down payment and frequently did not look at cash flow creating financial instruments that may have benefited getting into a home, but often with adjustable rates and little down payment. And in many states a circumstance where there was not personal liability, you created instruments that had significant moral hazard.

In not looking at past credit history for character and not fully vetting for cash flow, many of these loans, particularly a number with fraud, were destined for failure. Packages of loans that had almost 100% financing, low rates, little personal liability, and low payments made it attractive to gamble, so even speculators bought homes. The long-term fixed rate mortgage route to home ownership had little in common with these financial hybrids. The shame or character aspect of previous times also left modern culture when people looked at walking on obligation freely accepted as an economic, not a moral decision.

These packaged loans often private label without government guarantees were bought throughout the economy and interestingly in much of the rest of the world where investors did not understand the background but gambled on American debt and America's image. The failure was devastating. But many other countries independently followed our model with their own form of housing finance. So much money went into housing because of the demand generated by easy finance that it led to substantial overbuilding and the natural laws of supply and demand quickly took place. This impacted valuations and for the first time home prices started falling, default ratios went far beyond expectations, and the reality of the situation dramatically impacted Wall Street and the international economy because it brought a flash of reality to perception.

The high leverage ratios were now a major factor in the failure or reorganization of many institutions because the credit markets seized as the temperament for risk changed dramatically. It should be noted that much of the government action and inaction did a tremendous amount to create this situation through both Republicans and Democrats and particularly the lobbies that included both. There were many opportunities at Fannie Mae and Freddie Mac for reform, as well as examination of the Community Reinvestment Act implications to risk, but they were quickly dismissed in Congress. This was a political moral hazard frailty, as well as an economic miscalculation of leverage and cultural submission to political and economic greed at many levels.

At its core, it was a cultural crisis caused by the creation of moral hazard and an excess of greed, fraud, and a complete lack of individual responsibility both in corporate governance and in individuals who looked at opportunities. They speculated on them, without a true appreciation of individual responsibility or risk. The bottom line here was not a great need of financial regulation because much regulation existed. It was the failure of will to aggressively use that regulation because of the political and the cultural environment that we Americans desired—wanting an ever greater life without recognizing the implications of the larger scale problems that existed.

These were not unknown issues. As community bankers, we saw many of these problems early and certainly never ventured into subprime loans even at a substantial cost competitively. It was a case of the government rewarding the taking of risk and often punishing the most conservative institutions competitively. The honest obey the letter of the law, the marginalizers do not care, and regulators too often ignore issues in good times. The marginalizers often take their money and leave the repercussions to fall on the honest and their customers.

The very nature of banking had a philosophical culture shift. Bankruptcy moved from a cultural shame to an economic tool. After the depression legislation had separated investment banking, which had a culture that looked to profits from commercial banking, which had a culture of focusing on the balance sheet. So once the new legislation let large banks combine both commercial and investment banking, you had all the assets bet behind a much more intense profit motivation. This changed the dynamics and the regulators were not focused on cultural change but compliance. Incentives drive action; cultures add the temperament to the size of those incentives permissible.

The foreclosure crisis that resulted from these massive failures and the "robot signings" in foreclosures that have not followed true legal procedures give a perfect example of the decisions we are going to have to make within a system. I thought particularly interesting one case reported by the media where an individual sued the bank because its foreclosure was ineffective, and he wanted to punish them for their attitude in taking his house.

However, it was noted that he had not made a payment in about eight years, and had refused to vacate the house. The bank may well be guilty and may deserve reprimand and some loss, but usually banks' losses are passed to shareholders, pension funds, or individuals that invested in them for their retirement plans. The doctrine of "clean hands" applies. If they fail, it may be taxpayers that pay, but it is often other more conservative banks and their shareholders that have to pay through the FDIC insurance guarantee charges.

For much of history the core object of the field of finance was the accurate judgment of risk, which allowed money making by the judgment of investments or interest rate. With recent investment banking, the culture changed as you focused on selling risk to others rather than maintaining it. Risk control was less important than camouflaging it or minimizing it for sale. Legality put focus on technical disclosure, not substantial representation. Community banks still do finance the old way having to make money by judging and retaining risk. It is not the financial process that changed as much as the culture, which removed the necessity of the judgment of risk, as risk was shared with ever diminishing responsibility for the integrity of the process.

The ultimate problem with Dodd Frank legislation is that it grouped all institutions together rather than addressing the moral hazard culturally. All the consumer regulations are compliance and the industry will simply find revenue sources elsewhere. The issue that was not addressed was the greed and lack of accountability, which were not a part of serious reform. Finance has to require substantial retention of risk in order to culturally force responsibility.

This is not to say that much of the corporatist aspects of America driven by lobbying of government are positive, fair, or should not be changed. We are attempting to use a political solution that is affected by special interest to redistribute income on a political framework. This often benefits the very people that take the risk rather than the responsibility and are supported in the times of failure. We need to make these decisions on a cultural framework of what is fair. There must be regulation that keeps people honest. Too often the Democratic Party looks at redistribution because of its base. Too often the Republican Party goes for business because it is looked at as being its base even though much of big business has very questionable problems of greed in the size of its salary remunerations.

We are thus with choices between two extremes when in reality the Democratic Party ought to be looking for economic justice because of its base and at how to create opportunity that more effectively makes America competitive. And the Republican Party ought to be looking more at how to police business and the market system with ethics that are peer generated in culture beyond compliance to avoid government regulation.

How we solve this crisis is absolutely critical to the coming generations because it will set the trend and stage as to whether we are going to look realistically at the problems we face or simply continue on down a path of inertia. When you have a big balance in the bank, writing excessive checks is not a big problem. When you have a very low balance, you rethink your priorities and eliminate wants while satisfying needs. America's margin for error had a big balance, which we have drained over the last several decades due to our affluence and our desire for immediate gratification.

This recession, and the slower growth that will likely follow, will begin a deleveraging of America that will change the nature of society and its values. Second mortgage loans or home equity loans for vacations will be seen at their true long-term cost. Temperament will be changed, which will begin the debates on political and economic issues such as deficits, debts, and taxes. But the key is an innovative faster-growing economy that requires a focus on the vital drivers of growth and unburdened by the weight of government.

Too often the focus is on what is wrong, particularly in government, rather than what government should do well to help the economy. It does have a place with visionary and effective investment in infrastructure, general research and development, value creating education, and in some ways as a catalyst of private investment through sound policy and regulation. We are at such an economic state that government will not be able to pull out of efforts. In reality we have already engrained them too much. How they act will be more the question than whether government is required to act. Government's recognition of moral hazard is the most critical issue because that relates to sustainability through its impact on culture.

One of the best descriptions of how economics and culture come together (and thereby the moral hazard of politics) is set forth in the consulting method of my friend Peter Strople and his "Instant Change" concepts. He notes you no longer have 20-year strategic plans when the average tenure of a CEO of a large corporation is four years. The national culture reinvents itself every three to five years with new values, expectations, customs, and behaviors reshaping lifestyles and commercial experiences. The Language of Conscience Triangles provides a guide to the riverbank as instant change helps navigate the fast river.

Peter believes that the most effective people require a different set of skills for effective and rapid decision making capabilities. While The Language of Conscience Triangles take this approach on a macro level, his writings focused on the micro or more focused skill set development. It primarily focuses upon the power value—adding relationships that facilitate instant change and theory validation. It focuses on "having a conversation with the right people right now to arrive at the right solutions for the right reasons."

What makes his approach fit so well with *The Language of Conscience* is the common factor of values-based motivation. It is the key to the macro approach of how the world works in contextual through and in the micro creation of relationships. Real relationships, as Peter calls them, "are about serving the needs of others out of a genuine sense of caring for their well being, offering whatever you have that they need without caring about payback." It is exactly the third level of culture where you work with compassion and service.

The two concepts of The Language of Conscience and Instant Change also agree that money is seldom the solution. Money is more infinite and generally available for practical situations, but time and wisdom are finite and harder to find. People admire those who are effective, lest they rely upon and make deals with those they know, trust, and like. It is why referrals, based on trust are so effective in today's environment.

Whether at a macro or micro level in a changing world, trust and respect are crucial to both relationships as is the ability to make a difference.

The relationship most in need of this trust and respect is government that must show it is deserving of trust and support. The best way is to have an organizing principle ruled by limiting moral hazard. For it is the moral hazard that makes government unsustainable and unfair, just like bad character and incompetence ruins business relationships personally.

THE THIRD ISSUE:
A UNIFIED CULTURE WITH COMMON VALUES OF RESPONSIBILITY

Let's place a high value on unity rather than uniformity.

—Dwight D. Eisenhower

We didn't all come over on the same ship, but we're all in the same boat.

—Bernard M. Baruch

An individual has not started living until he can rise above the narrow confines of his individualistic concerns to the broader concerns of all humanity.

—Martin Luther King, Jr.

The core of any effort to have an innovative growth-oriented economy and a smaller governmental intrusion into the lives of people rests with the culture of the people as we have discussed previously. Extremes of poverty and wealth normally show that there is not appropriate balance within the culture systemically and as the trends continue to separate the levels of rich and poor the society is pressed in all three areas of power. Solutions, however, go in several different directions. Redistribution is usually the simplest politically and often satisfies in the short term. But in the longer term, sustainability of growth argues for much more opportunity within the society, and in the modern technological world that is not easily done. It requires investment, quality-focused education, and a unified effort. Singapore became the example of a society that could make change several decades ago.

China has had a different path, but it's opening up created significant opportunities and is building a middle class. America has a very different problem. It is a mature society that has followed after Europe in creating a welfare state that places increasing limits on options but even more limits on the opportunities of future generations. That means change has to take place over time and has to be supported by the people as a whole. If not, a movement from one extreme to the other does nothing but disorient positive change and cause a lack of confidence. The culture is what ultimately matters.

The Chinese philosopher Mencius of the 4th century BC said that a kingdom could defend itself from the outside attack if the king runs a government sparing of punishments and fines, reducing taxes and levies. . . . As Mencius noted, it is the protection of the people that wins the unification and that in turn gives strength.

What is particularly necessary in the United States at this point in time is a philosophy that changes focus to culture and the battle of conscience versus convenience rather than the existing politics of small versus big government in the creation of a dependent social state or the economic class warfare of pitting rich versus poor. The unification of the people on such a new cultural philosophy would reorganize the economic and political arguments accordingly and would hopefully allow the sacrifice necessary to make appropriate economic change and provide opportunity. America is very close to a tipping point of dependency as has been seen from the previous economic and political trends. The appropriate area of focus needs to be an appreciation of the power of culture.

Economically, the term "middle class" describes a stratum that is relatively broad in a democracy. The cultural equivalent, to which this group gives a significant base, is the cultural core of a society. It is the broad-based range of values that determine the power of culture in society. In a democracy it is in part the independent to moderate center that determines the direction of the country, in economics it is the middle class, and culturally it is the broad core. Thinking in context requires us to understand the similarities and relationships of all three of those independent groups with the cultural values being the most significant in setting the goals and directions of the others.

The Power of Ideas to Transform Societies

Horace Busby, who was mentioned before, was a primary advisor to President Lyndon Johnson through much of his life and was one of my enlightening friends. He was a close friend of my father and after my father's death when our paths crossed, he spent significant time giving me a perspective on how society changes. Most problems are not new, so history becomes a great teacher.

One of the things that he emphasized to me was the very unique situation America faced in the early 1900s—not so different from today.

It was a society that had great problems and was in despair. There were divisions in American society that appeared would never be mended. Divisions smoldered between the North and South over the Civil War. There was a racial division between black and white that was particularly pronounced and difficult to bridge. Also there was significant friction between labor and capital and conflict between economic forces more than between people who were often almost sacrifices. But the worst and potentially most difficult division in his mind was between the mass of the poor and the limited number of rich who controlled much of the nation's wealth. This division seemed to be leading to class war.

It was a time when society saw very few positive things and a great many potential problems. But what occurred built the very best of America and took us to our pinnacle—a step by step progression that might not have had a clear model but had a cultural ethic of strength. He also noted that the 1920s was when it began and that prohibition was not an achievement of hatchet-wielding little old ladies but instead of employers addressing the problem of drunk employees limiting productive workforces (not unlike our modern healthcare).

The tenements that had been filled with huge numbers of immigrants over the last several decades were impacted by charitable efforts particularly by women of means and culture who did not want to see wasted lives. So they organized sports, language schools, and helped create jobs. Women began to vote in 1920, and tremendous changes were wrought in the political agenda at a statewide level, which impacted society at the time.

Society changed how it looked at the world particularly in education, nutrition, and health. Education became important, and there was peer pressure to finish high school and to adopt healthy practices. In an effort to mold the young, families were molded as well and processed the information they took home. There was a new realization that citizens could live together, work together, and jointly make progress for a better existence. Horace or "Bus" always noted the very great dangers of that period.

In the 1930s leaders recognized that the U.S. was near a chasm of revolution and that what America appreciated in this focus was that people must have a stake in it. The greatest invention of that time was the even level monthly mortgage payment, which transformed a nation of tenants into a nation of homeowners and basically laborers now had equities. Everyone had a stake in the system and began to appreciate it as such.

There were many things done to help move from that almost doomed attitude of the early part of the last century. But what made it succeed is that the leadership authored changes specifically that focused on holding society together keeping it from turning on itself, and thereby transforming it to move in directions more toward peace, unity, and "opportunity for all" systems.

"Bus" told me that story many times with an appreciation of how society can often save itself. He noted that Russia and America were very similar at the turn of the last century, and many thought that class warfare would turn both into communist nations. The two nations went on very different paths primarily because Russia reacted to the changes forced upon it while America primarily transformed its reality and its vision through its concept of conscience at the time.

Today, some of those very concepts have been lost or at least misunderstood. The greatest problem of our financial crisis has been the extreme amount of money going into real estate that was originally perceived to benefit the poor. But in reality it simply became a vehicle for the greed of financiers and a vote-buying effort of those in politics. Sustainability and responsibility are absolute keys to any society. And compassion, which does not recognize the moral hazard of losing individual responsibility and sustainability, simply moves us further down more negative paths. Individual responsibility is lessened by dependence on government largesse. The dignity that gives our character is reduced.

The reason the housing crisis impacted us so greatly is that it exposed a tremendous amount of leverage within the system and the lack of responsibility and concern for the greater good that was found in many of the policies that aimed at short-term remuneration. What brought America out of the Great Depression were the actions of the business leaders and CEOs of many companies both large and small that took a great responsibility to help put forth the programs that rebuilt society. They realized that for the longer term you had to have a strong middle class to provide the buying power and the sustainability that an economy needs. One of the points that "Bus" often made to me is how the greatest success of these efforts to build a middle class came in the fact that in 1981 America reached the stage of becoming a true middle class society when middle class income taxes paid by households and individuals with incomes between $15,000 and $50,000 paid more than 55% of the taxes.

Today we talk of how we can put evermore taxes on the rich. While there is certainly an issue of fairness in that they have more assets that society protects with tax revenue, it is also clear that we are moving society by policies that move closer toward class warfare and miss the great lessons in the early part of the last century. Policies providing growth and opportunity for the middle class so they can have a greater share of the system are critical. Our educational systems as well as our incentive systems have failed in keeping our middle class competitive. Those are issues that we must look at in detail as critical issues for the future.

While figures can be viewed in many ways, I think it fair to say that the share of income tax burden in 2008 gives an interesting perspective. The highest 5% of earners accounted for about 35% of adjusted gross income but paid about 59% of the total income tax. The bottom 50% of filers paid only about 2.7%, and many got earned income credit, which led to refunds. The top 10%, those with AGI's of about $114,000, had about 70% of the tax burden.

Thus since the early 1980s, we have moved dramatically from a middle class dominated society that gives stability over the years. Partly it is because of stagnating middle class salaries or from structural changes in taxes and the economy. But the point is clear—we either have to provide more opportunity and national competitiveness or we will eventually drive out capital and economic incentives. Both Republicans and Democrats must rethink the importance of the middle class and look to growth policies that are sustainable. Government redistribution does not create wealth or innovation as effectively as markets.

The most core issue of our economic concerns is the weakening of the middle class in the last decade, but the very significant economic disparity between the wealthiest several percent and the vast majority of society affects what is the cultural core and brings the question of what is economic justice to the forefront.

The problem is not solved by protests of anger because the solution often put forth for the problem is redistribution when the ultimate solution for us and our children is wealth creation. What are destroying the middle class are healthcare costs, education costs, lack of opportunity for meritorious advance by hard work, and the other drivers we have noted. The belief that taxes on a limited segment can let government solve the problem is unrealistic in view of the magnitude of the figures. The reality is that the government is broke—worse it has debt increasing at rapid rates that have to decline and that will only exasperate the problems of the middle class core. You cannot rebuild a middle class by redistribution—the middle class core has to be rebuilt by the dignity and opportunity of work and individual responsibility to be sustainable.

The twentieth century social welfare state has reached its limits in Europe, and is an example of the fact that as in the United States, the government is broke because the country is broke. The last decade our use of debt mitigated reality, but now we should see our choices clearly. Unless we rebuild the economy with sacrifice, there is no strong engine for future growth. Taxes must be changed by reform more than symbolic increase. Regulation needs new theory and focus for effectiveness and not prevention of innovation. And most of all, government and business need to look to personal and institutional responsibility and accountability as core principles. While in reality that is far easier said than done, it is truth.

Today we get so much advice from our "experts" that we are over impressed by their data and do not analyze their wisdom. We miss the fact that experts often talk and argue so much with each other that significant ideas are missed. The bottom line is that we must rebuild our middle class core values to improve our middle class economy. Middle class values and economic opportunity do not come from redistribution but from wealth creation of an entrepreneurial environment and culture that must be created and preserved, not drained of its strength.

Class warfare and war on internationalization are dangerous policies. While excellent in short-term politics that pull the emotions of envy and convenience, they damage the problems' cure. It is far better to unite producers (workers) and investors in growth policies that focus on wealth creation rather than on less productive efforts that primarily game the government's tax and subsidy systems through special interest legislation and system dominance created by the elite in most fields supported by a partnership with the bureaucracy and lobby influenced legislative process.

There is a big difference between big corporate business and small business free enterprise. The former uses regulation for protection and benefit; the latter is burdened far more by sapping opportunity. Politics has to give way to economics, and it will only happen if culture rejects the tools of convenience and puts more conscience and moral hazard into policy. That is very difficult to sustain politically, so it will take educating generations on how to think about national issues.

We need to understand how our leaders think and where our resources are invested or spent. Several generations set a trend for the future—the future is what they make it by their policies and vision or lack thereof. There is no better example than modern China and what happened in the thirty years since its "opening." While Chairman Deng looked for what would give results in the modern world, he was not inconsistent with the Taoist Sage, Lao Tzu who noted that "the more prohibitions there are, the poorer the people become." But if government does not control forcefully, what structures society?

The Three Levels of Culture

While the *Rule of Law* is the strict line that tells us how much we can exercise free will in regard to other members of society, there is an unenforceable morality through courtesy, common tradition, and mutual respect that men owe each other. How they interact and what they demand of others that are not required by the law is really the culture of obligation or the culture of morality. The strength of this inner set of responsibilities is what builds a society. It might well be looked upon as Confucian because Confucius dealt with the obligations of each man to another as well as the obligations to government. It also is distinctly Western because it is in effect the Golden Rule. When the sensitivity to that diminishes and we let ourselves be controlled by emotions incited by robot telephone calls, telemarketers, or road rage, we then are sorely tempted to resort to ever lower common denominators of activity and behavior. That is the slow draining of much of the appreciation that we should have for the mutual powers of obligation that restore society. Reorganizing obligations is the mortar of a strong society and family.

In the family we focused on relationships with others and even when we did not agree, we knew that the best answer was to come up with a solution. Ultimately we did not want to lose the common relationships. While we may preserve the family, preserving the relationship between families is equally important since that is the concept of the fraternity— how we all fit together. The West may use "fraternity," and the East may use "harmony," but the historical principles are the same.

It is this unenforceable set of obligations that we must strengthen. And it is society's morally enforceable characteristic that we often refer to as character.

This is particularly important because character is the operational approach to enforcing conscience. Where conscience may give us the strategic imperatives, character gives us the obligation and necessity of fulfilling those conscience driven expectations.

Individual responsibility could well be considered the tactic or the method that we use to implement character since it requires us to take action. In the current trend of our society, taking individual responsibility is becoming less and less an option because we have instead moved from our system of obligation to each other to the legal system. And the legal system often punishes the acceptance of responsibility rather than encouraging it. Thus, the existing system has to be changed in the way that we think about issues or it will simply take this binding common thread in America to lower levels.

China prides itself in a different situation—its legal system is developing, even though slowly, to give rights. But it has in some cases a strong internal culture that recognizes dignity because of its past values and much of its Confucian background as also influenced by Taoism. Law is in some cases different from justice. The West recognized this in the creation of the Courts of Equity when common law became too technical and justice was lost.

The Chinese are coming at the issues from the justice concept trying to work into the legal approach because they think in culture but have had it overwhelmed by the regulation of central government. Each country is going to have to find a way to strengthen fraternity and harmony to rebuild this culture of moral obligation to establish the strong basis needed for the future.

The concept of "Enlightened Conservatism" that is reflected in *The Language of Conscience Evolution* is a cultural philosophy with significant economic and political overtones derived from it. It is the organizing principle within a harmonious society that a person would give to every other person the same rights and personal dignity that they would wish for themselves. In order to be effective it has to have a strong cultural commitment to character and moral obligation.

To accomplish this, you have to strengthen those principles through education in the organizations and institutions of your society. And also the government must use moral hazard as a critical factor in its determinations in the longer term of actions taken. There are no immediate solutions to the problems of today because they are so vast and almost unfathomable in view of their interrelationships to each other.

It is often said that conservatives lose principles when they compromise and thus become moderates. This is not an unusual observation when many in politics use the convenience of transactional politics to reach an agreement. The difference with enlightened conservatism's approach is that it is transformational and tries to keep ultimate principles of conscience while recognizing the reality, which is the core of true conservatism. Reality often requires adjustment to the undesired because facts do not allow and ultimately require action. The difference is why you do it—the motivation and the ultimate set of goals for which a difficult choice is made. This is why moral hazard is much more of a concern with Enlightened Conservatism where it may be less in moderation and finding a shorter term solution.

All that can be done are trends and movements that change the direction and help position future generations. I have often been asked about the balance of charity and obligation. The term "Enlightened Conservatism" was given to these writings years ago by the Quorum Report, one of the premier political newsletters of Texas. It is a very appropriate term. Rather than using compassion, which tends to be more liberal and conservatism that speaks for frugality, it uses enlightenment for a very specific reason. Compassion and conservatism tend to not necessarily fit together in a political term because it is difficult to be compassionate when you are forced to cut expenditures. "Enlightened Conservatism" and the books that describe it try to more appropriately play choices between wants and needs with the creation of the system that more broadly supports and enhances charity and private support beyond government assistance.

This distinction is important because individual responsibility becomes the determining characteristic of an enlightened conservatism. Compassion has to be shown to those that deserve it because they are not able to change their circumstances themselves. But private charity will often not support the "free rider" concept where people simply want support from others even though they have the ability to do more themselves.

Society owes support to those that are most needy, but it cannot afford to support a significant number who simply want to take advantage of the system. Need-based support and political entitlement are different concepts and have to be separated in analogies even though needed support is often a part of entitlement. Each entitlement needs to be analyzed independently. The obligations created that have to be honored are not sustainable without a significant cut for the quality of help to the people that are most needy. It is not compassionate to ultimately deprive those most in need from support by trying to be overly gracious in the concept of entitlements. Individual responsibility and character are diminished by policy through moral hazard when government takes the place of private judgment, which effectively develops the enforceable aspects of a moral society.

The final culture is one that is really a tactic and technique for the creation and building of this character and obligation. *It is the culture of compassion and man's obligation to another.* In the culture of obligation we do things for others because we have the expectation they should do them for us. In the culture of compassion we instead do something for someone else not expecting anything in return because our values let our own actions to others define us more than their actions to us. These are the teachings of the great religions and many of the great philosophers. This is the culture of conscience and stewardship of service.

It is important to understand that this needs to be a private undertaking by the individual sector and not by government. To simply vote that someone else should be taxed to do these things without a sacrifice on our part is not true compassion. It may give us a good feeling that these things are done, but government creates very little and often in giving to one purpose deprives opportunities in many others.

The nonprofit sector by which people take on these actions is the best sector to implement this type of compassionate and harmonious society. I served on the Board of Covenant House in Houston where we helped homeless children. The greatest impact was not the money that was raised and spent. It was the time individuals spent taking the kids to games or cooking pancakes for them. Showing individual care could actually have an impact.

The same is true of the benefit to the giver. Mrs. George Brown worked with me on the Texas Commission for the Arts and taught me a great deal about the difference between culture and society. Many people do things for the image, but others do it because they believe. She instilled in me a greater understanding of the benefit you get from the personal satisfaction that you have done the right thing for the right reasons. Charity and an absolute concern for others are critical in building a society that recognizes personal dignity.

People who care about others more easily lose the prejudices of transactions because they are caught in a transformation. America must strengthen its nonprofit systems as it relies less on government support because of financial problems. China, as it experiments with its new systems, will have to put in nonprofit systems and learn about them to remove the harshness that market systems can provide as it implements those systems for necessary growth. The Chinese have studied the sections on Non-Profits in *The Language of Conscience* and termed them communist capitalist organizations. They could function in a market economy but were consistent with their principles of support of the people. Mutuals are a far better way to privatize them to oligopoly of a few leaders as Russia demonstrates.

The demographics of the world and the current trends can be read in many ways. But most people see the economic ranking of countries by size forty years from now to be China as number one because of its great population and growth rates, followed by the United States that will remain competitive because of its great current strength, then India, Brazil, and possibly Mexico if it is able to address its current problems of violence. Many of the other countries of the world will follow closely thereafter.

Europe will remain significant but because of much of its demographics perhaps will be less relevant as it has to face the challenges currently seen in the Euro zone in working together as a unit. With these factors, it becomes increasingly important how China and America build their relationship and learn from each other. Both nations have many other influences, but whether they are competitive or cooperative in various areas will determine the future for the world as a whole.

The Cold War had been the organizing principle of the world since World War II. People might be tyrants or corrupt, but they fit in one category of the Western Alliance or the Soviet Block. That organized how people thought about a variety of things. After the Berlin Wall fell this changed, and there has been greater cooperation in the world, which has led to a great amount of economic growth.

With the emergence of China as another super power, how the world looks at its future may well fall in the hands of the leadership of America and China since they will set the tone for what becomes important. That tone will either be set by the politics of nationalism, the self-interest of economics, or if they can build a base of cultural harmony, problems will still exist but may be solved more thoughtfully.

The three cultures that we described—the Rule of Law, the culture of moral obligation, and the culture of compassion, are always present in both countries. As each seeks new systems, the question is how high they will be elevated in the discussion. There are no certain answers; there is only the ability to find compromise.

The key is whether that compromise is found at a technical or tactical level on smaller items or a fundamental cultural agreement that can move from the top down to help prevent the type problems that exist. I would venture that it is not a political solution but a cultural one where such a base should be built and that requires both countries to understand each other far better not just at their leadership level but internally. Both countries have much in common in their love of family and their concerns for dignity.

The Challenge of Intersecting Cultures

Samuel Huntington's classic work on "The Clash of Cultures" gives a clear understanding of the power of culture in shaping the future world. The clashes between the cultures of the Middle East philosophically or religiously and the significant variations in the cultures of the rest of the world make its integration a critical part of how well the world will succeed over the coming generations. Bridging these cultures will be the most important issue that can be accomplished. The unification on the basis of values is essential if you want to fully develop the economic opportunities between various countries.

The political lines of the past are being increasingly shifted to the core value entities that represent populations. When those divisions cannot be accomplished within a limited geographic area, you have different cultures that compete rather than coordinate, particularly through immigration, and the chance of conflict is increasingly great. There are many different theories on how to address these issues. Some look at a concept of relativity and almost total toleration between cultures to avoid conflict.

This is often described as the salad bowl approach because the various cultures fit together in a common society. The other concept is the melting pot, which tends to try to find a common transformational set of values on which they can all agree. Even though the cultures may have their own independent characteristics, the core values are enhanced and are the basis of how the different groups can work together politically and economically and operate culturally in a common moral agenda. This is the core of *The Language of Conscience Evolution* in its efforts to find the principles of cultural transformation and then align both political and economic factors together with them.

Because of the complexity and tremendous diversity of the world, there is never going to be the opportunity to build what many feel is a common utopian world. However, what you can find are ways to align interests and build common values that make everyone's environment far safer and far more prosperous.

This requires diverse groups to look at things from their interests and to appreciate that almost all of these cultures are built on an appreciation and the strength of family and the values like the Golden Rule and common good that often emanate from family. It is the core of the cultures that give hope that you can have both fraternity and harmony and they can eventually be interchanging words.

If we are to study how to bring about changes both within our society and the world, we need to use several areas of focus. China plays a significant part as a proxy for Eastern culture because of its dramatic impact in the modern world, particularly as it uses its Confucian Institutes to not only bridge language difficulties but also create more understanding. How Western culture and Chinese culture interact and how bridges can be built is perhaps the core issue internationally. Understanding each other matters greatly and is one of the great weaknesses that currently exist in the world.

Chinese approaches to business governance will have a tremendous impact on world standards as it invests throughout the world. And those governance standards will in large part be driven by how China looks at the culture it desires moving forward. The interesting thing about China, however, is that it is largely a Han significant majority with limited immigration. Its culture has absorbed outside forces for a great number of years and transformed them within its existing culture.

The United States is extremely different. It is a more open society that has invited people from all over the world and to a great extent has been built on a melting pot of immigrants that adopted the character-based values and quality that America offered. In the current more difficult economic situation, immigration is viewed differently from the past, and there is not a full appreciation of the impact that this will have on American society. The appropriate case study might be the Hispanic immigration and population within the United States that is by far its most rapidly growing component. It will significantly impact its economics and politics beyond just the changes in culture. Both of these are significant issues that need to be understood.

Both America and China may be gradually forced to move to an open society, with an ethos of meritocracy, efficiency, and results that could triumph over the historic structure of form, title, and position. Such would be an innovative society in which the culture of the people coming energized the society as a whole by giving it incentive and a sense of destiny. Both nations are going to reinvent themselves; the ultimate issue will be to what? One thing is certain, the effect they will have on each other will shape the results.

The Critical Importance of China to America

Understanding America's Current Strategic Financial Partner

If you fully appreciate that economics, politics, and culture are related but also have separate characteristics, you can more appropriately appreciate the current Chinese relationship with the United States. China has changed greatly in the last thirty years since its "opening up." A significant portion of that has been driven by economics. The West's increasing use of technology had given it significant advantages, but Western affluence had also given benefit competitively to cheap labor. As Chairman Deng moved China from communism to market socialism with Chinese characteristics, it was driven by the necessity of employing a significant number of people at a high level of economic growth to maintain stability.

As we noted before, a growth philosophy eases a great number of problems. When everyone's status in life is improving, even in smaller increments, giving hope for the future, it is quite different from a more economically advanced society where growth is limited and there are increasing focuses on divisions that help fracture the cooperation of the society. The direction in which society is moving is in some ways as important a concept to one's personal dignity as the level of wealth they maintain.

The contrast between Europe with its unsustainable entitlement models and China with its growth driven model provide interesting dialectics. Both require delicate balance and supportive national will. In Europe efforts are being made at the margin to put in more market systems. In China there are efforts to protect domestic industry, but these are more at the margins that have limited effect on the momentum of the system's expansion. Internal inflation, conversion to a consumer economy, real estate stability, political leadership transition, and other issues will be more indicative of policy direction.

To develop economic growth and bring in investment, China needed a pricing mechanism because it did not have markets and used the United States' economy and the dollar because it was a world's reserve currency as a base for comparisons. That has led to many of the current pricing issues, but China's development will make its goals for the future somewhat different from the past.

Amid much discussion of the fact that China has primarily changed economically, there is a significant note—it has not changed politically in the centralized control of the Communist Party. But the most significant factor that I think has not been fully appreciated is that there has been a renaissance in ancient Chinese cultural values. During the time of Chairman Mao, the party rose to power from all of the internal dissent and external invasion of China. At that point the equality of communism was the theory promoted by the power of the state.

It should be noted, however, that Russian Communism looked more to the theories of Marx that dealt with workers in more industrialized circumstances. In the Chinese Civil War, Chiang Kai-shek had co-opted many of these groups and the base of the Chinese Communist Party largely came from Mao's leadership of the rural peasant farmers that became its largest constituent base. There is a different culture between rural and urban settings that is sometimes unappreciated in the impact on value systems.

What you have seen in recent years is more of the renaissance of Confucian values and the other large components of Chinese culture. While Confucianism is not a religious concept of a god, it is a philosophical concept of reciprocity. The Silver Rule of Confucius is effectively the corollary of the Christian Golden Rule: "Do not do to others those things you do not wish done to you."

China's political transition in the next years will celebrate the 90th birthday of the Communist Party, but also give great credence to the Confucian Renaissance in values. Chairman Mao Zedong viewed Confucius as somewhat of a reactionary. But today the revival of the study of classical Chinese philosophy has been seen as a bridge and a key to the development of nationalism to other cultures through efforts like the Confucian Institutes. This nationalism is in areas from art to literature to Chinese traditional medicine, but its key may be its ethical traditions that can build a strong culture. This ethical historic cultural base is in some ways the equivalent of the Western legal system. They operate in different ways but are aimed at similar levels.

Modern China is not as pyramid power-driven as it might appear. Perhaps 400 key leaders dominate direction, but term limits and a system of collective decision methods make consensus important. So what organizing principle directs the transition to and from the new leadership will matter greatly. Among the forces shaping it will be several historic thoughts.

The traditional values also include the "Legalism" of Han Feizi, which has similarities to the West in Machiavelli's *The Prince* in that it is a doctrine of power and was favored by Chairman Mao; however, modern approaches make it much more of a nationalistic cultural base.

The restoration of traditional Confucianism and Renaissance values would be very nationalistic. If it became a dominant ideology of the state, it would develop into an alternative to Western Democracy built on Chinese cultural values of ethics and obligation.

The third alternative is a modernized Confucianism that takes the core of ethical values but blends them with the traditions of the West and the market systems that move close to establishing a cultural democracy with Chinese characteristics.

It is of course possible, but not likely, that the Party will let the default ideology of Western Democracy become an ideology. But for this to happen, the citizenry has to learn the responsibility of citizenship. China would then become more Western. However, that faces cultural hurdles.

To understand China's evolution we must be mindful that China suffered greatly during the Great Leap Forward when Chairman Mao tried to push the country quickly into a more modern state. The failures of information and accountability led to great famines. The Cultural Revolution that followed dramatically changed the landscape of China opposing many of the existing values, particularly parts of Confucianism, in the education system that many felt was too rigid. This upheaval changed Chinese perspectives for a generation.

Older family cultural values were present, but current political values tended to dominate. After Chairman Mao's death, the new leadership under Chairman Deng made significant changes. The "Great Opening Up" of China economically then began and his visions reshaped the Communist Party to a more modern economic perspective. They also began the more public revival of many of the ancient values. I think there is nothing that says more than the incredible presentation in the recent Olympics. The central figure of one of the most glorious presentations was Confucius and his interest in wisdom. That scene, as a point of focus to the world, said a tremendous amount about China and what it wished to put forward to define itself.

Years ago, Milton Friedman was quoted in regard to a question about how he saw the future of China. Since the basic philosophy of his economics was freedom of choice, I thought his view was a particularly accurate and prescient one. He noted that the first freedom China has approached is economic. Following it, you worked to get civil freedom, and eventually you reached political freedom.

The more I thought about his observation, the more I realized its affects in China. Economic freedom is taking more hold in China as their Constitution now includes private property rights. It is also moving more toward understanding the Western Rule of Law and is adjusting to many economic international standards with the World Trade Organization. The civil freedoms—freedom of speech, freedom of assembly, freedom of the press, and many others that are a part of the American Constitution, have to be acquired. But they have to be understood before they can be acquired. A component of that civil freedom, if you wish stability, is for the people to realize that obligations go with rights.

China's Desires and Fears

What China fears because of its history of internal turmoil and revolution is instability. What it most desires is harmony with opportunity. Thus, if their leadership is effective and does what is best for the people, the leadership is normally left in place and some rights that are not granted are not demanded. However, with modern communication and the impact of the foreign world on China, China's greatest problem currently is how to evolve into a Chinese form that is more democratic. This is a significant challenge with its mass of people, many in undeveloped areas, who have to learn concepts of civil obligation as a base of thought.

This focuses on the power within the Party at the highest leadership levels. Foreign media refer to two groups. One is called the Princelings who were the heirs of the influence of many generals and early Party founders. They are often focused on Party dominance. And the second less conservative establishment believes that China must open up more politically to involve the people to gain stability. In effect, it is the same argument that we have in the West between the impacts of small or big government, only in China it is a little more focused on the power of the Party. This evolution is best understood if you look at the ideologies that China has followed.

The Chinese Communist Party started with Marxism as a base. It changed into the thoughts of Chairman Mao. It then moved into the philosophy of Chairman Deng and then to the Three Precedents under Chairman Jiang Zemin. Now these have reformulated into the Harmonious Society. The trend of that ideological thought is extremely important. People often have specific images of China, particularly during critical events. Pictures are often not as accurate as videos showing the movement of trends. The largest single problem that China faces is corruption.

An intense centralized bureaucratic system gives significant power to bureaucracies, and market economics have only served as a fertilizer to that concept. The Chinese have a strong sense of morality, but corruption does not fit into morality exactly the way it does in the West. It is more an economic system vice that is punished. It is unique in the different way it is viewed. China was often dominated by conquerors or opposing armies demanding support and tributes which made it a way of doing business. It is significantly resented by the people and is one of the greatest potential causes of discontent at the lower levels and might cause significant negative repercussions for the Party.

This is one of the reasons that the leadership of the Party is so concerned about that issue as well as the fact that the renaissance of Confucian values with the Harmonious Society sets a different set of goals. If you are to build common support and harmony for sacrifice and stability, you must have more ethical sharing. This will make economic governance of companies an important focus.

The nature of the Internet is to decentralize. Existing systems have to adapt with modern communication. The Chinese Leadership fully understands this. However, the question is how and what or whose approaches to follow. But to be successful, any new leader will probably have to move this direction if he wishes sustainable success. Using the Internet to promote cultural ethics sets a different tone. It is not what you oppose but what you support that often defines you.

The reason that China and its future is so intertwined with the United States is because we buy huge amounts of its products that are often produced very cheaply, which significantly helps the American standard of living. As we noted, how much you can buy with your money is probably more important than how much money you make. Cheap Chinese goods allow us a higher quality of living. And by creating jobs, it does the same for the Chinese.

The problem is how to handle the financial imbalance this creates. If we decide that we want to increase our production in the United States through tariffs or reevaluations of the Yuan, these are not one-sided events. Making Chinese goods more expensive to make ours more competitive means that the middle class has to pay significantly more for them. This diminishes their standard of living. Many of the political answers to the relationship do not fully comprehend unintended consequences.

As companies do business in China, there are many difficulties and opportunities that have more favorable outcomes if you start with a strategic view of what you want to accomplish long term, and then go to the aspects of making a deal. The first is the mountain view of how the country operates, which needs to be understood. Then you can navigate and hire assistance for the valley of the trees below once you see the right direction. Companies come to China for two basic reasons—to sell to the Chinese market or to export. You have to learn the governments at the federal, provincial, and city levels. China is so large that it operates less like the states of the U.S. and a little more like independent countries in the Euro zone.

While many have predicted China's demise for years, they have been proven wrong because the Chinese government fully understands the constant instability it faces with all the problems and gives more focus to them than is appreciated. They will have many domestic problems—particularly inflation, environmental problems, and a financial system that is weakened by the fact that credit is allocated rather than market driven. There are demographic problems with limited social nets now that many state-owned companies are no longer the primary source of benefits. But they are researching health options from the West and moving heavily to prevention and wellness. They will minimize their difficulties because crisis forces them to adapt as they have for several generations.

The greatest difficulty many companies face is finding the right partner to help them understand and work in the market. It is a critical choice because the wisdom and connections of the partner makes a huge difference. But relying on the partner alone is often dangerous for if you split with him, or he demands more, he is the one with the market and the contacts. So strategic thinking makes sure one builds a wide array of contacts and relationships with a vision to the long term—not just commercial activities but joining into the culture. While contracts are normally honored, the government has more say than other countries, so understanding the system in advance is significant. Getting a contract is important, but the licenses needed may be more difficult and another governmental issue. While corruption is often referred to as a major problem by even the government, it is often more domestic. It is not necessary for foreign companies to succeed but can become a significant problem because of business practices if it is not closely monitored.

China has come a very long way. Its leadership understands the issues and is moving in a positive direction even if it is a plodding advance. As China becomes a major power, the governance and intellectual property issues will be increasingly important to them. Most developing countries do not have a long-term vision to own intellectual property. China understands its position is not going to be the same in the future as its educational systems drive innovation. Self-interest is a powerful tool when understood.

Like any country, business is not easy, and success depends on factors beyond your control. But early preparation makes a big difference in how you set perspectives and goals and can minimize the chance of failure. China is not a place to use a roulette strategy but a poker one, which commits smaller but increasing amounts of money through management as you acquire more information and can make more thoughtful decisions.

China also is one of the largest creditors of the United States in its government bonds. It was necessary for them to finance the American deficits so we could buy products from them maintaining their stability to add jobs and growth. It has been a circle between the two countries with China as the financing agent as well as the seller. They are selling us items basically on credit. Many protectionists attack China as a mercantilist economy taking advantage of the U.S. But the difference in this example is that they are the principal financiers and have to worry about what happens to us because much of their financial worth is our debt. They have lost money as the value of the dollar has deteriorated.

Another critical issue is that China is using their massive resources to acquire oil, minerals, food sources, and other assets by purchase and contract worldwide. They have national energy policies and expand political influence by loaning to countries on the basis of these contracts for infrastructure improvements, which are often built by Chinese companies and expand their influence. Many in America complain of this, but the issue is not the Chinese doing things intelligently, it should be our failure to have a similar international energy and resource policy. Their actions are showing our failings that only we can address.

Chinese funding has had a huge effect on many of the natural laws that would affect the United States. Generally, many of our less thoughtful financial efforts would have been reflected and had negative impact in the markets, but the constant need of the Chinese to purchase our debt stymied the normal historical approaches. The solution to the problem will come from China having a larger consumption society that generates its economic growth from sales within more than having to make sales without.

America needs to change its reliance on debt to more self-sustainable competitive practices that may require significant adjustments and lead to long-term stability. Both sides need to look carefully at how to view cooperation. Presently, there is little cooperation since discussion often looks from a zero-sum game when there is talk of protectionist activities on both sides.

There are challenges with China and with the United States to have fair trade because free trade itself has very significant consequences. However, if you are to avoid major disruptions, any real change will come from policies over periods of time. The greatest concern is the Chinese opinion of the value of the dollar. Because of their significant holdings, they are increasingly concerned at the declining value of the dollar and are now looking at making many foreign investments primarily for resources using dollars.

They will look to diversity risk through currency agreements with other countries, but that takes time, and they are locked for the short term to the U.S. However, their loss of confidence could dramatically affect the level of the dollar in its effect on the market's psychology. That is a major unknown that will hopefully never be tested. They may buy less current new debt, but the existing debt is a significant issue in refunding.

At a time when American investment, particularly in real estate and infrastructure is quite limited, there is increasing pressure and opportunity for the Chinese to invest in the United States as the Japanese did. This would be highly beneficial for both countries. It is not unlike the stability that followed the huge increase in oil prices several decades ago. Large amounts of money were flowing to the Middle East, and unless methods were provided to recirculate those funds, a crisis could evolve.

The Chinese fully understand this issue from their history. In the relationship with the British where much of the silver of the world went to China and the British had to find products to sell to the Chinese. In part, this led to the heroin trade and a particularly difficult period for China. The trade representatives of both countries discussed the economic benefits and understood most of these issues. The problem, however, is the commitment and will of each country's leadership to focus on the most critical issues. It is a difficult political issue. A cultural bridge could be part of a longer-term solution. Unilateral action, although occasionally politically blustered, is not a solution because the nature of both sides is to respond and a trade war would be devastating to confidence.

Another one of America's problems is that we focus on the symptoms of China's problems, such as the unwillingness to allow the renminbi to appreciate. We also focus on domestic protectionism and foreign investment and put it into an aggressive planned strategy that may overlook the real cause of government coming to increasingly hard choices. China is having to choose between the State Centralism of the past and new Market options.

These are difficult choices to keep stability, and decisions may be more based on keeping stability than adding aggressiveness. The world is more complicated for the Chinese, so more thought needs to be given to causes of actions rather than the actions themselves. The Chinese, if they do not wish to be misunderstood, need to make these choices more transparent as well.

When the United States adapted NAFTA as a trade relationship with Canada and Mexico, as well as with numerous individual countries since, it basically lowered the tariffs that American goods had to pay to go into those domestically protected countries. The difficult side of the trade agreements is they also helped those countries grow and become more competitive. As they were becoming more competitive, the agreements had significant impact on America's middle class because work could be shifted. Perhaps an engineer would cost $50 per hour in the United States but $10 in Mexico and $5 in China. With the Internet and modern communications, cost savings in services were moving just as they are moving in the production of goods.

Attempting to stop those efficiencies within business only makes you less competitive. The secret is to improve your competitiveness and to better use your advantages. That seldom occurs when you have times of affluence and no pressure. But as the pressure of crisis arises and the burden of recognizing indebtedness and unsustainability of programs is evident, these pressures require change. As noted below, the key is not to jump out of the airplane with a parachute that slows descent, but to figure out how to keep the plane flying and head for the horizon.

Personal Experiences with China

On Monday, November 22, 2010, in Section R-1, *The Wall Street Journal* presented a thoughtful set of presentations from interviews with the CEO Council. They covered the many challenges of the current economy, but one of the most thoughtful presentations was a section called "Parting Words," an interview by Alan Murray with Lawrence Summers the Director of the U.S. Economic Council who would be leaving at year end. It noted that Mr. Summers had been a key architect of the Administration's efforts to deal with the economic and financial crisis, and he gave his perspectives of the financial actions taken by the Obama Administration and healthcare. However, the key points of Mr. Summer's parting words, as shown in the byline, were that China was the most important issue of our time.

As a man of significant intellect who was privy to all of the issues facing the country, how he focused on them was revealing:

> *I think that when somebody writes the history of our time fifty or a hundred years from now, it is unlikely to be about the great recession of 2008. It is unlikely to be about the fiscal problem that America confronted in the second decade of the 21st century.*
>
> *It will be about how the world adjusted to the movement of the theater of history toward China. . .*
>
> *A reading of the long sweep of history suggests that rapidly transforming economies in a rapidly transforming global system produce histories that aren't always happy ones. So our wisdom, their wisdom, the way in which we interact, is going to be of the utmost importance.*
>
> *Ultimately there is going to be one thing that is most important, and that is going to be how the world sees the power of our example. It will be the power of our example and the power of our economy that ultimately will be this challenge and that is why, frankly, the question of how the United States relates to China in this world and what our example is, is so much*

more important than the question of how the media relates to Washington, or even the question of how Democrats relate to Republicans. And it is the central American challenge going forward.

China and the Texas Third Coast of Thought

I think Mr. Summers is absolutely correct. Your generation will be most impacted by this, but it has dramatic immediate effects. I first became focused upon China shortly after leaving college and helping form the Texas Lyceum. Dean George Kozmetsky had formed a very significant think tank on the effects of technology-based clusters of companies that developed economic growth called IC^2. I had the opportunity to get to know Dean at the University of Texas School of Business. He became a mentor who spent considerable effort on the Texas Lyceum and a number of other endeavors of my younger years. He taught me a great deal.

Even though I had no real interest in China in the early 1980s, he was already predicting the tremendous impact China would have as he worked internationally to take abroad many of his thoughts of economic growth through technology. He had watched the development of Singapore and noted its significance. He explained the importance of trade and the significant impact of education, research and development, and finding, developing, and using the finest minds available. He was a man of significant honor and one who, along with my father, helped shape many of my thoughts about the obligations men have to society.

During these years I served as President of the Texas State Chamber of Commerce before the series of mergers that resulted in the modern Texas Association of Business. As is historically shown in *The Language of Conscience,* I had the opportunity to play a significant role through Texas House Speaker Gib Lewis in the creation of the Texas Economic Development Commission. Through Texas Lyceum programs, much of our generation learned the significance of interacting internationally and why public policy matters.

A good history of policy arguments that blended into ultimate actions can be found in the work of the Texas Public Policy Foundation for conservative positions and the Center for Public Policy Priorities, which presented more progressive arguments. But both have appreciated the importance of conscience, the former through the recognition of obligation, the latter through the promotion of compassion. There are many organizations that have affected the ultimate policy mix as well as these think tanks, and on health care the Texas Health Institute has done very significant work in not only policy analysis, but unifying opposing positions.

Many more specialist organizations exist in the areas of education, legal reform, business advocacy, etc., which are involved in the power of change, but the easiest understanding comes from looking at the model from the broad top down understanding of the key organizing principle arguments. The top down analysis of ideas has to recognize the actions and impact of individuals and activist organizations that battled on behalf of these ideas to enact them. But Clio's approach is to look back at history from the perspective of time and judge what is most important at that moment. What exists in Texas today can be looked upon politically as a conservatively dominated policy agenda, but I think the reason for it is as cultural as political. It was the culture that accepted the blend of arguments.

The people that move to Texas usually do so because of those values. If it is a cultural power, the Texas Model can evolve into one that has a realistic view of necessary change that addresses some of its weaknesses. If it is a political model, then extreme partisanship will dominate. The need is for a new paradigm with an organizing principle that is based on common good from an enlightened perspective. That requires think tanks and leaders to broaden how they think of issues. It requires a new perspective of thought, which Clio would see as a turning point of thought.

It was the Third Coast of Thought that significantly impacted all of these issues. Texas is a low tax, limited regulation, small government model that is business friendly. As such, it has been creating jobs through economic development with its culture and recruitment in the benefits offered to relocating companies. Much of this effort is described in *The Language of Conscience*. The study group for the creation of the Economic Development Commission recommended two bills—one for a Strategic Planning Committee that made recommendations independent of politics, envisioned as a professional entity like the Federal Reserve. (Unfortunately, it never took hold because of the nature of politics.) And the other created the Texas Economic Development Commission by consolidating functions and adding efficiencies from existing separate agency efforts.

However, the discussions of the assembled experts and leaders made us recognize the tremendous importance of trade to jobs and standards of living, and the power of technology. Our proximity to Mexico sensitized us, and both issues were addressed. The Committee requested assistance from the Federal Government's Commerce Department to help tie our strategies to the Government's efforts in consulates worldwide.

We learned that business organizations helped coordinate private business efforts since foreign trade efforts by government were limited. If there were no interests worthy of expenditure, then they did not occur. We boosted the Texas Secretary of State's protocol functions and built more coordination with the private sector. The Texas Economic Development Commission was envisioned as a catalyst for private sector efforts more than a government agency expending money. This has traditionally been the "Texas Way."

But what we appreciated from the insight of the Commerce Department was that much of the rest of the world, particularly undeveloped countries, operated differently—government played a much larger role. So formal protocol approaches were critical. While the direct result of this Speaker's Committee may not be as obvious today, its membership of senior legislators, economists, business leaders, and organizations learned a great deal with a more common model in mind for state development. It affected many different efforts that followed. Texas had a number of visionary leaders from technology recruitment to infrastructure, and they benefited by creating a sense of evolutionary change. The Texas Lyceum built many of these issues into its programs and Journal, and they helped crystallize support for the transition of the state economically—if not directly in legislation, then in the perspective of thought.

The Texas Lyceum had been asked for input by the Speaker's study group and included many of these subjects in its programs. NAFTA was being discussed, and because of Mexico's existing trade with Texas, was generating excitement. This was all occurring in the late 1980s when Texas was in significant economic difficulty. The benefits of trade, as well as the costs in jobs, were discussed at various events. Senator Lloyd Bentsen was the leader of the U.S. Senate Finance Committee and later Treasury Secretary who helped make the focus clear over the years. The Texas Lyceum began in 1980 but now is on its 31st President and 25th Public Conference. But throughout that history, it viewed Texas as a culture and its purpose was developing ideas that brought people together for a common goal. But it helped bring an international force to discussion, often with the assistance of the large oil companies who were active internationally.

I spent the late 1980s and early 1990s fascinated by Mexico and the emerging globalization it represented. I met Dr. Felipe Ochoa Rossi, who led Pro Mexico, a group of major Mexican businessmen who worked on NAFTA. He also shared my passion for ethics and conscience. He and my Mexican friends taught me a great deal about the importance of recognizing the culture of a place you are trying to understand. He understood Mexico as few others in culture, in economics, and in politics. He became a great asset for our bridge with Mexico and understanding the benefits of trade intellectually and realistically. Mexico was 1/30 of the American economy then, and he could show the impact and need for growth. The smaller size helped focus on the key factors for success.

The Texas-Mexican border for a hundred miles on either side was a combination of both cultures. The Maquiladora system of joint manufacturing was a specialization of manufacturing, U.S. technology, and cheaper Mexican labor to cut production costs. The problem was that the two countries did not bridge culture well if you were not from the region of intersection. Most of the experts on Mexico seemed to live in New York or Washington.

Over the years, I had the opportunity to work with Felipe and many of the other Mexican leaders in helping American companies come to Mexico and giving insight to Mexican companies about the United States. Felipe worked significantly with organizations he created such as FIDIC's Task Force on Integrity, (International Organization for Consulting Engineers), and also diligently worked on South American governance efforts to stem corruption. It was in this area that we found significant common interest. On many occasions I was invited to witness the signings of various ethics agreements promoted by the Consultants throughout Latin America. We gave them insight as to governance approaches in the United States. Felipe's work on international protocols attacking corruption will be guidelines for the future.

The years spent watching Texas develop its business model made me appreciate the interaction and the context of trade. Trade operates based on competitiveness, and if you are competitive, it can serve as a significant leveraging factor in sales, growth, and profits. The monopolies of Mexico suffered when they had to compete. However, if you become noncompetitive, then the same leverage can negatively impact you, particularly if you run significant trade deficits that only make you less competitive in the long run as they become substantial burdens.

Texas built its model not from theory but from the creation of will, knowing that it needed to move into the technology sectors and into research and development. They also realized that the programs built over the last thirty years were ones that matched its culture, its economic advantages, and its political system. *The Language of Conscience* talked about all three. In particular, the culture of Texas was one that dealt with reality. The Arts were prominent, but there was probably less appreciation in Texas of "Picasso's Bull's Head" Sculpture (of a bicycle handle bars and bicycle seat put together for creativity) and more toward a bronze sculpture of a bull's head with the bull attached. Work ethic, personal dignity, charity, and a sense of individual responsibility permeated not just a culture, but also the economics and the politics. It was a meritocracy with opportunity. You were expected to do your best; you got governmental assistance only if you truly needed it.

My work with Mexico and Latin America only made me appreciate more how the effects of culture fit into context with the three powers. I spent considerable time at Mexico's great Museum of Anthropology, which gave me an appreciation that I had not seen in the short lived American history of the development of civilization through many eras such as the Mayans, the Aztecs, and many others. The same site often thought of as a vortex, was the Plaza of Three Cultures in Mexico City and as such brings an appreciation of how the past hopefully carries forth the wisdom that the prior civilization learned.

China's Emergence

When I first went to China in the mid 1990s, it was very different from now. Yes, the small airport and limited development showed the beginning of the economic transformation that has led to a huge modern airport for the Olympics and almost over development in some areas. But these were the handshake and smile, not the heart and mind. As a Westerner from a different culture, I assumed that the way the Chinese thought and their customs were related to their economics.

As we became more affluent and progressed up Maslow's Hierarchy of Needs in the U.S., our focus changed, as did our style. We focused on business results quarterly and used golf, cocktail parties, and power lunches to create sophisticated business connections. The slow moving protocol, elaborate cultural banquets, careful toasts, and carefully scripted meetings of exact formality were remnants of the Imperial Culture. At first impulse, a Westerner perceives them as dating their culture to a time long past and a major modern weakness to business and politics because of the delay it created. That is a very misleading impression. The reliance on historical culture shows respect for the past, but it is also a well-learned and understood cultural power strategy that gives and retains power over its control and timing of the process.

The Chinese are long-term thinkers who concentrate on the biggest issues. We think in the short term; they have a different focus and respect for the wisdom of ancestors, and history is a method culturally to maintain that perspective. It then directly impacts how they think about economic and political issues. It helps bring more Harmony in focusing on cultural values rather than political and economic interests alone or primarily.

There is no question that this has some disadvantages in the modern world, but it also gives strengths. The key is for both sides to understand each other. *To work with China you must understand how they think otherwise you will not change what they think.* The same is true of the Chinese needing to understand the West.

Once this barrier is broken, progress on issues is possible. Formal meetings must have protocol, but it also allows delay for a reason and strategic advantage. Informal meetings, where people get to know and trust each other are key, but getting to those levels is hard. Meetings are usually different from Latin America where you develop the agenda more when you are there in person. A successful Chinese meeting ought to be a ratification, refinement, and celebration of an already agreed general conclusion.

Where a meeting is held can have great significance not just in image but success. The level of the person you meet is critical since your level of peers judges you. So who heads delegations on each side makes a difference. With whom you take a picture matters because it gives insight to your honor and degree of influence. How well you understand Chinese history also matters because it makes these factors easily understood and appreciated.

Your success can be judged by whether you get meetings at high levels, where the meetings are held, the length of the meetings and if your host extends them, and whether the host bids you farewell at the formal area of your meeting, walks you to the exit, or very rarely, takes you outside to your car. Each is a showing of a higher level of respect that is conveyed to the others present.

When I first came to the formal setting of two large chairs in the middle with tea between them and a translator's chair behind, with a row of chairs on either side leaving open all in front of the two main chairs for the host and the head of the delegation, I looked at it as old fashioned.

After years of perspective, I see it as a very strategic format not only of control and image, but also of balance. Once the Chinese perceive that you understand it, the refinement of the process lets you see exactly how they feel about issues and you by how they use the process. If they want to move quickly, they can. True mutual understanding is the great factor that will determine how well the two powers interact. In both cases it starts with understanding that culture is the power of history affecting today's perspective and that the U.S. has a history in hundreds of years and China in thousands.

Simple as it seems, this has true impact. Both countries need and can learn from each other, but only if they listen to and comprehend each other. The key common interest that is the big issue is conscience and fighting not only corruption but also a culture of dependency and convenience. Now is a pivotal time, as civilization has to choose a renaissance of conscience or a less sustainable world of convenience. This is the bridging issue from which solutions to other issues can be positioned and is key to both cultures. I have seen this truth from personal experience.

This background with Latin America, the understanding of the components of Texas Economic Policy, the Texas Lyceum Conferences of the era on politics and their impact, along with my participation on various policy groups gave me a very different insight. In October 1994 a delegation, including the Lieutenant Governor of Shandong Province of the Peoples Republic of China, visited Texas to further the Sister State Relationship that had been previously signed between Texas and Shandong Province. It was the first time I met Ms. Vivian Lee and Mr. Ted Li who coordinated the travel and activities for the delegation through their company Omega International Travel. Dr. Ray Perryman, who had served with me on the Commission creating the Economic Development Commission in Texas, hosted seminars on NAFTA and the Chinese Delegation had attended one. The Chinese had visited with him about the appropriate way to approach the State after direct contact had been lost since the Sister State arrangement was signed. Because Ray was aware of my experience with protocol missions as the International Committee Chairman of the Texas Association of Business and understood our protocol efforts for the Secretary of State's Office, he asked me if I could assist them in making the appropriate contacts.

Formerly a Lieutenant Commander in the Naval Reserve (on active duty during the Vietnam era in Rhode Island and Florida), my impressions of China were shaped by that period. However, after visiting with one of our Senator's about the delegation's importance and how to proceed, I was told that Shandong, a leader in oil and agriculture, was the Texas of China. I was advised it was well worth the time and effort to build international relationships because of trade and China's place in the future. This was consistent with what Dean Kozmetsky had told me years earlier. So after learning the past history of the Sister State effort, I found that the appropriate vehicle currently would be a meeting with Representative Bob Hunter, chair of the Cultural and International Affairs Committee of the Texas House of Representatives that had jurisdiction over these areas to be an appropriate vehicle.

I helped arrange the meeting for the Delegation with the Committee. It was also attended by Speaker of the House, Pete Laney and representatives of Governor Ann Richards' office on behalf of the Governor's Economic Division that had replaced the Texas Economic Development Commission. It was agreed that the appropriate actions regarding the Sister State Agreement would be coordinated with the Governor's Office through its Economic Development Department, the Texas Association of Business, and other entities who would work with Chinese groups to build better trade relationships. The Texas Legislature and the Legislative Committee would be happy to consider any additional legislative efforts to enhance the relationship as the discussions proceeded.

In November 1994, the State of Texas elected Governor George W. Bush to succeed Governor Ann Richards. This created a complexity—the contacts made with Governor Richards' Department of Commerce were directly with individuals on her staff and the change of administrations changed the contacts. Since I had hosted the delegations in Austin, I was asked to assist in re-establishing the relationship and was invited to Shandong Province. I traveled there in April of 1995 with Mr. Forrest Roan and Mr. Bob Reeves who had also been involved in the process. I took with me a flag from the Texas Legislature and letters from Representative Hunter conveying the interest and relating the previous discussions, materials from the Texas Association of Business that offered assistance and contacts for future communications and visits. I also carried a letter from the new Governor George W. Bush to the Shandong Governor designating Mrs. Brenda Arnett, the new Director of the Texas Department of Commerce as a contact person to move the relationship forward. After the trip, we brought back letters of response to the various entities.

During that trip I had also given a copy of *The New Legacy*, a book I had written following the creation of the Texas Lyceum, to several of the Chinese leaders who wanted to learn more about Texas. On the trip to Shandong, we had been given an opportunity to see the Confucian Temple in the city of Qufu. This was of particular interest because it gave me an opportunity to appreciate the significant cultural history of China and the power it had within Chinese society. There were many similarities between the rural value-oriented cultures of China and Texas. Much through the efforts of Ms. Vivian Lee, who had moved to San Antonio with a branch office of her company, the relationship was continued as other Chinese trade representatives and officials visited Texas.

Developments 1999 to 2004

In September of 1999, I was invited to attend the 2550th Anniversary of the Confucian Festival in Qufu. *The New Legacy* had been partly translated into Chinese by several of the leaders involved in the Confucian efforts at Shandong and gave an insight to many commonalities of the two cultures. Simultaneous with this Festival, the Government of China had opened the Confucian Museum in Qufu and during the activities asked Ms. Vivian Lee and me to assist them through an agreement to help the Confucian Museum bridge with the West so that many of the core principles of Chinese philosophies could be better understood.

This was done with the Star of the Republic Museum at Washington on the Brazos in Washington County, Texas. The museum served as the historic center of Texas and was where, as a nation, Texas had written its Declaration of Independence and Constitution in 1836. While that may have seemed an odd choice, it was largely symbolic—both recognized the importance of values in culture from the rural frontier family based perspectives.

In August of 2000, a Delegation from Shandong and a committee associated with the Confucian Museum traveled to Texas to make a presentation of the Confucian Analects on gold leaf to the Star of the Republic Museum. Receiving them were House Speaker Pete Laney, the Star of the

Republic Museum Director, and representatives from Washington, D.C. who brought appropriate congratulatory documents. It was interesting that a tea pot, a gift from the Empress of China in 1839 to President Sam Houston as a gift recognizing the Independence of Texas was placed with the Confucian Analects showing the long standing relationship between Texas and China. Over the following years, various Chinese delegations that came to Texas often visited Austin and left items to build the collection at Washington on the Brazos. Among those delegations was one from the Central Party School in Beijing. A cultural effort became a way to enhance political understanding of different systems.

Ms. Vivian Lee also presented to the Central Party School Press and Leadership a copy of *The Language of Conscience* because it is primarily a guide to ethics as a core philosophy of both culture and politics. The Central Party School, as one of the premier organizations of Chinese leadership, is the executive training site of its senior leadership and a significant source of its ideology and strategic planning. It was focusing heavily on understanding market systems and the interrelationship between Chinese culture and these systems.

Corruption was a significant issue to them, and *The Language of Conscience* included the writings of many of the major ethics organizations in the United States and the West. The book's uniqueness is that it independently recognized that the great areas of power, economics, politics, and culture were the very same as the core of the Communist Manifesto in its belief that the economic system created the nature of the culture, which drove the intellectual or political thought.

A year later, the School decided that this book would be worthy of publication and study. The book also served as an explanation of the use of nonprofit entities, which were referred to by many at the School as "Communist Capitalist Organizations" since they had a capitalist philosophy of markets but for the support of the people in the non-investor owned concepts. Its systematic description of the creation of the Texas Lyceum, the Texas Economic Development Commission, the work of Texans for Quality Education, the legislative efforts for the Arts and Humanities Commission, and the context that culture played within each of these relationships fit closely to the critical areas they were studying in the development of the Harmonious Society.

The Central Party School Press undertook to translate and publish the book in a joint effort with Ms. Lee's Tejano Publications, which helped bridge translation and implementation issues. They noted to me that while they translated and published Western books, this was the first to be translated and printed under the insignia of the School. While publication of the book would serve as an appropriate bridge, it was also to begin an exchange of ideas in a method helpful to the School in learning to better inject the writings of its scholars and philosophers into Western thought so China could be better understood. The School wished more of an engagement with Western literary sources but wanted to do so in a way that would let them understand the West more clearly at the inception.

While the book publication was in process in September 2002, a delegation headed by the Director and General Editor of the Publishing House of the Central Party School visited Austin, Texas. They toured the State Capitol, the LBJ Library, and visited with the University of Texas Press, which explained in detail how journals were developed that helped cultures understand each other. The University of Texas Press is well known for its specialty on Latin American literature and how it has thoughtfully developed collections. Tours of the State Capitol gave insight into the uniqueness of the American system. That evening the Dean of the LBJ School at the University of Texas hosted the delegation explaining how American universities presently perceived interaction with China and how public policy issues were researched and taught in the United States.

In February of the next year, another delegation from the Central Party School visited Texas as part of a tour including the Secretary of State's Office and the Governor's Office. They were shown the various historical sites in Austin and given a more thorough understanding through the State Capitol of how the legislative system effectively worked and was coordinated at both the state and national level. The Federation of our system was of significant interest. A number of the distinctions between the Chinese system and the American system were discussed.

The delegation also visited Dean George Kozmetsky's Institute of Constructive Capitalism for an overview on how technology drove the American economy and how education and public policy played key roles. Dr. Kotmetsky had been heavily involved in the creation of a joint private sector, government, educational institution partnership referred to as HARC. The Houston Area Research Council was located in the Woodlands and for years helped serve as the coordinator of the Texas Lyceum. Since the Chinese operated in a system where all these forces were automatically consolidated in the State Council, this was seen as a vehicle of interest. Ms. Vivian Lee and Mr. Ted Li later followed the concept in creating CHARC, a similar entity to help coordinate Chinese and American efforts.

As mentioned in September of 2004, I traveled to China for the book release with Ms. Vivian Lee and Mr. Ted Li, who had played a key role in the publication effort. At this particular meeting, the Central Party School signed an agreement with Tejano Publications, LLC to bring certain types of writings—particularly in the areas of philosophy, management, and culture from the West to the School for publication. And similarly they agreed to assist the Press in taking the books of Chinese leaders that were particularly appropriate for the times, such as Mr. Zheng Bijian's *Peaceful Rise—China's New Road to Development*, to the West so that scholars could better understand each other.

The second part of the formal ceremony was to recognize the publication of the Chinese version of *The Language of Conscience* and to present it to different universities and agencies that it might benefit. The book was already being sold in bookstores in China through the Press distribution channels and was used in seminars at the School. A presentation was made by one of the leaders of their Philosophy Department. He made a clear point that one of the positives of the book was that it was written in an attitude of not telling others what to do, but why we had done what we had. It revealed our intent giving it more merit.

This particular meeting looked at the formation and strategy of how appropriate literature from the School on the "Harmonious Society" and the "Scientific Outlook on Development" could be more appropriately placed in venues where they could be studied and understood by the West, and how more Western corporate and government management could be implemented in China. Bestsellers were available, but scholarly works, particularly in ethics and management systems were needed. Because of rapid growth, their experience with market transparency, governance, and enforcement systems was limited.

One of the great difficulties is that there are often more than 100,000 books being published each year. In the United States there are only a limited number of major commercial publishers looking at bestselling books rather than more specialized intellectual ones. And the intellectual presses are different in nature as seen from the discussions that had taken place with their delegations. The fact that the School was such a fundamental leader in

Chinese thought and that its white papers are studied by many of the most knowledgeable publications of the West ought to give its writings significant impact. However, many in the West did not understand what the School was because of its private nature, and this created a significant challenge. There was no comparable institution in America. The School needed to define itself and its goals to the West.

Dr. Song, one of their leading philosophers, stated how *The Language of Conscience* could benefit the School in its efforts to combine modern economics with past cultural values through conscience. In the discussions, it was noted that in the West and the East there are many different ways to look at information and relationships.

But if you are trying to bring out the best in people and have the greatest success, the best method and the most appropriate bridge is to have an organizing principle that promotes conscience and its effective force of ethics. Confucian philosophy, which was the core of Eastern philosophy, noted that if one word might serve as a rule for the practice of all of one's life, it would be the word reciprocity.

As part of the meeting, the three case studies that I had written in *The Language of Conscience* were discussed. The issue of ethics that was particularly important because China is fighting to build a culture that eliminates corruption being enhanced by the addition of market economics and materialism. There was an interest on the part of the School to bring leaders in these fields to the School so they might build relationships with international organizations in ethics and governance.

They were particularly impressed with the Texas Lyceum as an organization that trained leadership by bringing public involvement more into the process. And the method by which it worked was of significant interest because it gave insight on how Western leadership was created and very diverse groups interacted to create and analyze policy.

The School studied methods and information from around the world and found this to be a very unique approach that fit well with their concepts of building a Harmonious Society. The Lyceum and the concepts in the books focused on "contextual thinking" and how the powers they studied related to the second area—leadership.

The third area, the effort of Blue Cross Blue Shield of Texas sponsoring the Caring for Children Program was significantly important because health care was a critical long-term issue in China. What was unique about the approach for the Caring for Children Foundation was its creation of nonprofit efforts to achieve a portion of what was needed rather than accomplishing it through government or commercial efforts.

China has non-governmental organizations but learning how to make them effective was significant. Russia had privatized with Oligarchs, but the Chinese were looking at ways to "privatize" government entities more consistent with communism and mutual ownership or nonprofit concepts. The Caring for Children Program demonstrated efficient ways to use and create entities of public service. The leadership of the School suggested that efforts be undertaken to use *The Language of Conscience* "as a bridge on ethics, morality, and cultural values with the West" through the publication agreement with the Press and by the interaction with other entities.

The School indicated an interest in building a relationship with the Texas Lyceum, which trained leaders based on nonpartisan principles since it included Republicans, Democrats, and Independents and was fundamentally based on the Aristotelian principles of ethics and vision. There was also an interest expressed to moving forward with the activities of the Press in meeting various publishing organizations in the West and continue building relationships with ethics related organizations.

Shared Events 2005

As a result of this meeting, a delegation from the Central Party School attended the 25th Anniversary Gala of the Texas Lyceum in January of 2005 and presented a copy of the Chinese Edition of *The Language of Conscience*. These were presented to Mr. Walter Tomlinson and Mr. Jordon Cowman, who were the Chairman and President of the Texas Lyceum.

At the Gala, the Chinese Delegation again met with the University of Texas Press and with representatives from one of the major speakers' bureaus in the U.S. acting as an agent for many American writers. Both gave insight and understanding into how the various commercialized organizations worked, as well as the expectations of major authors since it was also the purpose of the School to bring more Western books to China. Concepts of where rights could be acquired were discussed as well as the importance of intellectual property rights.

The Delegation also met with the leadership of the Texas Commission on the Arts, discussing possible joint activities in literary areas. It was not lost on the Delegation that the Honorary Co-Chairmen for the Texas Lyceum

Gala were every living Governor and Lieutenant Governor of the State of Texas from both political parties.

Even though they had often fought politically, there were concepts that could unify all sides. The Lieutenant Governor of Texas had suggested to the Lyceum that it undertake a study of the critical components of growth and the challenges Texas would face in the next twenty-five years. The Chinese were interested in working jointly to study the removal of impediments to trade and investment and assist mutual benefits of growth and cultural interaction.

In September 2005 a delegation from the Texas Lyceum went to China at the invitation of the Central Party School. Mr. Walter Tomlinson, Mr. Jordon Cowman, and Mr. Dougal Cameron joined me for a week of activities and meetings. It included an ethics seminar with scholars from the Central Party School, and representatives of organizations such as Dr. Felipe Ochoa of the Task Force on Integrity, as well as letters from the Ethics Officers Association and others indicating their willingness to work with the School. I had the opportunity to also include different groups attending the Beijing Book Festival, who gave insight to the School on how university presses and intellectual presses operated.

They gave their thoughts on the best ways to approach having scholars' works read in the United States so that appropriate bridges could be built. *ForeWord Magazine,* one of the premier institutions working in partnership with major American universities' literary departments gave insight on the current state of exchanges and what might be done to better enhance them. Ms. Vivian Lee hosted all the group's leaders at her Lu Yang Compound in Beijing, an over 600 year old compound that had housed members of the Foreign Legations—including an historic dinner as of the time of the changing of Dynasties in appropriate dress of the period. It was interesting that you had a number of nations again in the same walls but with a common purpose of designing cultural bridges and understanding more than political protocol.

The following year, a delegation from the Texas Lyceum visited the Central Party School and signed a formalized Collaboration Agreement discussed at their previous meeting, and in the interim, had received the blessing of the various necessary entities.

Several things had become very clear to the School and the various participants after visits to the United States. While the School was well known and understood by most of the significant players of China, it was not an institution that would be similar to others in the West. As a result, its scholars and their writings were not fully appreciated more broadly for the importance they have within the Chinese system. Major media organizations such as the *Economist*, the *Financial Times*, and *The New York Times* understand and covered specific things done by the School and the white papers released and cover them, but in other media there was not a full understanding.

To have more focus for think tanks and others, there needed to be a prioritization of their importance and connection to the issues in the major Chinese institutions. You might find some titles from the West that might profit the Press, but would not accomplish the major goals helping the Press present the evolution of the School's developing concepts in an appropriate manner. (Over the years that has changed. In *The New York Times*, Friday June 24, 2011, on page A13, one of the best articles on the School described it under "Shaping Lives." Increasingly the West understands that, "The training ground for the future leaders of the Communist Party of China is like no other university or college in the country." In the article by Li Jing and Pin Yining:)

> "This might be the most mysterious school in China. The gates are closely guarded by the People's Armed Police, 24 hours a day, seven days a week. Headmasters of this place, a training ground for the future leaders of the Communist Party of China (CPC), are always one of the country's vice-presidents, if not the president. Former headmasters include Mao Zedong, Liu Shaoqi, and Hu Jintao. . . .
>
> "The speeches that top leaders deliver at the Central Party School, and their articles printed in the school's publications, often signal new strategies and policies that will be adopted by the central government. . . .
>
> 'Officials might be discreet in talking to strangers or in public, but their internal discussion in class is unbounded,' said Wu Zhongmin, a professor at the Central Party School who focuses on social justice research. 'Sometimes their opinions can be really audacious and revolutionary.'
>
> "The Central Party School is a place where officials and researchers debate the future of the country and the Party.
>
> "They have to face the problems and find ways to solve them. Speaking empty words or simply flattering makes no sense here.

"Discussions are closely linked to the most pressing social problems, such as illegal land grabs, the inequality between rural and urban areas, and corruption. . . ."

This is an article that ought to be read in its entirety for anyone wanting to understand policy development in China.

Possibilities for Better Understanding

In that early period, I noted that a book that could serve as an introduction to the Central Party School in the West would be particularly helpful. It would note its history, its influence, and power, and the main points that it wished to put forth—books that had been suggested by the School, *Peaceful Rise—China's New Road to Development,* by Mr. Zheng Bijian, and Dr. Wang Weiguang's *A Scientific Outlook on the Development for an Overall Balanced Socioeconomic Development,* as well as the writings of several professors on the development of the concept of the Harmonious Society.

Since these would be new philosophical approaches from China, I suggested that it would be very handy to have them consolidated into a set of ideas that Western scholars who met with the Central Party School could read in advance. That let both the Chinese have some understanding of the dialectic of Western thought and the Western scholars have a better understanding of the new Chinese philosophy. It would show a respect to both sides and would allow time for focus on issues that mattered and would give depth to the level of discussions.

Similarly, as relationships developed it would be worthwhile for the School to work with many Western Journals where articles could be exchanged. Collections of writings at universities were key approaches to concentrating thought and study. The Exchange of Scholars was already a goal of the Collaboration Agreement with the Texas Lyceum.

This concept also required that you develop a set of Western thoughts that could parallel the Chinese thoughts so that their Marxist dialectic could effectively help the Chinese understand different Western systems and how many of the Western concepts could be integrated into modern China. I had written a number of articles on small government, value-based cultures, which the Quorum Report had called "Enlightened Conservatism." In part, I explained where it could be adapted and was a Western parallel of their

"Harmonious Society" and that both were based on conscience and the concept of fairness. It was a cultural philosophy rather than a political one, but it contextually integrated economics and politics.

The greatest intellectual benefit of such a comparison would be to have a joint system that compared different cultures by the forces of change and the status quo, which are often in or out of balance according to the personal dignity or "face" that a person held. If there were stability and satisfaction, the change interaction with the status quo would have stability. But when significant imbalances were present, there would be discontent. In both societies, the powers of economics, politics, and culture were the three primary powers where different functions could be placed. And the methods of analyzing them would be analytics, measurement (and prioritization), and trends (timeframe impacts).

These would be combined with an understanding of the importance of the three determinants of culture, which were predominant in *The Language of Conscience*. One was the Rule of Law or Discipline in Society, which was how the law was enforced. The second was the Rule of Obligation primarily from Confucius and Christ that looked at morality and what each man's obligation was to each other beyond the law (occasionally referred to as the unenforceable law of courtesy and honor). And the third or final concept being compassion or a culture of service where men helped each other without necessarily feeling they should receive anything in return. If the final culture was created, then society and civilization would be elevated because effectively you would be using the Golden Rule as well as the compassion shown through a civilized culture determining policy.

Civilization itself has stages as it rises from the anarchy of a valueless society to a civilization driven by noble ideas until it disintegrates to a lesser stage as those ideas lose force. China's history shows those trends. They are why culture and its power are appreciated. The comparison of similar values in the West could help the cultures understand the most critical common points to bring out the best in people. A book that helped bridge thoughts could be of assistance.

I volunteered to undertake writing such a book from this joint perspective but requested the rights to the writings of major Chinese scholars that had been discussed so I could have an orientation to read before meetings. This was consistent with the goals of the Collaboration Agreement with the Texas Lyceum. And it was from this effort that the book *Instilling Values in*

Transcending Generations was written focusing on the principles needed to be taught to each generation since change takes place over time. I enhanced the Triangles that had been developed for *The Language of Conscience,* updating them with thoughts and ideas I had encountered at the School.

Continued Relational Growth 2006

Also in September of 2006, I returned to Beijing to meet with the School and present them copies of *Instilling Values in Transcending Generations* so they might be familiar with them on the first trip to the United States under the Collaboration Agreement. The Texas Lyceum and the School had undertaken a five-year effort detailed in *Instilling Values in Transcending Generations,* which primarily involved an exchange program of leaders from both groups. In America the Chinese wanted to learn more about civil liberties and the American systems. In China, the Lyceum leaders wanted to learn more about how China thought in its future vision of the world under the Harmonious Society.

The leaders of each of the delegations from the School to the United States were often from the six members of the Board of Directors of the School. They were very high ranking delegations including select members of different departments having specific interests in building bridges with other academic institutions and methods to refine Chinese thoughts on the market and political systems.

When I was in China, I was also asked by the Ministry of Commerce to deliver a speech at their annual event at Xiamen that dealt with impediments to trade and investment, a theme that had resonated since the Sister State effort. I called a number of Texas business organizations and interested professional lawyers, accountants, and executive search firms.

It was a good case study in that China looked at being competitive through cost where Americans looked at the development of markets by oftentimes stimulating interest and need. The Chinese understood how to produce a product cheaply, the Americans how to create a demand for a product.

From a number of the questions revealed, I also created a two-volume set taking the books as a unit and writing a lengthy Foreword that updated much of what had been learned into a continuing context. The combined set was an eBook entitled *Understanding Enlightened Conservatism.* It focused on the concept that if every man grants every other man the same rights and dignity that he wishes for himself, then there is a significant balance in society.

This concept of dignity is fundamental within democracy in the West because it is the essence of legal rights and their enforcement and the respect that ought to be given with it. It is a concept I also found to be prominent in China, particularly with the concept of "face," where sharing of obligations and responsibilities and showing respect was a key. More than taking legal approaches to try and explain the differences in the cultures, doing so from the more cultural approach of dignity made things far better understood. This was true as the basis of working out problems. I had not looked on dignity as such a key until the evolution of these discussions. It becomes a lynchpin in many issues if analyzed accordingly.

Also in September of 2006, a delegation from the Central Party School visited the United States. We adjusted the agenda for areas of interest expressed to me when I was in China and included some very specific targeted meetings. I remembered how Dr. Milton Friedman, the great American economist, had noted that the evolution of developing countries like China moved first through economic freedom, to the development of civil freedom that required an understanding of obligations and responsibilities, and finally to political freedom where they elected their leaders. The most critical part of this evolution dealt with learning the obligations of citizenship as they acquired more freedoms. If this was not learned, there was instability.

The institutions in the United States taught and developed this over many years, and one of the most beneficial aspects of the Lyceum/Central Party School exchange would be the ability to show higher level leaders of China exactly how these institutions worked and, through a comparison of efforts of the joint book, how they interrelated to each other systemically. During this trip, we visited three major Texas cities, as well as Washington, D.C. The visits were specifically targeted to understand questions that the Chinese had asked.

Upon their arrival in Houston, they were hosted at a reception and the next day visited with the Houston Endowment—one of the most significant organizations in Houston dealing with nonprofit institutions and their use in accomplishing many common purposes unifying people's private activities in the place of government. This was a prime example of how private money could be relegated to societal needs. They visited the

James Baker Institute at Rice University, one of the premier think tanks that looks at international activities.

They also attended a dinner given in their honor by the Lyceum at the Federal Reserve Bank of Houston and were briefed on economic issues and how the Federal Reserve was a very independent institution dealing with monetary policy. The dinner included presentations from the Mayor of Houston and the County Judge welcoming them to the community and expressing continued relationships in the future. The Houston Partnership, the major business organization of Houston, expressed its interest in working with the School and explained the unique relationships between Houston and Mexico. The Chinese were significantly interested in how NAFTA worked and how trade problems were addressed since they were now part of the WTO.

The delegation also visited one of the major churches in Houston and learned how the religious system in the United States combines with family values to impart and instill cultural values within society. They wanted to visit with individuals rather than people of prominence to better understand how Americans lived. So I brought them to my home in Brenham for a dinner. Mr. James Dick, international pianist and long time friend, was kind enough to give a concert. Not far from Brenham, he built the famed Festival Institute at Round Top, Texas. His motto has always been to "never dream the ordinary."

Huge structures arise from the wooded landscape as a testament to the concept of excellence and giving to others. James spent his summers teaching young musicians from all over the world and has given many a free concert in support of our efforts to have the power of culture understood by those in politics and economics. Confucius taught certain arts for the same purpose. Aristotle looked at virtue from a perspective of excellence. Success in any endeavor usually requires more than raw talent at its highest levels. It takes commitment and endless practice. Brenham had history, but it also had the essence of excellence to be appreciated.

We visited Washington on the Brazos where the delegation presented a copy of the Chinese Edition of *The Language of Conscience* as well as some of their own writings to the collection that included the Confucian Analects. The delegation visited the George Bush Library at Texas A&M University and the Bush School, visiting with major international scholars including a number of Chinese students attending. They interacted with A&M professors and students.

Perhaps one of the most significant discussions there involved the concept of democracy emerging in China. When asked by one of the students, the head of the delegation very thoughtfully detailed a progression. He noted that the benefits of democracy were understood in China, but China currently has a significant problem—the need for generating significant growth economically to keep stability. Because of the poverty levels in the rural areas and the need to take both education and opportunities to a great number of people, the Party fit like an umbrella over the various institutions of government and life, but primarily focused on the creation of stability. Democracy is beginning at the higher levels of the Party in leadership elections, as well as being tested in some smaller areas.

For democracy to be expanded, a thoughtful process has to be put into place and would move down from the Party to the rest of the country as this was accomplished over time. Its characteristics may not be the same as the West, but many of the principles and values are jointly understood and appreciated. The history and culture of China are different from the West so China would develop its own visions. Just like Chairman Deng's observation that it did not matter if a cat was black or white if it caught rats, the terminology was less significant than the actual result.

Following those presentations and exchanges, we had a dinner at Dougal Cameron's ranch, and the delegation was shown Texas rural life. The next day they visited the famed Round Top Antique Fair area. It was amazing how much common interest in history both Americans and Chinese have in their appreciation of antiques. They also visited James Dick's facilities at Festival Hill in Round Top and learned of its devotion to excellence in mentoring the younger generation. They then moved on to Austin, Texas, having dinner at the Headliners Club composed of many different organizations in the Austin area. These included think tanks and major public policy institutes such as the LBJ School of Public Affairs represented by their Dean who later gave the delegation a tour of the School and the LBJ Library.

All the Chinese are extremely impressed with the Presidential Libraries that contain documents written by individuals that give the history of an administration and are open to the public. It is also amazing to them that anyone can walk into any Representative's office at the State Capitol. There was much discussion on the differences between the Chinese and the American systems in these regards. Part of it was the political basis, but another part of it was more cultural structure.

China had always operated in more of a hierarchy from the times of its emperors and as such the very nature of the culture needed to be understood. This was equally true in many cases with the Internet. While much of the West criticized the Chinese for censorship of the Internet for political reasons, a significant portion of that censorship also relates to their cultural concerns on individual dignity, and the belief that many criticisms should not be made public.

These distinctions are important. We found that if we could find common ground on concepts like dignity and justice, then that may be more important than the exact method for getting there. Too often the form becomes an impediment to the goal, and many of the efforts of these visits were to try to look in depth at what actually can solve problems and build relationships.

After special visits to the Texas Capitol, where they learned of its operations, they had dinner in their honor hosted by the Lieutenant Governor and attended by a number of business, educational, and civic leaders from Austin. The following day the delegation went to see the operations of the Dallas-Fort Worth International Airport and had a reception with major business leaders. Then in the evening Mr. Trammell S. Crow hosted a final dinner at the Crow Museum of Asian Art. The program was designed for three cities that fit the relevance of discussion of the Triangles. Houston had been formulated primarily for economics, Austin for politics, and Dallas and Brenham for culture.

The delegation then flew to Washington, D.C., where they received a Congressional Tour of the Capitol and a cultural review of the city and its various monuments. It was interesting to see the number of books on culture that were bought by the delegation to give insight on cultural issues.

A final reception was hosted by the Fund for American Studies that had done a significant amount of work in Europe helping Eastern Europe convert to market systems. The President of the Fund had also written the introduction to *Instilling Values in Transcending Generations,* and, thereby, was familiar with the efforts of the School using the books as a bridge on morality and values between the countries. Many of the other Washington think tanks attended the reception and discussions provided insight from both sides as to how interactions might better help us understand one other.

One of the significant distinctions I tried to point out to the Chinese is how multiple parties can work. They have one Communist party that may have disagreements but has to find harmony because it is built on consensus. The American two-party system of competing ideas and often-hyper partisanship is more difficult to understand from their perspective. My point was that some partisanship is necessary for the full discussion of ideas. Principled debate is the very core of a Democracy or Republic. The flaw is shown when the system of decision becomes political and driven by convenience primarily rather than conscience for the common good.

But convenience over conscience in any system, including theirs, leads to failure. It is no different from corruption in market systems. They become ineffective because there is no free competition, which is the driving force of markets. So systems need to be designed and evaluated on how they can perform on the conscience or convenience axis. In all cases, the key factor is cultural ethics must be supported.

Insights of 2007

A return visit of the Texas Lyceum delegation to China occurred in January of 2007. After visiting the Central Party School and discussing plans for the future year, the School briefed the delegation on many of the changes taking place in the development of the Harmonious Society concept and arranged a fieldtrip to Shenzhen.

This particular trip was extremely helpful because it included an understanding of the history of economic development and planning that took place in China, but how the Central Party School facility in Shenzhen studied the significant change in the city's culture. This gave the Central Party School a model of the values they needed to apply within the educational systems so they would appropriately prepare society for China's evolution to a higher level of economic activity.

In effect, Chairman Deng had created Shenzhen as the new and modern China. As it had grown to a city of eight million, a building showed those levels of growth from an engineering and technology standpoint and where the new areas over the next twenty or thirty years would evolve. But also the School studied the change in corruption, morality, and other areas that were enhanced by the mixture of Western markets with the pressures of competition and the Chinese system as it existed. They could see where China would be twenty-five years from now if values were not taught in the school system. What you quickly understood is that China was a very focused and strategic society with a leadership that thought in terms of generations. They did not observe it by things happening presently but how trends are established.

Shenzhen also had two theme parks that gave focused understanding of the various cultures in China and how China tended to see the world. One theme park gave insight to China and the different regions, while the other was a theme park where the Chinese could get an understanding of the rest of the world. Watching the families there reminded me of taking my children to Disneyworld—entertainment with education. The new China is not the old China economically, but modern China may be finding many of its early cultural value roots. What was included in the parks told what they valued.

On this trip, the School also brought up their interest in one of the other parts of the case studies in *The Language of Conscience*. One of the examples that I had given was an effort I made in previous years with Rogers Coleman, President of the Texas Blue Cross Blue Shield organization, to help form the Texas Caring for Children Foundation.

One of the great tragedies is that a number of children do not get healthcare when they need it for lack of resources and they suffer permanent loss in areas such as hearing. I had seen this problem when I was on the Board of Covenant House in Houston. After the formation of the Caring for Children Foundation, we used the knowledge gained there to also give guidance to the State in its future policies and undertook many of these goals.

The Chinese were very focused on the Texas Blue Cross concept since it was non-investor owned and from that operated as a successful business entity, but did so for the benefit of its members. If it made profits either new services were provided or costs reduced after retaining reserves for growth and contingencies.

Since health care was a critical emerging study issue for the School, this had significant interest for them. The Chinese save perhaps 40% of their income due to the uncertainty of health care. Because of this interest, I suggested taking a member of the Blue Cross Blue Shield Association on our trip to China to explain the concept. The Association had an interest in visiting with the School and learning more about China.

So in early April of 2007, I returned to China to introduce the Blue Cross Association to them and presented to the School the new eBook of

Understanding Enlightened Conservatism that had pulled together many of the thoughts from the previous visits. I also had the chance to present the books to the Counsellors of the State Council for their cultural collection and to Tsinghua University for its library collection.

In the Chinese system the Party, the government, and the military are three distinct power bases. The Party determines much of the ideology and the training of the leadership throughout the government, military, and Party. The State Council, effectively headed by the Premier, is the pyramid of all agencies, state-owned businesses, and other institutions. The Counsellors are a group of perhaps forty people who are retired or are experts in various fields who are advisors to the Council and to the Premier.

While the Central Party School deals with theory, the Council deals with the practicality of making issues work and evaluating them for implementation. During the Blue Cross delegation visit, there were significant exchanges on how the medical systems work for both countries for a better understanding of the complexity of the issues involved.

Eventually, the Association entered a Memorandum of Understanding for study of the issue with the School and Counsellors. While this focused on understanding each other's obligations, the side benefit of bridge building provided an understanding of how traditional Chinese medicine aided in wellness and a better understanding for future problems, as the SARS possible pandemic had just crystallized. Health is a global issue in today's environment.

As the Chinese designed their systems, they needed to understand how the Western systems functioned and how to eventually integrate to them. The West could learn much from traditional Chinese medicine. While the West would use the electronic medical records as a catalyst, the Chinese looked at other catalysts, but had significant focus on medical ethics being upgraded and non-profit formats.

In May 2007 a second delegation from the Central Party School came to the United States and visited a separate set of institutions. This delegation traveled from San Francisco to Washington, D.C., for a welcome dinner and combined a tour of the Capitol with a meeting of the National Endowment of the Arts. The leadership of the National Endowment explained how the funding of the cultural arts took place in the United States both through state and individualized efforts. They noted how little direct exchange there had been with China but how this was an area of increasing interest. Later an evening tour was given at the National Cathedral in Washington, D.C., a significant landmark of Washington where many state funerals and other activities were held.

The following day was spent at the Capitol as part of the Lyceum conference that featured a number of speakers on world trade. The conference was organized in different segments and was held by the Lyceum in Washington on a regular basis so Texas leaders could interact with national leaders. Many of the Texans in various Washington agencies were members of the Texas Lyceum and helped coordinate the speakers. A significant set of perspectives from Democratic and Republican leaders were presented, and the delegation had an opportunity to understand how the Lyceum worked in developing and analyzing subjects as well as creating interrelationships between various parties.

A former senior editor of a news association hosted a lunch with a briefing the next day at the National Press Club. It demonstrated how the press in the United States works and how the Club itself was one of the major venues for speakers wishing to address the media in Washington. It gave significant insight to the delegation as to how the news media in the United States functioned at the national level, which had been an important factor in the development of civil liberties.

The following day the delegation flew to San Antonio, Texas, and toured the Alamo seeing much of Texas history in its long-standing cultural relationship with Mexico. The next day they had meetings with the San Antonio Free Trade Alliance looking at methods by which trade and investment could be enhanced. They then toured the University of Texas at San Antonio with a dinner that evening in Austin.

This delegation also visited the State Capitol with an explanation of more detailed aspects of how government worked. The Texas Legislature gave a special recognition to the delegation. At a lunch at the Headliners Club that included various Austin officials, the delegation was given a gavel by the Lieutenant Governor of Texas, which was used to call the Legislation in session. After a series of afternoon tours and a dinner at the home of a Lyceum Alumni, they attended meetings with the Asian Society, and a series of meetings with universities and groups. The tour had been arranged to facilitate an understanding of how different civil liberties had to be matched with the development of civil obligation through the various institutions. The point focused on how teaching values and obligations was essential in building the foundation for civil liberties that led to political liberties.

Intellectual Building Blocks Refined

In March of 2008, I accompanied a Texas Lyceum delegation to China for the formulation of the 2008 plan. Discussions continued with the Central Party School Press in refining ideas from both countries presented within the intellectual arenas, primarily through the concept of a joint journal, and reviewed the great efforts over the last three years to familiarize the parties with each other and to understand different systems more accurately. During that time, a significant amount of material had been developed to build an appropriate foundation for a forum in the United States and in China. Here, each step had built on the last and taken ideas to another level.

The original suggestions in the Collaboration Agreement had begun with an exchange of scholars, but had been accomplished by a joint effort on books to set a foundation of thought by which a forum and journal could be more appropriately created, grown, and scholars could be added. For the Chinese one of the significances in coming to the United States was having their speeches put into the proper context to help minimize levels of risk associated with being misquoted or misunderstood.

From their trips, they had seen that the American media system is very different and very open as compared to China. It would dramatically benefit the American/Chinese exchange of ideas for Chinese leaders to make major speeches at major institutions. These types of opportunities could certainly be arranged as was seen from previous trips.

However, there was a desire to learn how systems worked effectively before proceeding publicly. The essential issue was to see that the key points being made were well understood. Between translation and differing audiences, that was a challenge to be thoughtfully addressed. What the Chinese prioritized was often not the focus of American media and audiences who looked at more general issues. The concept of using the books, journals, and finally presentations seemed more logical to assure that everything was in proper context and serious discussions could be accomplished.

Culture was the critical base issue. Economics tends to be a discussion of rich versus poor and politics of right versus left. But culture tends to be conscience versus convenience or in the terms of the Chinese writers, often selfishness versus the common good. A joint journal would thus be appropriate because it would be a way that such context could be provided and scholars work disseminated with economics and politics brought into the mix. The concept of the Triangles was also discussed as methods by which a forum could be designed. The Chinese felt that the Lyceum concept of exposing them to all three major powers in each of the trips was particularly helpful, and they had done the same for the Americans visiting China. It helped put the learning experience into context.

The significance was that the books written were not important alone but were really the joint development of a concept. It is the concept that is described in the individual books that is vital. The books simply showed the evolution of a journey on a conceptual thought. The ultimate issue is one of trust, and trust is accomplished by having a common vision and working toward it.

I stated many times that how you think about issues determines what you think about the issues. I also mentioned that there would be a need to add certain institutions to help in the difficult areas of economics, politics, and culture. In particular, I suggested the inclusion of Dr. Dennis Kratz the Dean of the University of Texas at Dallas School of Liberal Arts and also the founder of that institution's Confucian Institute. The University of Texas at Dallas has one of the premier translation centers for Chinese in the United States. One of the problems in working with the Press was having quality translation facilities. This relationship could tie them, with the insight of the Confucian Institutes, to the West and also with the other translation institutions.

On this trip I was joined by Jim Windham, a noted business leader and writer, who had an interest in working on the journal as an editor with Dean Kratz, and also with Mr. Jim Kozlowski and Mr. Dougal Cameron who had many ties with the business communities in Texas. Former Texas Secretary of State Geoffrey Connor also attended and explained the best ways for the government protocol agencies and other institutions to work together. I brought letters from the Houston Partnership that had worked extensively with me and the Ministry of Commerce in developing ties over the years. Houston and San Antonio are at the core of the United States relationship with Mexico. We previously brought letters from an organization representing the State of Texas and the four neighboring Mexican states on how the entities could work together with the region because of the work with NAFTA.

Many of the people, who wrote parts of *The Language of Conscience* or subsequent books, were Chairmen of the Trade Subcommittee of the Ways and Means Committee in Washington and Chairmen of the Ways and Means Committee in the United States Congress. They were directly involved with NAFTA and the WTO membership of China. This gave insight to the logic and level of thought within the book on trade issues and why concepts like the three-country interaction could create jobs in all three countries, but had to be based on cultural understanding and trust.

Another development that the Partnership emphasized was the significant impact of the renovation of the new Panama Canal allowing larger ships to come from China, Korea, and Asia into the Port of Houston. It might well change many of the shipping approaches of the Mid West to the Gulf rather than to the Pacific decreasing costs for all and adding convenience. The Chinese also gave a tour of Port Tianjin, giving the Texas delegation an overview of the trade issues and complexity as well as the detail of planning that had gone into that Port complex. The difference between American and European expectations and obligations in China was interesting. Again cultural and legal systems were significant—Europeans seemed more used to regulatory uncertainties.

In October 2008 the Central Party School Executive Vice President led a delegation that visited Houston. The delegation attended a forum with the Greater Houston Partnership in increasing trade and investment between the two countries that had been a discussion point of the previous Lyceum trip to Tianjin. An area of common interest had been a research project on removing the impediments to trade and investment between the two countries and also including the concept of NAFTA.

The Houston Partnership detailed the five major issues they thought could be of the greatest significance in building bridges and offered their assistance to continue working with the School in research on the best implementation opportunities. The Vice President then gave a formal presentation at a luncheon hosted by the Texas Lyceum and the Greater Houston Partnership at the Federal Reserve Bank of Dallas, Houston Branch. The audience included the business leadership of Houston and many of the leaders of the Houston Chinese community.

During a tour of Houston, the delegation had an opportunity to meet Rockets Basketball player Yao Ming, visit a number of significant sites, and travel to the Star of the Republic Museum at Washington on the Brazos where copies of the Vice President's speech and books were included in the collection of the Confucian Museum exchange. After additional meetings and tours, the final day culminated in a dinner at the Petroleum Club.

One of the significant aspects of this particular visit was the presentation on the *Peaceful Development of China and Chinese Renaissance* that was made by Professor Li Junru, the Executive Vice President of the Central Party School to the Texas Lyceum and Houston Partnership at the Federal Reserve. He discussed the Peaceful Development of China, the Chinese Renaissance, and the relationship between them. From a historical perspective the peaceful development of China seeks to realize a century-old dream of making the country strong and making the Renaissance of Chinese civilization come true. He noted that the Chinese nation had overcome many hardships and "without the renaissance of the Chinese civilization, it is hard to reach the real peaceful development."

That is a significant point since it shows the tremendous importance the Chinese place on their historic culture. He noted the three challenges that China faces from resources, the environment, and a series of dilemmas in socioeconomic development. To solve those questions the Chinese government advocates the Scientific Outlook on Development, which requires them to put people first and pursue a comprehensive balanced and sustainable development. It is a concept where China realizes that it needs to improve the quality of civilization culturally and economically. He noted that peaceful development requires a civilized China to stand firmly in the family of nations. And most importantly, he noted that the peaceful development of China and the Chinese Renaissance is a long-term historical process that requires the efforts of generations. There is a sense of historical mission and social responsibility within China.

One of his other major topics was the Chinese Renaissance in a Harmonious World, which was a recognition that the Chinese people have to join hands with the people of other countries. It was a feeling that China should respect the path and model of development people of every country chose to follow in accordance with their actual conditions.

I was particularly interested in his description of the kind of the Harmonious World that was envisioned. He noted:

A harmonious world we Chinese people conceive might be pictured as follows in five aspects. Politically, all countries should respect each other and conduct consultations on an equal footing, in a common endeavor to promote democracy in international relations. Economically, that they should cooperate with one another; draw on each other's strengths and work together to advance economic globalization in the direction of balanced development, shared benefits, and win-win progress. Culturally, they learn from each other in the spirit of seeking common ground while shelving differences, respect the diversity of the world, and make joint efforts to advance human civilization. In the areas of security, they should trust each other, strengthen cooperation, settle international disputes by peaceful ways rather than by war, and work together to safeguard peace and stability in the world. On environmental issues they should assist and cooperate with each other in conservation efforts to take of the Earth, the only home of human beings.

He stated that this was a set of ideals, but was also a good aspiration. And the problems that came with such a set of goals are ones that cannot deny contradiction and conflict. In addition he emphasized the need for handling and settling disputes through a proper approach and a mechanism of coordinated differing interests. He spoke of the need for emancipating minds because human history has shown nothing can be done by fighting a World War, block politics, hegemonism, or by the clash of civilizations. He noted that in the 21st century Chinese citizens must have political, scientific, humanistic, ethical, and occupational qualities. Improving the whole citizen's quality involves an arduous task not only by standardized schooling but also by every citizen's self-education and self-practice. He pointed out that the Chinese will absorb the wisdom from home and abroad and ended with a quotation from Fei Xiaotong, a distinguished sociologist who passed away years before. He said, "As every nation should value not only its own merits, but also others' merits, and treasure shared merits to achieve great harmony of the whole world."

His speech recognized that China had an intense nationalism and appreciation for its culture, but the ultimate issue to creating a World Harmonious Society was the process by which people could work together. The fact that the Peaceful Development of China was so directly connected with the Chinese Renaissance of its values was a point I think that many missed, but I tried to emphasize as being particularly important.

Continuing the Foundation

On March 23, 2009, a delegation from the Central Party School led by Mr. Sun Qingju, the Vice School Master of the Central Party School, and a number of other significant leaders went to Dallas, hosted by the Confucian

Lyceum Institute and the University of Texas at Dallas. In this particular visit Mr. Ross Perot visited with the group for several hours for a tour of his facility and explained through exhibits his views on the importance of character and many of his perspectives on a broad range of issues. A luncheon was hosted by President David E. Daniel of the University of Texas at Dallas, and in the afternoon they toured the Dallas Arts District through the courtesy of the Director of the Margaret and Trammell Crow Collection of Asian Art. It was shown how Americans were bridging with China through cultural areas and the possibilities that could take place in exchanges of exhibits.

That evening Mr. Trammell S. Crow hosted a dinner and reception at his home. The following day a breakfast was hosted by the Honorable Geoffrey Connor, the former Secretary of State of Texas, who explained and answered questions regarding Texas, its protocol systems, and his experiences in leading delegations from the State of Texas to China. Later in the day, due to the Chinese interest in understanding health care, a visit was made to Blue Cross Blue Shield of Texas where Dr. Paul Handel, the Medical Director of HCSC, explained overviews of the interactions of American medical systems and the Chinese cultural medical approaches.

The Federal Reserve Bank of Dallas provided the delegation with a tour of their facilities and discussions with President Richard Fisher and other Bank officials that gave the Chinese an insight into the independence of the Federal Reserve and the actions it took to preserve the value of the dollar. President Fisher had been with Secretary of State Kissinger during some of the most significant early breakthroughs and was able to add historical perspective.

A representative of Rutgers University as well as the University of Texas at Dallas and several others discussed the potential exchange of articles by leaders of the two countries for publications in respective journals. Rutgers University publishes the *International Journal of Governance* that helps build transparency in systems and putting forth modern management techniques.

In October 2009 a delegation from China visited Texas after meeting with the Wilson Foundation through its Kissinger Institute in Washington, D.C., as part of an exchange program. The delegation was from the Counsellor's Office of the State Council. Its major functions include organizing the Counsellors of the State Council to carry out research and investigations on critical areas of work that are particularly difficult. They serve as advisors to the leading officials of the State Council in many areas including laws, regulations, and strategic research.

The Counsellors have contributed greatly based on their in depth research in regard to the opening up of China. The Central Party School provides training support for the leadership of the Party and deals in philosophical issues of ideology. The Counsellors to the State Council are a similar high level research and thought organization, which deals more with execution and implementation of policies. The relationship of the Counsellors with the Wilson Institute involved a series of exchanges. The Lyceum and the Confucian Lyceum Institute had independently visited with the leadership of the Wilson Institute because of its ties with China on previous occasions. The delegation was headed by Mr. Chen Jinyu, the Chairman of the Counsellors of the Office of the State Council.

They stopped in San Antonio, Texas, for a reception hosted by Ms. Vivian Lee of the Omega International Group in context with efforts being made between the Council and Bexar County to develop international ties and jointly study the issues that could assist in investment, particularly for the Chinese in the United States. Bexar County had been very successful in attracting foreign investment, from Toyota and other companies, and this effort included a number of San Antonio leaders.

It has continued over time and has been very thoughtfully organized addressing specific issues of bringing foreign investment back to the United States to create jobs. Because of San Antonio's close ties to Mexico through NAFTA, this has been an effort that has involved the three countries. The greatest problem found over the many years of the State of Texas working with the Ministry of Commerce was how to develop mechanisms that effectively helped the Chinese understand the American legal system and the uniqueness of many of our laws.

Mexico had systems more similar to China and by understanding how the three countries worked in their specializations there could well be mutual benefit. Many of the containers that were shipped to the United States return to China empty so the ability to coordinate sales of American goods that could be shipped cheaply back to China was an enhancement to both economies. Following the tours in San Antonio and interactions with various organizations, the group toured the YO Ranch to see how rural Texas operated and to understand the rural history of Texas and its similarities to many of the cultures of China.

As a result of that trip, I had the opportunity to visit with Chairmen Chen in depth on the concepts of the books, particularly the *Essentials of The*

Language of Conscience which had been written in part for the last visits of the Central Party School as a base for both sides for common forums and seminars. The previous materials we had given to the Counsellors were dated. He had particular interest in our views on current market collapse and the failure of financial institutions. Greed and failures of regulation and governance were significant issues being addressed by the Council. I noted that Premier Wen, whom Mr. Chen advised, was someone I respected in that we jointly looked with great admiration on Marcus Aurelius and his book of *Meditations.* I noted that several of Premier Wen Jiabao's speeches dealt very closely with his concepts that much of the current financial problems were cultural rather than financial except for leverage in that there had been a lack of individual responsibility and far too much greed and fraud. His comments often referred to "putting the blood of morality into the veins of businessmen." Chairman Chen and I discussed the efforts for ethical governance of corporations by their boards and management issues.

Health Care and a Rare Opportunity

In January 2010 the Counsellors of the State Council invited me to China to take part in two activities. The first was a set of discussions with the Counsellors regarding health care. They wanted a presentation using my books as an analytical base for studying the new American approaches to health care with comparisons to what I knew of the Chinese system. I compiled the history of American healthcare and its reliance on private insurance as well as how the system had evolved and its differences from China. I also brought opinions of different experts on how the wellness and prevention of the Chinese system could be coordinated with Western approaches. The need for medical ethics and governance were key discussion points since the Chinese system was incentivized in the provision of services and medicines.

Ms. Vivian Lee and I then observed the meeting of the Kissinger Institute of the Wilson Foundation and the State Counsellors. This brought together people with knowledge of the various governmental functions. They described how government effectively worked and the difference in systems so that they could be fully understood, giving an excellent understanding of how other major efforts were addressing the same issues.

In May of 2010 the Central Party School with a delegation hosted by the new Vice President of the Central Party School, as well as a number of other educators, was returning to China through Mexico City. In

Mr. Li Junru's previous trip to Houston, it was anticipated that as part of the effort to understand the opportunities of doing business between Texas, Mexico, and China there would also be a continuation of the trip from Texas to Mexico. Due to other scheduling difficulties, the Chinese visit to Mexico had to be cancelled, but the School had a desire to learn more about Mexico and NAFTA and the joint benefits of three-country trade.

This was particularly important due to the construction of the new Panama Canal, which would allow supertankers to originate in China and Korea, go through the Canal and come to the Gulf Coast. As mentioned earlier, the Houston Port was one of the few deep-water ports well suited to handle this type traffic. The issue had been discussed in the previous meetings where the Houston Partnership had explained its critical issues. One of those was the continuing desire to work more closely with them regarding impediments to trade and investment. Ms. Lee and I had been asked by the Houston Partnership to assist them in putting together the different parties to this effort.

Dr. Felipe Ochoa, a premier consultant in Mexico, who had worked with the Houston Partnership and the Central Party School on ethics in the past, had attended the Houston meeting and was asked by the Central Party School to be a primary contact in Mexico so they could visit with institutions and bridges could be built. Since both the School and Dr. Ochoa were familiar with *The Language of Conscience* and the related books, having contributed to them, it was a basis of the approach to build trust on many of the concepts.

During the trip to Mexico City, the group visited with Grupo Carso and Mr. Carlos Slim and his family. Mr. Slim had read many of Dr. Ochoa's presentations on Mexico and China and gave his insights on how Mexico functioned and learned Chinese interests and perceptions. In the afternoon the delegation was shown the culture of Mexico through the museums, Chapultepec Castle, and a tour of Mexico City.

Later in the day they had an opportunity to meet with UNAM, one of the great universities of Mexico, and learned how cultural relationships could be expanded, particularly in some areas of common study. The murals for which UNAM was famous were explained. And visits to Teotihuacán and the famous pyramids of Mexico gave an understanding of Mexico's culture and was the equivalent of the tour of the Great Wall and the Forbidden City. Later they had the opportunity to talk with leaders of the Mexico City government, who described the new medical complex being jointly built in which Chinese medicine might well interact with the use of traditional medicines. They also met with the leaders of the power company of Mexico, the CFE, and various business leaders who explained the opportunities in Mexico for cross-border trade.

Promise for the Future

Perhaps the most recent visit of a Delegation from the Central Party School showed the most promise as to the integration of global systems on the Rule of Law and Corporate Governance. In July of 2011, a delegation traveling in the United States, headed by the Chief Librarian of the School, Professor Chin Gaotong, visited Austin where they were given tours of the Capitol and appropriate recognition. I hosted them for a dinner where we discussed the very significant expansion of the School Library, not only in size and electronics, but also in its focus on critical issues.

The Language of Conscience Evolution focused on the fact the culture developed the law, not the law the culture if you wish it to be a successful society. Law can force culture through regulation, but unity and sustainability require public support over time. The other issue was ethical corporate governance. Our discussion focused on the new "super section" of the library on the Rule of Law as their main policy and executive training institute researched the impacts of valuation created by private ownership, intellectual rights, and the corporate governance necessary in Western systems and its enhancement in their own. I explained the purposes of organizations like the Governance Institute of the Conference Board and referred back to the writings in the book series on the Better Business Bureau. China uses a cultural system to think of "justice" more than a politically-based legal system. Blending those has challenges but could solve many of the problems American companies are having in China if arguments are explained in that context. The use of a great library as the center of intellectual property appreciation and governance, and prioritizing it in unique ways intrigued me. The School's library will not only have the selections of modern libraries but is a library of forward thought for policy makers and, as such, plays an organized role. We talked of the Triangles and the contextual thought presented. The School's ideas have much in common with them and I agreed to assist particularly in the area of the Rule of Law and the necessity of ethical governance culturally.

I noted that what is needed is a catalyst particularly in corporate governance and Rule of Law issues between the major Chinese institutions and Western organizations. The future creation of something similar to a Language of Conscience Center as a nonpolitical forum of interaction might create a unique forum for thoughtful and effective discussion of issues. I very much think it could make a difference if the right groups are involved for the right reasons in the right process. The global acceptance of market property rights is what maintains values and all nations have a major part in establishing it for a successful global economy.

While there have been other delegations and trips, often with the Chinese Ministry of Commerce or American institutions, I have listed these at length because they are the heart of those relating to what I would call the development and mutual understanding of The Language of Conscience Concept. None were that critical on their own, and many involved different people that took institutional positions. But what you must get from them is that great change or opportunity usually comes one opportunity at a time, but it is the commitment to develop and passing it on that matters.

If it is a family business or a family value legacy, the commitment to its future matters. My impressions of China are totally different from my first visit. Even today there are those that will tell me I am simply being "snowed" by Chinese propaganda as they wish to create an image.

Perhaps, but most of those friends have spent little time learning the fundamentals of where both nations are headed. China has a lot of problems that I would like to see handled differently, but that is also true of America and every country. Things are what they are, and the issue is how we all change to bring out the best in us. You will have to understand, and navigate your way in what may become the Asian Century or the American Renaissance if we adopt proper policies, but China and America are in it together and will have a huge mutual impact on each other. Never underestimate it. You have to stay educated and watch. This history of our work with China gives me insight to them because it is at their levels where they decide policy and teach those below. The Communist Party may fail for some reason, but it is more likely to evolve. The question—"How can the West work with it for the best outcome?"

When Dad ran for Sheriff, he never hesitated to take positions and defend them. He taught me that you defined yourself by your enemies and your friends. They showed your level of commitment and where you stood. He made it clear that if you look for a friend you usually find one and if you look for an enemy you usually create one. How America looks at China and China looks at us matters greatly. Whether you want a friend or an enemy is often created by this.

He made the observation that it is best if your enemies are weak, corrupt, and stupid for obvious reasons. They are not only less effective, but also usually on the wrong side of values. So when you have enemies that are strong and smart, you need to reappraise where you are to be sure you are not in the old story of the cobra. He was so self-confident that he saw only a big rat when he tangled with the mongoose that was a lot faster and bit him in the head. As Dad also noted, some societies believed you defined yourself by the power of your enemies, and most of them are probably extinct. Finding ways toward Harmony should be a goal and an action of strength not weakness.

You cannot use current philosophy and assume it will stay the same, so you must protect against that possibility of change. Both sides look at what is written above and have it as their perspective. In these situations, if there is honor, the warrior's heart lets a great deal be done out of respect and common values. Neither China nor America are weak, unintelligent, or socially corrupt in their best motivations. So the key is to understand each other and bring out the best.

China is in a very unique period, particularly for a rapidly rising power. The Cultural Revolution and the economic hardship of The Great Leap Forward drastically altered their ancient culture of Confucius, Lao Tzu, and Legalism. China has partially opened with its economic policies, but it is seeking a blend of a new system as it moves forward. It has been through the progression in recent years of Marxism, Maoism, Deng Xiaoping Thought, The Three Precedents, and now The Harmonious Society as implemented by Scientific Development. How will that define itself, and what will be America's new vision? Most critically, how do the visions see each other? We should always remember to carefully determine how we think of others. General Dwight Eisenhower made a critical observation of quick reactions when he noted "to a man with a hammer, every problem looks like a nail." Relationships are not just political/military, but economic and cultural.

My View of China's Future

China's path to "democracy" is cultural rather than political, for democracy is a culture of responsibility and goes beyond just political vote counting. Elections require campaigning, but governmental success requires substance and the sustainability it has to generate.

I am not sure that anyone in the West fully understands the mix of changes occurring in China since it is difficult for the Chinese themselves to do so. You have a huge nation at different stages of development adopting market systems while trying to bring back past cultural values. You have political leaders that both value the stability of the past systems and those that see the need for change because of a rapidly evolving world in which China will be playing a greater part.

The Internet and communications will naturally decentralize what is largely a centralized structure. So what will be the new organizing principle or mortar that keeps stability? The way people prioritize those issues will make a huge difference. What I have experienced is that the leadership in China is highly intelligent, focused, and though there may be significant internal disagreements, they understand the need for a unified effort to maintain the growth and stability so the country will not descend into chaos. If you look at America and our partisan policies, we do not have any more certainty than China. Both countries have diverse groups and cannot be characterized easily.

Much of the world looks at China's growing military strength and places the mindset of the past in judgment. The older political/military organizing principle looked at gaining international influence and military bases. While ever present to a degree, it misunderstands the new organizing principle of controlling food and resources for your future population and control of cyberspace.

China understands that shift, and its international efforts in Africa and the concept of a joint "dry canal" in Colombia are better explained by it. The important consideration is that nationalistic politics as an organizing principle is much more of a zero-sum game than economic principles that can be more win-win with trust and cooperation. The future will be a focus on resources. America needs to understand that and create policies accordingly as China has. At that point the issues of how to position and cooperate become clearer.

The economic needs of the future will shape future politics, the question is how—the answer depends on the parties.

The old way of looking at China is best understood by the concept of the politics of geography and the culture it provides. When I joined the Navy under the Ensign 1955 program, I attended Officer Training School and Naval Justice School in Newport, Rhode Island. One of the new things I learned was the significance of the thoughts of Alfred Thayer Mahan as to sea power in his "The Influence of Sea Power upon History, 1660 – 1783," published in 1890 in shaping the world's navies. It also made him a premier geostrategist. His was an expansion, in many ways of the military strategies of Antoine-Henri Jomini and in some ways Carl von Clausewitz in that they both focused on and learned the functions of the permanent elements of warfare.

Von Clausewitz's famous aphorism that "War is the continuation of policy by other means," recognizes the context of the broader power of economics, politics, and culture. They are part of a bigger picture. China for example is a country surrounded by mountains and deserts with a history of controlling its immediate interests, but not historically aggressive. Its lack of sea power is a key strategic weakness. This is why it now has its first carrier and an ever increasing submarine fleet as well as a focus on weapons to compensate for a lack of sea power. I had an opportunity to attend several Conversations with the Country on the next American Maritime Fact Sheet. It is very worthy of contemplation because it foresees a world where cooperation matters and it generally receives equal consideration to the "fears of war" military confrontations that the media often places on headliners. We make our future world, and while it cannot be based on trust alone, trust is a necessity for more positive involvement of sides. Bridge builders are key; both China and the United States have much at stake. China will wish to control its region of influence out of national security just as the United States does, but how the countries work together and with the rest of the world matters. I have included the U.S. Maritime Strategy as a reference to one of the best forward thinking documents of the day:

Maritime Strategy Fact Sheet

"*A Cooperative Strategy for 21st Century Seapower*" recognizes the economic links of the global system and how any disruption due to regional crises—

manmade or natural—can adversely impact the U.S. economy and quality of life. This new strategy charts a course for the Navy, Coast Guard, and Marine Corps to work collectively with each other and international partners to prevent these crises from occurring or reacting quickly should one occur to avoid negative impacts to the U.S.

Why Develop A New Strategy?
- *World prosperity and security depends on free use of the seas.* Markets crave security and our vital interests are best served by a stable global system.

- 70% of the world is water, 80% of the world lives within a few hundred miles of the oceans, and 90% of our commerce sails across it.

- The world has changed since 1986 when the last maritime strategy was developed.

- The new strategy will meet emerging challenges in an uncertain world.

What's New in This Strategy?
- *Signed for the first time by the service chiefs of all three sea services*, the strategy draws the Navy, Marine Corps, and Coast Guard closer together to provide a layered defense of the homeland and work to protect and sustain the American Way of Life.

- The new strategy provides the right balance of forces to conduct traditional combat missions and *raises the prevention of war to a level equal to the conduct of war.*

- It elevates Humanitarian Assistance & Disaster Relief to core elements of maritime power. *We've always done this, but now we'll plan to do it.*

- U.S. maritime forces will be employed to build confidence and trust among nations through *collective maritime security* efforts that focus on common threats (proliferation, smuggling, piracy, terrorism, etc.) and mutual interests.

- The new Maritime Strategy raises the importance of working with international partners as the basis for global maritime security. Although our forces can surge when necessary to respond to crises, *trust and cooperation cannot be surged.* Relationships must be built over time based on mutual understanding and respect.

- *The strategy was shaped through a partnership with the American people.*

- The American people want us to remain strong; they want us to protect them and our homeland, and they want us to work with partners around the world to prevent war.

America, with coasts on the Atlantic for trade with Europe and on the Pacific for trade with Asia, has great advantage if it controls its trade lanes and those of others. Mahan understood this gave military and economic advantage. Trade has been the key to wealth and will remain so. The engagement of China needs to be in a joint effort to protect trade, which is important to both. Perhaps one of the best American strategies is this new maritime policy developed over the past five years at the Naval War College in Newport where Mahan taught. Rather than military competition, ethical control of the seas needs to be a shared burden. China and the U.S. must look at military cooperation in a new light beyond politics and recognize the economic implications.

The Chinese must be concerned about the outside world and its view of China because they understand the significant part they are obligated to play. But at the same time they realize, more than many Western governments, the problems that lurk domestically in the form of an aging population, inequities within the country, trade imbalance and inflation, and the challenges of maintaining rapid growth rates for stability.

The leaders in China today have a system that is different from their better-known Communist Party predecessors who had significant individual power. Instead it is the Communist Party System that effectively bends leadership to a consensus. The question is what will be that Communist Party vision and the principles that it entertains? There is no question that personalities are very important, but in effect the Politburo Standing Committee could well be looked at as a singular unit because of how the systems work to produce a unified final product.

What is key are the thoughts being put into that system. Usually they emerge from the Party advisory groups with its premier think tank, the Central Party School in Beijing, and the State Council that unifies many of the realities of governing. Not at all lost in this mix is the power of the people because of their satisfaction or dissatisfaction. The leadership of China has a great concern for what happens at the lower levels of society because they fully understand that the stability of the country depends on how people perceive their position. It is probably best called their sense of personal dignity because it is not just where they are materially although that has significant impact in judgment.

But because of China's past culture and its strong families and the core of responsibility there, the concern is about the life their children will lead. These are issues that are critically important. What ultimately is it that the people seek and value? The answer will differ in different societies. Throughout history, from China to the ancient Greeks, it is recognized that two drivers within society often have impact—the materializing of consumption and the nobility of the spirit of sacrifice for others. These are other ways of saying convenience or conscience, but the mass of a society creates a peer pressure one way or the other. China and America are now at a point when the society will confront choices on the blend of these forces moving forward.

Perception and Possibilities

My perception from my visits with the Chinese is not certainty as to which path they will choose. One extreme could be the central authoritarian power of a Mao or instead the renaissance of the cultural powers of Reciprocity of Confucius. In all likelihood, the Harmonious Society in its next stage of development will be the traditional change versus the status quo position of history—just amplified. China is in the process of an evolution of thought, and the best place to fully understand how it is thinking is to look at the issues about which they most want to learn and try to see how that thought pattern evolves. You have to temper that with the fact that China is not unlike the West in that it has significant political pressures within that are not fully understood except in their internal orientation.

From the West we look at China and if it takes an action, we often say it is being assertive, it manipulates an undervalued currency to gain trade advantages, enforces its power with neighbors, and it focuses on its actions with North Korea. But within China the average person probably does not think that China is acting strongly enough and that the West does not understand China and often acts in hypocrisy. The views domestically and internationally are quite different. China has a growing nationalism that results in part from the past patriotic education given by the Communist

Party and a media that describes issues from a Party perspective. The Internet and social networking increase pressures. That puts significant pressure on the leadership trying to manage China's emergence in the world, an emergence where China has a difficult time matching Western diplomatic expectations. The Middle East is a prime example. China often sides with Russia on less stringent international sanctions on Iran, so China and Russia are grouped as allies. But in reality their interests are very different. Russia is helped by the instability in the region because the price of oil remains high and it sells oil. China has to buy oil so it wants the cheapest price stability would bring, it has opposite interests to Russia. But it does not want to concede international powers to interfere in what is perceived as a domestic sovereign issue which is key to China, so it has the same position but different logic. You should not automatically characterize China without looking at its core concerns. They may be different than perceived.

The West recognizes the significant growth of China and puts high levels of expectations on it to assume much greater international responsibilities and be magnanimous in dealing with others as a significant power. Nonetheless, it is often criticized because it is put in a group that is seen as authoritarian. The Chinese have to overcome both a bias and a selective view of their actions.

These dual perceptions are going to make it ever more difficult for the Chinese leadership to manage expectations both domestically and internationally because the perception gaps of what actions should be taken differ. This is why highly emotional issues such as Taiwan and the feelings created have a significance that is not fully appreciated in the West even though trade is ameliorating many of the problems. Longer term, the geopolitical controlling issues previously described will continually require the countries to work together as economics presses both.

One of the greatest problems China perceives from the West is its criticism of China on the "lack of democracy" and primarily an analysis of that concept of democracy from political grounds. The West, particularly America with the Constitution and Bill of Rights, views issues from a political system. Ours developed over many years with executive powers evolving from Monarchs, the Senate from the power of Nobles, and the House of Representatives from a democracy of the people. Our cultural experience led to our balancing these three sources. Machiavelli is one of the best sources here in his *Discourses*.

It would probably be far more appropriate to look at China's evolution to democracy from a cultural approach. In America our system politically deals strongly with individual rights. China often does not think in terms of individual rights as much as it tends to think in the terms of individual dignities. The two can be brought more closely together by a thoughtful approach to systems.

Both China and the West need to understand the concept of the "Rule of Law" more clearly. The same is true with different parts of market systems such as governance and intellectual property. However, the Chinese in studying the American system, realize that in many cases our legal system of rights has gone far beyond the comfortable tolerances of their cultural systems. We have replaced some individual representation with more limited legal duties. They understand concepts in the sense of our Courts of Equity more than technical common law.

Their concepts of the use of the Internet give a degree of insight. The West looks at censorship from a political viewpoint of the right of speech. The Chinese also look at the Internet as a threat to the existing culture because the ability to criticize is taken much more personally in China than in the West. The concepts of courtesy, shame, showing respect, the need for formal apologies, and the power of protocol are all strong traditions arising from older Confucian concepts of obligation and imperial heritage.

Their way of thinking about many of these issues may be quite different from how the West often perceives them. In the West we tend to look at corruption as an ultimate moral issue. It is looked upon negatively in China, but in some ways is more dealt with as a negative economic issue. In many of the discussions we had with the Chinese delegations, these types of questions often came up.

One of the best examples was a visit by the delegation with a very large Episcopal Church in Houston. The church leaders, after following my suggestion of showing how the family sections of the church helped develop and instill values in youth, explained the more religious aspects of Christianity and the church functions. However, the method by which the Chinese looked at understanding the West was a very thoughtful one that created complexities. They studied the Western market system very closely and had methods of thought on how to categorize each institution within it.

So one of the very first questions asked of the Ministers was, "Who exactly owns this Church?" That was an interesting concept to try and explain. Each following question showed an intent desire to understand that the framework in which the West is often presented as an entity, many times misses issues of context. It is really neither side's fault.

I remember when *The Language of Conscience* was translated and about to be published, I received requests for clarifications and sources since the Chinese often go back to the original quotation. One of the clarifications came on my concept of discussing taking my family "fly fishing." Of course, we in the West understand the term to be using a lure that looks like a fly to ride on top of the water at the end of the line of the reel, usually on rivers or creeks, so that it and the hook that it covers is struck by the fish to catch them. But in the actual context of reading the sentence, if you were not familiar with that terminology, you would logically get back the questions, "Why do you catch flies? What do you do with the flies once you catch them? How do you really catch the flies in the first place? Could you describe the goals more clearly?" Anytime you deal in different languages and different thought processes, it is particularly difficult to have a full understanding of what both sides are saying.

When you deal with different languages, people prioritize things differently. Our language in the West is more linear with letters, words, sentences, paragraphs, and pages. The Chinese language of over 30,000 characters is much more conceptual.

This means that it becomes increasingly important to find common ways to think through issues that build joint mental models. That was a significant effort of the program of the exchange with the Lyceum and the Central Party School and a major part of the effort in writing the books. Beyond just having common language and a common understanding of issues, such as civil liberties and obligations, the core is to have a common belief that is transformational and helps you work together.

That is why we use the concept of *The Language of Conscience*. It was the one common theme that quickly emerged from the conversations. The Chinese believe heavily in family; they understand the power of culture, and that became a very common theme of how to build mutual understanding.

Both sides have to work at building a common mental model or it does not work.

The Chinese are moving to democracy more in the form of creating their own approach and direction. But as noted, it is more from a cultural aspect that reforms the values of their society by the renaissance of the older values of Confucius and their many philosophies on harmony. The legal or political concept of democracy will be slower coming but will be built because of their increasing wealth and trade. At some point, with all their engineers and creativity, they will be demanding intellectual protection.

The trend is more obvious than the current time although there will be intervening periods of regression and adjustment. Power of direct control is evolving more into influence that affects power stemming from many different sources. But what is recognized in China is that the ultimate power comes from the people—their Revolution began there. Whether or not the Party recognizes the tremendous impact the Internet and media, particularly the social media, is having that will affect cultural values will be critical.

Nearly every Chinese leader with whom I have spoken had a full appreciation of the fact that the Harmonious Society is necessary if you are going to bring about sacrifice and change. And you are going to have to devise a set of cultural, political, and economic principles that evolve as a planned unit in order to keep stability and consistency. They often look at the West and many of the ways we approach problems as quite different because of our gridlock.

The distinction between the two systems is significant; the Chinese lost organized value systems of the last decades and are looking at how to restructure them into society, primarily to fight corruption and materialism. They are focusing on what needs to be added, which is easier to see. America is having a value system gradually eroded, but while the slow loss is perceived, it is not as clearly identifiable. What both can learn is why values matter and appreciate them more clearly so that their recreation is most effective.

What I tried to explain to the Chinese are the powers of democracy and market systems. Many of the current failings and issues that they look on as hypocrisy are really not the fault of the system, but of corruption, greed, arrogance, and men's personal desires as opposed to a more common good. Systems are computer hardware, and the quality of the people in them is the software that determines results. Do not judge good hardware, however, by the failings of software.

The best of Western culture and its democratic and economic systems comes from the true concern of the people that originally were the base of the Constitution and Declaration of Independence—they were the common good. These two documents were based on conscience and values, and they looked to a responsibility of the people, particularly the leadership, to move good. These principles and open acceptance of others built what some call American Exceptionalism. But there can be many exceptional societies if these cultural values dominate.

China's sovereignty has had many invaders, but it has converted nearly all to its culture. That is a point of strength. Confucius taught the responsibility of leaders and the people to follow them. It is much of that cultural approach that still permeates China. In a sense, if the leaders do the right things, the people will tend to follow more than the Western system where the wants of the collective individuals and different groups drive the system. The two systems are quite different, and thus the cultural power of acceptance and respect within a concept of Chinese democracy is probably the form that will evolve.

The leadership thus must find how to continue to satisfy the people once the materialism of economic growth and a rising standard of living is reached. China is at that point now, and you see the concepts of Scientific Development beginning to try and address it. Concerns for the environment are dramatic for the Chinese people—the tremendous concerns for integrity within the Party because of the great problems that corruption is causing at lower levels—these are issues that are significant within their ranges of consideration.

The Chinese more fully understand the concepts of Western democracy and governing, but how do you bring the people to have an understanding of those issues? They understand the responsibilities that the West wishes to impose upon China as an emerging power, and the need for taking a more active role because of their position; they are not sure how to explain this domestically where perspectives are different. China has many potential domestic problems that are being enhanced by the rapid growth that make the system less stable and limit actions.

Dramatic Changes

It is important to understand how dramatically China has changed over the last thirty years in its period of "opening up." Its economic growth rates have usually averaged between 8% and 10%, which is absolutely remarkable and has given stability to the country. They have moved a great number of rural farmers into industrialized opportunities and have made remarkable achievements in increasing the standards of living, particularly in their cities. Even though China is now the second largest economy in the world behind the United States, it has very different characteristics. China presently is only a $5 trillion economy while the United States is closer to $15 trillion. Thus, it is only one-third of our GDP. It is the growth rate that is significant, and it will be harder to maintain as the economy grows—already labor costs are increasing and affecting competitive advantages.

The economy, moving farmers into industrialization still has significant work to do within the rural areas while many of the easiest conversions have been accomplished. China realizes with its success it needs to transition from what was one of the world's largest export models to a consumer driven economy. It is necessary for China, but also necessary for the world. The world worries about China's currency values, but the Chinese will worry about them even more because of the impact on inflation. What is of benefit to the United States and the rest of the world is the opportunity for growth in their domestic industries in selling to China. That is the key transition point, and hurdle that must be addressed. The fact that the United States needs to move from a demand-driven consumption economy to a supply-oriented production one, will itself pressure the Chinese system since we are a premier customer.

China is in a period of leadership transition and when transition happens there is always significant uncertainty and tension. The United States faces many of the very same issues as it transitions from a debt-fueled economy, which in recent years China supported, into a more productive realistic fiscal model. The critical point is that these two are not separate but combined and have to be seen as two of the largest parts of major global concerns. Simple rhetoric or nationalism accomplishes nothing—the ultimate best decisions for both countries rest in the ability to coordinate.

In 2012 there will be a significant leadership change in China. Traditionally, before such changes and for several years thereafter, there is more rigidity within the system. It tends to be the same with American elections where positioning is particularly important and the ability to take actions fits into certain windows. China's new leadership will thus begin showing significant thought and direction around 2014 although there may be indications before then. At that point a new government is in place and the domestic and international issues have to be balanced. After the financial problems in the West have tarnished capitalism's image and the apparent gridlock of America's politics, comparisons to China's more centrally planned system will grow. But it is important to understand a centrally directed system is only as good as the leadership making decisions.

China's recent leadership has adapted extremely well, in particular the economic planning of Premier Wen Jiabao. If wrong decisions are made, central direction can be painful as the Great Leap Forward proved. What is making China unique is how they are going about thinking of issues and consequences. It is the level of thought in policy. America is capable of the same things in its adaptable market systems if they were allowed to freely function. Systems do not perform in theory but in the reality of how they are impacted, directed, and constrained.

Within China there are several "hot button" issues that are similar to the West. The term "universal values" or in Chinese *pushi jiazhi* has come to represent a variety of concepts. Most commonly associated with it are issues such as freedom, democracy, human rights, and also the economic considerations that fit with them—the more liberal position within China. It is more of a direction toward a Western model of government being subservient to the people as opposed to the more conservative "socialism with Chinese characteristics." This is a more cultural model where the people obey the government, and the reform is more directly through the internal promotion of Chinese Confucian values, which focus on social harmony and moral rectitude. In some ways the United States with its positioning of the Republican's stance on smaller government, lower taxes, and libertarianism would be closer to the liberals, while the Democrats that believe in much larger government, heavier and stricter regulation, would seem to fit a little more with the conservatives.

Like American elections, China's future probably will be determined more by the internal desires of its people than ideologies. The reason for this is the dramatic transition over the last years and the evolution of the Communist Party and its leadership to meet those needs in order to stay in power.

The current concept of personal dignity may well be determined by the meaning given to, and desire for, "Xiaokang." For several thousand years the Chinese have used that term from the Book of Songs to refer to the "good life." With time, technology, globalization, and "cyberization" the good life is no longer the existing older values of peasant life but more a desire for opportunity, requiring education, a desire for job security with health and retirement, and the expectation of at least a moderate level of prosperity that would be considered middle class.

Due to China's rapid growth, this is being achieved in the cities. But it also must occur in the rural areas where more than half of the population is still in difficult circumstances. The rise of a middle class is essential, but an increasing problem related to prior success and inflation will burden this group that now has high expectations. China's planners will have increasingly complex challenges to bridge options requiring an international strategy.

Within China, there are the normal two competing concepts—change versus history. The status quo of history will be competing for that vision of the good life. Will it be economic or cultural or a blend of the two? On one side, the more liberal economic concept looks at the modern world and strategizes how China is going to provide that opportunity for increased growth and both domestic and foreign investment. Within that concept is more of an internationalization or Westernization of China that understands the necessity of the Rule of Law, the protection of intellectual property.

The need for international investment expertise in areas like risk management and financial planning, and its attitude of responsible position within the world as a great power requires movement in areas to allow necessary change. These are composed of both rights and obligations that require education and sacrifice on behalf of the people so goals like innovation and critically important joint international efforts can succeed. The competing conservative perspective looks at the traditional Chinese values and a concern for traditional morality that will be replaced by materialism. They look with disdain on Western media, which lowers the dignity of others for entertainment. They also see great dangers when cultural values are lost. And they search for a path that can best embrace both concerns.

Any combination or balance must also recognize the change social networking media has made. Now the ease of cross sharing makes change certain. The key is to build an appreciation of the traditional values and morality as a vital part of that media. Men and women instinctively know the value of the Golden Rule and the Common Good.

A combination of both will probably emerge in China, and it is how that balance is effectively put together. There are no easy answers, but the Chinese have extremely intelligent people within their institutions who understand their problems, their strengths, and how the traditional Harmonious Society of China is probably their solution.

What needs to be appreciated within China is how much has been done over the past years to prepare their children. Recently, there was an outstanding article in the January 8-9, 2011 issue of *The Wall Street Journal* on page C2. The article gave great insight to the Chinese mothers' demands for a regimen for their children historically and how parts of these areas were changing today as innovation and creative thinking were particularly necessary. It also included the results of the program for international student assessment tests of fifteen-year-olds in reading, math, and science that are conducted every three years. In the latest tests, conducted in seventy-five economies in 2009, Shanghai scored highest. China provided scores from selected educational systems, including Shanghai, Hong Kong, and Macao. The source of *The Wall Street Journal* article was the Organization for Economic Cooperation and Development. The interesting comparison, however, was where the Chinese students stood compared to the rest of the world and the position of the United States. In reading, Shanghai was first, South Korea scored second, Finland third, Hong Kong fourth, and the United States trailed at a distant seventeenth.

In math, Shanghai was again first, Singapore second, Hong Kong third, South Korea fourth, and the United States trailing significantly at thirty-first.

In science, Shanghai was first, Finland was second, Hong Kong was third, Singapore was fourth, and the United States trailing at twenty-third.

These statistics speak volumes for the competitiveness of educational systems in taking tests, the focus for the Chinese. They show that there is great talent within China, and the massive numbers of Chinese compared to other countries being educated at this level gives some significant indication of trends over the next several generations.

What China lacks, and the middle class will increasingly demand, is an environment that allows opportunity for wealth creation, creativity, independence, and a broader thinking for the discussion of ideas. Social networking, and all other related changing technologies, will greatly enhance this in the coming generations. The Western strength in education has been its creativity, which led to innovation and the commercialization of markets. China will eventually succeed here as well.

There has been rigidity in thought in the past, and the question is what will structure the way of thinking moving forward. Social networking may let you have a thousand friends, but it does not create extremely close relationships or depth in understanding people. These are created by values and maintaining them while allowing much of this growth in opportunities will be the ultimate determinant of China's success.

An Economic Glimpse

Economics pushes liberalization as China begins to compete in the world and its true impact is fully realized. Culture pulls from the other direction in keeping with the historical status quo. A method of thinking, and thus a necessity for educating not only children for the next generation, as well as current citizens who lack a background in much of this thought, is probably what would best be called "Contextual Thinking."

If you are able to think balancing economics, politics, and culture then you will be able to judge how you think about being in the middle class and enjoy the individual dignity it provides. These issues will be at the forefront of China's discussions and the focus of its leadership. China has been studying this issue for years. It simply reaches a critical point at this stage because of what is happening economically in the rest of the world and its desire to secure the resources necessary for its citizens' growth.

Going back to *Peaceful Rise—China's New Road to Development,* it recognized years ago the challenge of resources for every Chinese to have an American standard of living. The multiplier or the divider is far too great. The Chinese realize that satisfaction and harmony are cultural issues, but culture will have to evolve to allow more creative thinking for the nation not only to be competitive but also to reach that level of cultural dignity. The process may be different from what the West would suggest. But the realities of the future, if the Chinese focus on their ultimate best interest, will make many of these changes occur.

The query is how to do so without dramatic instability within the system. That requires the people to understand that if a government does not provide the support, then they must jointly do so in a private way to replace it. This is mirrored in the United States. We must realize that rights require obligations to be met so stability can be maintained. Debt lets you avoid reality short term but is very inefficient in the long term.

The bottom line is that your generation and your children's generation are going to either suffer or benefit somewhat equally with the Chinese children of the future. If ways can be found that are win–win for all concerned in this time of transition by the Chinese opening their markets and America helping China in creation of one of the largest domestic markets in the world's history, then everyone will benefit. Gridlock would cause far more serious consequences than people anticipate because of the interrelationship of the economies. The rest of the world will play a major part, but the first actions will be by the two most significant players.

Whether in America or China the concept of Contextual Thinking, best defined in the Triangles that were created to describe it, is a balance between the need for innovation and for temperament. Temperament determines whether you take risks and is often the stimulator or depressant to innovation or creativity. Temperament judges the risk and the reward. If there is relative danger with little benefit, then generally structured thinking and not adapting change is the choice. There is little incentivizing the taking on of risk. And the more intelligent someone becomes, the more they recognize this.

Many in the West evaluate China on the business model of a mature corporation. They focus upon the weaknesses and the negative trends that can also be detrimental to lower margin businesses. However, China has evolved into a very rapidly growing business model. As a result, its greatest problems will be similar to those of a company that is growing too fast and has a significant amount of imbalances to rectify and control. Many of the existing problems are solved by rapid growth as the maintenance of stability of the last twenty years has shown.

At this stage, however, China's next transition must look at the significant pressures being caused by their success in education where they now have a much larger well-educated workforce with less opportunity. Low-level jobs will never satisfy the personal dignity of well-educated youth. The cost structure of housing in many of the major cities has dramatically increased, moving beyond the affordability of many within the middle class. The inflation rate will increasingly become a significant problem. And if materialism reaches Western standards on a large scale, you will have a consumer economy as well as massive need for resources.

All of these considerations will require a very different business model just as the West has to adapt to significant changes in its debt-funded model.

How the two interact, or do not, will truly be the question of the next decade. If the world can find ways to specialize such that there is increasing growth and prosperity for all, standards of living can continue to increase. If there is deterioration in cooperative efforts, then in all likelihood the sustainability of the current system will create significant difficulties for all.

Growing companies have to react more quickly to changes and have many more challenges allocating resources. This often leads to a more decentralized leadership. China's ruling party has seen significant changes during the "opening up." The absolute authority of Chairman Mao or Chairman Deng moderated where there are significant forces that must be coordinated by the leadership rather than directed by it. Just like a growing company, the ultimate solution is to have a vision of its destination and an operating set of concepts that help to pull together the diverse parts.

China is perhaps looking in the right place when they talk of the Harmonious Society because it is at least a framework that would be developed to give an image of a goal that helped unify the parts. Where that may be a vision, educating and piecing together the parts, particularly where international affairs are also involved, will be an incredible challenge.

Looking at investment and trade impediments, you begin to realize that the issues are both short and long term but ultimately require a framework upon which trust as well as legal protections must evolve. For example, China needs to become a much larger percentage consumer economy, both for Western and Chinese interests.

Chinese standards of living need to improve in order to have middle class opportunities and standards. That requires a much more sophisticated banking system that manages risk effectively. With inflation, assets become quite expensive and hard to purchase by simply saving cash. Inflation creates substantial problems. The American banking system went into extremes as America became a debt-dominated culture, but in the early stages it is an extremely beneficial aspect. Having mortgages that can be paid gradually or having cars where monthly payments diminish the high significant initial cost are important.

There is no question that financing can be provided in different ways, but often what you get is a financial sector, not an integrated financial system, providing an ultimate use of funds and building in much of the safety required. Things like title insurance will probably be a long time coming in China, but some types of guarantees that affect the same transparency and reduce legal uncertainty of properties does become necessary. As the Chinese study the Western system in preparation of a consumer economy, these are issues that increasingly will be important.

On a similar note, China has largely built its economy on moving lower-cost labor into more productive arenas. They are now being challenged in that low cost environment. Countries like Vietnam and Bangladesh have forced them to step up the quality of production and sophistication of product levels. That requires significant cooperation with Western technology experts, who have great fears of doing too much with China because of the potential loss of technology and the creation of a major competitor.

An example would be oil and gas drilling with new processes such as fracturing, which opens up great amounts of shale gas that could be of tremendous help with China's reserves. In sophisticated microchips and other products, China may import 70-80% but would like to make them domestically, eventually importing 20-30% and shipping the rest for sale abroad.

Obviously, Western companies like the idea of current markets but fear what the production domestically in China could do to their market, not to mention what would occur in their markets worldwide because of Chinese cost reduction processes. This is not an unknown circumstance on both sides; the problems are fairly well recognized. The issue is more how to build a relationship in which both intellectual property protections and trust exist. That will require additional thought and research jointly between the West and China and vehicles that allow such discussions.

Too often both sides go in with transactional mindsets wanting to protect what they have and get the most from the other side. This is simply traditional business. A much more transformational approach allowing guarantees on both sides and ultimately involving the highest levels of Chinese government in looking at its transitions in modernizing society is needed.

The issue of Corporate Governance will be far more important than the Chinese realize. As they need to develop these relationships domestically and abroad, they will need to learn and adopt many Western practices of running corporations both in goals and culture. Governance is the way the leadership of a corporation sets the standards and vision. It is very Confucian in nature with focus on the fiduciary responsibilities but also efficiency is looking for best practices in oversight.

Joint efforts with groups in the West such as the Conference Board, which has specialized in these areas, would benefit both countries dramatically in protecting intellectual property and building a framework with other institutions for cross-border investment. These are areas like the military training of forces—they can be described, but the experience, coordination, and an appreciation of their context to other issues make them a sophisticated technology to be done properly. How well this next stage of economic development is handled—the creation of true world-class international corporations—not just in size but also in corporate responsibility, will say a great deal about the vision of China's new leadership. China will be changing the method of its growth when this stage is attained because it is a more sophisticated approach to wealth creation than its first stages.

If you look at why the Chinese need to save such large amounts, you start with a cultural understanding that Asians save much and consume little culturally. Asians often save one-third of their after tax income. This is not only true of individuals but is also true of many of the state-owned enterprises that comprise the Chinese corporate sector. These funds are retained and historically have gone into developing additional facilities. Between a relatively under-valued currency and the low cost of retained capital, there has been a significant excess of funds for the economic development necessary to create jobs.

However, you attain a level where capacity is not as essential as balance within the economy. This is particularly becoming clear as the debt driven Western economies deleverage, and Western consumers spend less thereby dropping the Chinese trade surplus that has been the business model of the past.

China has kept its higher growth rates by boosting fixed investment in commercial and residential real estate as well as public infrastructure and manufacturing capacity. However, after a certain time, if the demand for products is limited, much of that investment becomes increasingly less productive. You reach a certain point that you build excess capacity and your financial system generates weaker and weaker loans if it is financing increasingly less viable products.

Our Similarities and Differences

The Chinese have all the same concerns as Americans. They worry about retirement, health care, emergency costs, and their children's education. In the West more sophisticated financial systems dealing in everything from annuities to retirement planning, health insurance, and developed credit models have allowed Westerners to almost go to the excess. There is a balance that the West is learning in its retrenchment from too much debt, which became a cultural liability versus having too little leverage and inefficient systems to shift risk and temperament.

Risk, temperament, and contextual thinking all become very important when you try to shift the cultural attitudes of a nation. Generations have to be educated. The Chinese look at the West and its failures in the current economic recession as showing the weaknesses of the market system. But these weaknesses have been greed, corruption, and irresponsibility. If those characteristics were removed and the appropriate balance that helped to develop America maintained before excess, the system would be of great help to the Chinese as they move to the next level of development.

The increasing potential inflation in China and the perhaps $300 billion trade surplus annually has already begun to push the Chinese to invest abroad. For the past decade they have primarily invested in United States government debt. But in the last several years there has been much more effort to acquire foreign companies particularly in energy and other natural resources, technology, and financial institutions because of the need for converting their domestic economy concerns. In the future, with China's concern for the value of the dollar, international purchases will become more common, particularly as expertise is developed.

How the Chinese handle their foreign acquisitions will become increasingly a trademark of their business practices. What style of governance will take place and with what motivations? China today gives contracts for resources and then lends to governments on those contracts. It is highly effective in controlling future resource needs. But company acquisitions become a more complex endeavor if it is to be successful. The ethics of Chinese corporations will, in part, determine their partners level of ethics and significantly impact standards, so if the Chinese demand and train ethical governance as they move abroad they can impact their own risk and help set higher global standards.

A benefit of the foreign investment will be that the Chinese will have to learn more about American governance standards due to legal compliance. This will also be of significant benefit within China where often transparency and Western governance standards have not been applied to their larger corporations. Leadership in China is increasingly looking to put more transparency within systems to fight corruption, and this will be an area of mutual concern.

The more the Chinese understand Western systems and governance, like the research presented by the Conference Board, individual director training such as the National Association of Corporate Directors, and peer ethics with the Better Business Bureau, the easier it will be to develop these systems. Accumulations of knowledge from American corporations will better the Western opportunities for them to understand the importance of protecting intellectual property. The discussion forums for these issues, between the private sectors of both countries will be increasingly important. If discussion forums do not take place, there will be tension in Western economies for Chinese investment just as there is presently tension over the restrictions on Chinese purchases. Chinese independent private company initial public offerings have become a significant concern for U.S. capital markets due to weakness in accounting and governance. While the Chinese government has worked with large state-owned corporations to move toward governance standards, the fact that China is tarnished by the IPO problem is not insignificant. Chinese leaders understand face, image, and general reputation matters so governance will ultimately be addressed.

One of the concerns privately discussed by Western companies is the level of Chinese espionage, particularly commercial. While China felt it very necessary to catch up with the West through learning as much as possible, this creates an increasingly difficult circumstance for a joint effort environment. As we said on the issue of regulation, if a regulatory agency deals with intimidation as a method, it is almost impossible to build trust and cooperative status because of the fear involved. The two are quite inconsistent. Normally a balance must be found for a workable relationship to most effectively function. The same is true in trying to make commercial joint ventures.

The difference between China, the United States, and a number of other countries is that almost all nations capable use espionage and cyber spying for national defense reasons. In *The Art of War*, Sun Tzu makes clear the need for the best and most accurate information.

The United States, however, does not focus on commercial espionage as a method of business as many other countries do. This is a critical difference that is the core of intellectual property. Cyber theft of intellectual property is a huge deterrent in the trust factor of joint efforts and a critical area to be addressed at this point in time. Governance is the best approach to change this culture, but it takes the national leadership to mandate it.

The general philosophy strategically, from a military perspective, is to judge carefully where your partners are presently, but also what would happen should their attitude change. Both on Western and Chinese sides, that set of concerns exists and is a reality of history in both directions. The key to creating a Chinese market for American goods and in bringing Western technology that builds their middle class and standards of living has to be more cooperative. And because the discussions are technological, more guaranteeing of not only intellectual rights but trust, both sides feel that this is impossible.

I would hope that would not be the case when I see the strong culture of China and appreciate the strong power of the Rule of Law in the West. But these are discussions that must take place on a common ground of candid, thoughtful discussion where neither side gets offended. This blend of integrity is what a conceptual The Language of Conscience or other Governance Center would have as a core mission.

This is often difficult in the political arena because there are national interests in both directions with politics behind them making discussions much more rigid. However, institutions might well have success in working with their governments, focusing on the most key issues and looking at a longer-term transformational approach headed in the right direction. The same is true in China but will inevitably need the blessing of the leadership and expertise of the Central Party School and high levels of the State Council.

A more critical issue for China will be how to address converting its health care sector into a system that is both able to minimize cost, give some security so there will be less cash retention and more economic spending by its people, and the coordinated prevention with the West of potential pandemics. One of the most thoughtful approaches in this arena was the creation of a national trial through the work of the Central Party School and the Counsellors of the State Council working with the City of Xinxiang, Henan, and HAAA, a health care entity largely representing American interests. While it is a processing effort primarily, it has given the Chinese a much better opportunity to understand how the nonprofit, non-investor owned health systems of the West function.

The effort was not instantaneous. An appreciation of the need for it grew from the original discussions on *The Language of Conscience* and the nonprofit nature of health insurance explained in the Caring for Children

Foundation. I had the opportunity to introduce the National Blue Cross and Blue Shield Association to the Central Party School and the Counsellors for the State Council in years past as was reflected. From those original efforts the several Blue Cross plans with the city developed methods for learning how transformational types of issues could be discussed and implemented.

The same types of smaller projects will probably be started in many areas of China. These are important because first-mover companies have great advantages in China in that they better understand how the systems function. The Chinese wish to learn the best of technologies and to do a significant job in their research. Finding the right approaches, hopefully by the Chinese government working with broader-based American associations, may be the best method for discussion. Wellness and disease prevention are global goals and priorities.

My Observations

No one was more surprised than I at the interest of the Chinese in publishing *The Language of Conscience* and the efforts we have made these past years. But in retrospect, it was an appropriate base for study in their search for this balance of economic opportunity with traditional values that will define their middle class. My family values were very similar to theirs, but mine were directly adjusted by the market economy of the West. I am certainly no expert on China and have been there only eight or nine times.

But what I found unique were the discussions with the Chinese and their interest in understanding how the principles covered in *The Language of Conscience* were used to unify people, bring about sacrifice, and more importantly, instill values in the context of how economics, politics, and culture work together.

The places that I believe they have helped the Chinese have been to look at Western systems from a cultural perspective. *The Language of Conscience* begins with the need for providing an individual dignity to those you meet and looking at how you build trust, or lose it, on people's actions, and what they value. If you begin with that, you see its effects on society. It is not a study of morality, but a *study of the power of morality*. It is not inconsistent with what the Chinese are looking to build in their Harmonious Society. *Then cultural principles forming their Harmonious Society parallel the principles of moral hazard that need to be built into our Western political legal society.* Their new society needs sacrifice in the beginning, but it will grow and needs to grow quickly because its aging population provides a significant demographic challenge.

What type of society will the new consumer-focused China create? If it is totally materialistic, with its tremendous numbers of people, the careful thoughts in the presentation of China's Peaceful Rise give significant insight to the problems within and internationally in the consumption of resources that would be involved. China's leadership understands that a great part of its job is not only to educate its people but also to understand the values they must hold to have a balanced society. Whose values will be taught? The old patriotism of communism alone is no longer effective and will not be. A new set of ideas must be put forward, ones that define the Party. That definition will become clearer with the new leadership but like geopolitics much is already set in trends and constraints. The broad needs will not change and the wants will have to be addressed.

If they ever move to democracy, the government and the Party will have to learn to have much greater trust in people. That requires people to understand the obligations and the benefits of civil liberties. And the only power within China that can help that is cultural. The political base has not been trained or educated to the fact that the West took centuries from the evolution of the Magna Carta to reach many of its current systems. When Alexis de Tocqueville wrote *Democracy in America*, it was in preparation for ideas for a French system that was dramatically different.

All democracies have different forms. The question is one of justice, dignity, and rights. All systems vary, but a critical point to be remembered in the coming discussions is that the competitive world is creating a need for both order and innovation. Order is often top down, and innovation and creativity bottom up. Regulation is a tool of top down control politically; wealth creation is an economic force from self-interest. The American Constitution is bottom up in that it says not what government must do for the people but what it cannot do to them (however, America has expanded government power as its trend).

The Communist Manifesto sets government as the core, which is top down, but the last 30 years has reduced government by giving markets and private property a place. It is the future framework of "Socialism with Chinese Characteristics" that has to be decided. Will it at the core be communism with market incentives or market capitalism with strong controls—or neither and address the middle class or a "xiaokang" of cultural dominance into which economies and politics are evolved? That is probably where "The Harmonious Society" will evolve just as "A Revitalized American Exceptionalism" will require the same things in the U.S.

China has one of the oldest existing cultures dating back 4,000 years. The Cultural Revolution may have tried to change it, but its renaissance is now blossoming. It is the core that holds the Chinese people together. What is often missed is that America and its great systems of democracy resulted mainly because we are a nation of immigrants. People came from everywhere to America, and we had to have systems that looked at rights between different groups. China is a very insular nation—one that does not have great numbers of immigrants that affect its internal aspects. The Chinese culture, looked at broadly, has absorbed almost every group that has come into China. You must look from that cultural perspective.

If the concept of personal dignity based on conscience is the core of the Harmonious Society, you have the problem of how China builds new economic and political systems from the cultural values that matter. This is why their great think tanks look at theory and executive concepts using ethics of common shared concerns and rights to build them. There is a need for any sustainable system to have deferred gratifications and wellness to sacrifice for common goals. If it is not ethical or perceived fair, there is automatic discontent.

The economic system under such a concept is not going to be the same as the West. Western approaches of total free enterprise have greater highs and lows in economic activity. It is more a shareholder-based concept. China's culture might well work more like a nonprofit. As we visited with many nonprofit entities in the U.S., this was a very significant area of interest to them. As previously stated, they often called such institutions Communist Capitalists because they were made to bring about efficiencies and compete like a mutual or nonprofit that operated as a capitalist company but the benefits went to a much broader base of members.

Their interest in these concepts, as opposed to Russia's concepts of oligarchy, is significantly different. The Chinese people would react very poorly to the Russian system out of a significant concern for fairness. This requires looking uniquely at issues such as corruption within business and government. Many of the writings in the books dealt with peer pressure and how to maintain transparency. Those were of interest to the Chinese as was how organizations like the Better Business Bureau could be used to apply peer pressure and give awards for integrity.

The other side of the economic system must also be understood—what the Chinese learned in the Great Leap Forward and the Cultural

Revolution about the problems of the "free-rider" concept. Since incentives matter, there must be balance that removes the worst problems of pure free markets. Yet there cannot be a lack of incentives or you will have no growth, no success, and a lack of stability. Thus, a concept of conscience dealing with obligation and with compassion is critical. Obligation requires a rule of law, equal opportunity more than equal results, but it also requires a strong private system as well as careful government focus on charitable needs or those unable to care for themselves. Service organizations and nonprofits for charity have a huge part to play in market system operation.

In China the family takes care of this responsibility respecting dignity. Thus, the balance in the economic system driven from a cultural perspective may be quite different in the United States. We have a tendency to grow government believing that money solves the problems when it may, in effect, cause them. China has already had the problems of massive central government, seen those issues, and is looking at their reform.

Political democracy, from a cultural aspect, is also somewhat different. When I was in law school, one thing we studied most intently was the English system where English Common Law became so technical that even a missed comma or a misstatement through a pleading often caused injustice. The English came up with a system of *Equity* and a number of doctrines that brought justice back into the system, not so much on technical legality, but instead on doctrines such as the "necessity of clean hands." You cannot recover if you have done wrong in the process.

Many of the concepts of equity sought ultimate justice then adjusted fairness processes technically. China may well evolve a fair legal system using its cultural past. The same justice can be sought, but it results from a different way of thinking about the issues. The greatest challenge for this bridge will be the infringement of intellectual property. China is just adopting private property concepts so it will take time to evolve.

The most important issue that our children and grandchildren in both America and China will face is how well they are able to work together. The first issue is how to understand each other and discuss rather than criticize. When we first began the exchanges with China in Texas, they were protocol delegations. They thanked each other, were courteous to each other, had a formalized approach, but in many cases had difficulty with long-term results.

As the relationship with the Lyceum and the Central Party School, and later the Counsellors of the State Council were built, the levels of discussion changed. There were often different people but because of the growing familiarity with ideas and purposes that had grown, you saw more unique relationships. They became more institutionalized. The field trips we would go on in China gave us more insight that Americans often did not understand. Watching how the Chinese studied the cultural changes in Shenzhen— how they viewed the loss of values and then implemented them in their educational systems so that China would not lose them twenty years later when it became more like Shenzhen—was a remarkable lesson to me.

This observation made me fight even harder to have the great classics still taught in our universities. The values are perhaps more important rather than the technical aspects of an education. To say ethics should not be emphasized in its own course because you could have a math course instead, misses the fact that ethics in working with other people has a great deal to do with conveyance of what you would learn in the math course and its purpose. The Chinese understand that reasoning better than the West. They see it from values lost to be regained.

Another clear observation is that the United States expects quicker changes and adaptations than are realistic for the Chinese. Domestically, they have remarkably taken 400 million people from poverty, but they have 800 million more in the rural areas. Internal stability puts limits on the size and speed of changes, but the modern world will make many of the changes. The way they have done much of this is not just manufacturing and trade, but infrastructure and construction. These latter approaches are maximized and if their banks lend on margined projects, they add to an existing bubble. These are Western systems that helped in these areas in the past, but they have to be adapted to Chinese culture and economics. Lending in the future may be more to individuals than institutions, and that is quite different.

How the Chinese perceive our efforts and intentions is a critical factor since the U.S. and China are linked. The Chinese think conceptually and by their thought connect dots to show intentions. Americans often try many different approaches to issues and have interest groups that force some smaller changes domestically. In the U.S. we are used to inconsistencies. We give price supports to produce and then buy excesses. We think more like lawyers who make several inconsistent arguments in a case. They think like engineers—everything has to be understood and balanced for something to work, particularly in critical planning.

This leads to real misunderstandings. They can see certain independent actions like arms sales or trade restrictions and connect the dots into a scenario that makes sense of the dots but may be incorrect. So having vehicles that have a more factual assessment and understanding is critical. And it needs to be created as a win-win situation, explaining concessions on either side.

We should not lose sight of how differently we think, as we deal with common forces, powers, and motivations in any system. In America it is said we think like Chess—which is a game of attrition, all players exposed and on the table, a strategy of dominance. The Chinese are compared to their game of Go—an ongoing battle of containment, more pieces with some off the table that can be introduced at any time, and a strategy of patience and conservative use of resources.

In reality we need to invent a new game with parts of both as a team effort to push the score of common living standards ever higher.

The Cleavage Point on the Diamond and the Canary in the Mind Shaft

If you analyze Chinese politics, economics, and culture and how they are contextually affecting each other, you see two competing factors. The historical culture that pushes toward individual dignity is emerging strongly while at the same time the existing political system, which is the historic centralized organizations, continues a desire for control to maintain stability. These are two forces that will probably be more settled in the economics of China than might be perceived. When Chairman Deng opened China twenty years ago he brought in free markets, but China has traditionally kept its own approach to market capitalism. It has evolved a new type of state-directed capitalism.

Many countries have had state-controlled companies that were in effect almost departments of the government, but traditionally as market systems move forward, they were privatized. This was the case of much of Latin America when the Western example of market capitalism was adopted through many of the proponents of the Chicago School with Chile being the first. However, the corruption and greed that were revealed in the financial meltdown have had much of the world questioning the Western model. Too often they focus on capitalism as the problem rather than the cultural failures that diminished it and needed to be prevented.

The Chinese political system has maintained control of many of the major industries. They are also being prepared to be the Chinese economic champions moving abroad. They are seeking a more sustainable model that redesigns capitalism more in keeping with their political structure. This is a model that is increasingly being compared to the Western market model by emerging countries. While the Chinese often note that this provides a more stable approach to economics than the wilder swings of the West, they feel it can also give a corporate infrastructure internationally as they continue to not only buy resources, but companies through their reserves in much of the rest of the world.

This fits with their political system in that there has always been the close relationship between government and business in China. But it will mean that China's major companies will become increasingly outward looking and will need to build expertise and skills as they acquire foreign companies and have the necessity of facing governance and accounting standards for stock exchanges. The problems that they will face in these arenas are significant. Just like in the United States, if the government picks winners and losers, the results do not show the benefits of the competition of the market and often are inefficient uses of capital. One of the few offsets to this will be whether the Chinese can learn Western governance standards, and while maintaining control of their national leaders, they put a degree of independence within the boards of those companies that have them operate more efficiently and with more of the Western style of governance to look at performance and incentives within the organization to bring the best of market systems. The competence of leadership both in the government and in the corporations will determine a great degree of the success of the model. In effect the government remains the shareholder, but has a more independent, performance rewarded management.

The concepts of ethical governance are ones that both the West and the East will inevitably need to learn if the conscience-oriented aspects of culture are to grow. How the economic sector looks at issues such as greed, fraud, private property rights, and corporate practices will matter a huge amount in shaping both the culture and the politics of the future. As several of my friends in the Task Force on Integrity noted, *there are only a few places that the rubber truly meets the road,* and that is where you begin to see the direction of the future.

Perhaps the best demonstration of how increased governance in state-owned Chinese firms could benefit, is the transition it could provide as firms evolve in the economy. *The Wall Street Journal* of Thursday, February 23,

2012, led with a front page article "New Push for Reform in China" (Influential Report to Warn of Economic Crisis Unless State-Run Firms Are Scaled Back). The World Bank and the Development Research Center, a think tank that reports to the higher levels of the State Council, issued "China 2030," which predicted the significant need for scaling back state-owned enterprises and making them operate more like commercial firms. The concern was decelerating economic growth under the existing Chinese model as it reaches certain plateaus for developing countries (Brazil and Mexico being examples) once certain income levels were reached. A key point noted was that "It isn't known whether "China 2030" will project a certain growth rate when released next week. But current forecasts by the Conference Board, a U.S. think tank, see the Chinese economy growing at 8% in 2012, and slowing to an annual growth rate of 6.6% from 2013 to 2016. . . . While some reduction in the rate of growth is inevitable—China has been growing at an average rate of 10% a year for 30 years—the rate of decline matters greatly to the world economy."

But changing systems and addressing the powerful entrenched forces in the existing model will certainly be a major political and economic issue as the forces of change and status quo are culturally shifted. The World Bank helped China with its early reforms and is respected there as is the Chinese think tank, so this will raise the issue of governance change clearly. I use the term governance change, because corporations are directed from the top in the Western system and the directors set the vision for the corporation by their oversight of performance and efficiency, but also by their impact on how employees are compensated with incentive systems to accomplish results and where the company's money must be invested for the future success. These considerations require a more individualized focus for the company than the state-directed model where it is more influenced by government policy and needs.

China normally takes actions with planning and a long-term perspective. The need for growth may accelerate these considerations, but it is also likely to take a more thoughtful cultural-change approach to what will be a tenacious internal discussion of political and economic considerations. In the years I have worked with the Central Party School and State Council on ethics issues, governance was always in discussions because it was a key method to fight corruption.

What this report does is to bring in the second issue of governance—how to make the company more efficient and competitive by asking the right oversight questions and helping provide focus. The Chinese government will need more input from the companies as a source of information as they go abroad about changes that are needed to be competitive, and a key initial change would be culturally to adopt more Western governance initiatives. This would be a logical bridge between the two opposing forces of defending the interests of the status quo and bringing change. Those running corporations would have more of an opportunity to shape what they think should be the evolution of the firm while the proponents of less state authority would see a beginning step that moved toward both efficiency and ethical culture. It would be a middle ground to allow observation of change and a gradual evolution of approach.

There are many sensibilities that have to be addressed in developing a Chinese approach to governance—just like the Rule of Law needs to be explained in the sense of Cultural Justice. Governance will be the key first step of discussion strategically if a sound system is to be evolved, but it will require the highest levels of the Chinese government working with Western governance organizations to blend concepts. It will take time, research and training. Institutions like the Central Party School will need to develop and teach courses toward that end, and the State Council will have to heavily promote the concept. The benefit will be a much better working relationship with the rest of the world as more common governance practices become established. This is a key point on the cleavage point of the diamond not only of future Chinese economic success but also global ethical governance.

If the Chinese are able to learn Western governance and see its benefits, I personally believe they will move more toward market systems and in some ways toward more of the aspects of the Western style of political democracy. If they move heavily to a state-dominated system, they will face the problem of how to bring efficiency and integrity to the culture of corporations. Eventually they will become less efficient and less competitive in the international realm. This may occur over several decades but what makes China the unique place for this type of experiment is its appreciation for the power of culture. It may well be able to use the creation of ethical standards to bring efficiency and judgment to its boards and shield direct political involvement or at least mitigate it.

To accomplish that, both China and the West need to cooperate in helping each other. The West needs to bring the best governance practices to China, and the Chinese need to assist in promoting them internationally. They are in the interest of both countries and most certainly in the interest for the world.

Because of the power that economics has in shaping the interests of politics and ultimately the values or lack of values in culture, what happens in the giant corporations of China as they begin to move externally will be one of the critical factors that ultimately will impact many other decisions.

In the future, China will be increasingly analyzed and every small action given meaning. That is a less accurate way of judging their attitudes and progress than looking at the composite of actions over the span of the last thirty years. There have always been episodes of tightening and reaction as limits are reached in the existing structure, but China had a general march forward as it adapted to the modern world. New leadership had more exposure abroad, older leaders looked to their legacies with care, and trends mattered. That does not mean China will make the right decisions or that older values of conscience will prevail, but the trend has been more positive.

China will do what is in its best interests politically and economically, as is natural for all nations. But the key is how they perceive those interests and how broad a common good is sought as a personal benefit. That is where cultural argument is needed to show where the best common interests can be found. Modern economics and nationalist politics will create frictions. Common concern for the future and the type of cultural ethics that will dominate the globe reinforce the significance of values. The natural trends of history and common need will argue for more cooperation if the opportunity is given.

The Critical Importance of Hispanics in America's Future

While Dad had very much of his focus on dignity, individual responsibility, and honor, Mother came at the issue from her family history a little differently, but to the same results. She believed very much in the concept that one's reputation was what was the most valuable thing in life because it conveyed the truth of how you lived. She believed that character was what you did when no one else knew and emphasized the importance of that concept. But she also felt that you had an obligation to leave evidence of your beliefs. To her, a satisfying life was one lived by principles and that truly showed compassion. It probably was best expressed by one of her favorite passages:

> *A good name is more desirable than great riches; to be esteemed is better than silver or gold.*

—Proverbs 22:1 (NIV)

She did not view this in the terms of receiving honors but in showing a commitment to doing the right thing. In her era, shame was a major consideration. Honor truly mattered and good intentions and works were expected—not to bring reward and recognition but as an obligation. Mother taught that the essence of Jesus' teachings was that people were far more important than things, and you should be concerned for all people. Materialism is secondary.

In your generation, I hope you remember both Dad's and Mother's key concepts.

An Award Worthy of Mother

If you are diligent in life, you usually receive recognitions of one type or another. It may be based on your contributions to an organization—financial and/or personal. It may be in recognition of a unique distinction that you hold or a variety of other circumstances. The award says a great deal about the institution giving it as well as the individual receiving it. To me the truly significant awards are those that are not based on money, influence, or any consideration other than purity of choice for a thoughtful set of criteria.

Mother would have been most proud of a distinction or honor that I was given in March of 2011 that was quite unusual for me but very much in keeping with her judgment criteria. It was also one that provided a significant education for me and a confirmation of my faith in people and conscience. I was advised that I would be the first recipient of the Cesar Chavez Legacy and Educational Foundation's Conscience Builder Award for the dedication that I had shown over the years in support of personal dignity. Since I had had little interaction directly with the group, it was not one that came from my support or significant personal ties. It was one truly based on their efforts to create an external award that recognized their principles and at the same time several internal awards that recognized dedication to them. This award was given at a dinner in San Antonio prior to the organization's co-sponsored march with the City of San Antonio for Dignity and Justice, a long-standing tradition within the city.

Since my background was that of a capitalist and a former President of the State Chamber of Commerce, as a business leader who has been an advocate of free trade and the right to work, as well as one with a conservative political background, I seemed at first an odd choice. However, the more I read of Cesar Chavez's history and the significance and dedication that had been given to many of the principles he proposed, the more I recognized that similar to my experience in China, powerful cultural values overcame economic and political interests to unite. This was an organization and a movement of which I was thoroughly aware because of the significant distinctions having been given to Cesar Chavez in a Presidential Award of Freedom and holidays in his honor. There are also many streets in different cities named after him, just as Martin Luther King's have been, in recognition of a culture he symbolized.

As part of the process, I got to know a number of people like Jaime Martinez who had kept the flame alive through the Educational and Legacy Foundation for many years. They gave me an insight to the struggle that had taken place and presented it in a different light than I had seen from my vantage point in college during that period. I had the opportunity to meet one of the other great leaders of that era in Dolores Huerta, the Co-Founder of the United Farm Workers. She had been a school teacher who saw the poverty of the children, their lack of shoes and food, the lack of restrooms for laborers, and workable conditions, and had become an organizer for their efforts. Her Foundation today spends all of its money on scholarships. She still dedicates her life to the effort, and the many placards of his picture in the marches speak to the respect she holds. Her obvious commitment when she speaks to groups and thousands of people tells you a great deal about her life.

Dolores and I became good friends with a significant mutual respect even though we did not agree on a number of political and economic approaches. We certainly were in total agreement on the importance of dignity and the understanding that the only way you solve problems is for people to come together with respect and the desire to find a common end. She was a legendary hard negotiator as I have always tried to be for my principles, but the question is often how you can make a deal. The political extremes of today start at such wide points they seldom have a possible compromise. It is increasingly difficult in partisan politics to find a common ground that can be transformational. So everything is a difficult transactional approach that may give each what they want but seldom does the country any good by making the hard choices of sacrifice that are necessary for our children.

I saw Dolores as one who had the children as her ultimate goal. And if you had valid arguments for reaching that goal, she would consider them. Her arguments would get a far greater consideration from me because of my respect for her and her son Emilio who took the time to help educate me on a great deal of history. The next day I was invited to participate in the March for Dignity. Not to do so after I had just been given a rather exceptional award of conscience for my support of dignity would have seemed quite hypocritical. Because it was a form of communication in which I had never fully participated, I was more observant than normal.

In my German heritage in the smaller town of Brenham, I had participated in our Maifest Festival and its parades from the time I was about three years old and through all of my children had a lifetime of involvement. The Maifest parade was in many ways a showing of our patriotism and our heritage. It was a way of remembering our past. But the parades that I knew were only one of a number of different gatherings.

As we watch the riots in cities in the Middle East, the protest demonstrations, we see the extreme of these parades. So it becomes very important to separate nonviolent acts from those that often in the media reflect the violence of protests and riots. A march in recognition of a purpose is more cultural and has a significant symbolism and a much different purpose than a violent protest.

The march of 25,000 to 30,000 people was lined up as far as you could see with its black eagle of dignity flags of the movement and often American flags attached to it. Families walked together, in some cases children in strollers. What you had was a culture reminding itself of its history and showing itself its influence and dedication not to ever go back to a time of lesser dignity. It was a time that families passed on values. Every event that I attended had a Pledge of Allegiance, a military presence with the flag, and symbols of patriotism with invocations, blessings, and benedictions. They were cultural events that were dedicated to values. In many ways I was probably considered an outsider, but I was made to feel completely welcome.

The introduction and the person giving me the award was Raulito Navaira, brother of Emilio Navaira, both great Tejano music stars. And each time I was introduced they quoted the comments of Little Joe, one of the most prominent Tejano icons, on *The Language of Conscience*. The comment in each introduction referred to how he viewed my book and very accurately caught what it says:

> *Hispanics, through music and the arts, which are an expression of the soul, will continue to define our rich culture. Our culture's character is defined by either*

character or convenience. Skipper, "The Texas Prophet of Conscience" wisely realizes that Hispanics will not allow politicians to identify who we are. The Language of Conscience eloquently articulates our values—God, family, and serving others.

—Little Joe y la Familia

While this march was nonviolent, traditional, and focused on bringing sensitivity and appreciation to issues of dignity and justice (and teaching the next generation), it taught a lot about social gatherings. This was more the old school approach of Martin Luther King that emphasized awareness. With the cuts that will necessarily come in social programs and the increasing financial pressures on society, expressions of emotion are going to increase dramatically. The Tea Party is an example as is the movement to Occupy Wall Street. Social media makes it far easier to rally your supporters, but it is less effective in converting people who are not in your "network." All of these social movements have to reach maturity if they are to have impact and that involves the ultimate goal and some plan to be pushed to get there. Whether they are violent or involve conflict is a very key consideration that distinguishes and defines them. Who are their spokesmen and image defining leaders? How are they structured to function, a top down system or a more bottom up one of individuals?

The march in San Antonio was very constructive and focused. Even it was an effort to refine goals and build a new vision. It is not enough to show influence, you must detail what you specifically wish done to have power. Political leaders only look at the effect on elections. The greatest power comes from a system such as the Tea Party efforts that changed an election, and its power is that it had a system of ideas, not necessarily one leader who could be attacked. Ideals can be expressed in systems that unify, and men can express them in leadership. The focus should not be on the crowd but on the goals that can survive them.

With the demographics of the Hispanic population of Texas and America, you will see an ever greater influence and impact. What I saw in my experience confirmed to me that their decisions ultimately will be based on what is best for their children and the preservation of their families. That is their key issue and one for which they are willing to sacrifice as long as it is with respect and is part of a much greater group.

The question for America will be with whom can they join for transformational cultural values? Or will only transitional politics be available? It is an uncertain issue of the future.

One of the other guests honored at the event was Eduardo Ibarra, M.D. of Puerto Rico. He emigrated from Mexico and did his medical training in New York. He was honored for his work, providing clinics in support of the poor. I greatly enjoyed my visits with him. He gave me a set of principles that he thought carefully defined many of the Latino values. He called it the "Latino People Manifesto" and had presented it on the 200th Anniversary of the Mexican Independence at midnight on September 15, 2010, at the Lincoln Memorial in Washington, D.C. It is interesting how closely many of his core beliefs match the writings and principles in *The Language of Conscience* Triangles. With his permission they are included here:

Latino People Manifesto

There is a sole Humanity, beyond the borders that separate People. Human Rights belong equally to all, although we have different origins and diverse ideas. There is a unique dignity that is part of our own existence and it belongs to all Human Beings. Only equality grants us true liberty.

Let's not contend against individuals, ideologies, or political organizations. Let's fervently dedicate our fight to the defense of the Universal Human Rights.

No law should promote discrimination against any Human Being due to the color of her or his skin, origin, language, religion or economical status. No law should undermine the Human Rights and Dignity of the People, being our People or any other People.

The laws and projects of Nations, should promote wellbeing and opportunities toward a better living, not only for their own inhabitants, but for all the Human Genre. Migratory laws of nations should be deeply humanitarian in order to allow all the People of the world to share work opportunities and wealth. Law and order should prevail in all nations, together with mutual respect between all People and Humanism as a means and as an end.

A Nation's progress can only be measured in its bestow of justice, and the summation of wellbeing of all of its people. Pride in our origins leads us to dignity in our destinies.

Perhaps the best understanding of the core of bridging cultures was given that evening in a speech by Isidro Garza, Jr. before the presentation was made by Raulito. I include it and my acceptance not out of pride, but to focus on how issues can be handled to be transformational. While a part is repetitive of previous discussions, both sets of comments serve as an example of a case study of a bridge built on joint ideas while the participants are quite different.

The 2011 Cesar Chavez Conscience Builder Award
Presented by Isidro Garza, Jr.

It is in trying times such as those experienced in the mid '60s and '70s by the farm workers that courageous leaders with strong convictions, such as those of Cesar Chavez and Dolores Huerta, make their mark in the legacy that is forged for our children. In his struggle for clean water in the fields, portable restrooms, and a decent wage, it was human dignity that was central. On the farm workers' flag, the red is for the sacrifice, the white is for hope, and the eagle at the center is for dignity. The organizing principle behind "La Causa" was and continues to be the core values of honor, courage, and respect for the rights of others. "El Respeto al Derecho Ajeno es la Paz," President Benito Juarez (1858). "Peace is defined in the respect for the rights of others."

It is in today's world-in-turmoil, with its global economy in disarray, that we look for leadership to help charter us through these storms. We have accomplished much in viewing from whence we have come, but with our increasing strength come greater responsibility in this charting of destiny. More than ever ideas matter because how we think about issues determines what we think of them. Today, we not only seek justice and personal dignity, but economic opportunity, strong families, and most of all a greater future for our children than our generation has had. These things we cannot do alone, but are impacted by others. How we refine our thoughts, values, and actions moving forward is strategically important, but it can never leave the principles of our legacy. We must start by defining ourselves and what we value most. Personal dignity and justice come from Conscience, and it is this value that is the organizing principle of our organization and history. Tonight the Conscience Builder Award will be given for the first time and will henceforth be given annually to recognize this principle and to bring into our community others who share it as their core value. We recognize that awards define people, but recipients also define the organization giving them.

We are honored to have amongst us a person who has dedicated his life identifying unifying principles, which are basically the same principles that Cesar Chavez lived and died for: conscience over convenience, the golden rule— to treat others with dignity and respect, as we would like to be treated—and service to others. These unifying core values, a culture, "Nuestra Cultura," that bring a balance to politics and economics; politics is usually driven by expediency, immediate gratification, convenience, Democrat versus Republican, and economics, usually driven by long-term effect, rich versus poor. This is like a chariot being pulled by two horses . . . each trying to go their separate way: one wants to go to the right; the other wants to go to the left. It is neither to the right nor to the left that we want to go. So it is that third horse that is put in the middle to complete this troika, a culture of conscience that sets the course for the greater common good and which brings fairness and prosperity. That middle horse of conscience has spokesmen that may be very different but contain the same message. I, like many feel that his forthcoming book, "The Wisdom of Generations," may be a bridge between many diverse groups that currently differ in economics and politics by decision-making that demands the recognition of long-term economic realities and moral hazard in politics. It is a book of advice to his children that lets them understand their future is linked with our children's future and those of others worldwide. It is philosophy of expansion and growth not division. These are thoughts commonly held that will prove to be the bond for a harmonious generation.

Cesar Chavez, labor; Skipper Dippel, capitalist. Cesar Chavez, Skipper Dippel: two people with very distinct backgrounds and upbringings. They have spoken that we must think beyond ourselves and serve others. . .that our futures are in our own hands and what we make of it. What can be common between these two seemingly opposites? Cesar Chavez's view of life from the "surcos" (from the fields) and Skipper from a middle class home in a small town where his father was sheriff, and later a banker to a record of academic achievements, the U.S. Navy, and an extensive career in business, literature, and political leadership. He is a capitalist who has been President of the Texas State Chamber of Commerce, served on a Federal Reserve Bank Board, and numerous business organizations. It is the core values that both lives exemplify—strong family commitments, values passed on to them by their parents, and the driven talent to lead both as organizers of people and creators of ideas—ideas that center upon an epitome of a culture of conscience that brings out the best in men and makes them define themselves. They may have done it in different ways, in different eras, and with different styles, but they never gave up, and they stood in controversy.

In 1980 Skipper founded the Texas Lyceum Association, which recently celebrated its Thirtieth Anniversary with a record that brought together all genders, races, religions, and political affiliations to talk with dignity and intelligence on the future of the state. I was fortunate to be one of the first attendees and what impressed me was not just its openness, which was unusual for the time, but the motivation. The Lyceum was the grove of trees where Aristotle taught wisdom in thought and ethics. It did not tell you what you had to think, it helped you learn to think well. Skipper has believed that in determining facts you have knowledge, but wisdom requires adding values to it. His is a new way of thinking for modern times, which helps organize and prioritize thought. In his lifetime he has led many state efforts on education, economic development, the arts and humanities, and is probably best known for a series of books, The Language of Conscience Evolution, which have been used globally in understanding the contextual nature of politics, economics, and culture

Cesar Chavez. . . .Skipper Dippel, much more alike than different—they both epitomize an honorable culture of conscience.

So, you see it is the commitment to these common core values that define Skipper, and also define those of our Hispanic community, which are fundamental to "La Causa de Concencia." It is for this reason that the 2011 Cesar Chavez Conscience Builder Award goes to Mr. Tieman "Skipper" Dippel.

And now to present the award we have this year's Grand Marshall, Raulito Navaira.

Acceptance Speech
Cesar Chavez Conscience Builder Award
March 25, 2011

After a Presentation such as that, the only appropriate words would be, "What would Cesar say?"

He noted that if you really want to make a friend, go to someone's house and eat with him. . . . The people who give you their food give you their heart. That is certainly an appropriate sentiment tonight, and I can only express my appreciation for this distinction and wish you to know that I fully appreciate its significance.

As one grows older and gains experience, he realizes what is truly important in life. My father taught me early that you do not judge a man by his handshake and his smile, by his job or his clothes, but by his heart and his mind, which is all that mattered. Cesar Chavez noted the very same thing about La Causa, "There is no turning back. . . . We are winning because ours is a revolution of mind and heart. . . ." While we sit here as men and women today with our sons and daughters, those of us with age appreciate the fact that we are here only for a small period of time in the record of God's creation, and more importantly if we wish to affect the future we do not do so by material wealth, but by the ideas and the values that we put forward through our children. For Cesar and I would agree that there is no better way to learn than what he called the Book of Humanity.

As I look at the audience tonight, I see older friends from the past. But more importantly, I see the young leaders that will accept the challenges of a current world and its difficulties. I am very much reminded of the story on the Internet of the old Indian Chief who was teaching his grandson to be a warrior. He noted to him that within each of us is a battle between two wolves, a good wolf and a bad wolf. The good wolf uses the forces honor, respect for dignity, and conscience; the bad wolf uses pettiness, jealousy, greed, and the other power of convenience. The Grandson asked, "Which wolf wins?" The Grandfather answered, "The wolf you feed the most."

Tonight, we are here to feed the good wolf. The recognition of conscience and the personal dignity and justice that are essential to it are critical factors that bridge all cultures. As Cesar Chavez noted, "You are never strong enough that you don't need help," and the ability of people to work together is essential. We have much more in common than we would ever expect until we learn about each other.

The story I have told my son Tee many times is the same that my father told me, that his father told him. Before the Great Depression my Grandfather Henry had begun the Brenham Wholesale, but with the Depression he had to let half of his staff go and pulled my father back from the University of Texas to help him with the business. The first thing that Grandfather Henry asked my father to do was to take a knife and try and crack some eggs with as little damage as he could and to very carefully make not too intrusive slices in several flour sacks. My father thought that the pressure of the Great Depression had impacted his Dad's mind and questioned him. Grandfather Henry made a very clear point to him. He noted that the people that he had to let go came back every day or so to see if there was work, but there would not be any for a long time. They were people who had helped him build the business, and he owed a responsibility to them. If he offered to give them products, only half would take it and their dignity would be hurt by the charity. If my father did his job of inflicting limited damage, then Grandfather could ask them to help him by buying damaged goods at a low price they could afford, and his obligations would be honored while they maintained a dignity that was deserved. Those values were taught to me and I taught them to my son. And I expect him to teach them to his son, just as I would imagine many of you have done the same to your sons and daughters in carrying forth the power of history and the values you have moved to the next generation. That is why we are all here tonight. We are different in some ways but the same in values.

The challenges that we face as a nation in healthcare, education, job creation, and our national deficits are waiting to be addressed. And unfortunately the self-interest, greed and arrogance of many looking to their own convenience are in many ways letting the bad wolves win. The good wolves have a great concern for their children and realize that their future is going to be bound with the future of all other children and must find ways to maintain the family values and responsibilities that have been our heritage and that have built our country into the greatest economic engine the world has ever seen.

The Language of Conscience Evolution is based upon the concept of "Enlightened Conservatism," which basically holds an organizing principle that every man owes every other man the rights and dignities that they would wish for themselves. Its trademark is a triangle where the forces of change and the status quo of history are balanced or unbalanced by personal dignity. It is very similar to the eagle at the center of your flag, which represents its key point: dignity. There are three powers in the world that affect this dignity: economics, politics, and culture. Almost all other factors fit into them in combination or directly. Economics is often driven by rich versus poor; politics is driven by right versus left. Both of these are driven by the interests of individuals, not by their values. Culture is the power of ideas being moved forward by history, usually through the family unit and is very different. It is driven by the values of conscience versus convenience with conscience being driven by both obligation and compassion. Obligation must often be met in order that compassion is sustainable. It is not right versus wrong, but whether one cares about others and the future or only themselves at the present. Our adversary in this modern world is convenience, which asks the question, "What's in it for me?"

The Cesar Chavez organization is an extremely influential one that plays an activist role in the direction of the Hispanic movement. It will become increasingly important as the demographics of the state and nation increase the influence of the Hispanic culture. The new census shows that 37.6% of Texans are Hispanic, and 48% of the children under 18 are Hispanic. It is an organization steeped in heritage that understands the cultural power for which Cesar Chavez dedicated his life as well as many others present have dedicated their lives to the concepts and ideals that are conscience. The question many ask is "In what direction will this heritage move?" "How will it adapt its key principles of dignity to also strive for an ever-increasing economic pie where everyone's share grows, rather than arguments over division of how to split slices?" "How will it move to further its goals of opportunity and middle class jobs?"

The creation of this award based on conscience and defining culture as its organizing force rather than one recognizing politics or economics says a great deal about the ideas and interests you value and your vision. It says a great deal about your appreciation of family. We are no longer Anglo or Hispanic or any other race. Under conscience, we divide ourselves differently. We recognize not only multiculturalism as a necessity in the modern world, and the necessity of diversity to unify people. But we understand that the great question is whether we emulate the likes of Gandhi, Martin Luther King, and Cesar Chavez in reunifying these diverse groups into a melting pot based on character and morality among men. That also brings about the greatest economic growth. A decision process looking at the future of our children is essential or we will simply let the various cultures be a salad bowl of absolute toleration that looks to relativity and political correctness.

Character is destiny and this award says a great deal more about this organization than it does about me or the ideas that I represent. In adapting to the modern world, it is an organization that has defined itself by character, a devotion to family, and the respect for personal dignity by embracing an intellectual approach that looks at how to make the world competitive for our children even if we must sacrifice in the process. We must come together and bring our mutual thoughts into harmony. We must have a new way of thinking that sets a paradigm to continue the cause of dignity from the past but blended with the economic realities of a global competitive world. Cesar noted that we need to care not just about ourselves, but also our community. We are part of a greater whole. It is that whole that must succeed. In the modern world you must be seated at the table or you may be on the menu. And when at the table, you must think strategically. If you want to be transformational, you must have a common vision with at least some of the others at the table, and it will usually be value based. If not, you can only trade for transitional or self-interest. For all of us in America, we need a new common vision for our children's future.

One of the best ways to make this point is the example of the question of the man driving a two-seater sports car by a bus stop where he saw three people waiting for a long delayed bus. One was an old friend who had saved his life and was desperate to get to a business meeting, another was an older woman who had medical problems and immediately needed to get to a hospital, and the third was a beautiful woman that he saw as the love of his life. The man was forced to make a choice.

Should he honor responsibility and take his friend to whom he had obligation, should he honor compassion and help the old woman as he had been taught, or should he invite the potential love of his life out of convenience? Those are in many ways the choices we have now as we look at our deficits, our debt, and the great competitive challenges facing our nation. People argue each of those approaches. The answer is best found in a new paradigm of thought that looks at the contextual thinking of how all of the parts can be put together. A better answer would be for the man to give his car to his friend on the condition that the friend drive the older woman immediately to the hospital on the way to his business meeting, and he would remain and wait for the bus with the potential love of his life. How you think about things determines what you think about things. That is what tonight is all about. I see a modern vision of what guides a very powerful movement. For a generation you have fought for the Cause. That cause at its core is conscience, and it can be the unifying concept of a far more powerful integration with those of similar beliefs.

There will always be a battle for the soul of civilization in every generation. There will be a battle between the leadership of conscience and convenience, but conscience has to be the transformational power of a common vision of several groups to stand in a new paradigm. Small steps set the direction, but as Cesar Chavez showed, they leave big footprints in history if they have the power of conviction. Tonight we are trying to do our part to unify those fellow believers of conscience. The world is about to enter one of the great battles in this war between conscience and convenience. Whether we take a small step tonight or if it becomes a giant one, the important thing is that we take it together in united heart and mind, parents and children.

One additional benefit of the event was the inclusion of four other organizations that represented Think Tanks or associations on health care, education, and businesses that attended and built ties. Substance needs to come from opportunities or as Mother would say, "you leave evidence of your beliefs and concern." But this event gave me a very different insight to the Hispanic Community.

The Undocumented Hispanic Population, Immigration, and the Future in Context

One of the most significant domestic issues that will affect the United States economically, politically, and culturally will be how well the current Hispanic significant demographic will be absorbed into the existing U.S.

population. The immigration issue is one that splits the country politically because it involves a division between the Rule of Law in its strict sense and the Rules of Equity, which in many ways look at the situation of children facing deportation that were raised in America, often originally without their choosing. It looks at the fact that our country has not enforced its borders for many years and those actions are more harshly visited upon groups that should have followed the law, but in many cases came to America the only way they could because of the values and opportunity they felt it provided for their family. Politics is used to divide on these issues and it becomes increasingly important to understand how the future may be very different from the present. It is a hard issue for "conscience" because obligation of law and compassion for justice conflict. It is an area you need the out of the box "sports car" thought.

One of the great demographic problems of the developed world over the next few decades will be the decline in population in many of these countries. In the early inceptions of Europe and America, having large families in an agricultural society was a significant benefit because they provided labor and in many ways ultimately provided for retirement. Today, in a more industrialized and increasingly service driven economy, children are a significant expense and thus the number of children has dramatically dropped in many nations. That is one of the significant problems economically causing the potential deficits in Social Security and Medicaid and a great number of other programs. The number of workers supporting each retiree has dropped substantially and as populations may shrink, the stability of the society will be challenged. While at present, there are fewer jobs because of technology and globalization, and thus immigrants are looked upon competitively as a cost to American society, in the not too distant future that dynamic may well change and there will be a necessity of attracting additional workers for societies to remain competitive.

The educational quality of your workforce is going to determine how economically strong a nation remains and with that economic strength its political influence and power. These are issues of context that have to be considered in how America looks at setting its policies. Because of many of the past eras, this is a difficult hole from which to try and extricate ourselves currently but it will be one of the most important domestic issues that America will have to face. How to think about these issues is increasingly important. Several friends of mine have worked a great deal with the immigration issues because of their professions. Gordon Quan and Charles Foster of Houston have an international firm that has given unique insight into many of the core problems of how to view this issue. Charles Foster has often written on the depth of problems that must be faced, but in my conversations with him over the years one observation he made to me was particularly important. This Cesar Chavez Award gave increasing credence to the strength of his observations.

Culturally he felt that while there were differences, the huge wave of Hispanic immigrants was not that different from other large waves of immigration throughout American history. The common denominator is that uniformly all the large prior waves were viewed with a high degree of suspicion believing that they would never be real Americans—that they would not assimilate. All of the issues that are often brought up on talk radio and by others about large scale Hispanic immigration from Mexico and Central America were also said about prior immigrant waves. The truth was that for the most part the Hispanic children assimilated at about the same rates if not somewhat better than the immigrant groups of the past. There has always been prejudice and misinformation.

However, he noted that critics do have one very valid point in that unlike other immigrant groups, this large Hispanic wave of immigrants and these undocumented residents share an almost 3,000 mile border with the United States. While they are far more distributed than is recognized, the largest numbers still reside in the Southwest, an area that was historically a part of Mexico. Thus it is an area of deep ties culturally with Latin America from the food we eat in Texas even to the names of our streets and cities. The critics have noted that this group of immigrants is different in that they are not coming to start a new life in the new world because of the values and culture, but only for employment. There may have been some truth to that in the early waves of immigration. The higher percentage, however, is coming like the immigrants of the past for a better life. As Charles noted, some come initially only for temporary work, but once they get here they realize how dangerously difficult it is to cross our southern border and make the logical decision that rather than keeping their family ties by going back and forth they stay.

In the long run we have been more successful at fencing people in than fencing them out. Thus they not only stay, but also often smuggle in their spouse or children on a one-time basis to reunite the family in light of the difficulty of going back and forth. With the drug cartel violence along the borders of Mexico and the United States this has only been enhanced. From a political point of view, the answer is relatively simple. As Charles has noted in his writings, we need circular immigration and legal options so that people who come can go through the normal channels rather than having to be smuggled into the country. Others that just want to come and work temporarily can do so by a temporary work visa. But under our current system there is no legal way for blue collar workers to enter the U.S. This brings the necessity for a rationale, which points out the need for comprehensive immigration reform. Many of his writings and those of others have dealt with a variety of ideas on the issue. There are significant issues of automatic citizenship at birth and the integrity of the order of the formal immigration process. However, there is a rigid bureaucracy and gridlock. There is no right answer, but we must find a just one.

The difficulty is that it has become a major political issue argued from the extremes. If it is looked at more as a cultural issue it has more of a chance of being absorbed. If the residents come to be Americans because of its values and opportunity they need to be asked not to leave their cultural values behind or the appreciation of their history, but to understand and address that they are being given opportunities by our culture. If they come solely for jobs, then the method must be one that allows jobs formally only on a temporary basis. If they come to adopt the cultures and the values that have been the American ideal then they may fit much more closely into our society than one would think. As workers are needed, these are values we need to seek.

The borders have to be enforced because that is the necessity of a nation. But if that is done effectively, I think the American people might be far more understanding of a system that blended the Rule of Law with the equity of justice in finding systems that could solve the problems faced in this arena. If the issue is one driven politically for which side a group will vote then it becomes incredibly divisive. If the issue becomes one of a common appreciation of values there is far less danger and far more understanding.

My experiences with the Cesar Chavez Legacy and Educational Foundation gave me a very different understanding of where the future of the Hispanics may lead. The people to whom they showed the greatest respect were not necessarily politicians, but were their Tejano music stars, which carried forth their culture. What they valued in leaders like Cesar

Chavez and Dolores Huerta was not necessarily the politics in which they found themselves, but the values that they wanted for their children. Those will end up being common values and increasingly both political parties must realize needs placed on us by the future economic competition of the world. The Hispanic culture has always been wary of government and its involvement in its activities. They believe very much in opportunity more than dependency and as such may well provide a significant boost to America's productivity if they are properly assimilated and educated.

When I chaired Texans for Quality Education and worked to create the Economic Development Commission in Texas, my significant concern was the Valley of Texas. Our weaknesses in education, our drop-out levels, will make it increasingly difficult for us to be competitive. We may have great research universities, but what will really determine our strength is the overall education of our entire workforce. I do not believe that the political parties themselves will change as much as I believe the people within the state, if common involvements between the cultures can take place, will help solve the problem by finding more opportunistic solutions.

One of my long time friends, Pablo Schneider, writes columns on Hispanic Board of Directors Leadership and the "Changing Face of America." Some of the observations in his writings give a different context to how we look at the difficult problem of solving the illegal immigration issue and the necessity of blending it with other future challenges. The issue is not fully appreciated unless you are from Texas or one of the other majority-minority states of California, New Mexico, and Hawaii. It creates a different dynamic, and the U.S. will gradually become a multicultural country over the next thirty or so years. So this is an issue that is important to what the values of the culture will be, and economically because of American demographics with declining workers and a growing retired population needing a strong economy to support it. The politics of today needs to appreciate the context of these situations in its decisions if we are to compete as a nation and build a new dynamic model that rebuilds the middle class.

Pablo wrote one section of a recent article "The Changing Face of America," which I think conveys this thought:

In his intriguing book, The Next 100 Million: America in 2050, *demographer Joel Kotkin looks at how America will change as it grows by 100 million people over the next forty years. The conclusions of that book*

combined with the projections of the Pew Research Center are no less stunning.
America will become a majority/minority country. Anglos will comprise less
than half the population, African-Americans will remain at their current
percentage of the population, Asian Americans will grow rapidly on a small
base, and the number of Hispanics will nearly double. Two-thirds of the next
hundred million Americans will be Hispanic. These Hispanics, who already
account for 56% of U.S. population growth and 47% of consumer spending
growth, are critical to the current and future growth of the population and
economy of America. (Pew Hispanic Center)

Pablo also notes some interesting observations in that 61.9% of Hispanics
are U.S. born and 38.1% are foreign born. There are approximately 11.2 million
undocumented immigrants in the U.S. The Department of Homeland Security
estimates that this includes 6.3 million from Mexico (56.2%), 2.4 million from
other Latin American countries (21.4%), and 2.5 million from elsewhere
around the world (22.3%). Between 2000 and 2008 approximately 9.5 million
immigrated legally to the U. S. including 3.9 million from the Americas. More
than 19 million Hispanics are eligible to vote, 12 million are registered to vote,
and 9.9 million voted in the 2008 elections. Hispanics represent more than 9%
of eligible voters nationwide (Pew Hispanic Center).

As the demographics of Hispanics increase with their location in critical
states the political impact will be of growing significance; the issue will be
how they choose to align their values and interests. The current political fight
over illegal immigration pits the rule of law against the cultural sensitivity of
dignity in how the country addresses a problem that was caused in history
by the inaction of others. Thinking out of the box to achieve not only
justice as a majority sees it, but solutions to other problems will require a
rethinking of interests on both sides and will depend upon what values the
American Hispanic population considers most important.

In Texas, the Hispanic population is not Mexican. It is Tejano with its
own music and vision. They see their future in a different way than those
only here to earn and return to Mexico. This is a distinction often lost in
policy setting. If we want them to assimilate and work with us, we cannot
divide politically what we need to blend culturally. The illegal immigration
requires an understanding by Hispanics of the necessity of a closed border
and a process. The fairness of that process and how we work with existing
inequities is far from clear, but a great deal will depend on the perception

of the nation on where the values and loyalties of the growing number and power of the Hispanic people lie.

Power, Culture, and Naivety

One of the interesting things about life tends to be how images are sometimes associated with efforts. One of the most difficult images to convey is the true belief in character or symbols of great strength and not weakness. Whether it is the Christian martyrs or the many people over the generations who have worked in nonviolent protests to bring about change, it takes an appreciation to realize that the strength derived from ideas is often in the end what overcomes the great current power. I learned this from my father. His image of "the Peacemaker" and favorite eight cell flashlight, "the light of enlightenment" could just as easily have been described as a minister as would be his true image of a sheriff. In reality his beliefs were very close to the same. The groups that I have described, the Central Party School and the Counsellors of the State Council in China or the Cesar Chavez Educational and Legacy Foundation are not what would be considered naïve or passivist organizations. They probably represent the most significant strength within their respective sectors in the creation of ideas and their implementation whether it is through mandate or marches.

Another organization that has given me insight to a different culture is a Jewish one and through it and its efforts I have seen that cultural power is perhaps the most significant power for sustainability and will. The best example of this cultural power of will is the experiences I had in Colombia.

Colombia: A Case Study in National Will
A Culture of Violence Challenging a Culture of Conscience

In late March of 2012, I accepted the invitation extended to a group of officers and directors of the Jewish Institute of National Security Affairs to visit Colombia and be briefed on the changes that had taken place in the country over the last ten years. The Jewish Institute of National Security Affairs, better known as JINSA, has a membership of approximately 16,000 and has a long history of being devoted to building relations between America's military and law enforcement with Israel and intently supporting the national security of the United States. When I was first asked to serve as a director almost twenty years ago, I was hesitant because my background is that of a Methodist, and I had many time constraints. However, I soon learned that it was an organization that focused very strategically on the most critical issues of American national defense and had an advisory board that was composed of many retired American military and senior law enforcement officials. It matched my interests in coming from a law enforcement and military family. I have participated with JINSA for twenty years, and have been increasingly impressed with the researched focus that it has on emerging issues. It is one of the premier organizations in writing on terrorism through its journals and its Law Enforcement Exchange Program (LEEP) between the U.S. and Israel, which is headed by a former Head of Counterterrorism at the FBI and has trained many senior American law enforcement officials on the intelligence techniques and the methods to identify and fight terrorism.

When JINSA suggested the trip to Colombia it marked a unique choice. Colombia has had a reputation for many years of being extremely dangerous with a great amount of drug activity. Revolutionary groups such as the FARC, new criminal threats like the BACRIM, and the remnants of former notorious drug cartels have presented great challenges.

Anyone watching the two documentaries about Pablo Escobar, primarily "The Killing of Pablo" and "The Two Pablo's" that compared his life with one of the Colombian soccer stars, saw a dramatic history of how Colombia had become virtually a failed state. Upon Escobar's death in 1993, a period of drug activity and violence characterized the country and was the theme of many movies including one of Harrison Ford's. Colombia was one of the most dangerous places in the world, and the city of Medellin was one of the world's most dangerous cities. This trip allowed an opportunity to explore the changes in Colombia in large part because of the involvement of the American government at the request of the Colombian people, and to serve as background for an article for JINSA's highly regarded *Journal of International Security Affairs*. It also brought together a group of leaders whose opinions could be of help in telling the story of the change, not only in political arenas but the increasingly important economic ones.

Of no small concern was the increased activity of Iran and Cuba in the neighboring state of Venezuela and the potential linkage of terrorist groups with the drug syndicates found in the border areas, which were uncontrolled. Narco-terrorism was becoming an ever greater problem, and because of the drug pipelines it also had the ability to smuggle weapons and people, a continuing and major threat to the hemisphere. Many of the terrorist groups found their sources of income in the drug trade as well as kidnapping and robbery. Colombia has been America's staunchest partner over this period in a very critical time, and can be a cornerstone in Latin America, but few people understand the present Colombia and its significance.

What it has learned in fighting economic narco-terrorism is very similar to what Israel has learned through its law enforcement and military in fighting economic political terrorism. This is a threat that is particularly important because many of the same transnational criminal organizations have moved up Central America into Mexico and have formed partnerships with the major drug cartels located there. This put them on the border of the United States. And being a Texan concerned particularly with this area, I wanted to better understand the core problems that exist. Strategically, the issue is not just the American border and the attempted prevention of entry; the problem is far greater because of the sophistication of these groups. They are able to build their own submersibles and submarines and understand how to use the laws of coastal territory to avoid interception as well as creating networks of businesses, bankers, and lawyers to protect their interests. So to simply focus on a border misses the strategic problems that have to look at a far larger and broader challenge.

Mexico is facing this challenge now. In 2003 Colombia finally faced it dramatically after the El Nogal Club in Bogotá was bombed on February 7, resulting in the deaths of 36 people and the wounding of more than 200. Blamed on the FARC, the attack was apparently meant to dissuade President Alvaro Uribe from his attempts to change the direction of the country. In horrified reaction, the Colombian people said "No More!" and the FARC suffered a tremendous decline in popular support from that point forward. The El Nogal bombing began a formation of will that saw a violent but dedicated effort to change the nature of their society. What created and sustained this national will was what I was seeking to understand when I accepted the invitation. It is the most important cultural power because it drives the politics and ultimately the economics.

There is a point where anxiety, which is the fear of economic or political pressures or threats, turns into anger, which pushes or supports action. That point of change from anxiety to anger involves a judgment that is complex and contextual. It involves at its very base a consideration of fairness and what should be rather than what is. That inner balance that gives the strength to overcome fear is ultimately how conscience and fairness affect personal dignity.

This was a story I wanted to hear directly because the reality of life is that conscience is often greatly challenged by the threats of evil, which push for convenience. As a conservative who views reality as a person who believes in the ultimate power of conscience to give the strength to build the foundations for a greater society, I wanted to see how theories of character, of conscience, and of will interplayed with the use of power in the most difficult of circumstances. What lessons could I learn from the Colombian experience?

JINSA is an extremely well respected organization in law enforcement and the military because of its depth of research on these issues and its efforts to pinpoint the most critical actions. It has been one that not only understands the power of force, but that also understands the power of the higher ground morally. It was the Executive Director of JINSA, Tom Neumann, who first suggested to me the idea of writing *The Language of Conscience*.

This trip to Colombia perhaps taught me more than I had expected. The delegation was composed of several JINSA directors and members, headed by James Colbert who serves as the Director of Policy for JINSA and writes the reports of these visits. A full report will be found in the *Journal of International Security Affairs*, and much more information can be found on JINSA's website at www.jinsa.org. The delegation was led by retired four-star Army general, James (Tom) Hill, who served as the head of the U.S. Southern Command from 1992 to 1994. Gen. Hill had participated extensively with President Uribe (ultimately making 34 trips to Colombia within a 24-month period) and the American effort through Plan Colombia. His commitment exemplified the involvement of the American government to help the Colombian people overcome the problems that their democracy faced. He was joined on the trip by Major General James W. Parker, USA (ret.) who had commanded many of the American Special Forces in Colombia responsible for a great degree of the training of Colombians. Maj. Gen. Parker's career had placed him at the epicenter of the Army's Special Forces and gave me a great degree of insight into the codes of honor and dedication that were taught and were a part of the Special Forces. These were even more intense than those I had seen in my Navy experiences.

Their observations combined with a full week of intensive briefings from a number of sources strengthened my belief that the principles of conscience and honor were at the core of any successful change from an almost failed state to a truly vibrant and responsible democracy. It is the will, the level of dedication, that matters and what I wanted to learn was exactly what helps create or maintain that national will.

We began with a briefing by the leadership of the U.S. Southern Command in Miami, Florida, which gave a historical overview of the last twenty years of Colombia and what the challenges had been to the country as well as the various groups that had influenced it. The joint task forces of the military with many other agencies that were represented in the discussions showed that the Southern Command, which has responsibility for everything south of Mexico including the Caribbean, has an incredible challenge. However, even though I am from a law enforcement family and one that has a significant commitment to the military, I was incredibly impressed with the level of intelligence, focus, and attitudes of everyone that I met. I have attended a great number of bureaucratic organizations in my lifetime in various countries and in various aspects of economics, politics and culture, but I have seldom been as impressed as I was on this trip by the briefings of the U.S. Southern Command and the dedication as well as their justification of how money was spent on behalf of Colombia. The American military's approach to this issue is not fully understood and if it was I think would be one of the highest and best uses of American influence and power that I have ever seen. The same is true of the Joint Task Force with law enforcement agencies. Often thinking is rigid in bureaucracies—again, General Eisenhower's point that to a man with a hammer, everything looks like a nail. The innovation and breadth of understanding and thought here was adaptive.

It is important to understand that what was done was at the invitation of the Colombian people and to a large extent under great difficulties because of American law and regulations. Because of the Posse Comitatus laws, the military can serve only against terror and military threats. It is not allowed, apart from certain exceptions, to be involved with criminal activities that normally fall directly to law enforcement agencies and civilian jurisdiction. This was a significant problem in Colombia because the national police had to attack crime through its civil justice system and its military had to attack the terrorism of the FARC revolution from a national security perspective. The army and the police are not combined either in the U.S. or in Colombia (although in Colombia they are both under the Justice Department), and Colombia served as a prime example of how coordinated joint efforts needed to occur. At the same time because of the significant violence and the human abuses that take place in this type environment, many guidelines in both countries were passed to try to guarantee a respect for human rights and the conscience that needs to be the basis of conduct.

We proceeded to the American Embassy in Bogotá and were briefed by the heads of various departments of the Embassy. I did not realize that the U.S. Embassy in Bogotá, Colombia is the second largest American embassy in the world, second only to Iraq. It has been the center of understanding Latin America. I can only express significant admiration for the people making the presentations. They generally appreciated and gave credit to the Colombian people for being the core of the desire to build a new country and to establish a Rule of Law. They had good leaders, a dedicated military and police force, and a national will that was built to emerge from the violence. It was the support of the institutions that ultimately made the difference that has changed the very nature of Colombia, but it was not an easy task. The part that America played in not only training the police and the military, but far more importantly in giving insight to the institutions of democracy and justice was absolutely critical. The embassy staff conveyed through their very presentations their respect for the Colombians in how they gave the credit. Nonetheless, as we visited with the heads of the DEA and a number of other departments for briefings on the complexities of what was involved, it was very obvious that America had put some of its very best officials in Colombia and you had a team that was very deserving of respect and credit. I have encountered over my many years many briefings that were somewhat a protocol function simply to satisfy egos—that was far from the case here.

This was a group of people that knew what they were doing and understood in depth exactly what they were fighting and why it was important. It did not hurt that the JINSA directors have never had a reputation for being shy or less than direct, but again you could see that the money that America had spent in helping Colombia probably only equaled a few days of the Iraq and Afghanistan war. But it has made an incredible difference because it was very thoughtfully and intelligently used and strategically pinpointed where it needed to be. The fact that much of what had been conveyed from America was not just its support, money, and training, but a greater insight to its institutions, its values, and the soft power that America ought to be using in much of the rest of the world had been very well demonstrated in Colombia. Their court systems, even the vetting of units to see that there were no civil rights violators included, were ones that impacted the culture of performance and the evolution to professionalism.

The next few days were spent visiting the equivalent of our White House, Pentagon, and National Police Headquarters. We had the opportunity to meet the senior leadership of the military and police including advisors to the President, a member of their Joint Chiefs of Staff, and many of the leaders of their National Police. They described in detail what they had faced and oftentimes with the clarifications and the insights of the two generals that accompanied us you saw the incredible challenge and risks that were taken in bringing a sense of order. But in each case the fact that the people supported the effort became increasingly important and necessary for change.

To this end, James Colbert had foreseen the need to experience the profound changes in Colombia made possible by the reduction in violence, and made plans to take the group for a few days to the city of Medellin, which had been almost impossible to reach except by plane in the difficult days before. It is Colombia's industrial city and potential tourist destination. You could see from all of the presentation that we had significantly increased safety in Colombia, as statistics in some ways even preceded the people's changes in perceptions. It certainly preceded the changes in the perception of Colombia in the rest of the world. The city of Medellin was beautiful and we had the opportunity to visit with the city government showing how they had put in significant crime control, how kidnappings were now almost nonexistent, and how their crime statistics were greatly improving. It was a beautiful city that in the future will inevitably become a significant place for tourism.

While it is a city of parks, the most significant place within the city was a hillside covered with what I would call shanties. It was called Santo Domingo and was formed by the many displaced people that criminal gangs forced out of their homes and eventually much of the population there had great difficulty surviving. It was so dangerous, run by gangs in the earlier part of the century that even the police and military could not go into it. It was in fact one of the most dangerous places in the world. The government built the equivalent of a metro train out to the center of the area, and then built a cable car system with eight people per car at a ticket cost of 95 cents that went through three stations to the very top. It dramatically cut the time to the city from several hours to less than one, and almost tripled the income because of peoples' ability to get to work more quickly and to come back and spend time with the family. It was one of the best expenditures of money that a country could have made. Our group walked through most of that area with no difficulties—only kids playing soccer. And while it undoubtedly has crime, it was obviously a very changed place from what it had once been. The tour for me ended in a place that answered most of my questions about what affects a national will even in times of violence.

On some rocks from the highest center of that group of colonias emerged a three-story black glass structure, which towered above the shanties. While it had a much more appropriate name, Parque Biblioteca Espana, it was called the Spanish Library because it was part of a library system, but this one had been built with a grant from Spain. It was the symbol of the change in Santo Domingo and the surrounding colonias. As we entered it we saw the auditorium, which was a place for performances and meetings. We then went to the library, which was a place where books were made available so that education could become more of the center of opportunity, and more importantly the significance of education to rise above the problems that were faced was made paramount.

In another section computers that could begin to teach computer literacy to parents and children were made available although only on a timed basis because the number of people limited use. But most importantly before we left, they took us to a special room that had innumerable pictures and volumes that was effectively a place for an oral history. It was a place where the people brought and told the stories of their families. It was a place that they showed their existence had mattered and they showed the existence of their ancestors and of the pride that they had in them. This helped answer my question of what gives people the will to make dramatic change. A telling sign is what they do after they achieve freedom. They focus on what they missed most, which often is the loss of what caused the change in will. It confirmed to me that personal dignity, the control of one's own life, and a satisfaction with it is more than a general observation. It is an intense inner judgment in which fairness and conscience play a great part in temperament. Hardship can be endured if it is shared and fair, but dignity requires respect and a common concern.

In what had been the worst of places, after the national will strengthened, what was demonstrated was a valuing of family and individual dignity as was shown in the creation of the histories that were the core to which education and economic opportunity had to be added. Those were the things most sought by the people that they put in after they had the chance to be rid of the violence. They are also the very things that when strengthened would prevent the violence by keeping the national will strongly against it.

What Colombia showed me is that the principles of dignity, honor, and the family values that we are taught are the core of a national will both in maintaining it and redeeming it when it is lost. Colombia will now face a great challenge because it still has the battles to be fought with terrorism and crime through its political, military, and law enforcement, but it is winning and strengthening the battle of its internal cultural will. Ultimately the great test will be an economic one—whether Colombia is able to build the economic base to supplant the narcotics culture. There are no simple ways for this to happen, but economics is now possible because you have security. Without security there could be no investment of economic services. The Free Trade Agreement with the United States is a strong beginning and it gives that opportunity. Much of the concessions in that agreement were given by the Colombians not by the United States, but it recognized Colombia as a place to do business and showed respect. Colombia has great unexplored oil reserves and desires for manufacturing. With security, these are their areas of development. Government must now help develop the private sector and encourage the international private investment that is quite different than normal government functions.

One of the high points of the trip was the opportunity to visit for an extended period with former President, Alvaro Uribe. He is the man that is probably more responsible than anyone for the change in Colombia by his force of will and his election as President. His parents had been killed by the FARC and he was dedicated to a set of principles that mattered. Few people have impressed me as much as he did in that conversation. He was humble, thoughtful with his words, and extremely courteous, but showed an iron will of consistent belief. When people spoke about America having to cut its budgets and that what support was available for Colombia might well be limited as it would be to the military and many other agencies, he noted one important thing—money was significant, but it was not nearly as important as the respect that America could show Colombia and the image that it cared about what Colombia did and became. That was as important as any financial aid. Respect matters.

What this trip showed me was that national will has many factors, but the core factors and values that are important remain the same. You can fight individual problems, but the ultimate solution is a society of fairness and conscience that prevents the deterioration into the disintegration of the values that are the cement of society. There are reactive efforts and there are proactive efforts. For the national will to remain strong for character and for values prevents a great many of the problems that we too often anticipate and inevitably have to face when we look at issues that weaken that national will by taking attention from what are the most important items of family, personal dignity, and contextual thought on how the three great powers of economics, politics and culture inevitably fit together. The will comes from a respect for ideas. In America they are embodied in our Constitution, which is the ultimate definition of man's dignity. Unlike other countries where the military and law enforcement swear allegiance to the government, America swears allegiance to our Constitution—the ideas that give us unity and will.

One of the best observations of history was made by Sir Alexander Tyler in *On Athens* circa 1787:

From Bondage to Spiritual Faith

From Spiritual Faith to Great Courage

From Courage to Liberty

From Liberty to Abundance

From Abundance to Selfishness

From Selfishness to Complacency

From Complacency to Apathy

From Apathy to Dependence

From Dependence back to Bondage

Colombia has moved through the cycle from bondage to violence back to courage to almost liberty from it. America is at the point of apathy to our great principles and our national will must be regenerated before we have dependence on government and debt rather than the courage, which gives liberty.

JINSA also gave me a far better understanding of the Jewish community and how powerful its culture has historically been. In these most trying times it has been their strength. One of my long-term friends Fred Zeidman explained to me how the family concepts of Judaism were very close to much of what I write of Christian families. He noted that the Jewish concept of charity (tzedakah) is linked to justice (tzedek). It is the means through which justice can be brought to the world by addressing the injustice of poverty, lack of resources or hardship. It is part of the overall concept of "repairing the world" by addressing the injustice of poverty, lack of resources or hardship. It is part of the overall concept of "repairing the world" or "tikkun olam" that is the object of the Jewish people's partnership with God. Much of it ties back to Rabi Hillel, a great sage from the time of the Second Temple who said, "If I am not for myself, who will be for me? And if I am only for myself, what am I? If not now, when?" The Jewish practice of keeping the Sabbath from Friday sunset to Saturday sunset allows for twenty-six hours of being unplugged from the world of work, technology and obligation, and a chance to slow pace, reconnect with the family, intimate community, and God. It is an island of time of rest, reflection, and reinvigoration. To the Jewish community, the Sabbath creates structure, meaning, and depth to life and provides a framework for family togetherness—at the Sabbath table on Friday night and Saturday afternoon. Family is the core of the culture.

Family and worship are two components of the Sabbath, but the third is study. It allows for the study of the religious text in an organized manner and in a long summer Sabbath there is a tradition to read "The Ethics of the Fathers—A Compilation of Ethical Sayings from the early part of the First Millennium." These help cement the family identity connecting with the past and bringing a new and deeper understanding of the current day. History is not in the past for the Jewish people. They entwine it with each Jewish person's individual identity—familial and collective. A Jewish person moves through a matrix of identity from personal (who they are), familial (where do I come from—who is my family), and collective (who are my people). I wrote in several of the books of *The Language of Conscience Evolution*, I have great respect for the writings of Maimonides, the great medieval Jewish scholar, legal authority, and doctor who synthesized science and religion in his writings. He harmonized science with the laws of nature and he believed that human beings are not perfect, cannot know everything, and are necessarily limited by their status as corporal mortal beings.

This is a reality that seems to be overlooked by a great many people today. It is not far different from Confucius' observation that it is difficult to teach an arrogant man because his mind is already full. Today our educational systems pit theologians against scientists when in reality Maimonides understood that something can be logical in a scientific consequence of a natural event but that does not mean that it is not miraculous in itself. Tom and Fred's contribution to my education of Jewish philosophy over the years also gave me one very significant insight. The Jewish people have been tested over several thousand years, but the essence of family and community and the core set of values have been their greatest strength and cause of survival. They have often been persecuted for those beliefs particularly the belief in one God when ancient societies had many, but it has served as the absolute core of their strength. From the existence of Israel to the part they play economically in much of the world, family is the core.

Thus, if there is one point that should come to you as children and grandchildren it is that the power of ideas and the force they ultimately provide are never to be underestimated. There will be good times and bad, but it is the strength that not only lets you survive them but grow from them. Whether it is our American heritage that is so well described by Alexis de Tocqueville, or the Chinese heritage of Confucius, the Hispanic heritage of dignity, or the Jewish concepts of justice, they all have a common thread. Stalin mocked the Pope in how many divisions he could muster, but he never fully understood that the divisions were not often visible.

Summary

Many years ago, Baylor University asked me to do an oral history on the founding of the Lyceum and a number of the activities in which I had participated subsequent to it. I took from that experience an interesting observation. They were not only interested in what happened, but they were interested in fully understanding why it happened. Many times in history, events are recorded. But the actual reasons are obscured because many explanations are given by those that were not there.

As I look back on my life, the choices I have made, the actions I have taken or not taken, the successes and the regrets, I find like most people, I could have lived a very different life. You would probably ask me why I have spent so much time writing a personal guide on public policy and China.

The reason is that I hope you will be leaders, and to be such you have to understand a greater picture. Only if you are leaders can you direct your own future, otherwise you just concede it to others. You do not have to be in politics that as Mother often said, has two tears for every smile. But you can affect thought. Our Baby Boomer generation has burdened you with debt, and debt impacts growth eventually as well as freedom of action. You will have to act more intellectually if you are to maintain your values and standard of living. But how you think, and how your nation thinks, are the greatest legacies we can leave you. Fortune can take all from you but your soul and mind. It is all that you truly own because it is your essence of free choice. The rest you only have in custody from our Maker for a period of time. As they say, the evil on earth proves the existence of the Devil, and then he proves the existence of God.

VIII A CHEAT SHEET FOR CONTEXTUAL THINKING

THE ORGANIZATION OF THOUGHT

In the modern world, as in the past, there is limited respect given to "great thinkers" of their time. Former ages had John Stunt Mill, Karl Marx, Tolstoy, Gladstone, Edmund Burke, Jefferson, Lincoln, Keynes, Hayek, Gandhi, and so many others. Today political leaders and pundits give opinion and shape emotional ground. Many leaders like Christ and Confucius were only appreciated after their death when the wisdom of their thought was needed. Today we have specialization of our great minds and the need is to find ways they can cooperatively work to define, shape, and support organizing principles of society. This is not done on talk shows or in elections but is essential for thoughtful decisions. The Internet should make such cooperation much easier if you define a framework for discussion. That was the purpose of discussion in many of the later books in *The Language of Conscience Evolution*. You need networks of specialists from all cultures working together with a common heart and a transformational goal, each adding a piece. There is no one great intellect today capable of this—only a process.

The Panama Canal in the early 1900s searched through great American engineers with different talents, but the most needed talent was a conceptual thinker, who helped organize a process and then got the buy-in from a skeptical Theodore Roosevelt. Action had to wait on thought and planning. Similarly today, we need the Fox and MSNBC viewpoints to inform us.

But we also need a fact-based system of assessment that primarily shapes how we think about issues so we can judge the information presented and shift ratings-driven media back from emotionalism to logic. That requires a faith in people, which is often challenged by the modern world. But I still hold that if you can instill the Golden Rule of Reciprocity, it is a determining factor. Cultural power defines personal dignity, and is a greatly underappreciated power. How do you create sensitivity to it, and how do you think about it in terms of forces and powers?

Having discussed a wide range of issues, history, and process, we reach the point of how you bring it all together. We are in a new environment with new information that is going into old systems of analysis that may not prioritize it effectively, we may miss key items of importance (the black swans of current financial discussion), and may have a method of thought or analysis that is not appropriate for the future.

We have discussed the lessons of the past and the big issues for the future, and one truth must be perceived—a strong and successful society must sacrifice and use wisdom in its choices and needs to have an organizing principle of strength that brings harmony to the individual, the political body that is the state, and the fraternity that is the culture. Liberty, opportunity, and innovation are all derivatives of a cultural fraternity of the Golden Rule and Conscience. This cultural integrity or morality is not the government itself. Because once society replaces the cultural integrity with codes of law, we are a nation of complainants and dependents. The Chinese philosopher Lao Tzu noted that "the more law and order are made prominent, the more thieves and robbers there will be." Law is important for the basics to keep order, but morality between men is what keeps the peer culture.

So what we must concentrate on is how to build that culture. You will always have convenience; the hope is that only conscience dominates. Toward that end, I have included an edited presentation from *The Essentials of The Language of Conscience* that may help reform many small shotgun pellets into a rifle bullet by focusing on a target. It is repetitive in some areas to accomplish this end. But its purpose is to connect the critical dots of these issues into an easily remembered conceptual diagram. It is presented first as a summary of many of the key issues we have already discussed and how they fit into this framework.

INTEGRATING THE INDIVIDUAL WITH BROAD SOCIETY

The Tao of the Triangles
Bridging the Individual, Government, and Reality

The reality of the world is that economics and politics are essentially driven by interests while culture is more often driven by values. Personal or national interests are thus more subject to the temptations of convenience where values derived from the experiences of history better recognize the wisdom of conscience as an operating principle. Thus conscience with its emphasis on character-based individual responsibility politically and its emphasis on ethics and opportunity economically, form the best base for a unified and stable society. Those cultures corrupted by convenience lose the benefits due to corruption in economics, which limit the benefits of markets through limiting competition and opportunity. They lose the political mortar of the support of the common good by restricting personal dignity.

One necessary realization is to judge the line between personal dignity and the entitlement of political correctness. The Golden Rule understands that there is a balance in one's individual rights and obligations to others so you do not impose on their dignity. Jefferson's observation of this balance in government was that if the people feared the government it was tyranny, but if the government feared the people it was liberty. In culture the common defense of each person's personal dignity gives empowerment and respect. But imposing unbalanced expectations or criticism weakens this power and respect and brings resentment undercutting support for the principle. Sometimes the greatest damage to a concept is done by its most intense supporters losing the sense of balance and pushing extremes that weaken or destroy their primary argument. Hypocrisy is the usual result of this imbalance and needs to be demonstrated as such to force discussion of the alternate principles at play.

The physical sciences at their highest intellectual levels in the 20th century were dominated by the search for a unifying theory between the theory of relativity, which promulgated rules for the great objects of the universe, and the theories of quantum mechanics, which proposed new rules governing subatomic physics. Their perceived incompatibility has been the subject of many years of debate among the world's leading scientists.

In a somewhat analogous way, the same is needed for the social sciences, but they are more difficult because the free will of the people differs greatly from the objectivity of physical science. Nonetheless, there are parallels worthy of study as to how this effort can be approached to at least discover common ground and threads of understanding across cultures.

In Eastern philosophy there is the concept of the "Tao" or as it is translated in the West "the Way," which has many definitions but effectively is an effort to bring unity and enlightenment between the individual and the natural whole. It is a concept of balance and understanding. While it is more identified with Taoism attributed to Lao Tzu and Chuang-tzu (with the Tao Te Ching and the Chuang-tzu), which look to finding the basic rules that organize man and the universe or nature, it is a concept that is in many other writings of the East because it is really a search for balance and harmony. In the West philosophers such as C. S. Lewis had their own Tao. Adam Smith, the father of markets with his "invisible hand" of *The Wealth of Nations* focused upon self-interest, but his life's main work, *The Theory of Moral Sentiments*, was a Tao in its own right of how different things balanced. Stability is the value sought of such concepts, so issues such as order, balance, and harmony are key to their organizing principle. One cannot understand China by only looking at modern China; its culture has roots in millennia that serve as a rudder to its direction. Mencius, perhaps the most prominent student of Confucius, looked upon the protection of the people as the key to unification and this included a government that was benevolent, spared punishment, and reduced taxes.

The question is what can we learn from this set of concepts in how to understand and define an organizing theory that can help humanity work together in a coming set of probable crises as unsustainable trends reach climax. Trends are particularly important because they help counter the short-term focus that blames a current event for a problem. Usually a problem eventually results in the inception of a crisis being recognized, emotional politics and media seize upon a symbolic example, and often the bigger picture is clouded. Problems normally are caused by long-term failings and are seldom solved without long-term solutions that require understanding to sustain sacrifice.

We cannot greatly affect the laws of nature; we can only understand them and use their reality in giving us guidance in our decisions. We can only affect how we work as a unit, so our unofficial Tao is to look at the relationship between the individual and the government that is the unit that sets the policy under which he lives and determines his individual dignity.

There are many theories of philosophy, but all come from different eras with different levels of technology and political theory refinement so they are not as applicable in an exact form. But lessons can be learned from them and mistakes avoided in the moral hazard of public policy. While we might outline these theories and identify their sources to put them in the proper context, they are individualized as to ideas and often meant slightly different things in their day. Aristotle often talked of virtue in his books on ethics. Although virtue had some of the connotation of values we have today, it focused on excellence as virtue because the time had a different focus.

In more modern times a good example would be the dominant theories competing in economics. John Maynard Keynes' work largely defends heavier public spending to offset lack of private spending in a crisis. The opposite thought is found in the writings of Friedrick A. Hayek that defended the private sector benefits and free trade. There are many studies and much mathematics defending both. Keynes seems more logical in the short term, Hayek in the longer term. Much depends on how you view the issue. Keynes' point that if you run deficits in the short term you ought to run surpluses in the good times is often overlooked. Simply, do you pick a quick fix for the short term or a more sustainable long-term policy? Often you need a combination. These can be argued by the political extremes as one or the other. But balance and good policy should recognize that levels of debt increased in the short term have consequences for the long term. Trade impediments to ease short-term unemployment hurt ultimate competitiveness and not all spending, whether private or public, has equal consequences. And most of all, values are simply a reflection of opinions of the future income streams. A balance is necessary between consumption and production, for imbalance in either direction has consequences.

So clarity of policy, as much as policy itself, has a significant impact on private involvement when taxes, inflation, security, and many other factors are included. There is probably a need for both policies in a crisis, but the secret is how you affect the balance and recognize the best and the worst of each. Key concerns are sustainability and stability of support or will. It is easy to talk of long-term change, but unfortunately the will deteriorates unless controls are forced. That takes a different mindset than political extremes. It requires a more educated or aware public, leadership, and media. It requires as true family values, a balance of short-term benefit as pain for longer-term goals in a form worthy of sacrifice.

One of the important developments deserving the careful attention of the West today is the evolution of the Harmonious Society in China, which was recently placed into its Constitution. As we noted, China has three principle streams of religious or philosophical thoughts that inform individual goals in life—Confucianism (Philosophy), Taoism, and Buddhism—but its culture is a synthesis mainly of Confucianism, which focused on teaching government officials ethics and competence so they could serve as models for the people. The Taoism of Lao Tzu added the skepticism that often had unintended consequences and legalism that is a bit more realistic in part paralleling the theories of Machiavelli on reward and punishment shaping conduct. Chinese ancient culture kept unity by balancing Confucian morality with the compliance of legalism. It is no different from Roman Marcus Aurelius' observation that a man must be upright, not be kept upright. The culture sets the stage for how you choose to balance the values in society.

There is a blend of theories, but both idealism and realism are needed in shaping policy. That is a given. The problem is how to develop a theory that makes the best balance for the longer-term interest for the greatest good while protecting the rights and dignity of all. This brings to the forefront the necessary understanding of important considerations for man's dignity and equality and also the limitations. There must be some rules. If we had total free will there would be chaos, but what are the limits and nature of those rules? Equality is the key consideration of this concern with the individual component of the Tao. It is the essence of fairness that keeps harmony. The individual wants as much independence and dignity as he can have as a trait of human instinct. Fairness would seem to be total equality of outcome. But this conflicts with the reality of the laws of nature in many ways. I would like to be treated equally with Yao Ming in salary and contract, but it is highly unlikely that would be the case since the laws of economics and nature recognize that scarcity of a product like talent gives it much greater value. So equality must be restricted to at least equal opportunity to match the realities of nature.

As Communism and other systems found, removal of incentives from one's own efforts leads to the "free rider" concept where some do not work if they do not have to do so. There is a great difference in compassion for those that truly need help (which the government and private charity must address) including efforts to equalize opportunity and redistributive philosophy itself. The arguments are often mixed in "compassion," but true compassion includes recognizing that conscience is composed of compassion and obligation, and obligation requires sustainability or you hurt those most needing help in the long run by weakening the support system. Thus, "harmony" requires systems that build in all generations and will improve over time because they are sustainable.

This leads to a very critical issue. People are equal in their rights and dignity, but ideas (often realities of nature) are not equal. Some ideas are much more important than others to the ultimate well being of society and the individual. This is the effect of the limits of the natural law of the Tao. So we must consider both sets of interests as we look at options and their intended and unintended consequences. The equality of individuals is bottom up in direction; the prioritization of importance in ideas is top down. Yet they ultimately work into balance through the natural laws' reality. The question is how you can get a better and more stable balance with the greatest possible dignity for the individual.

This is why the current fixation with "political correctness" can be so devastating if not fully understood. *Political correctness is the political interests trying to sway cultural values.* If every disagreement is "racist," the concept moves from a significant issue to political chatter, which lowers the concept. Words must be used carefully without hypocrisy to protect them in fairness. The solutions are not to condemn actions, but would be far better answered by positive cultural efforts to build bridges. Issues of political correctness are often very important individually and deserve support, but when they distort thought on the ultimate importance of ideas, they have significant consequences. They can often focus on relatively unimportant issues for the long term and draw all attention from the critical issues that are ignored until it is too late and crisis has greatly limited options. They made people afraid to discuss critical issues, which is the cultural solution. They often take place in political theory by extensions of good intentions.

Communism started with the focus on the necessity of one greater virtue of equality that was separated out of the balance of the Tao. But its singular focus on equality in extreme led to good intentions being gradually counterproductive in the lost sense of human nature and the natural laws of markets and competitiveness that come from the innovation of an incentive-based society. The "free rider" emerged and ruined the true concept of "equality."

The new Harmonious Society in China seems to be an approach that is seeking the balance of the more complete Tao. Capitalism has had its own problems with excesses. Adam Smith talked of the benefits of self-interest, but greed and the corruption it often brings in the extreme are an extension of the problems of markets that do not have the internal ethics necessary. They became counterproductive to markets because they limit its key competition. The West is seeking more balance in a Tao that reemphasizes the common good over the excesses of the few. The "free rider" in the West has been the undeserved compensation of a limited few through crony capitalism. It similarly violates the fairness of the Golden Rule.

The world has moved through eras of the dominance of the three great societal forces (or powers)—economics, politics, and culture. In the 1960s, politics dominated with Kennedy-Johnson, Khrushchev, and Mao. That era of Capitalism versus Collectivism changed when technology gave great benefit to market systems and the world had to adopt competitive adjustments. Reagan and Thatcher brought economics to the forefront in the West, Deng in China transformed thought, and Gorbachev adapted Russia. But that economic era is now moving to the cultural era wherein corruption and terrorism, the excesses of economics and politics, boosted by globalization and shortages, are forcing changes in approach. New ways must be found to solve problems, and the cultural approach requires an understanding of the forces fighting within it for dominance of the culture—conscience or convenience. They will always both be present, but one or the other dominates the nature of the society.

Government has regulation to try to control corruption; but the more regulation often the more opportunity for corruption, so you have to develop a culture of conscience and individual responsibility rather than dependence to ultimately solve the problem. That is necessary in all the considerations of government if you are to avoid moral hazard. One issue of the future is the size of government because it in turn affects the nature of the culture (dependency versus individual responsibility) and economics (big business to cope with regulation or true small business opportunities). But even more important is the efficiency of government in how the money is spent—wasted or invested. Big government normally takes from the private sector market-driven investment to redeploy the funds to less efficient use.

The truth of our budget, and most developed countries' budgets, is that growth is the only real solution even though cuts, efficiencies, and reengineering are desperately needed in government. Policies have to take into account both considerations and be symbiotic rather than offsetting. One reason the term enlightened conservatism was chosen was that you have to have conservatism in using resources, but how they are used needs to be a strategic multiplier of growth. These choices are not as complicated if political interest is removed. There is presently a bias in our policy to the older in our society that directs resources for their security, which will be unsustainable so it will be adjusted by reality. Growth will require more investment for the young to make them competitive to drive the economy and provide more sustainability to the reformed programs for the elderly. Government does not create wealth, so boosting private growth, opportunity, and confidence is the key.

One of the basics of politics is buying support economically. It creates a substantial moral hazard because everyone wants benefits for free. Government addresses "needs" of the deserving, but also provides the "wants" of entitlement for political support. The population has to be educated to think not of just the benefit offered but of alternative uses for spending, including not spending at all and leaving reserves for crisis. Where the money being spent is sourced is critical, whether it is debt or increased taxes. Who would spend it and does the efficiency of spending all matter? When America had great prosperity, these issues were often overlooked. But today our greatest threat is not foreign military power or even terrorism—it is the challenge to the economic base that supports our strength. We must use comparative thought on resource allocation, which has to be an automatic of any new paradigm of thought for contextual thinking.

As emphasized, moral hazard is a major risk of public policy because the general interest of the common good is disorganized while the special interests are very organized and normally well funded. This is why the decision process not only needs to be transparent but understandable. Reporting news of what happened is one thing; fully explaining why it happened and the consequences is something else. There are many "whistleblower" institutes and groups but most have a special interest agenda themselves. Our greatest challenge will be building respected sources of information that present in a consistent style so that complex issues are understood and coverage is broad. This makes it convenient for the powerful to have conscience since it would also be convenient.

The Role of Leadership

I am told that leadership is what should be taught rather than values because to teach values you have to determine whose values to teach. *I have never understood that argument since leadership is a style with versions of intimidation on one end and transformative value-based leadership generating popular support on the other. Leadership is simply putting a set of ideas into action and is judged on the efficiency with which it is done. The existence or absence of values is the ultimate defining characteristic.*

The essence of politics is leadership and the essence of leadership is managing change with an understanding of both where a society is and where it needs to go. To simply complain or study accomplishes little unless it is a brief delay in a longer journey of action. Good leadership is ultimately making decisions, and making them with wisdom. You must not only understand where you are but how you got there by the three powers, and you must anticipate the effects of change through the three powers of economics, politics, and culture. Leadership has many characteristics, but in the case of the Triangles it focuses on managing change from the status quo that history has presented with an understanding of timing and risk. Timing and risk both require a judgment of the dedication of those following, which is found in the more general term of personal dignity. It may have other economic and cultural connotations, but from politics it is Sun Tzu's key factor of dedication or strength of will. The speed of change and the risk factor are thus affected by how well followers are educated as to a leader's vision and how it affects them and their families. As Dad always noted, people are seldom for or against you, just normally for themselves.

The force of change is often one that separates or pushes apart the existing system, while the force of current equilibrium created by cultural values passed forward by history and the inertia of the system of economics and politics tend to be consolidating factors. This constant tension to pull apart the system and to pull it together rests in the judgment of personal dignity, but the power of each force can be limited or increased by how personal dignity is perceived, which is often about how you think about issues. A reasoned system will have different results than an emotional one because the nature of the intensity given to destructive or constructive impacts would vary, particularly in crisis. A reasoned system would need to consider the contextual powers and how they were impacted as well as the moral hazard of change or retention of the current system on the cultural component.

Understanding leadership that can bring change of a transformative nature brings the obvious conclusion—it has to be so strong it takes people out of their comfort zone and expands their temperament for risk. This requires a leader with certainty and with the communication skill to convey necessity of change and inspire confidence. In the modern complex world that is more difficult. It is easy for there to be protest against evil, but how to correct it is the goal and it must have some consensus to succeed.

This requires a process of thought that gets to the big issues but organizes a consideration of anything relevant in the process. I think it was Picasso who was asked how he sculpted a monkey. He replied, "I take a big lump of clay and take away anything that is not a monkey." We have to do that to find the big issues that matter, but then we need to build a core motivation of conscience-based action that is logical to explain options and consequences. It is for this the Triangles were designed and become a common denominator of thought. Transformation is effectively innovation and the same way of thinking needs to be in business and politics but must have cultural value systems as its guide rails to stay consistent and build unity for risk and sacrifice.

Ultimately true leadership can be viewed as the shaping of cultures and developing them with the strength of stability. A leader not only must consciously create an effective culture that gains the buy in of the people but also develop secondary leaders to preserve and expand it. Whether the culture is a value system or economic process, or often both, it requires both top-level strategic leadership and lower-level operational support. The bigger the organization the more important this is because size often brings varied and diverse units that normally adopt the characteristics of the local leader and local practices. In these cases the key is often the dominant value culture emphasis since economic systems often localize. Cultures constantly change as leaders move and new parties or conditions are added, but a culture that has excellence shapes the changes to itself rather than change with the new tide. It is the reason so many organizations from the military and law enforcement to corporations build and train systems, which are really cultural supports. Leaders think in these terms if they want success and internal strength for crisis.

Today, if we start taking away the clay to reveal our problems, one big remaining one is the decline in income of the average family over the last decade, which is more prominent at the bottom of the economic ladder. The Census Bureau statistics show a 14.2% decline in household income for the lowest fifth and a negative 7.8% for the middle fifth. Even the top fifth declined 5.8%. One great additional problem is that American upward mobility is diminishing and the hope many have for their children. For this last decade politicians have had many short-term efforts to have government disguise the real problems and move money from investment and innovation to subsidy. The financial recession exposed what we had done to deteriorate the balance of our financial model. We relied too much on debt, mainly consumer debt, and used government to subsidize its problems rather than addressing the problems. With technology and globalization already costing jobs, increased burden on productive sectors only makes the problem worse. The response of the corporate elite is to influence tax policy by its lobby, which only distorts correction more. Government pushes consumption without the balance of earning it. So if we are to use the monkey analogy, what we have to create as a big idea is a new vision that is not from the extremes but from logical goal setting with an understanding of consequences. Our organizing principle is the critical choice in how we make decisions; the wisdom of past generations indicates this requires starting with our failure rather than continuing to argue over our interests.

The Triangles are designed to make a leader think through all these factors to refine a decision and adjust it to reality while trying to bring out the ultimate best in and for those following. If economic support is less, cultural belief replaces it as an example. A leader today has to worry about the short term as much as the long term because real change takes time and often sacrifice, so it has costs often in one's own career. But if a true leader has a cause, he has also built strong followers and looks not to what he achieves but what a cause achieves and places the battle flag in the hands of the next generation. That gives you the best way to judge a leader. What are the men like that surround him? Do they abuse power and succumb to corruption or do they respect honor and look at leadership as a true responsibility. Who does he keep as key advisers that give insight to thought? By this analysis we have difficulty finding leadership today because we expect others to lead us when we need to create a culture expecting and supporting such leadership if we wish it to be competitive.

If this is a modern battle, how do you develop the leadership to wage it constructively? John Kenneth Galbraith, a thoughtful social critic, concluded that all great leaders have had one characteristic in common:"the willingness to confront unequivocally the major anxiety of their people in their time." But the fundamental issue today is probably not responsiveness to their anxiety, but the education of the people on what their true concerns and priorities should be. It is not a cult of personality or celebrity, but a trust built on reason and accountability in pursuit of a vision. That requires conscience rather than convenience to transform society because you must change society not just adapt to it.

One of the most necessary abilities to gain, usually through studied experience, is when to bridge conflicting issues and when to force a choice of a path. You want to avoid unnecessary battles, but you have to force decisions that are deemed critical. That requires knowing where you are headed and if the issue is strategic, operational, tactical, or only choice of a technique.

However, the reality of the often perverse incentives of government is that they sometimes work differently because the focus of government is and will always be short term and fixed on the mood of the people. As a result, the next election matters in the West, and stability has priority in the East. So these realities will trump grand theory unless it is built into a realistic power base. That is what is greatly lacking in the world today. Good government requires an educated population to appreciate and support it. The materialistic benefits of money from government often overcome this concern of the people because there is limited economic benefit in being for ethics or common good. If people appreciate a system of thought that gives clarity to self-interest and the benefits of the common good, it imposes a base discipline on how they think and even instinctively react. Ideas have power and if they are allied with another power base, there will be a political leadership that will push them in self-interest. Conscience is powerful among the average people when they work on a local level because it affects relationships and how things are accomplished.

But as one rises in levels of power, arrogance, financial considerations, and election burdens, all work to change the nature of leadership to the convenience model, which is extremely powerful and usually dominates. The answer to that is to use convenience to help conscience by building a culture that appreciates competence and conscience to the point that it becomes the political power base of those rising in leadership. Unfortunately, this is a very difficult thing to do and can only occur by finding common ground in ideas and a willingness to sacrifice over time. It will happen in the future only if crisis demands change, which is usually the catalyst as people try to seek a new approach.

Having answers in place when a crisis does finally demand change is critical. Emotional solutions of the moment are easy to sell to the public;

complicated realistic solutions that usually require pain and sacrifice need time to prepare both in concept and in explanation. There is no better example than the current strife in the economics of Greece and the riots over change. These same issues of sustainability will become more widespread throughout the world and at all levels of government. The question is what force will be the driver of the solution—economics, politics, or culture. The outcomes can be quite different.

Many in history adhere to the concept of legalism (reward and punishment) or reality as an environmental factor produced by the nature of the times. We often refer to them as the realists. Machiavelli and *The Science of the Thick (Skin) and the Black (Heart)* are more extreme political versions. On the other hand, the idealists believe that man has an internal conscience for good that can be developed and asserted if taught to be appreciated. Christ, Aristotle, Confucius, and other moral thinkers develop these principles. The environment determines a great deal, but if one examines the Chinese reaction after its recent earthquake, the reaction of the world after the September 11th terrorism, and the charity after the floods in Southeast Asia, it is evident that men have a natural understanding of their obligations to others. There is much evil in the world, but there is also great charity and goodness. It is the development of this good that in many ways should be the goal of society through its institutions.

The historical defense of these concepts come both from philosophers like Immanuel Kant who looked at man as more logically understanding and developing these values, and the more spiritual defenses of writers like C.S. Lewis who studied many of the legal and belief systems of history and illustrated all the commonalities of values over time and place. This concept holds that man is possessed of a moral sense that is "written on the heart," or a natural law. While similar to physical laws, the social natural laws are often distorted because we have free will. Others believe as Lewis that they have a divine component. His defense of God when challenged that there was unfairness in the world was to take the logic that if you did not have goodness in you, how could you recognize the unfairness. You do not know a line is crooked unless you can recognize a straight line.

So the creation of a culture that has a balance to reality but a push toward conscience as opposed to convenience because it instills individual responsibility and favors the common good succeeds as an organizing principle. That leads to the creation of the Triangles and *The Language of Conscience*

Evolution. To bring cultural change you need a different type of leadership. James Macgregor Burns' 1978 book, *Leadership*, identified two basic types and defined them best. One is *transactional leadership* where there is an exchange often based on trade-offs among competing interests—budget negotiations, jobs for votes, or similar situations of the traditional power relationship. Burns' second concept, *transformational leadership*, is more complex because it creates a vision and focuses on the needs and motivation of the followers. It builds a mutual trust from common purpose and a commitment to unity. It also has the strength of making followers into leaders. (To me, this is the creation of the Western "Uncommon Men" or Confucian "Gentlemen.") It is the last concept to which the Triangles were designed. The Triangles do not try to tell the answers but just help to focus on the questions that build mutual understanding. They train followers to be leaders through education and building common trust.

The quotations and writings of *The Language of Conscience* are not new or that different from much of historical context. But they are synthesized to not only the modern environment but, more importantly, future trends so popular enlightenment is reinforced. You set a context of thought that can have a consistency and sets the context of how decisions are made. The reality is that growth brings complexity, reformation requires simplicity, and so the Triangles serve as a thoughtful matrix.

These categories are but a summary rendition in organized form of the critical issues we have discussed from family to society, but they are organized into a way of thinking that is more aligned with future paradigms.

Reviewing and Understanding the Levels of the Triangles

We have looked at change (of addressing knowledge) versus status quo (of history's existing wisdom) and how one perceives and accepts his place in life through the prism of his all inclusive "personal dignity." Man creates this "personal dignity" from his evaluation of economics, politics, and culture (including factors that are combinations like environment)—the three powers that affect him and his future as he refines his judgments through analytics, measurement of levels of importance, and trends that give him foresight. It is how he views his satisfaction with the control of his life and his future. If he accepts conscience, individual responsibility, and economic justice as his goals, he fights to build and maintain a culture where the discipline in society is the Rule of Law that is above any man.

The Rule of Law seems a simple concept. But if you look at it contextually, it is far better understood as a blend of the three powers. In its essence it is a system of order that gives the fundamentals to the three powers. It shows ownership economically, which allows private property. And with public ownership documentation systems making it transparent, it allows effective commerce. In politics it grants responsibilities and rights, which define the limits of the powers of men and governments. In culture it should show fairness and justice that is transparent, so it gives dignity that builds the support for the system. It is the base of men's obligation to each other that society enforces, but it also can change in unique ways. An example might be the concept of credit. The word "credit" comes from the Latin meaning trust. So an economic concept is really based on a cultural value. When trust is lost, credit greatly diminishes with significant political consequences.

This is the story of our last credit crisis. The Rule of Law got so complex that it created almost non-transparent and massive credit instruments that were often properly disclosed legally but not fully understandable and often with questionable ethics. The Legal System was technically in place from a political concept but lost its cultural trust, which caused economic chaos since even now the ownership issues are unclear. The concept of the Rule of Law thus needs to be broad. Just as English Common Law became so technical that it lost power, and the Courts of Equity had to be created to restore the cultural trust that was lost.

Where the morality of the Golden Rule fits with Confucian concepts of obligation and Christian morality to create a peer pressure within society for ethical behavior, it reduces the need for government that is the accumulation and enforcement of all laws. Cultural ethics sets the peer judgment of juries. Unless society elevates itself to privately handling problems, government is required to do so. The larger the government, the more reliance there is on it economically, politically, and culturally until individual responsibility ebbs to dependency and ultimately unsustainability at higher levels of development.

One of the great questions is how to understand the nature of the process of change. Change has several component parts. The first is the creation of an idea and its validation and refinement. The second, and equally important, is its effective implementation. Both must be in focus. A strategy of implementation must be a part of creation, and implementation requires focus on the true ultimate goal rather than less important tactical parts.

This set of Triangles was developed during the writing of *The Language of Conscience Evolution* as a quick summary of the critical issues in the process of thinking in context. It can serve as a "cheat sheet" or summary to help make sure all major concerns have been addressed. It has also been called a "Rosetta Stone of Cultures" because it deals with forces and powers similar in all cultures and allows a thoughtful comparison. The aspects that explain the sections in more detail, as well as the process, are all found in more depth in *The Language of Conscience Evolution*. By going to the summary book, *The Essentials of The Language of Conscience,* the last part has the indices and overviews of each book for easy reference or the website at www.thelanguageofconscience.com provides a different overview.

The concepts related to the Triangles began as we first formulated the process for the Texas Lyceum and what we called The Third Coast of Thought. It needed to be a method of thought that built upon itself a continuingly greater refinement. Too many efforts have a tendency to be short term and provide a feel-good meeting of current perspective. Efforts of substance need to build upon the knowledge learned to ever increasingly refine it and test against reality. Many of the concepts of the Triangles were added, changed, or reconfigured over a thirty-year process as the book evolution shows. It incorporated early the concept that the core or cement of an effort was driven by the perspectives and motivations of the participants.

One of the projects that gave insight was one undertaken with Brenham National Bank over the years in helping teach financial literacy. Too many students do not understand how finance works and the more they can appreciate the significance of maintaining a good credit rating the more it emphasizes how you must have discipline and character for whatever information is taught to have any true effect. It is not the information but the increased discipline that is the key. When I helped start the Texas Caring for Children Foundation that supplied health insurance to children, we were often thanked by parents who noted they thankfully did not have to use it. The problem was that the concept was also preventative by design since it reduced costs and problems by diagnostics appointments. Even well intentioned efforts need careful thought and education for success.

Those interested in the political evolution could find much in the archives of Harvey Kornberg's Quorum Report, or if the focus was economic in the archives of Ray Perryman's Perryman Report. As you teach your children and perhaps want more emphasis in specific areas, please refer to the other

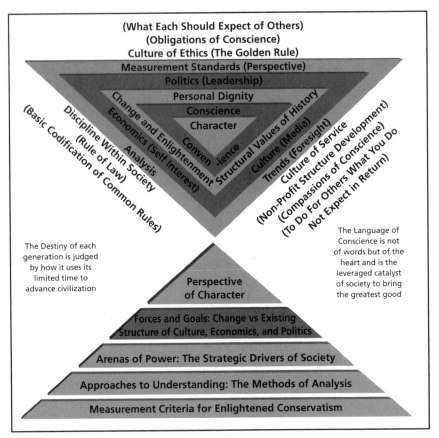

books in *The Language of Conscience Evolution* for more specific reasons and details within the Triangles and the methods of instilling values. It is not your teaching but their learning that matters.

The simplest of questions for the organizing principle of a society is often overlooked in the political rhetoric and economic self-interest of any era: do we want a civilized system of orderly process (civilization) or do we want to be governed by our most base instincts? The answer to that would certainly recognize the benefits of civilization for the rights, dignity, and opportunity it gives in theory. But if we look at actions through this prism, reality is different in that many political approaches bring out the worst in us rather than the best. It is why The Golden Rule is such a valuable tool. There are injustices that must be opposed, but how to do so and why need focus. A vehicle like the triangles uses motivation of responsibility and conscience to try to keep the value of civilized behavior rather than base instinct at the forefront not only of how we think and how we explain our decision process to others, but also how we teach our children.

In the realistic world there is not a list of "to dos" and "not to dos" that does not change with new facts. There are guides and theories that help greatly, but what is really required is what we have discussed as a way of thinking. The subconscience is far more powerful in many ways than the conscious in that it stores experiences and creates instincts. It is what creates the "culture of our lives" in light of what experience has taught us. The Triangles are not a set of guides but triggers to help organize a way of thinking and help one better define the real questions to be asked. Everyone has a different background that makes them unique. But if conscience is their inner goal and operating principle, this set of thoughts will help magnify their abilities for leadership and analysis because it shapes a contextual thought process rather than a single focus.

If you do not have a set of guidelines when you talk to others, you seldom have success in serious discussions. But equally important is attitude going into the discussion. The Triangles provide order to discussion, but this focus on conscience to build trust is equally critical.

The Triangles focus as much on trying to create a positive context as they do logical wisdom. No matter how good answers may be they have to be implemented. In public policy a parallel is the theory of choice of growth or division of the pie—which under convenience is usually an argument of taking more from someone else's piece versus the conscience of all growing bigger pieces by concentrating on expansion of the pie rather than division. Division usually means losing the principles that make it grow and substituting a different organizing principle.

It is in this context that the Triangles were created to blend the individual and government to reality. Cultural context is critical because it sets the stage for how things are judged or in an international world how they are understood if translated. Accurate translation and understanding must have the context in which the concepts are presented. If you look at most famous writings that have affected society, they are not often so much definitions but set the context. Confucius is known for the Analects, which are mainly a collection of sayings. The Bible and the Koran give guidance as to ideas that are organizing principles that can be adapted to the times.

The Triangles are an accelerated learning and analytic process and can best be viewed much as with the evolution of the level of games. Tic Tac

Toe is basic as a game with a few squares and pieces. But it evolves into checkers, which has more pieces and more rules but the same squares and game concept. Then it evolves into chess, which is more complicated, but has the same basic squares and pieces that move differently. For the Triangles in the interplay of conscience versus convenience, the objective is really the search for character and individual responsibility, the places where the organizing principle begins. It is the province of the idealists who believe that man can be taught and guided. It must be the dominant theme that gives us context, but we must look to reality and the natural laws in determining the balance in the Tao the Triangles create.

Forces are the basis of reality. The key forces are change and the status quo of the current structures brought forth by nature. They are what affect stability itself and the rate and degree of change in stability. So they must be studied, prioritized, and understood and the probable consequences of their effect and duration evaluated. But their effect on stability and the system of the Tao is best judged by the impact on personal dignity.

Personal dignity is not just a cultural concept of gaining rights and respect, which give a fullness and satisfaction to life. It also affects economics and politics contextually because it creates a powerful way of thinking. Perceived affronts to dignity drive action as strongly as any motive. Economics depends on innovation and the drive that the self-interest of opportunity brings, requiring such a cultural mindset to be most effective in developing human potential. Such dignity also creates the political appreciation of the assumption of responsibility necessary for democracy and a Rule of Law. If one has a sense of worth, they look at the necessity of preserving it. Perception of personal dignity reflects the degree of control one perceives he has on his life and how satisfied he is with it.

Change is a certainty in life, but the uncertainty is whether it is positive or negative. The degree to which we can shape the effects of this change rests in whether we accept it or try to direct it. Change ultimately leads to our future, but that future is not inevitable but influenced first by our thoughts and then our actions. We have to envision a better future and create a compelling vision of where we wish to go or how we wish to live; with that vision we individually and collectively can generate a will to put it into practice. Ideas matter in the creation of transformative visions so a process of how to evaluate and ultimately manage change positively benefits from a framework of perspective. This is one of the benefits of the triangles.

Understanding the impacts of change helps create an understanding of what to anticipate and how to mitigate difficulties or expand positives.

Personal dignity is not just a feeling; it is an internal operating system that helps organize thought. If you have no dignity and are downtrodden, you accept life and direction. When you have dignity, you innovate and preserve it. This is why it is the balance between change and the status quo since it is usually the initiation of action through frustration. The revolutions in the Middle East are perfect examples because they are largely inspired by frustrated youth that cannot reach potential and through education and modern communication now realize it. As we noted previously, social networking embodies much of this desire for recognition and dignity. It will be a major impact on the future as will be the desire for more depth of trust and deeper relationships.

But personal dignity as it is used in the triangles is not frustration and rebellion, which do not address the creation of the culture of dignity but only the immediate relief of a burden. Personal dignity is the creation and maintenance of an ongoing system of contextually related ideas and obligations that go with it. The key is not one's individual feelings but the fraternal feelings with the rest of that society. One can demand courtesy, but respect has to be earned and that respect is usually judged by one's adherence to a moral code. The establishment of that moral code is difficult, long developing in its definition and preservation, and seldom fully appreciated.

It is the determinant of whether the public sacrifices, dissents, or revolts. This is where the Tao of the individual must be represented in his equality, and the best means of keeping stability is to appeal to the fairness within men that they wish at least equal opportunity and equal rights and dignity that they would grant to other men. If not, there is no stability and significant change. The effect on their children greatly influenced this. The rate of change is what is often less important than the direction if they see their family will be a beneficiary of their work. This comes from the installation of conscience and its parts both obligation and compassion. Conscience also allows sacrifice for the future to be an appreciated trait that has a value and recognition of its own. If society does not reward behavior in some form, it is diminished.

Nature's Reality and the Three Powers

The next issues in understanding the reality of nature are in understanding the three great powers that cause and are affected by the change. Economics, politics, and culture all have crucial roles and understanding their powers to influence incentives and interrelationships to compensate for each other's weaknesses and strengths is critical. Each society may have very different characteristics from others in these rules and regulations and form, but whether conscience is present in them is the key.

When we consider the contextual thinking of how the powers fit together, we need to realize that free markets are the equivalent of democracy within its parameters. You are voting with your spending. Free markets also parallel increased personal dignity culturally because you are given more opportunity for risk and expansion. The characteristics of different power systems overlap and often are consistent in balancing out, although in interim periods of time differences can occur. It is in looking at the trends over longer periods that you see the direction of change, although often variable, and there are always exceptions from special circumstances. Natural resources may provide income and overcome natural forces demanding economic change, for example. The point that should not be lost is that usually great reward comes from great risk. Innovation is risk based and it is what leads to increased productivity, which enhances the standard of living.

Democracy is not the same in different cultures; the Rule of Law is applied differently in cultures. *There is argument of "Exceptionalism" be it by America or other past societies. To me "Exceptionalism" is found not in geography, achievement, or even power, but in the core values of the society in how they treat the average man. The most exceptional society is the one in which every man grants to every other man the same rights, dignity, and opportunity that he would expect himself and is willing to stand and sacrifice for a system of government that provides it—even if he realizes change takes time but direction must be secured. This is often not a government that protects all by heavy use of law and regulation. These are burdens upon one's dignity and desires for free will. But desire for security leads to dependence just as free choice can lead to error. The balance comes from a society that cares for its most burdened not from force of law but strength of heart, for that preserves everyone's dignity.*

Economics is a complex subject, but the Triangles focus on the highest growth available with ethical responsible values rather than greed. Two things usually generate high growth—one is innovation (often effective education) and research that has opportunity and pushes productivity. The second is incentivizing the population to work harder by giving them reward for their efforts. Men deserve the right to their efforts, and it should not be confiscated from them beyond what is necessary for the realistic common good. That is economic justice at its core. These economic goals normally require smaller government with less regulation providing more opportunity for the middle class to see merit succeed. Regulation is the bane of small business as are excessive taxes that drain capital.

The third level is the necessity of making decisions based on facts that give evidence to a competence that can provide confidence and educate the people to the available options. Analytics is not just a determination of the critical true facts, but it is also the comparison of differences in options. These differences are in many forms. One analysis might be economic; a different analysis might be from a moral comparison, and another by political interest. The point is that analysis of fact is knowledge, what it means in broader contexts of options is wisdom.

Analytics, or truth from facts, is the basis, but it must have two other critical considerations. Second is measurement or prioritization because in dealing with ideas we have noted they are not equal. Some will have much greater effect than others. Third is the understanding and study of trends. If not, you begin intergenerational conflict and lack of sustainability. There is a great difference between changes that are cyclical and may self correct to a degree and change that is structural and is long term in nature. Time is a great change agent, and it is essential that vision be long range. While these are generic components that are not new, the problem is that they are seldom actually used as a composite to find a Tao for government or for working between societies in a world that will require serious discussion. Transformational leadership needs a process to both build common goals and to agree on the facts so that tactics are consistent with strategy. Political correctness, hypocrisy, arrogance, and self-interest are just a few of the impediments to serious discussion and the seriousness of the times will demand order, usually enforced by reality.

Perhaps no part of the Triangles will become more at issue than the trend analysis about generational frictions. We covered in earlier discussion the fact that technology had replaced many good paying middle class jobs, not just in America but Europe and other nations, and increasingly in developing nations. The huge debt load America and much of the developed world took on, beyond just real estate, had the impact of both keeping the older generation working so less of the existing jobs opened, and creating a debt burden that will cause increased taxes and limited spending that will impact innovation. Our universities have created an educated class worldwide that is having great difficulty finding work but is educated enough to have expectations and realizations that their concept of personal dignity is being negatively affected.

Throughout the world, whether it is France, Greece, Egypt and the Middle East, or China, the frustration of youth at the burdens being placed on them by debt and its cost on creation of jobs and high economic growth is increasing. Their expectations were that an education would allow them opportunity for the middle class life, but they often now have both high personal debt to service and an increasing understanding that private sector jobs are difficult to create. What was true of the value of a college education thirty years ago is minimized today by more college graduates in competition and technology-impacted job growth, and less valuable skills for actual needs in the economy.

Bringing their concerns into public policy considerations will be necessary and will greatly shift some of the decisions on revamping public pensions, health care, and what is affordable from government. The educational system will have to address these issues far better than it has. Its goal has been to educate, when it needs to be focusing also on the creation of opportunity in what it teaches and how it prepares students to use their education. The youth are not finding a place in modern society, and society is not utilizing their talents for the creation of productivity. There is public policy fissure between the old and the young, and it will be increasingly apparent to all as the choices become narrowed.

The Triangles also envision a mix of perspective of thought for a balanced judgment since a lawyer or a philosopher thinks in different terms than an engineer or a CEO. Legislatively based Senators, for example, have a different focus from executive-oriented governors. A blend of not only knowledge but also expertise on theory and execution is required since both are necessary and complimentary. When the principle of common good is lost to individual self-interest, the system loses its key systemic force for action. Today many principles affect all branches of both Congress and the Executive branch because of campaigns. There are no real center-weights to this special interest government except competing special interests. The shift of focus must be mainly to ideas, but that leaves the question of how to spread the ideas effectively. The Internet may be the game changer.

In the three powers, it is critical to get the big ideas right. You cannot manage everything, and ideas may be conflicting and impact efficiency, so contextual prioritization is necessary. Explaining that logic and getting it accepted are at the core of any set of ideas that shape options. Like an appellate judge who focuses on the few really big issues out of the context of the action of the trial, we need to focus more on the big things that matter.

Today there are many views on the problems of government. But the basic issue is where we started in our individual and family values and how they have evolved. Serious cooperation usually means defined discussion well-prepared and refined over time in a certain context. The military approach to reality is very appropriate here. You need what is called a Warrior's honor for real success. It combines integrity with power and cooperation with strength that aids commitment. People have definite self-interests. You can talk with them and work with them in common intent, but the reality is that you also are concerned as to what happens if others change in nature. So you evaluate what their capacity is to hurt you in the military, business, or politics. Discussions need to be comparisons on all the above items because they are very different as a package than just an individual part. They set the context that both sides understand is needed to be candid about their concerns.

The Ultimate Chess of the Triangles
Strengthening the Magnetism of Conscience

However, the ultimate Chess of the Triangles is in the final set of ideas relating to these critical components of culture. To create an understanding of how policies being developed need to go back to the concerns of what the policy does to add or minimize the moral hazard in the creation of a culture of responsibility is the basis of strength of any society. The final level returns the thought to the individual and his dignity even though the realities of the natural laws have been added to the process in the center step. The three components of the Triangles' culture are critical to understand if you are to instill values in transcending generations.

First is the culture of law and how it is enforced. This is the common protection we have and comes from the existing cultural value we will jointly protect. How we change these laws often depends on how well the people are educated since there are restrictions on the common man, but also are his greatest protection.

The second culture, that of the obligation of conscience or morality, is accomplished in part by an understanding of the Golden Rule of doing unto others as you would have them do to you, which creates the sense of obligation beyond that required by law. It is the obligation code that Confucius promoted in the creation of a society of Gentlemen. It is what we do because it is right and moral to do it. It is an unenforceable but required obligation of civilization. It determines the amount of law necessary because it affects what people will do among themselves to enforce the unenforceable issues of morality through face and the culture.

The third and final culture to be developed is compassion, or what we do for others without the expectation of return to us. It is the service in nonprofits that take the harshness from the market system and develop this charity and sense of individual responsibility, common good leadership, and humility to the service of others that builds the individual responsibility and character with which we started.

We move from an organizing principle of conscience to the reality of nature and to the reinforcement of those balanced policies to develop the culture that set the context. The Triangles simply place the need for the creation of such a balance or Tao in a common format. The basic strength is that growth in all areas has added layers of complexity and interconnected relationships. Change is very difficult on a piecemeal basis. Therefore, to reach a goal each decision needs a simpler, coordinated vision to help restructure. Since stability is the key and the fairness of conscience helps create it, this Tao of choices helps any reformation at almost any level.

Each user will have his own opinions. Those that use it will refine it; those that do not would be asked to develop their own if they can do it more effectively rather than criticize what others believe. It is an effort to bring out the best in man although any presentation of values stirs emotion. The key is whether a great enough nucleus of thought and use can build support for its method. In many ways, it is simply a vehicle to convey ideas to the next generation. If it assists in a common conversation and context, it will enable the most critical ideas and values to be passed on and their importance fully appreciated. Many define history by the great men of each era and their impact, but reality rests on the great ideas that emerge and transcend history.

One of the things we must always remember is that the world is a very complex place and there is much we do not know of reactions or natural law. All our experts are usually only right for periods of time; conditions change and they are less accurate. We are far better off looking at the trends of history and seeing how we can judge events in the scope of time with the understanding of how limited our options can be. I think one of the best observations in this regard I have seen is Nassim Taleb's observation in *The Black Swan*:

> *We act as though we are able to predict historical events, or, even worse, as if we are able to change the course of history. We produce thirty-year projections of social security deficits and oil prices without realizing we cannot even predict these for next summer.*

—*Nassim Nicholas Taleb*
The Black Swan

My personal observation is that history runs with broad themes over time. Interests of individuals and nations push it in many directions in the short term, but cultural values of conscience usually reemerge when crisis finally occurs unless the values have become so weakened that they are no longer fully appreciated and seen as solutions. Like the geopolitics of old, predictions could be made of the future, partially by the geography of a region and benefits or problems it provided and the culture it created. Today other factors also set cultures and the cyber era presents a new geography in many ways.

Culture or what is passed forward is the power of history. The transmission of a way of valuing that is most important is conveyed in what I call the Language of Conscience. It is not just ideas but how the thought process organizes them to allow the most impact or power from them.

The greatest criticism of the concept is that it is theory while the world is reality. It is easy to talk of solutions if you do not have to vote for them or implement them. So theory to be effective needs to be the best way to organize the natural law and reality. The strength of such theories of organizing principles is that the whole will be greater than its parts if it is designed on a win-win concept of conscience as opposed to a zero-sum game of competitive convenience.

The greatest strength of the concept is that in modern day concepts of catalyzing conscience on common grounds in a way that leverages the good of many individuals in their values and compassion is critical to civilization's future core values. Materialism, individualism, and self-interest are well promoted.

Groups of conscience are like a shotgun blast, often small pellets perhaps with sound but that travel only a short distance. A rifle bullet, not only concentrated and more powerful but far easier to aim at a more distant target, needs to be thoughtfully chosen, which can unify the pellets.

The world moves in cycles, civilization evolves in values, but we are a very interconnected world. As the populations of less developed economies attempt to reach first world status, the impact on resources, environment, world health, peace, and the components of a civil society will be sorely tested.

Political power internationally is usually thought of in terms of military supremacy, but in reality it ultimately may be the economic and cultural power of the nation that supports it. A feared or arrogant culture generates opposition of much greater force. A weakening economic base is seen as a growing weakness that will sap strength. Our recent economic declines in the West, particularly in the United States and Europe have weakened us more in image internationally than is perceived. If we waste our economic strength on foolish and inefficient uses of resources, we follow in the steps of the Soviet Union and miss the lesson of China. Power is not just political/military; it is ultimately economic/cultural for sustainability. America is still greatly underrated in its strength and its ability to regenerate. We can shift from consumption to a balanced economy over the next decade if we can accept the sacrifices of retrenchment on debt. That is a question of will and is a cultural phenomenon.

Politics also has nationalism, which is a difficult place to build bridges. Economics has self-interest, which is often even more difficult. Only culture with a bridge of conscience provides the best starting place for the other discussions of reality because the world is a disjointed large family in one sense. Each division of it may have different cultures generally, but each has families where parents love children, the rule of reciprocity is understood, and conscience is more unifying than convenience.

In every society these are the "uncommon men" who value conscience, and the goal is to unite them into a common appreciation of basic values that adapt to their culture. Many talk of "One World Government" but that is unlikely and possibly dangerous since personal dignity often requires less law and more culture. A World Harmonious Society of culture might be a more achievable society of culture if it were based on conscience. Local administration is more sensitive to people and common goal issues such as the environment, health, finances, and similar areas where international cooperation is necessary already from appropriate partnerships. The issue is what should be an organizing structure for a World Harmonious Society and is a set of thoughts more than a political structure. The culture will create the law if it is to be successful. Politics often only gets in the way. It starts with how you unify the many pellets of conscience in the world.

When you look at issues in a singular way, they often appear different than they are in reality. In political terms when you have a shortage of revenue, the easy argument is to tax the very rich rather than cut jobs or services. It is argued that this is fairer and that they have more assets that are protected by society. To some level that may have merit, but usually the gain of the rich is from taking risk, and in reality in economics, you must build in consideration of the other consequences. Not only will the rich move at some level, not only will it inhibit growth because people will not take the risk when there is little benefit, but it is an unstable tax structure. In economic decline—the worst time for weakness, the rich are more risk based and usually get hit worst by the economic decline. Their income is most impacted, which hits the stability of the underlying tax structure. Simple answers leave out strategic issues of sustainability. We need to train ourselves with unity to look at issues more in terms of consequences not just short-term emotional expediency. There are arguments that taxing the very rich have less impact, but you also have moral arguments. Economic justice requires recognition at all levels and has to be argued equally. But equally important is that if you tax rather than develop private charity, that is a major alternative, you drive the system toward big government and dependence. Tax reform that shrinks the bulk of regulations increases efficiency and incentivizes private support.

The problem we all face is that issues are often not presented directly but a small amount at a time. We are at crossroads of our lives daily on issues of conscience and convenience, so recognizing these is a necessary part of our self-enlightenment.

We are constantly in a battle for the soul of civilization between forces of conscience and convenience. Convenience benefits from issues being viewed in silos from bottom up. Decisions made with this perspective are simple. If you look from top down and the long range it involves many more, often moral hazard decisions. So the key to restoring the soul rests more in how we think than in just making single decisions—and that requires both education and commitment to values of responsibility.

Big issues of principle are often quite different and usually have major consequences to us as we are torn between fear and honor. Issues of major principle are very significant because they are recognized to be "direction changes" for short or long term. The more extreme of them are those where honor was truly recognized as a core belief—Masada, Thermopylae, or the Alamo for example. This sense of honor of cause is often infectious.

When I was President of the Texas State Chamber of Commerce and the East Texas Chamber, I asked several musicians to help me convey the emotions that music and the Arts (as described by Confucius) had in shaping man's temperament. I asked them to play two pieces. The first was the *El Deguello,* which in history was first played in Spain by the Moors who entitled it with a word meaning "slitting the throat." It is a piercing bugle blast of modulated succession of low-c notes that meant no quarter. To any Texan it is well known as Santa Anna's battle signature, which was dramatically played at the Alamo as 182 Texans faced 5,000 or more Mexican soldiers on the last day of a thirteen-day siege.

History is often revisionist, but to any Texan, this is a story of ultimate honor. Whether it was a wise decision to battle from an old mission may be argued in history, but why they did so was the point. It was not a battle between Texan and Mexican but a defense of the Mexican Constitution of 1824 and its rights. The Deguello is to me the symbol of the brutality of power. (Another historian mentioned it was called the Song of Assassins and some felt could be traced back to the time of Herod's soldiers in the era they searched for Christ.) It is the song I would tell the audience that best represents the pressure on men's souls. It is the one with which we began our presentation on occasion and it set a very serious tone.

We ended with another piece, *The Impossible Dream*, from *The Man of La Mancha,* which traced back its heritage to Miguel de Cervantes (1547–1616) who wrote *Don Quixote de la Mancha*, a great piece of Western literature by an author who had spent a part of his life in prison and wrote a satire on chivalry. But *The Impossible Dream* is a song that brings out the very best in men. Perhaps it is foolish to chase stars, but it is such dreams from which courage evolves with a power that overwhelms the Deguello.

IX | A LETTER TO FELLOW BELIEVERS OF THE IMPOSSIBLE DREAM

CREATING, STRENGTHENING, AND SUSTAINING DRIVEN ORGANIZATIONS

An interesting article I read years ago noted the peak age of most professions. Interestingly that of a philosopher was in the early to mid sixties, much later in life than almost all others. It is perhaps not until you have grandchildren and have experienced the realities of life and the many cycles in which the present is often hidden that you have an appreciation of the flow of history. The writing of *The Language of Conscience Evolution* over a period of years began after the formation of the Texas Lyceum. The Lyceum has been an organization that for thirty years looked at certain goals based upon Aristotle's concepts of ethics and vision. It primarily focused on a stewardship of values, a concept of unifying diverse groups to bring out the best in society and then educating by studying public policy options so a more harmonious approach to solving problems could be taken. It was an effort to create that was neither partisan nor driven by individual ambition and purpose. It tried to create "Bridge Builders" who were not after personal followings as much as with other leaders to transform and inspire.

In the early years it often focused on members bringing their families so that it was not just the leaders, but also their families as a whole that got to know each other. (When your children play together, it is difficult to fault a fellow babysitter.) In recent times the organization has often met at Washington on the Brazos on March 2nd with their children to appreciate Texas history. In surviving thirty years and having significant impact by having many of the political leaders of both parties involved, the Texas Lyceum has served as a learning vehicle for the benefits and problems involving thoughtful public policy. From PBS presentations to Texas Polls it has tried to help the public understand issues, and in the presentations of its Texas Stewardship of Values Award promote recognition of true service for the best of motivations. It is a rare award that cannot be bought and is determined by all the former Chairmen of the organization looking at the broad historical scope of Texas.

The first book in *The Language of Conscience Evolution* was *The New Legacy* that was written at the suggestion of Taylor Publishing Company, the publisher, and *Texas Business Magazine,* which did excerpts of some of the lessons we had learned from the early Lyceum in an article in September of 1987, "The Challenges to Texas." Interestingly, it became more a book on culture than it did on politics or economics although both were involved. From a Lyceum nucleus of alumni, many different institutions were either started or affected by the friendships and the public policy interests that the Lyceum began. I spent time in the creation of Texans for Quality Education, Inc., the Texas Leadership Institute, the John Ben Shepperd Forum, and a host of other entities. But in each case over the years the cycles of economics, the changing of leaders and their interests, and the changing nature of what society valued tended to change each of these institutions, which is an ongoing natural phenomenon.

The very concept of the Triangles evolved from the point that change is constant and clashes with the historical status quo. It is the thoughtful management of change that matters. However, the nature of these changes and their ultimate impacts are often missed. People see the great impacts, but they don't see the slow erosion that changes the direction of rivers. Increasingly many of us involved tried to create organizations which leveraged the conscience and compassion of the many smaller organizations—in effect, networkers of networkers. When people are driven by service, and not financial gain, fundraising and resources are key. But also you had to build a resilience and adaptability into the organization for it to survive.

These organizations all maintained the "uncommon men" of service, Confucius' "Gentlemen," and the embodiment of a culture of service and compassion. When they lack that component they become stagnant and lose relevance. These men or women were the critical audience to assemble and educate. It was not what a new organization could do for them or them for a new organization, but how together we could use common resources to strengthen all and build a transformational network toward a common end. The challenge is to define what that common end is and how to assure equal cooperation to it. The goal has to be to show results, even if only the step in the right direction to be followed and grown. Most institutions start small but grow with time and definition.

Experience has shown that great theory often falls to reality. Each organization is pressed for volunteers and resources. Focus is short-term since most leadership is only for a year. The common goal is elusive and personal egos play big parts as each wants to leave a legacy. The Lyceum has been successful over the years by being a catalyst. It pulled together many groups on policy on the major issues facing the state and by preparing discussion strategy often brought competing groups into the limelight to show their work. It is not difficult in educating on public policy. All groups liked the opportunity to present their work if it was in an honest forum. The secret is in creating a trusted vehicle that respects all entities partnering.

I once was Finance Chairman for a Billy Graham Evangelical Association event in Brenham. We had to convince thirty-five local churches that the benefit of having the community excited and enthusiastic about faith overrode their concerns that support for it would come at the expense of their individual church budgets. It is not easy, but with history and thoughtful approaches, many times the parts are far more effective if you create a transformational whole. Much of my life has been in search of how to develop a system that could bring out the best of people and organizations as a leveraged catalyst for conscience driven goals. Free Enterprise and Democracy are both ideas that require an ethical and responsibility driven population. The biggest problem all of us have faced is the creation of a common way of thinking to unify thought and institutional support to promote and expand those ideas with integrity of purpose and vision.

In the early '90s in an effort to revive the original motivation of several of the institutions we previously formed, I was asked to write an article on leadership that turned into a book. It was written with no original intent of distribution because it focused on the lessons I had learned over the years from trying to use the nonprofit sector to balance out some of the extremes of market economics. It talked about the importance of culture as a bridge between groups within society and even nations. From my participation in politics I learned that there were three great powers, economics, politics, and originally media but in reality it should have been culture because culture goes beyond the media of the day and more effectively influences how people look at the things presented to them in making their decisions. Former Texas Governor and Treasury Secretary John Connolly was an early mentor and emphasized these three strategy points. *The Language of Conscience* talked more about why conscience is important. It focused on the power of morality, ethics, and individual responsibility.

Over the years I have been greatly impacted by the works of Alexis de Tocqueville in *Democracy in America* and his focus on the importance to early American values of many of the cultural aspects of citizen participation, nonprofit institutions, and civic organizations, and the unique relationships between early Americans. Values mattered. While there is some question that he actually said his often quoted concept that "America is great because America is good, and when it ceases to be good it will no longer be great" it certainly reflects a concise view of his vision.

Cicero similarly looked at honor in Rome with the highest of perspectives. I do not perceive Machiavelli to have been a fan of Cicero, but he was a fan of the fact that the Romans paid their taxes in private on a system of honor that he respected greatly. I would argue that Cicero's concepts did a great deal to affect that culture. Honor, and the Honor Codes that help personify them, matter a great deal in giving strength to cultures. I was raised in a law enforcement family and spent many years associated with the U.S. Navy. Their values shaped me by reinforcing what my parents taught me. If honor and conscience are where we start, how then do we make the right choices of competing needs? The concept of identifying wants versus needs is critical, but sacrifice of an individual, company, or a nation requires confidence that sacrifice matters.

A Catalyst Must Study Economics, Politics, and Culture in Context

I have over the years increasingly seen the interaction and context of power, economics, and culture and realized that economics, particularly the more extreme self-interest, is ultimately driven by the incentives that are in place for the organization from its leadership. If the vision is short term then ultimate damage to the institution over time was often overlooked, but incentives do matter. I have had the opportunity to work with a number of corporations and the culture of the corporation, what it values, has a great deal to do with its ultimate success. However, that is often not directly related to the marketplace and how it is perceived by a much more institutionalized investment climate driven for performance because of the incentives to those managing money. It normally impacts in less obvious ways in setting goals, temperaments, and risk, which gives more stability and sustainability. That change in culture over the years has come not only from the financial incentives of greed in the executives, and also the short-term perspective of performance, affecting incentives, but how money flows, and finally the part that government played often through the politics of the lobby to impact the regulations that often undermined market forces. Leverage, which was generated from these changes, was an accelerator of the declines, but the ethical cultural failings were more the moral hazard loss that was to blame. Greed removes natural protection by overriding the caution of more conscience-based temperament. It is harder to cheat an honest and less greedy man.

The way we think about issues and politics has to change if America is going to be more united and competitive. America has always rebuilt itself in challenge, but the question today is whether we have the strength of will to sacrifice for the policies that are needed. The same is true for the world as a whole. We must find growth that can be a win-win for everyone rather than many of the policies that in all likelihood will begin to take place that are effectively a zero-sum game.

Culture is the way to accomplish this, but the question is how you give it influence and power. Conscience is recognizable if people are sensitized to it, but conscience has to be looked upon from a perspective of power. Convenience is an extremely powerful vehicle particularly in the echelons of power. The more powerful people become, the more greed, arrogance, and disjunction from the average man takes place. Hubris affects decisions, and political and economic support drive judgments. Legacies matter more than thoughtful policies unless you concentrate on leaving thoughtful items that history will appreciate.

I have supported a great many people in politics and there are very few who have not disappointed me in that they have started with all the right values for which many of us sacrificed for them. What they forgot is that the people supported them because they supported ideas that were beneficial. Unfortunately, the more they enter the realm of politics and gain seniority, the more the principles fade and the issue becomes personal hubris. It is no longer that they look at how they fit into the overall system as an advocate for a certain set of ideas that can make positive change. But it is instead how the world revolves around them and how they will cement their place within the world. There are some that never lose those first perspectives, and their goal is not so much to look to their legacy as they look to the self-satisfaction in changed society for the better. But they are increasingly rare in an intense partisan system.

If we look over the lessons of history, we inevitably find many men that have been wealthy, but few are remembered. There have been many political leaders, but those often remembered are for the principles on which they stood or the lack of principles by which they inflicted harm. Machiavelli often thought that a philosopher that did not have the power of armies could not be effective. While I have great respect for Machiavelli's Discourses on Livy and the insights he showed in his writings, his removal of ethics from statecraft in *The Prince* is perhaps one of the key points of understanding the true distinctions between the power of conscience and the power of convenience. I would venture that some of the greatest proponents of conscience in philosophers and religions moved forward in history not because of armies but because of the power of ideas and the power of conscience within those ideas. Personal dignity is an inherent part of man and when suppressed to a breaking point, reasserts itself and appreciates systems that protect it. Unless you live without something you never fully appreciate its value. Witness the change in China from Mao to Deng, and now the resurrection of Confucian values, which in many ways Mao opposed through the Cultural Revolution.

As Lord Acton noted, power corrupts, and absolute power corrupts absolutely. The more you rise in power, the more arrogance, greed, and personal interests become focused because of the nature of power itself. It becomes the definition of convenience because staying in power becomes the ultimate goal.

Conscience, on the other hand, is quite different. Even at an individual level, a person of convenience has a significant advantage over a person of conscience in an individual sense because a person of convenience is not limited in actions as the person of conscience would be. However, a person of convenience makes few true friends. They have allies and relationships, but the very nature of convenience can become a liability since others can persuade their allies.

People of convenience are thus much more transactional in how they deal with each other and become allies for the moment. People of conscience also are somewhat different. They have an inner core, which brings them together with others of common vision. It may be that groups of conscience may totally oppose each other on political or economic issues, but the reason they do is highly significant because it also allows the opportunity for honest discussion and compromise.

People of conscience build power by unifying with others in a more transformational sense by which they look to change society to a common goal and a common set of ideas. Groups that may disagree with each other on some issues may well be able to come together for a broader issue on which they both agree if the system allows it. Often intractable issues that do not appear to be able to be solved economically or politically can be broadened with the addition of culture, and there may be opportunities to rethink how common ends could be formulated. It is through the nonprofit entities, the nongovernmental civil associations, charities, educational groups, etc., that people who may have more diverse interests have the opportunity to work with each other. We have a strong nonprofit sector in America, but it is becoming less influential as society looks more for government to solve problems. It is losing its power to bind as our organizations become more specialized than general.

The problem with this concept is that often conscience, and even the groups that support it, are not driven by economic or political power. If nonprofits are formed solely for economic or political purposes, they really do not fall into the case of a conscience organization, which has a different internal motivation. This makes growth and resource accumulation difficult since they must appeal to ever more specific interest groups. Our problem is that the big picture benefits are last in the need for specificity. In Texas the Regional Chambers of Commerce in the 1950s and 1960s argued for the common good and succeeded in positive changes. Then Political Action Committees were formed and were more directly involved. At first they were generally for the common good, but slowly evolved into industries—banking, car dealers, insurance, etc. Then they became even more specific such as independent bankers, large bankers, mortgage bankers, etc., as focus went to specific convenience.

In Congress there used to be a few committees, now we have subcommittees of subcommittees, so almost each Congressman has power in the media and in contributions because he has power over a segment of the economy. Vulnerable freshmen Congressmen often are placed on the Financial Services Committee because of its impact on fundraising. We have few organizations that integrate issues and even fewer that do so from conscience.

Organizations that support ethics and conscience have a tendency to be smaller and oftentimes driven by a select set of circumstances or goals. They are nonprofit and more academic, and they often have limited interaction with other institutions. Smaller organizations often have problems with funding and because of that are competitive with each other. Universities that deal with many of these issues also often have problems of academic jealousies and conceptual ownership. They deal in relativity and ultimate toleration, which does not fit with the necessities of having a set of values of conscience and morality. Building sensitivity to the need for ethics, morality, and conscience is the best ultimate goal, but it needs to be part of a more common approach so efforts reinforce each other.

We are in an area where multiculturalism has to be accepted as a reality necessity. We are in a time where diversity has to be respected since an accumulation of peoples and cultures are oftentimes the only way they can preserve the values they hold in conscience, but the great question is how we reunify these extremely diverse groups. There are many ideas in this regard but to me they fall into two basic camps.

One is that you reunify them on such values as conscience, morality, the Golden Rule, and the Common Good. Teaching character and understanding emphasizes these basic set rules of values by which men must operate. There are defined codes of honor and obligations between men. This was what Martin Luther King believed in placing character as the key component, as did Gandhi, and have most religions. But this concept is not necessarily a religious one of man to God but begins at its basics as a relationship of man to man and effectively is the embodiment of the three cultures discussed in the Triangles, the Rule of Law and Discipline in Society, the Rule of Unenforced Obligation and Morality, and the Culture of Compassion and Service. The purpose of that section of the Triangles is solely the creation of this culture.

THE PROS AND CONS OF TOLERANCE AND ACCEPTANCE

The other approach is one that believes that there will be clashes of cultures and that it is difficult for the many cultures of the world to fit together.

Thus, the best approaches may be more toleration and an acceptance of relativity in understanding each other. This is perhaps the more prominent view at most major universities, and it is not necessarily in opposition with the values discussed above. Toleration and relativity are positive values if used appropriately, but in extreme they are like substances that are medicines at one dose and poison at a higher level. If total toleration destroys values, then morality loses some level of common obligation; it cannot be relative and still have structure and importance. Understanding that the two concepts exist is important because they operate quite differently even though they use similar words.

This is similar to having a headache and one philosophy addressing it with an icepack, and the other with a hot water bottle. If you mix the two, you lose the effects of both. Toleration and relativity is not the same thing as a code of morality and character. They are important parts of character but cannot be so pronounced as to overwhelm the necessity of character. The difference is that if you have common character in morality, you pull people into a melting pot. But if you use toleration and relativity heavily, you tend to get a salad bowl. You can build a transformational set of ideas with a melting pot, but it is much harder to do so with a salad bowl of diversity alone.

Because of my military, law enforcement, business, and political experiences, the question most often asked of me is whether it is naive to believe that promoting conscience can change trends. The answer quite simply is that usually conscience comes back in the nature of man when it is needed. If you look at the progression of most democracies or civilizations, you learn a great deal about the fact that cycles repeat in history—not exactly, but in many of their basic characteristics. At times of crisis after human dignity has been crushed, the respect of dignity often emerges in its strongest sense, and replaces ideas. So in our present time the question for us is how we can try and avoid crisis by copying those times in history where thoughtful and intelligent cooperation does the most to minimize potential problems.

There is no way to change the nationalism of politics or the self-interest of economics. They will inevitably cause frictions. The question is how we can create institutions that let the potential impact of problems be seen and emphasize the benefit not only of conscience, but also of common interests in solving many of the problems. If you have expectations of ethics in politics and economics and reflect displeasure when it is not present, you change the situation. Common interest is seldom presented well. We have such institutions in politics in the history of the League of Nations and the United Nations. But they have not been very effective because nationalism inevitably affects foreign policy on a political basis. Financially, we have such institutions in the World Bank, the IMF, and a host of other economic agencies. However, these are institutions designed to avoid crisis and often have problems battling corruption. Too often you have the concerns of rich versus poor. One other concern of bringing unity is where an idea originates. If it starts with either of the combatants, it is often never considered jointly. If respected institutions of wisdom and integrity can originate ideas, discussion follows if for no other reason than preservation of image. These organizations will be critical if we are to end the gridlock of current politics.

Cultural institutions exist but not on a very unified basis in context that has the ability to be a working place for success. If there is a common need that eventually will necessarily be filled, it will be for an institution that can help unify these areas worldwide. The changing nature of globalization with communication and financial interaction will force change. America at its peak has perhaps 4% of the population of the world, but probably a quarter of its income, and maybe a third of its net worth. Three hundred million people have had a standard of living that the other six billion people in the world would like to achieve, and only a portion of them in the developed world is close. For the rest of the world to approach those standards will have tremendous impact. Recent media discussions of the 1%, note that perhaps half of Americans would be in the world's top 1% because of our much higher standard of living than undeveloped countries. Even if this is a high estimate, it has the benefit of focusing on the problem of resources.

As noted previously, one of the most significant books that has not been fully appreciated, *Peaceful Rise—China's New Road To Development,* was written years ago by Mr. Zheng Bijian. He was one of the significant scholars of China who pointed out very clearly that 1.3 to 1.5 billion Chinese cannot automatically have the same life standard as America. If you had that many cars and that much consumption, there would be tremendous imbalances created even if it was possible. (I paraphrased his writings with the permission of the Central Party School Press, in *Instilling Values in Transcending Generations.*) China's impact on the world is going to be extremely significant and how China addresses many of its issues will have dramatic repercussions. The emergence of India and Brazil, and potentially Mexico, follow the same trends. Europe's demographics will have significant impact upon it although it will always remain significant, but Asia and Latin America and eventually Africa, will be increasingly important players. How will they look at the world in 2030 or in 2050? You and your children will be greatly affected by that perspective.

The Creation of a Library of Conscience and an Institute for Cultural Ethics

When I took a tour of Egypt years ago to understand its civilization, one thing that impressed me was several guides' reference to the great Library of Alexandria and the tremendous amounts of knowledge that had been acquired in one place and time for the world. Before its destruction in the unfortunate fire, it had accumulated much of the wisdom of the world of the time and gave thought and understanding to how it all fit together in context. A library by its very nature has to organize its sections. It has to think through relationships and context. But the parallel that also must flow with it was one of Sir Francis Bacon when he talked of the greatest insect. He noted that ants are very impressive because they collect parts of leaves and other types of food, bring them to the nest, and store them accordingly. But a more sophisticated insect was the spider that created very intricate webs from within to trap the unwary and take advantage of its prey. The ant took from the outside world, but the spider from within. However, to Bacon the greatest insect was the honeybee since it both took from without, the nectar of the flower, and created honey from within that was useful to many. Such is the nature of how a great institution has to be built.

The Internet today provides far more knowledge than the Library of Alexandria could ever have possessed years ago. However, the Internet is like the ant. It simply categorizes and puts out great amounts of information. There are many spiders that use that information and warp it to their own purposes. The goal is the creation of a hive of honeybees that have not only the talents and the ability but also a more positive ultimate goal. This needs to exist as a place of respect and trust, so it must be an effort of many diverse parties to give it the credibility necessary. Trust and wisdom are the critical goals to be sought.

Socrates noted that to understand a thing you must first name it. We named all our programs and our values. What we need to create is a catalyst for the creation of a unifying vision that gives morality power. *The Language of Conscience* talks of "cultural ethics," but the problem with broad acceptance is what or whose ethics. There needs to be thoughtful and coordinated work in context to bring understanding. Before we can discuss balance of fairness of economic policy or political systems, we must find the organizing perspective that can get enough support to bring changes. It would be the solution to many problems.

I am amazed how many times today racism is a point of focus by the media when it was Martin Luther King who led the most successful effort against it with a vision to have "character" as the goal. Cesar Chavez had a similar vision of values in his basic appeal for dignity in "the cause." The term "Enlightened Conservatism" deals with joint dignity. You must push the positives not the negatives if you want unity. *The Language of Conscience* sought a method to explain and communicate the necessity and power of conscience. It is as consistent with the most modern efforts at organizing a society in China's new ideology, The Harmonious Society, to the movements in the West to bring the Rule of Law such as the World Justice Project. This is particularly evident if you watch Chinese efforts to engage the world with a developing World Harmonious Society, not of Communism, but of their ancient culture and language from their international Confucian Institutes. You better understand Confucianism when you realize that his view of marriage was not the unification of two people, but the interrelationship of two families. All types of institutions can be bridges.

In the West because of our financial crisis, ethics and governance are being redefined from just compliance to culture. Corporate or institutional governance is not just about an ethical leadership; it is the creation of a culture that operates with ethics out of sensitivity to the interests of the parties involved. It requires more disciplined thought, thoughtful creation and implementation of an operating culture, and efficiency looking at the most critical issues of leadership. They will fit with that culture, strategic investment that is the future of the company, and a clear understanding of the intrinsic value of the company, which requires how risks are managed and where earnings are actually made. Individual directors will need ever more professionalism and collectively they will need refinement creating a contextual strategic mind for the board to create that culture.

A confirmation of that trend is the new concept of "benefit corporations," a new charter available in seven states that allows a board of directors to consider social objectives ahead of profits and be shielded from the normal requirements of maximizing value for shareholders or forcing shareholder lawsuits. This alternative business model is for profit, but can sacrifice some value for broader purposes. This recognizes that capitalism can have evolution toward pubic interest as mutual and nonprofit organizations have already shown.

In the West many of our corporate failings have come from a lack of ethical, sustainable governance. In developing nations this will be a key consideration to refining their corporations for international involvement as well as internal efficiencies. The nature of the financial recession will require far better governance because of the challenges to be faced. Concentration on governance in institutions is not just ethics. It is creating a cultural value system of efficiency and sustainability as a vision as opposed to a disconnected battling operation of competing interests of convenience.

A good friend, Bill Ide, who as a former President of the American Bar Association, current Chair of the Advisory Board to the Conference Board's Governance Center, and one of the experts on the concept of the Rule of Law, put this in a proper frame of reference by addressing these issues in a defining proposition:

When humans choose to live together as a society, a form of social license is created as to how members will treat each other and be treated by the entity they have chosen to govern their lives. Typically constitutions, laws and other formal covenants governing behaviors are enacted, but the glue that allows society to function is the underlying culture. If the culture is not driven for the greater good for all, distrust will grow among the disenfranchised against those deemed to be profiting at their expense. At the ultimate political level, this could mean revolution. In a free market democracy, typically loss of trust builds demands for more government regulation.

The communist system rose from a belief that capitalism would not provide an adequate safety net for the disenfranchised and that commerce should be totally regulated. But that system ultimately failed to deliver sufficient efficiencies to provide for the overall good and market characteristics have returned. China, the E.U., the U.S., and all thoughtful advanced economies are seeking to determine the best culture to provide for the greater good of all. In the end, a society must have a culture where decisions are made for the greater good by political, business, and thought leaders to assure the right equilibrium between greater efficiencies and regulations to protect against exploitation. On the non-economic side, exploitation through hate, fear, and prejudice must also be prevented by the greater good culture providing education and rights for all. Self-regulation is the ultimate mode for achieving the right balance, but a strong and non-compromising culture for the greater good must be a given or the needed trust will not be forthcoming.

My definition of his proposition in simple terms is that if men do not want government increasingly in their lives and limiting freedom and opportunity, they must mutually enforce obligations of morality, ethics, and honor within society.

Toward that end, they have to create not just a physical center that can link many other institutions—but a network guided by a transformational common purpose to compile the information and thoughts on conscience from different cultures and synthesize and develop how conscience is put forward. Universities often ask questions that start first with, "Why should I be interested in conscience and what difference does it make?" And second, "How do you research and teach it? How do you put it in such a context that it is understood?"

The issue is cultural ethics. How do you teach the younger students what the important values to teach to their children are, and how do these different values become relevant to their own lives? The final question that is the most difficult is what to teach. Whose values do you teach? Too often in academia it is said that we must let people decide for themselves rather than determine what values are to be taught. *You do not need to teach conservatism or liberalism, ideology or religion, but you need to teach how to think from the perspective that conscience and morality must be part of each individual in how they look at life. You need to teach them the great classics, which include both sides.* It helps them to understand the need for individual responsibility, and the benefits of the common good, and the enlightenment of compassion and respect for dignity.

As I mentioned earlier, Cicero believed in honor. The opposite perspective, the cost of honor, is shown in the novel *All Quiet on the Western Front*. It showed the problems of honor in war and the reality of war. You need a balance, but if taught well, you understood that your life would be determined by what set of values you adopt. For students it would help shape what they study and the values they need to gain. This should define why students need an education. But it also allows them to focus individually on what they want to get from an institution. The Classics are necessary, but they have to be put in context with reality to have real impact. Universities must learn to look more to the real world for input. If not, the vacuum of trust will be filled by newly created solutions to the need. People do not wish to feel hallowed or without the control that a decisive personal mind can give in facing the future.

Through research, higher education has almost made a god of knowledge because of its impact on ratings and funding. They have minimized the more controversial subjects that sensitize to values beyond relativity and toleration. They are increasingly inefficient as funds so often go to administrative or private issue projects done in the name of education. America is trailing in overall quality of education, and it will be the subject of much discussion in reviving the economy. But I learned when I chaired Texans for Quality Educations, Inc., that money is not the key. It takes parents, the creation of interest in students, realistic classes that provide attainable education, and most of all a correct model of the world to fit what is learned in context. The Chinese have gained a lead in math and science performance at lower levels but have a need for the same type model of the world to create ingenuity and the values for a harmony in a society with such great numbers and such rapid change.

Strong cultural peer values that eliminate litigation and the need for regulation lead to smaller government and more opportunity in market systems, creating wealth and opportunity for the people as a whole. These are issues that are different in each culture, and there are no exact right answers. What does matter in a democracy is the concept of dignity, justice, and the Rule of Law over the power of individual men that create property rights and ownership. If you have the wrong organizing principles, you very seldom reach your ultimate goal.

Cultures differ because of history and geography. In Asia farmers grew rice, a crop you plant constantly, while America used wheat, which is fallow part of the year. So how time is used affects the perspective of work ethic. The secret is not the need to be identical, but to have common core principles.

If such an institution—we might call it a Library of Conscience—was created in the future, could it succeed? It is hard to say because any real change requires the ability to unify a significant number of people and the concept of power. What brings people to a common institution is their belief that they benefit from it.

The only way to put conscience into power is often to get people to believe so that it becomes convenient for those in leadership to adopt conscience. It is exactly that same process that becomes necessary in the development of institutions. In corporate America there are institutions in governance and ethics to which we give increasing importance and support because regulation will continue growing at an almost unbearable competitive level. This will happen if corporate America does not engage in its own peer pressure governance to correct the problems that exist.

The concept of broader cultural value institutions might seem naive in our modern environment, particularly with the world's focus on power as realistic judgment criteria. However, the social networking technology that has democratized information where it is less controlled by a few centralized institutions will evolve but will reach a quandary of trust as the experts and elites who controlled information use resources to influence the new methods. The quality and integrity of information will become an ever-greater issue. The use of the Internet for scams as it matured is a perfect example. Influence will matter increasingly. Bloggers of integrity will be sought out, but that is quite different from teaching a more democratized and powerful public how to think even if they think differently at the end of the process. If they think in terms of interests and not values you have very different results. We all have a confirmation bias tending to see facts in a way that supports our prejudgments.

If those prejudgments are to be cultural values and not economic or political interests, we have to see why that is ultimately in our best interest. That level of thought requires the combined transformational power of many in some institutional form to give it integrity. The public can get information and knowledge as never before from the Internet, but wisdom requires conscience to have a strong presence relevant to the times. Such a Library of Conscience cannot be of the old physical form but must be a dynamic technological one available to all who wish to use it. And it must be maintained with a diversity of interests that give it integrity, which in the modern world will require a multinational cultural concept of the Golden and Silver Rules of doing to others what you wish to be done to you.

If Marcus Aurelius was correct that a man should be upright, not kept upright, then before the "keeping upright" destroys the culture, we need to do some character building. And the same is going to be true throughout the world.

It is important to recognize that corruption and intimidation are worldwide problems as convenience uses them to accomplish its ends. Every country is seeing this problem expand. In some of the more developed ones like the United States it is simply less transparent and more systemic.

The solution is not in just one country because the activity can be taken elsewhere. It's a worldwide issue of whether civilization continues to accept corruption's growth. You will never eliminate it; you can only make it less significant and build a culture that helps retard it. China has significant corruption and recognizes it as a major threat where many other countries do not. Unfortunately the leadership's efforts have seemingly not had much effect because they are individualized more than cultural, and they have a hard time using traditional methods in a still somewhat unfamiliar market system. The market system in some ways can be a fertilizer for corruption if the proper safeguards are not in place.

China has been trying to learn Western ideas to combine with their own cultural and compliance approaches. I think China's sentiment was well captured in a paragraph in *The Wall Street Journal* of Monday, February 14, 2011, page A17, Graft Probe Sinks China Railway Chief by Aaron Back that noted: *In January, President Hu Jintao acknowledged the difficulties, warning at a meeting of the Central Commission for Discipline Inspection, the party's antigraft body, that the party faces a "grave situation and arduous tasks," and vowing to "combat graft strictly and punish corrupt officials severely" to win public trust, according to Xinhua.*

The key point is that the world needs not just a central location and coordination to learn how to build better systems and relationships with other law enforcement agencies for better cooperation, but a transformational attitude that will only come from strong leadership and public support. The Rule of Law is one of enforcement beyond just words, and the efficiency of it depends on a cultural perspective. If the people shun bad behavior, it makes it more dangerous. If they are corrupted to become a part of it, it only reinforces it. The Chinese understand this better than anyone, and their senior leadership is constantly trying to find new techniques as we saw from our exchanges with them. However small undertakings not built on major efforts will have little effect. This is a project of social science not unlike what the space program did for physical science. It needs an international joint commitment to a conscience to move civilization forward. Ethical governance is a similar necessity for corporatism and the lack of fairness due to wealth.

Everyone performs differently if they have to report to others and justify actions. In explaining, you often make clearer your logic and its flaws. You can teach the handshake and smile appearance, but you also have to give will to heart and mind.

America needs to reenergize its professionalism. China's business practices will have huge impact on world standards as they emerge as a large international player and a professional governance system will have to develop. How they train and certify a professional system will change Chinese practices over time because all rising leaders will need to learn and appreciate it to advance. This is why China matters in the formation of a Library of Conscience theoretically.

There are many associations of scholars, Institutes of Ethics, and governance groups that believe in these concepts, usually a specialized section of them. These need a common cooperative home, even if it begins small, that can grow over time as its value is perceived. The Internet itself may prove to be an option.

Studying conscience in culture directly affects economic and political systems if it can be implemented. That is why the division between people must be bridged. It does not matter if you are Republican or Democrat, Indian, Mexican, Chinese, or an American. You care about your children's future and are you willing to do things to preserve it? Or do you care primarily about just yourself and right now?

Before the majority of the world can look at these issues in the same way the wealthy do, we must begin with the understanding that charity and taking care of the most significant problems are necessary. But the greatest problems of the impoverished are an ineffective government and corruption. So you must solve both problems together. Nonetheless, unity from conscience sets the stage for the most rapid economic growth because it provides opportunity and hope. Poverty requires more serious focus on resources and a unity to grow more than wealth.

People have been criticizing capitalism for inequities and speaking of the 1% wealthiest negatively. But capitalism as a system, with political and cultural supports, is the best of meritocracy, opportunity creation, and wealth creation. Look at North versus South Korea, look at the former East and

West Germanys, and look at the policy changes of Singapore and gradually China. There may be flames to address, but market systems work. America has proved that just as much through the recent financial crisis that was multiplied in effect by financial leverage, but originated in a failure of public moral hazard and individual greed. What is wrong is not the market system, but the failure of the cultural value system to balance the market powers from excess. The inequalities that result further corrupt the balances.

Corruption robs the underprivileged of their opportunity, dignity, and self-respect in its unfairness. The issue is not that the poor cannot afford ethical conduct because of their condition, but their condition is caused by the corruption, which contaminates policy and programs. The government is ineffective and skepticism of institutions is created. This is why Confucius emphasized the need for ethical leadership and why Cicero promoted honor. The poor may have little, but they seek fairness in the system, and if the system to bring them out of poverty is corrupt, it is highly unlikely they will get relief. So, ethical culture is just a beginning.

These are the type relationships and studies that a major center on conscience could assist. Eventually, globalization and cyberization will make it an international issue more than ever before. You will never have a one government world or one economy because both are based on self-interest in politics and economics. However, you can have a common value of conscience and law internationally because the common good has significant values for all.

The great philosophers and religious leaders of the axial age set the general rules for conscience, but modern economic and political theories have diminished their power. You will not change power without calling on what it is in the soul of every man—his conscience for giving dignity and accepting responsibility for his actions and his family's future.

Even if we cannot change the world immediately, we can begin by passing on our vision, experience, and our way of thought to the next generations.

An Interesting Possible Catalyst

One place where such an institution may well emerge is the People's Republic of China where leadership has been very interested in this type of concept. China is already in need of this type of wisdom to set its future public policy. It is emerging from several centuries of economic domination and has to define its new character to keep stability. The last thirty years of its "opening up" has created a very powerful economic engine due to its large population. China recognizes the importance of market economics or "socialism with Chinese characteristics," and it also has a significant appreciation of its ancient culture and Confucian morality with the compliance of legalism, and the skepticism and enlightenment of Lao Tzu.

One of the key issues provided in my discussions with the Chinese over the years is that to me the market system was an efficient tool of economics. As they studied it they had questions as to when you became a market driven society, then an economic system, and the consumption and greed shaped not just economies but politics and culture was replaced with dollar worship. There is a point where market systems dominate beyond just economics and it happens when cultural values are weakened and a vacuum exists.

However, its leadership thinks in terms of Sun Tzu that recognizes the power of the moral high ground—just as their culture began with the Duke of Zhou's concept of the Mandate of Heaven believing that his side won because they were just and honorable. While corruption is a significant problem in China, personal dignity is a cultural characteristic of the Chinese that remains extremely important. Its stability is greatly underestimated by the West because China effectively has a set of cultural values that are strong but are being tremendously impacted by Western technology, which is a destabilizing factor in many ways. The Chinese government has a very difficult role in keeping economic growth to maintain stability from market economics and at the same time transforming and maintaining a "Harmonious Culture" that is not overly materialistic. The Chinese people's judgment of the leadership depends a great deal on its success and continuing growth but also fairness in its policies. But the challenges to that continued growth have to be addressed. China will have to evolve and the questions will be how and with what value system. There is no certainty with new leadership and possible economic and social problems. However, this is a more defined institutional process that gives insight to what philosophies they are studying.

China understands its problems far better than most other countries because of the impacts of the failed Great Leap Forward and the Cultural Revolution. It thinks of them in its Central Party School in theory and the Counsellors of the State Council in execution. The uniqueness of China's situation rests in the direct control of many of the country's institutions in a limited number of people. As *The Wall Street Journal* pointed out in an article entitled "China's Private Party" about the 300 "red phones" that are placed at the highest level, what will these 300 have as an organizing principle compared to our leaders reacting to 300 million Americans in our political system? The problems they have to solve create a need for the type of research and thought necessary on cultural conscience.

The leadership of the Communist Party truly affects the leverage of power and because it affects all institutions it has a much greater opportunity to impact the cultural values of the country moving forward. China's leadership has been insular, but its new economy will force it to interact with the world. Foreign investment is already growing significantly. How will it do so and on what platform of engagement since this can well affect business practices globally? Recently China has become more proactive and nationalistic in defense of its domestic businesses. Some of its businesses have relied on commercial espionage for growth and advantage. Both might be expected of a growing country desperate for stability. But now China is a major player in the world.

As it matures, the Rule of Law and strong corporate governance are a necessity. Whether it is developed and how well it is understood is one of the critical understated issues of the future. Will there be a Chinese Conference Board and Better Business Bureau? I think the answer is yes in view of the significant expansion of the Library of the Central Party School, particularly its focus on the Rule of Law and the work of the Chancellors of the State Council on Ethical Governance. The seeds are there, the bridges are being built, but this could be a greater catalyst internationally than perceived if supported by China's future leadership. The issue is not just the professionalism of ethical and effective governance, but a common concept to build bridges with more trust abroad.

China has the entire world telling it what to do and most "experts" on China seem to live in New York or Washington not Beijing, which clouds understanding. Chinese leadership processes and absorbs information, but they think from their own culture, politics, and history. The stability of the country with its many income disparities, corruption, and challenges dominates policy even if they recognize the necessity of morality in the economy. They focus longer term on what is taught in schools, but the days of nationalistic advertisements are lost in the reality of modern communication, so they must refine and choose a vision.

Nonetheless, there are three circles of significant leadership—past leaders respected by their tradition and legacy, the current leadership that has maintained stability and helped China continue outstanding growth, and the future rising leadership that has been more exposed to Western values. All three are important because transitions and transformations that are often in crisis require continuity. A slower implementation to a final goal is the Chinese way of thinking in bringing Harmony. They often hide their capabilities and rely heavily on patience. Projects have to have support both at the bottom and top of their system. It requires a more common vision even though there are very different groups in an intense political environment not unlike the West. The difference is that the American system was built for checks and balances on power—executive, legislative, and judicial to limit government expansion. The Chinese system until recently used government and central planning principles for growth but come from policy directed institutions with a leadership that needs to finally agree. There is balance in finding consensus, which will be more difficult as the economy presents challenges

What Chinese leaders are grasping to find is an understanding of the future world so they can adapt to it while developing their own country. The "socialism with Chinese characteristics" can be old style central planning with ownership and market incentives added, but which have more dependency. Or it can be more market-driven capitalism with a far greater use of nonprofit and governmental support to take the edge off pure market forces. The latter leads to more opportunity and innovation but poses challenges with stability economically, environmentally, and socially if not handled well. Bridging systems is highly complex. The real issue is the balance between the market economy and the cultural values sections which will determine the nature of the society and ultimately drive its politics.

The Chinese growth has been largely from taking rural workers and increasing their income and talents. But China now needs to build a consumer-based economy and develop productivity practices and market analogies similar to the West. The Chinese have recently given more focus to the importance of private property. One of the great problems with the West has been China's lack of recognition of intellectual property rights. However, as the Chinese develop more and more of their own products through their own processes and research, they will have a vested interest in making certain that these rules of law are applicable. What both the Central

Party School and the State Council recognize is they need a process where they can have more input from experts on market systems—particularly corporate governance and transparency procedures. To control the problems of markets they will look at Western concepts implemented in Chinese ways. By the Communist Manifesto, Engels noted that the method of productivity for economics drove the nature of society (culture), which impacted the intellectual thought (politics). So affecting the driving forces of economics with governance is a logical place to start.

There is rising concern in the West that future Chinese policy will increasingly demand surrender of intellectual property to gain access to Chinese markets. Many Chinese see this as a national right since they feel historically that they have been disadvantaged by the West's interventions in China. However, that has serious unappreciated consequences and moves toward a zero-sum mentality rather than a win-win mentality. China will ultimately do what it understands to be in its own interest. The discussions of impediments to investment and trade have been helpful since the issue is not just how the West is treated in China but also how their investments in the rest of the world are ultimately treated.

Innovation will be a critical issue to China, and regardless of the number of engineers, it is partially a culture and an art as much as a science. What the Lyceum exchanges revealed is the Chinese leadership's understanding of this concept. As China is increasingly forced to choose between a domestic protection strategy and an international cooperative one of the Golden Rule, the West has to seriously develop and explain the benefits of the latter not just from the bottom up issue of a singular trade policy but also the top down issue of China's ultimate position in the world. Groups such as the Conference Board are key, but the concepts need to be developed to explain China's ultimate interest.

At the same time the Chinese have their own culture and approach to thinking through problems. In the West we deal more with opinions where the Chinese tend to focus more on facts. The Central Party School Motto is "Truth from Facts." Most of China's leaders are engineers. Many are out of Tsinghua University, which was formed in part by a grant from the United States when it was believed that the amount of reparations being paid by China after the Boxer Rebellion were too high. This university was built on the concept of technology and learning interaction with the West. I had the opportunity to visit Tsinghua and present my books to them for their library. What impressed me greatly is that they have perhaps four million student applications for 4,000 positions. It is a great school for engineering and technology and is now internationalizing its base of social and economic thought through partnerships with premier institutions worldwide.

Quality education is greatly valued in China, and the competitiveness of its youth driven by this system will mean that China's intellectual property will experience tremendous growth over the next decades. But China must now build into its systems the concepts of the rules of law that not only protect the West so that they can exchange and grow intellectually, but to protect their own intellectual property for the future as they begin to take it worldwide. This is a cultural issue and a political issue of valuing the rights to one's work. Taking someone else's ideas for personal profit is no different conceptually and morally than stealing his money. It needs to be explained to the Chinese from cultural ethics beyond just criticism on legal grounds to be more understood and not looked upon as self-interest in the West. And Western demands must have "clean hands" where the legality of claims and patents are solid and justifiable or the concept of intellectual property is trivialized.

The Chinese want to understand the United States and Western systems and they feel we need to understand them to properly appreciate their concepts. I would agree that neither of us understands the other nearly well enough. In the next several decades, economics will cause innumerable frictions due to trade imbalances and politics because of nationalism. The only place a bridge can be built that helps discuss these issues in unity is the common interest of culture. The Chinese do not understand where American culture is going because we are changing so many of our past concepts. Simultaneously, China is making vast changes almost in the opposite direction.

This is why I feel that China is a logical place for such a "Library of Conscience" to originate. America if it wishes to revitalize itself is a close second in need. Its Confucian Institutes that have spread around the world teaching the Chinese language have been a remarkable bridge to Chinese culture internationally. However, what China truly needs within itself is a better understanding of how the rest of the world thinks so that it can understand its future cultures. And the only effective way to do that is to try to find common values of cultural conscience and expand them into how they are implemented in economical and political decision-making. This is a very different concept from a United Nations of politics, but it is a cultural equivalent based on the potential continuing revival of historical Chinese concepts bridging with Western principles that are similar.

If such trends continue, democracy in China may eventually take the form of an even greater respect and a protection of individual dignity more than the political civil rights of the Western systems. The fairness and owner-ship of property rights may well be more originated and governed by the Silver Rule of Confucius than by absolute legal systems implemented over time.

A Library of Conscience, developing these concepts we defined as a Language of Conscience would divide the challenges along the lines of the Triangles that have evolved from advice of the West and China. The divisions would look at economics, politics, and culture separately for detail but then can be unified to support each other—the method of thought, which brings people together and that is the cultural search for common integrity and the advancement of civilization. Few care about this unless a greater power provides a magnet of self-interest. In economics we need to look at the Rule of Law in fighting corruption. How systems can be built that "put the blood of morality into the veins of businessmen" as Premier Wen Jiabao says. But the service organizations of the world and the many nonprofit institutions that take these concepts to the individual would be consistent with these thinkers and much more empowered as charity and dignity receive more respect.

Over the years I have given to the Central Party School and the State Council examples of American organizations such as the Conference Board and its work on governance and the Better Business Bureau and its peer related abilities to affect economics through peer pressure. The ability to give awards such as the Better Business Bureau Torch Awards, if given by an entity that has a sacrosanct system of determining the recipient, could be a powerful international recognition of efforts. There are many organizations such as the World Justice Project that look to expand the Rule of Law and have done studies in its implementation that would be of great assistance to understanding the issues of international law. They also could learn from the Chinese system of cultural equity and how many of these principles might be adapted more appropriately for Asia to have an earlier and more pronounced recognition of issues such as property rights and man's individual dignity.

Research sections on trends and demographics worldwide could help people understand and solve impending problems. Such a series of institutes would allow China to expose the best-motivated international institutions to Eastern ideas that will have significant effect in this century. This project also needs to involve Latin America and Europe. They have the same problems and the same strengths of character that worry about family and its values. Mexico's great university UNAM with its cultural expertise would be ideally suited.

Any major research ought to include how to enhance and sustain conscience. Strategic planning requires you to define a product, which in its truest form would be an appreciation of the necessity and value of conscience and the ethics and individual responsibility tempered by the compassion it requires. The next consideration is the group of people to whom it must be sold which is universal. The final and most important question is how it can be successfully executed in an environment often hostile to it where its proponents are scattered. Conscience is ultimately personal and to force it rather than lead to it ultimately weakens it. Having a common concept to sell is the beginning. Adding depth, which brings together more diverse groups in refinement and understanding builds and unifies the base by changing from transactional to transformational thinking.

So tactics include many self-regulation efforts as well as individualized ones in each profession exemplified—all play key parts but are less effective as small individual guns than as bullets in a bigger gun. The Internet will be of great help in its use of peer evaluation of service on lists that rank satisfaction. This is self-regulation at a basic level. But to enhance the effectiveness of the product, they may need to change calibers of presentation, which should help them explain their relevance and fundraising. This is the nonprofit approach. Another tactic is to build a profit-based sustainable concept that goes beyond demonstrating need or creating peer pressure and helps build the culture into corporations. Consulting may help leaders understand how to do this to shape a culture, but the key is the commitment to leadership after training.

Military and police officers are often sought in successful corporations because they have disciplined leadership as well as codes of honor. There is no better way to inject conscience in business than to have it appreciated as the competitive advantage it can be as it limits the excessive greed and arrogance that weakens companies. From small businesses to large, the power of an ethical culture needs to be linked with sustainability. But that is weakened unless all society, rather than the individual group, is enlightened as well. Ultimately, faith-based conscience and ethically sustainable business concepts will be the two greatest drivers in sustaining political efforts that are weak if there are no cultural or economic underpinnings.

Hopefully, the Chinese realize that it cannot be based on their ideas alone or even in dominance if they wish interactions at high levels and credibility that brings others to such an institution. But it could help generate similar centers in other nations and be a method of uniting smaller institutions for exposure ideas and setting a framework of common understanding and a base for common discussion.

A case in point, Chinese and American military and law enforcement entities do not interact significantly, which is to the great benefit of those who would prefer that solutions not be found because it is to their economic and political advantage. The issue of conscience and the importance of codes of honor found both in the military and law enforcement are a common ground upon which warriors of strong belief in their own nationalities could still implement and more effectively impact the development of our children's world.

We must align international values, and particularly those of the Chinese because of their rising power, with the United States. To worry about whether a Chinese submarine is technologically superior to an American aircraft carrier, to me is secondary to whether or not the Chinese submarine aligns with the American aircraft carrier. If they were in alignment in the first place, fewer crises would occur—a political cold war equivalent would be devastating to economic growth and cultural ethics.

In a world where you have present alliances, your worries are always what happens if those alliances change and how badly your opposition can hurt you. A more careful understanding of the risks for both sides militarily and economically could change outcomes more positively. These are the type issues that a great institute could address.

To bring universities to study concepts of ethics is significant. But to bring groups like the Task Force on Integrity of FIDIC of the International Consulting Engineers that actually battles these type issues on a day-to-day basis and can suggest ISO style of governance impacting corruption, are far more important. Joint efforts of organizations of governance like the Conference Board would be ideal partners for the State Council strategies on transparency. If such ideas originate and have resonance, then governments internationally will have far less pressures.

There are many things politics does not allow government to do. But it takes respect and power to get ideas implemented. Only a few will ever be implemented, so they need to be the critical ones. Intractable issues and great difficulties will create friction, but this in its own way could do a great deal to provide a place that could be like the honey bee to bring ideas and options.

While many think Chinese leadership is very internal and focused, which is true in the sense of style, it is not correct to think that it does fully understand its options and the impact on its future.

China's leaders, particularly the new generation, will learn the lessons of leadership. History has shown that as power grows, it normally nurtures a sense of arrogance. And as global leadership burdens are placed on a rising power, it soon learns that the responsibilities are more than expected and there are true limits on the exercise of influence. This is partially due to the fact that the perception of the country changes as it rises in power and has the ability to affect others. The country is looked at differently as each action is analyzed. The United States has experienced a type of envy from other nations for years. As China expands its interests and influence, it will find the same phenomenon.

How it emerges will set the tone—whether tough or humble, or some balance in between. If it desires bridges, then it will need serious institutions to build understanding. Chairman Mao looked at power as coming from the end of a gun. And Confucius looked at power as being the concept of reciprocity. The future China is yet to be determined. If there is a negative in strength, the negative is potentially in how it is used or perceived to be used.

Other countries will react more positively to a World Harmonious Society concept if there is a greater level of trust. But if the nature of relationships changes, they will always be skeptical about how vulnerable they will be. Institutions that discuss and build solutions jointly can do well for both sides. The more people understand each other, the more their critical temperament is adjusted.

Regardless of whether or not China focuses on such a concept, there are many people who recognize cultural decline and its effect on civilization. Terrorism and corruption are two major results if not building a positive direction. Coordination is extremely necessary in times like these. China just expanded their resources to build the world's fastest supercomputer. It may be that China has the ability because of its structure to expend the resources and power necessary to create a "supercomputer" of equivalent cultural conscience in a Library of Conscience and the respected institutes. But to work with them, the West may have to create a supercomputer in a different way, unifying many smaller computers of conscience. Hopefully, there are institutions that would work with a simplified concept of goals and effort. What this entails is that an agreement is generally reached on the concepts to be taught with understanding why. Those that wish to, join letting the others go their own way in trying to find a better method.

During a delegation to Washington, D. C., one of the senior officials of the State Counsellors wanted to visit with me about some of the concepts in the books. When asked about what would be the best things to see in Washington, I suggested he join me for a special tour of the Holocaust Museum. While viewing the Darfur Exhibit we discussed China's negative press coverage because of its development of resources there and the indirect support that gave.

The Counsellor listened thoughtfully to all that was said and noted that China in no way supported genocide. He did not feel helping a country develop its resources should be read that way. He added that if that was true, the United States could be considered supporting of Venezuela's government policies since it buys its oil and allows its sale in the U.S. That is not necessarily the case, so conclusions must be based on fact not supposition.

The reality is that China strongly opposes genocide because of many of the problems of World War II and the Japanese occupation. In Shanghai, China helped rescue many thousands of Jews during the time of the Holocaust by giving them refuge. There were museums similar to this in China that might be possible partners with the Holocaust Museum. We all ultimately agreed that fighting genocide is important and seeing results make for sensitivity. But that shows the negatives. The prevention of genocide and much evil creates a culture of conscience that would automatically prevent it.

Too many American ethical efforts are theory with a significant pride of ownership and a detailed specialization. They do not address the broad crisis of cultural ethics and how it is taught with the values passed down. In America, the family was that core but today only half of American families actually have the two-parent structure that parallels the past. That makes it even more important for outside institutions to do their part in helping develop conscience where the benefit of a strong family culture is not present.

Why you do what you do matters in the judgment of others. It is not so much that you need a final arbitration of exact rules—in fact that might hurt. You must have proper hearts and minds that overcome the handshake and smile of image.

We need to find that same unanimity in how we sell, develop, and organize our private charity and nonprofits. It is not just how much money we make, but how we give it to create dignity and desire. An ethics movement that looks less at its individualized efforts and more at how it can tie those efforts into society will accomplish a great deal more. The benefit is that the vast majority of people working on ethics and governance do so because of a belief in the system. This gives a greater vantage point for seeing this level of trust and dedication to building a network.

Whether it is a great university, a series of universities, or a private institution that eventually becomes the core to unify these smaller entities into a "supercomputer" equivalent of whatever focus, its goal will have to be the inclusion of outsiders for a vision of how to promote the concept of conscience. It needs to not be a concept of "invented here" with a self-motivation. It will only work effectively if it conveys image and trust as well as a transformational confidence building governance system to unify for the greater good rather than just joining together to enhance personal benefit. In the American system this might be the formation of a foundation to support these principles that could work with foundations in other countries promoting the same principles.

THE IMPORTANCE OF THE CONCEPT OF MARKETS

A final concept that I think is equally important in the West, and eventually in the East, is the concept of markets. Throughout all of my life I have tried to work from the nonprofit sector because I felt it had more nobility than doing it for private gain. I have found that the limitations involved make it difficult. The constant effort to raise money and the constant competition of other good causes drains the forward momentum.

A commercial market can well be developed in home schooling, additional education, and corporate training to strengthen them for long-range stability and better governance. Recent polls show the greatest concerns of Americans focus on the decline of our values and concern for children. It may also be the best way to counter the market economy displacing values to become the market culture society. It battles from within. There is a growing hollowness of life and its purpose that aches to be filled. For-profit ventures may well be the vehicle by which much of the research of the "supercomputers" can be distributed as good ideas are at a premium. The point is that libraries, institutes, or systems must be built as building blocks for each other. They begin with a set of ideas, but make sure those ideas are broadened by the next level of thought in providing the questions to be moved forward. Too often seminars end with a good feeling but little real impact. What matters are continued study, development, and evolution with a contribution of many parties to bring about reality concepts that build systems.

A core study might be in China partnering to bring their most prioritized materials on their vision to a location in the West for exchange. The Confucian Institutes cover language and culture, the University exchanges are often individuals, and only a few high level exchanges begin to reach key policy groups at the Central Party School and high levels of the State Council. China needs and wants to be more understood by the West and vice versa. But there are so many books and agendas, and so little framework developing the full conceptual minds that much is overwhelming and in-effective. It is why prioritization was such a significant part of the Triangles.

When I presented my books to the Cousellors of the State Council, they gave me a collection of the Great Books of Chinese history. For *Instilling Values in Transcending Generations* the Central Party School shared with me critical works that explained the concepts of the evolution of the "Harmonious Society." The next stage ought to be a Center in China and in the West that made this sharing of common understanding more accurate, more focused on need, and open to expansion. When I say a library, I think the Great Books of the West and China are a worthwhile place to start, but the right scholars working together is where the magic could begin.

If these critical items are developed, there will always be a commercial market for them in all countries. The Internet will be a prime driver of this effort as it finds its own problems with credibility. People will seek that which gives them the mental satisfaction that maintains their health and allows them to look at a stressful life more appropriately. Even if nonprofits bring forth the right items, the markets will implement them if they fit the right needs. So the key is to remember the commercialization of ideas to use the power of markets.

Our markets today, at least in media, seem to be more the humiliation of people and the concept of celebrity rather than the advancement of individual respect and dignity. As crisis comes, the importance of these ideals will grow, and there is a substantial market if there is credibility. People will not want their children hardened by the principles of many reality shows when they realize the effort of a vacuum of corresponding positive values.

Those that sell positive values may well want to make a dollar, but if those that buy look carefully at the credibility of where the ideas originate and the history of the motivations of those involved, it will be a beneficial honeybee concept in having these ideas distributed. This is the ultimate goal of ethics, a sensitivity created to share common goals. How systems develop will depend on the times, but the fact that something has to be a catalyst to bring the right ideas forward and show that the value of the Common Good and the Golden Rule is unquestioned.

We are often told that concepts are dreams, but dreams matter in creation. Victor Hugo noted, "There is nothing like a dream to create the future." Dreams are ideas, and it is very hard to know the ultimate impact of ideas. Mother used to always use the old saying, "You can count the seeds in a fruit, but not the fruit trees in a seed." Unless you try concepts, little changes—so if you want positive change, you need to build a laboratory and an incubator for such ideas.

A GLOBAL CONSCIENCE FORUM

To explain, challenge, strengthen, and bridge the thoughts of such a catalyst of conscience as envisioned in the "library," there would need to be a forum. I have always been amazed at the energy the World Economic Forum has given to business and the many other forums, similar to the Lyceum, to thoughtful discussion of policy. Nearly all get their strength and support from the interrelationship of those attending. Where the Language of Conscience Center will have forums for discussion of issues, any real impact comes from the economic thrust that would come from searching for governance and ethics within worldwide business and how to unify relationships based on trust and deserved respect. By bringing together people, particularly those that need to meet, you serve a need that allows trade internationally, builds bridges, and creates a culture of conscience within those desiring to be a part. The higher the level of those involved, the greater the momentum.

The place it is most needed is the Pacific Rim where much of the world economic activity will expand—the United States and Canada, Mexico and Latin America, and Asia with China as the major player as its economy becomes the largest in the world. The ideas have to be developed, but there must be a way for them to be known and spread. These are the current three legs of the stool that could support the effort with balance between them.

The private sector is a proper vehicle because companies, individuals, and even cultures make their choices more voluntarily which is key for a conscience-based effort. Such an organization would have to rely on peer standards and broad influence beyond individuals or institutions but could grow into a mighty tree from a small seed in the world of today and eventually could truly be international and help shape global culture.

THOUGHTS ON NATIONAL DESTINY

In the modern world, one of the great uncertainties interjected internationally is the role that America will play moving forward and whether China, and eventually other countries, move into shared leadership positions. That is likely with the leveling of the world, but America still has a very dominant position with the exception of its fiscal position and economic deleveraging. In many ways America seems to be leaving the concepts that it invented and exported in free trade, free markets, and individualism as expressed by individual responsibility. Yes, they have had a very significant effect in creating an increasingly level worldwide economic playing field, but because of the current economic situation they are losing support from within. Because of the impact of the global crash related to America's economic system, there is increasing suspicion internationally.

What America originally believed was that free trade and open markets gave them an advantage because our system had meritocracy that gave us a competitive advantage. What we are now losing is our self-confidence both in our system and our moral leadership worldwide. That will be a costly retreat for our children. We must husband resources to help unburden their generation, but we must not deprive them of the engines of opportunity and thereby meritocracy.

In recent times I have argued abroad profusely that it is not the market system that failed, it was the cultural system within the market that drove it to excesses of greed, lack of responsibility, fraud, and most of all, a lack of conscience. America's problem will be how the coming generations address these challenges. I am amazed at the French riots, often with a great number of young people who took to the streets when the French government decided to move the retirement age from 60 to 62. Great Britain is taking a very different approach to its government's response to drastic cuts to the government budget. They also have had riots. In Greece riots protected the austerity of cuts without realizing without the cuts in benefits there would be no loans to pay any benefits. A way of thinking to understand options is essential. The outcome of these battles is as much cultural issues as economic since they are in part the defense of a way of life in these countries. In each case you are dealing with economic reality, some in denial and in the others a beginning appreciation for it.

Europe is becoming the classic example of how systems have to be changed to increase entrepreneurship and competitiveness so that private-sector jobs can replace unsustainable government spending. Asia understands this. The rising generations in India and China are not worried about how much time off they can have, but how much time they can spend to become more competitive. These are concepts that will become increasingly clear in the next decade but require a consistency of thought in an ultimate strategy rather than two sides alternating on shorter-term issues.

I think Ronald Reagan explained this issue best in 1964 when he noted:

> *You and I are told we must choose between a left and right, but I suggest there is no such thing as a left or right. There is only an up or down. Up to man's age-old dream—the maximum of individual freedom consistent with order—or down to the ant heap of totalitarianism. Regardless of their sincerity or their humanitarian motives, those who would sacrifice freedom for security have embarked on this downward path. Plutarch warned, 'The real destroyer of the liberties of the people is he who spreads among them bounties, donations, and benefits.'*

We can give government the power to discipline, but how much power we give them through regulation and control directly affects our economics, opportunities, and freedom within our culture. We determine our destiny, and if we do not take responsibility for it in shaping the great ideas under which we live, then we face the consequences. My generation has a mixed record—

your generations have your own era to live. I do not expect you to spend your lives in politics, but I hope you follow the family obligation of striving to be uncommon men and women to help make a difference. America will have a difficult decade as it brings balance to its finances, adjusts to its necessary sacrifices, and rediscovers what is truly important in life. I have the faith that its core values will reemerge in crises. You can design a future better than the past as the shift from consumption to production reinforces individual responsibility. These thoughts from the past show societies have been here many times before. How a society thinks is the key.

THINKING FROM THE EAST

Wisdom is recognizing what you know and what you don't.

—Confucius

By three methods we may learn wisdom: First, by reflection, which is noblest; Second, by imitation, which is easiest; And third by experience, which is the bitterest."

—Confucius

He, who learns but does not think, is lost! He who thinks but does not learn is in great danger.

—Confucius

When it is obvious that the goals cannot be reached, don't adjust the goals, adjust the action steps.

—Confucius

Meditation brings wisdom; lack of meditation leaves ignorance. Know well what leads you forward and what holds you back.

—Buddha

Words have the power to both destroy and heal. When words are both true and kind, they can change our world.

—Buddha

THINKING FROM THE WEST

We do not inherit the earth from our ancestors, we borrow it from our children.

—Native American Song

Science is organized knowledge. Wisdom is organized life.

—Immanuel Kant

I count him braver who overcomes his desires than he who conquers his enemies; For the hardest victory is over self.

—Aristotle

The function of wisdom is to discriminate between good and evil.

—Cicero

Knowledge comes, but wisdom lingers. It may not be difficult to store up in the mind a vast quantity of facts within a comparatively short time, but the ability to form judgments requires the severe discipline of hard work and tempering heat of experience and maturity.

—Calvin Coolidge

The price of greatness is responsibility.

—Sir Winston Churchill

Culture, more than rulebooks, determines how an organization behaves.

—Warren Buffett
Chairman and CEO
Berkshire Hathaway, Inc.

You cannot escape the responsibility of tomorrow by evading it today.

—Abraham Lincoln

X | Conclusion: Live an Enlightened Life as a Person with Honor

This is the advice that I can give you children and grandchildren or fellow believers in the idealism of honor. It is a lifestyle that you have to choose, and people are really only educated in it when they wish to enlighten themselves and take the time to learn. There are many that will challenge you because they have a different mindset, but do not let that criticism bother you. They simply do not understand the world the way that you will learn to and quite likely have not thought of it in the necessary contextual sense.

Political systems create dependency or opportunity depending on the economic model they allow, but people's culture ultimately determines their law and government. That is what you must always focus upon, as you become a part of the solution. To not be involved is to abdicate your and your children's futures to others. To magnify your impact, you have to become a leader. And you do that primarily by gaining the respect of others. So the life you live, as Karma would suggest, is what you create for yourself.

There is no great plan that can be put together for America or the world that is able to address all issues. Change is dramatic and rapid, and no one knows exactly where it will go. If you look at their track records, no pundits or economists have been that effective unless they look over time in the natural directions that demographics and issues will force. Observing trends is more like watching a video than a snapshot and gives important insight to direction. What they also teach you is that usually the future is built by changes and adaptations caused by shorter run policies.

The strength of a society is to have the cultural mortar of conscience, integrity, and responsibility that makes it see the long-term moral hazard consequences of short-term actions and address them accordingly. I think it is the best lesson taught by Clio the Goddess of History. The best way to help society is to simply take each of the critical decisions that have to be made and run them by factors of conscience and convenience that are similar to those with which we describe The Language of Conscience:

Character / Humility

Individual Responsibility and Honor

Morality (Concern for others and the future)

Obedience to the Golden Rule / Fairness

Appreciation of the Common Good

Respect for Individual Dignity

Respect for the Rule of Law

Recognition of Obligation

Recognition of Charity / Compassion

The Emotions of Love, Trust, and Faith

While the words are in some ways synonymous, they cumulatively describe a way of life that is less material, more reasoned, and for the most part would be more satisfying.

The Language of Conscience has been replaced slowly but surely with a Language of Convenience, which has a powerful and reactive set of forces that need to be reorganized as well:

Extreme Personal Self-Interest / Greed

Concern Only for the Immediate Materialism

Arrogance / Pursuit of Power

Use of Law for Personal Gain

The Emotions of Envy and Hate

The bottom line is that each generation can only pass on to the next what is important to them and that combined set of values is what affects your future. In America, the trends will be determined by the people themselves. There will be many who will look to relocate to areas of opportunity if the directions are such that they penalize opportunity here. Looking at Europe, particularly England, you have seen in the past great migrations of people to the United States but now you see them moving more to New Zealand and Australia. You see the Chinese study here and go back to China. We must welcome to America the minds that can help us grow and get them to share our values.

Several generations always determine the future of the society. The responsibility is yours—what you do for your children even if those generations preceding you failed in many aspects. America has a tremendous history and culture that still exists and the uniqueness of it is that it can right itself when it finally realizes its problems. Never underestimate the American people, but also never underestimate their ability to find the wrong path if they do not understand the reality of the situation. This is why education and context matter, and the greatest time you can spend is on efforts that move them forward.

Your generation will be joined with many others throughout the world in this same search. All countries have societies with those of conscience and those of convenience, and the true battle of the world's future may well be between them. Conscience would hopefully prevail unless politics and economics remove conscience as the cultural mortar. Be a bridge builder to them and to the next generation, and you will have addressed your obligation to humanity. If you remember that when your life ends, it is not what you leave, but what ultimately survives you that is the judgment of success of Clio's history, and that will help you to make wiser decisions as to what is truly important in the moment.

ACKNOWLEDGMENTS

My special appreciation goes to Congressman Kevin Brady and his Chief of Staff, Mr. Doug Centilli, for their efforts in preparing the Preface of the book as well as Former House Ways and Means Chairman Bill Archer and his long time associate, Mr. Don Carlson, for their efforts in the preparation of the section on my background.

First and foremost, I need to express my appreciation to Mrs. Judy Stockton for all of the time and effort she has taken to consolidate, edit, and organize the book. Without her assistance it would not have been completed or of the quality. I additionally need to thank Ms. Sylvia Odenwald, Ms. Carol Odenwald, and Ms. Edie Dunavan who have served as editors in the formal organization and review of the book. A special thanks to Ms. Sharon Jasinski who aided in its preparation. Numerous individuals have assisted in the preparation of the book by allowing the inclusion of their materials. Foremost among these was Ambassador Lyndon Olson, Mr. Jamie Martinez and Mr. Isidro Garza of the Cesar Chavez Legacy and Educational Foundation, Mr. Fred Zeidman with his insights on Jewish history, and Mr. Van Hoisington for allowing the inclusion of his materials. My appreciation also has to be extended to the Central Party School of the Communist Party, the Counsellors of the State Council of China for rights to republish materials and for the many efforts they have made in assisting me at bridging Eastern and Western thought and their openness to researching ideas that helped contribute to many of these concepts.

I especially need to thank Suzanne Leonard, Todd Nordstrom, Gordon Pennington, and Peter Strople for all their assistance, advice, and efforts to help perfect the book and its presentation and its conveyance to a more modern technology.

The efforts of Ms. Vivian Lee over many years in the development of the bridges with China and her support have been invaluable to the creation of this book. The assistance of her sister Vicky and her brother Sam is additionally appreciated for the insights they have given to Chinese culture. The insights of my friends, Dr. Felipe Ochoa of Mexico and Mr. Bill Ide of the United States in the sections on governance and ethics are greatly appreciated.

I am also particularly indebted to Bessie Burks, Milton Carroll, and Isidro and Martha Garza for their insights to the significance of personal dignity.

There have been innumerable contributors to the ideas and the thoughts of the thirty-five years during which these concepts and ideas have been generated. Many individuals, scholars, writers, and institutions have helped develop the concepts within and their ideas have blended over time with the general themes. While I have focused on giving credit to the origination of ideas wherever possible, it is important to recognize the catalysts like the Lyceum or many other institutions and organizations that became the melting pots where these ideas are blended into a greater product.

Most of all, I owe an acknowledgement to my parents, my sister and brother-in-law Deanna and Ronald Alfred, my wife Kitty and my children and grandchildren for the life experience that we have all shared and that shaped each of us.

ABOUT THE AUTHOR

THE HONORABLE BILL ARCHER
FORMER CHAIRMAN HOUSE WAYS AND MEANS COMMITTEE

Scott Bennett, the former editorial writer and nationally distributed columnist for *The Dallas Morning News,* described Skipper in terms of the 1953 Isaiah Berlin Essay, "The Hedgehog and the Fox, the Fox knows many things, while the Hedgehog knows but one big thing." He noted that Skipper was a rare creature who combines the best of both and that his one big thing was that conscience must be paramount for a civil society.

This is perhaps the best way to understand Skipper because the essence of his being and philosophies are inherently simple from a background that engrained integrity, compassion, individual responsibility, and driven dedication. They were the values of a small area in central Texas near where the Republic of Texas began with its deep Texan values and where a part of his family and mine were located. The complex side of Skipper is an intellectual capacity that was developed by a unique set of educational achievements and intellectual curiosity that led him to distill the detail of the realities of life in economics, politics, and culture into a set of ideas. These ideas helped originate the Texas Lyceum, which for thirty years has been the leading public policy and leadership training institution of Texas, to chair numerous public policy efforts such as Texans for Quality Education, the legislative efforts of the Texas Arts and Humanities Commission, to play a leading part in the Speaker's Economic Development Commission that helped define government in Texas as a catalyst for the private sector rather than a substitute for it, and most significantly a set of books entitled *The Language of Conscience Evolution.* The thirty-year span of these books shows the history of the evolution of the Texas political, economic and cultural growth of Texas' Third Coast of Thought over the last four decades. I was a panelist at the first Lyceum in 1980, which was unique in that it transcended many of the political divisions in Texas by appealing to a higher calling of stewardship. It was the first of many bridge-building efforts focused not on compromising one's beliefs but creating new ideas that recognize the reality of today's world.

Skipper's understanding of economic policy grew from serving as President of the East Texas Chamber of Commerce, the Texas State Chamber of Commerce, as a member of the Board of the Federal Reserve Bank of Dallas – Houston Branch, the Chairman of the International Trade Committee of the Texas Association of Business and in numerous other economic policy positions. His personal history as the President and Chairman of Brenham Bancshares, and as President and Chairman of Dippel Venture Capital Corporation gave him significant insight to economics particularly for the job creation problems of small business and the impact of debt on customers. He has a driving desire for deeper wisdom and knowledge, which is indicated by his holding a law degree with admission to a number of courts, a securities license, an insurance license, and a real estate license, largely acquired to know the fields.

He has spent significant time studying health care as a member of the Board of Directors and Chairman of the Finance Committee and previously the Strategic Planning Committee, of HCSC (Blue Cross Texas, Illinois, New Mexico, and Oklahoma), which is the largest non-investor owned health insurance company.

In the realm of politics, he served as an advisor to a great many Texas political leaders of both parties over the last years and supported both Democrats and Republicans, having been the Vice Chairman of Independents for both Governor Bill Clements and Senator Phil Gramm during the time Texas transitioned from a Democratic state to a Republican one. He served as an advisor to Democratic and Republican Speakers, and as a member of Senator Bentsen's Committee of 50.

But his most important contribution has been in the study of culture and the part he has played in developing an appreciation of the distinction between conscience (with its component parts of obligation and compassion) and convenience (with its self-interest and greed).

He has been a staunch defender of national security and defense as a member of the United States Navy who remained in the Reserve to become a Lieutenant Commander and who has for many years, even though a Methodist, served on the Board of Jewish Institute of National Security Affairs, one of the most committed American national defense and anti-terrorism organizations. His ability to bring unique and divergent people together has been acknowledged in many ways. House Speaker Tom Craddick and his predecessor, former Democratic Speaker Pete Laney co-sponsored a Joint Concurrent Resolution of the Texas House and Senate naming him the Prophet of Conscience of Texas in view of the contributions he had made. The Cesar Chavez Educational and Legacy Foundation in creating its Cesar E. Chavez Conscience Builder Award gave its initial presentation to him for his efforts and writings in support of personal dignity and justice.

Skipper has a tremendous appreciation for education and wisdom, which has focused on learning how to think because it determines what you think. His educational background began in the small town of Brenham where he was Valedictorian and Student Body President of Brenham High School. He then attended Blinn Junior College where he was Student Body President and Class President, as well as Salutatorian and continued to the University of Texas where he posted a rare 4.0 average at the University of Texas School of Business graduating as its Valedictorian equivalent with a Delta Sigma Pi Scholarship Key, and then attended the University of Texas School of Law where he received the Baker Botts Outstanding Freshman Law Student Award and graduated a Chancellor before entering the highly select United States Navy Ensign 1955 Program to become a member of the Navy Judge Advocate General's Corp. Education has been a significant part of his life and he greatly appreciates the impact it has on economics. He was recognized as a distinguished alumnus of the Brenham Independent School District, is an inductee of the Blinn College Hall of Honor, and served on the Centennial Commission and Commission of 125, which was composed of graduates of the University of Texas setting the future of that organization. He chaired Texans for Quality Education, Inc., which studied educational reform in Texas and was one of the Leaders of the Texas Commission on the Arts that showed the importance of culture in value creation.

The reason that this background is significant lies in the fact that *The Language of Conscience Evolution* of books are not theory but reality. Conservatism is primarily an appreciation of reality but it has to be adjusted to the times and it has to bring significant support within society in order to bring change. These books chronicle not only Skipper's continuing devotion to the same principles that he had when he ran for Student Body President at the University of Texas in the turbulent times of 1970, but also the evolution of how solutions need to be addressed as the world moves forward. The books have received significant recognition in the Book of the Year competition of *ForeWord Magazine* and the Eric Hoffer Award. Several have the rare Clarion Five-Star Reviews.

But most important of all, and the best way to appreciate the significance of thought, is the fact that *The Language of Conscience* was translated and published by China's Central Party School Press and has been used in presentations to the Counsellors of the State Council of China. When I was Chairman of the House Ways and Means Committee, one of the most significant actions taken was a passage of the Permanent Normalization of Trade Resolution between the United States and China, which prepared the way for its entry into the World Trade Organization. Perhaps no issue was appreciated so significantly as the potential impact of China's entry into the world stage. The Central Party School is the core training institute and think tank of China. It looks in detail at the power and ideas in the world. That these concepts were not only published by their Press, but also in doing so they noted its unique standing as a bridge between China and the West on morality, ethics, and cultural values.

The exchange efforts that have grown from the books are an indication of the commitment of the Chinese to these value-based bridges. In a much challenged world where countries will have to cooperate, the Triangles of The Language of Conscience may well be the mutually agreed orientation of thought. If so, it shows how individual efforts for principle make a difference. I wrote the Preface for *The Language of Conscience* and referred to my personal hero, Sir Thomas More, who recognized that ultimately ideas define men. Skipper's accomplishments are significant, but his importance may indeed rest in the seeds planted with *The Language of Conscience* and the concept of Enlightened Conservatism. They give a method of thought, which brings together opposing parties not for token compromises but transformational agreement origination in an analysis of logical options driven by the Golden Rule. The world is in such difficulty that it must find ways to look at the current situation not in theory but in reality, and find a path by which to proceed. Skipper's books and triangles remove the impediments of pride and self-interest to a degree where it is possible to allow ideas to solve crises. This has always been his focus and defines him better than all else. I salute my friend for his work and his lifelong devotion to the highest of ideals.

About the Author's Way of Thinking

Tom Pauken
Former Reagan Administration Official
Texas Republican State Chairman, 1994-1996

My longtime friend Skipper Dippel often writes that you judge a man by sincerity of handshake and smile while understanding the critical importance of character. Skipper is a man of good character who has devoted a lifetime to the preservation of those values that are the underpinning of a good society. His new book, *The Wisdom of Generations*, continues that quest to preserve and nurture those values that have made America such a great nation.

Skipper is a Conservative in the Edmund Burke mold. While a strong proponent of the free market, he also appreciates that the free market doesn't work without an ethical compass guiding our society, and that the government has a role as an umpire in ensuring that people play by the rules. He understands the importance of individual rights, but also the need for individual responsibility for a civilization to flourish. While economics and politics are important, it is the morality of the culture that is essential to preserve a free society. If the culture becomes coarse, then a society begins to decline and lose its way.

Skipper believes that wisdom is shaped by values applied to knowledge and ultimately is transmitted to the next generation by the family, not the government. He has coined the term "Enlightened Conservatism" to describe his views. Conservatism recognizes the reality of our human existence while enlightenment comes from the thoughtful application of history to that reality.

At a time when we badly need to bring our people together for the good of the country and the future of our children, *The Wisdom of Generations* by Skipper Dippel is an important contribution to building bridges between Americans of different political persuasions. Our present political climate is dominated by talking points, big money, and political consultants whose primary motivation is the gaining of political power. The question becomes: Political power to do what—say what is necessary to get reelected or make the hard choices necessary to get America back on the right track. In the post-Reagan period of American politics, all too often the focus has been on short-term political gain versus the long-term good of the nation. That is why it is so refreshing to have the voice of Skipper Dippel in his latest work yet again making the case for the power of good ideas to change the world for the good. Skipper's father had a conversation with his son as he was dying. I have quoted from that conversation often. Here is one paragraph from that conversation: "One certainty in life is that you are not always on top. There are many people who try to avoid the falls by changing philosophies. These are people of convenience. They're often successful in the short term, while they are on earth. But I have always wondered whether they were successful in the sense of eternity. I feel following conscience is a far better guide."

One other key concern in learning how to think is to realize that our own ambitions and push for excellence help us set goals that truly matter. A friend of mine, former University of Texas Football Coach Fred Akers, often told his athletes to remember, "Seldom, if ever, do we exceed our own expectations." He attributed it to a mentor who probably found it from another, but it is a truth of life. We cannot be more than we wish ourselves to be, so we must envision our future.

Skipper Dippel has consistently been a man of conscience, not a man of convenience. May his voice continue to be heard on these important issues that will determine whether our Constitutional Republic survives or whether our great nation declines and falls as so many other great nations did that came before us.

APPENDIX

FULL ENDORSEMENTS

"Over the next decades, the less developed economies of Latin America and Asia will play a major part in the world's growth, stability, and cultural values. How people do business—the level of integrity and trust will evolve in this environment and will shape the nature of the world. Where you invest, who you trust, how institutions are respected will come from that culture. Mexican leaders in the Task Force for Integrity have led a movement not only in Latin America, but worldwide, for integrity and Tieman Dippel has been their partner. *The Wisdom of Generations* tells their story, not only in Mexico and Latin America, but Asia. It is the defense of family values, integrity, and the necessity of institutions and corporations to adapt higher levels of governance, standards of competence, and responsible compassion if they are to protect market systems and what they can produce."

—Carlos Slim Helu, Honorary Chairman
Carso Group, Mexico City, Mexico

"One of the great challenges we face as a nation is not just in limiting spending to true needs, but making sure that the moral hazard in funding programs that contribute to a decline in individual responsibility and character are fully understood. *The Wisdom of Generations* provides an understanding that those in need are best served by the sustainability of the safety net, and their ultimate protection is from a strong nation that has the economic power of growth with fiscal responsibility, the political will to put the common good as a primary concern, and the cultural strength to recognize that character and responsibility only occur when the national will values character and individual responsibility above the convenience of immediate gratification of wants. When I was a District Judge in Texas, I saw what caused weakness of will in people that lead them to trouble. The same is true of national will, but the problems are hidden in our great bureaucracy. Skipper writes of the great contextual interaction of the personal interests of politics and economics with the values of culture, and every day with the decisions I make I see that interaction on a national scale, and I agree with his conclusion that we will not change the nature of politics or its effects on our economics until we decide culturally what values will govern us. The people rather than the political leaders determine our future by their actions or inactions. *The Wisdom of Generations* helps them understand the issues and challenges that face us as they make their decisions."

—Congressman John R. Carter, 31st District of Texas
House Republican Conference Secretary
House Appropriations Committee

Far too often we forget the power of morality and character to shape destiny. *The Wisdom of Generations* reminds us that character in a people is the ultimate strength of a society that makes it exceptional. For twenty-five years we have followed Skipper's efforts to build bridges within societies and between them, always on behalf of the principles of conscience, justice, and personal dignity. His writings are removed from the common thought of Washington and have a depth that truly understands creating and maintaining power for the right reasons. His views on contextual thinking will increasingly be relevant and perceptive in a world of limited funding and increasing change. Trust, to create intellectual power to solve problems, and the use of economic ties to prevent conflict will become necessities. *The Wisdom of Generations* should be read by anyone who cares about American National Security or wants to teach a child how to succeed in a difficult and increasingly challenging world. The key point taken from *The Wisdom of Generations* is that the cultural values taught to our youth influence our national destiny.

—Tom Neumann, Executive Director
Jewish Institute of National Security Affairs

"Skipper has spent much of his lifetime dedicated to and participating in areas that support American national defense. Perhaps his greatest contribution has been his long-standing argument that political and military security concepts have to be expanded dramatically to include economic security and cultural advocacy. Modern times have shown the economic limitations on our country and its future effect on our military and Homeland Security. The contextual thinking of how to build alliances and more efficiently position resources is now upon us. The bridges built through Skipper's writings on conscience and common cultural values serve as a powerful advocacy of Western values to many of the critical nations of the future such as China and Latin America. But his concept of Enlightened Conservatism may be one of the best ways to reunify the American people through character-based civic responsibility that can sustain necessary compassion. He emphasizes that *how* you think about issues determines *what* you think of them, and whether you think in values or self-interest is critical."

—Representative Michael McCaul, House Homeland Security Committee, Chairman Subcommittee on Investigations and Oversight

"As a former President of the Texas State Chamber of Commerce, banker, and conservative writer, Skipper, may have seemed an odd choice to receive the first Cesar E. Chavez Conscience Builder Award, but as much as the Award defined him for his dedication to personal dignity and justice, he defined the Award and the fact that Cesar was not driven by politics or money, but instead was dedicated to the cultural values of conscience, fairness, and the right to opportunity. While Skipper and Cesar are of different eras, backgrounds, and politics, they are very similar in their willingness to stand on principle and their compassion for others. Skipper's writings on the importance of personal dignity, honor, and the necessity of family values articulate our Hispanic culture, La Causa. While many of us may not agree totally with Skipper's take on all issues, one can attribute these dissimilarities to our distinctly different backgrounds and perspectives. Cesar's legacy was a cause to build, not to destroy, to unite, not to divide, as is Skipper's mission. They are more alike than different. There is much to be learned from his writings on how to create jobs and opportunity and is this not what Cesar stood for? America is better today because of Cesar; America will be a better country because of the effects of Skipper's writings. We will always be friends because we know the depth of each other's motivation for our children's future, and motivation comes from the depths of the heart and mind."

—Dolores Huerta, Co-Founder, United Farm Workers Union

"In *The Wisdom of Generations*—the most recent book in his *Language of Conscience* series—Tieman H. (Skipper) Dippel, Jr. makes the point that personal and family values form the essential medium within which ethical organizations and cultures either grow and are sustained, or wither away.

One hundred years ago, the Better Business Bureau (BBB) movement began. The BBB focused its original efforts on "truth" as a bedrock for retail advertising and marketing. Its founders did not base their efforts on law or regulation, for there was little of either in those early days of marketing. Rather, the founders of the BBB "self-regulation" movement built it on deeply held personal, family, and spiritual values.

As it was in the early days of the BBB, the organizing principles of Skipper's writing rely on his belief that a society of integrity and personal responsibility can foster cultures and institutions built upon mutual obligation. When individuals share common values, peer pressure can exert a powerful influence on personal, institutional, and societal behavior. His books refer to these shared values as "the language of conscience."

Today, more than ever, we need to build a shared, borderless appreciation for the obligations between men and women to deal ethically as these obligations may be difficult or impossible to legally enforce. This is the message of the Language of Conscience—one that is shared by the Better Business Bureau during its Centennial."

—Charles I. Underhill, Former President of the Better Business Bureau of Western New York, retired Senior Vice President and COO of the Council of Better Business Bureaus, Senior Consultant, Council of Better Business Bureaus

"Ancient Greek philosopher Heraclitus of Ephesus wrote that "character is destiny." This concept is clearly evident throughout the evolving writings of Tieman "Skipper" Dippel. I have known and worked with Skipper a very long time. He now has a large brood of grandchildren, yet I remember when his own three children were born. I am an economist by trade, and can best discuss his work in the language of my chosen profession. For instance, Skipper talks of economics as one of three integrated sources of power (politics and culture being the other two). He offers a concept, which he calls "Enlightened Conservatism" as a framework for much of his analysis. While I might give it a different label, there is something quite profound in this framework. Despite all of the current babble about the ninety nine percent and the one percent, as well as the corresponding railing over the supposed evils of the marketplace, there is some inherent nobility and fairness about a capitalistic system.

In the 13th century, Saint Thomas Aquinas, arguably the most respected theologian since the Apostles, wrote instructions for monks on how to establish proper restitution when an economic harm (such as theft or swindling) was at issue. Through this process, he developed a doctrine known as the "Just Price." This idea is virtually identical to what we presently dub the "Long-run Equilibrium Price," which is the basic outcome that unfettered markets produce. Although formulated centuries before trade and exchange of the type we know today governed economies, and in an environment where a good after-life trumped any notions of profit maximization, the "fair price" was determined to be essentially what markets produce.

Having said that, it must also be recognized that markets, while just, are far from perfect. At its core, a market is nothing more than a remarkable mechanism to organize the human response to incentives in an efficient manner without a great deal of effort. It is not a good device for caring for the poor, building infrastructure, assuring universal education, or any other desirable outcomes for which public and private interests are not perfectly aligned. It is in those arenas that the "enlightened" aspect of Skipper's framework must come to the fore. In fact, the "social contract" which lies at the core of Western (and, to a large extent, Eastern) civilization is one of the fundamental tenets emanating from a period that we call, appropriately enough, "The Enlightenment."

In *The Wisdom of Generations,* Skipper fuses these elements with a strong sense of family and community to provide a compelling narrative of the diverse challenges of modern life. I highly recommend this book to you."

—Dr. M. Ray Perryman, President and CEO,
The Perryman Group Institute Distinguished Professor of
Economic Theory and Method,
International Institute for Advanced Studies

"What is truth? What is justice? How do our views of trust, fairness, empathy and integrity shape our lives, our country and our world? In *The Wisdom of Generations,* Tieman Dippel, Jr. continues and advances the tradition of the great thinkers fathered by the ancient Greeks who have sought answers to these questions. In today's interrelated world of disparate cultures, how we address these issues has never been more relevant. The future of mankind shall be determined by how we respond."

—Paul O. Koether, Former Chairman
Pure World, Inc. and Kent Financial Services, Inc.

"Those of us in the Humanities are dedicated to studying the ways in which we human beings endow our life with meaning, especially the complex of values that guides our behavior. Skipper Dippel's thoughtful focus on values as the basis of understanding our own and other cultures not only marks *The Wisdom of Generations* as humanistic in the best sense of the word but also provides direction for those who want to help create a world that is more harmonious, equitably competitive, and perhaps even wiser. This is a profound and profoundly important work."

—Dennis M. Kratz, Dean, School of Arts and Humanities,
University of Texas at Dallas

"Economic growth and the jobs it brings are the critical issues of today and the future. The comparison of the Midwest Industrial Model and the Texas Economic Model are often presented for policy as contrasts. The Language of Conscience Series is a history of that Texas Model by a scribe who played a very active part in its development and has a unique understanding of it. While I do not agree on Skipper's defense of the Right to Work and Free Trade, I see great merit in his view that the strength of the Texas Model is a cultural one based on individual responsibility and governmental accountability, which ultimately drives economic policy. His vision requires an expanding and strong middle class, worker's dignity, strong ethical governance that removes crony capitalism, efficiency in government, and the creation of a competitive environment through education and capital investment to face international competition. That competition will force new management and labor paradigms. Skipper's value-based model may well become the best foundation for a new business model. Skipper may have been the President of the Texas State Chamber of Commerce and many other business organizations, but he understands the culture of labor and what it can provide. Labor can learn a great deal from him. He asks the right questions in a dignified way to bring out the best in people and systems to bring the unity needed for shared sacrifice."

—Dennis Gannon, Former President, Chicago AFLCIO

"Once again in his new book, *The Wisdom of the Generations,* Teiman Dippel has demonstrated that the practice of personal ethics is a key to a successful and well-led life. It is not possible for governments practicing democratic principles, or governments using other forms of governance to succeed without having its main participants operating in an ethical manner. The education of our children at any level, but particularly at the college level, must in some manner impart a sense of ethical behavior into their curriculum. Successful business leaders are well aware that having a reputation for ethical behavior is one of the keys to economic success. *The Wisdom of the Generations* provides strong guidance into how this can be accomplished."

—Dr. Charles R. Matthews, Chancellor Emeritus,
Texas State University System, and Former Chairman,
Texas Railroad Commission

"My Father, John Chase, was one of the first black students at the University of Texas when it integrated its graduate architecture programs in 1950. He left a lifetime of great physical structures, but his core effort was to serve others, and he was a leader of organizations like the University of Texas Ex-Students Association and innumerable public efforts to improve minority treatment, often through the belief you could do much more from the inside than from the outside.

Skipper and my parents became friends through the University of Texas, and he often asked Skipper to come to Houston when Skipper was President of the East Texas Chamber of Commerce to speak to minority groups from Rotary clubs to Texas Southern organizations. Skipper had my father's respect because he defined and promoted individual dignity at difficult times. They were alike in that both defended their economic and political perspectives, which differed, but came together on honor, family values, and dignity. The minority community has welcomed Skipper over the years because he opened opportunities like the Texas Lyceum, supported economic and educational opportunities for minorities, and pushed for financial literacy and individual responsibility. Even those that disagree with him respect his integrity, honor, and intelligence. When a legacy endowment was created for my father at the University of Texas and it needed several sponsors, my father chose Skipper to be one of the signatories. He and I have been lifelong friends, and I would recommend *The Wisdom of Generations* to all families who want their children not only to be successful, but to have a value-based satisfying life."

—Tony Chase, CEO, Chase-Source LP

"I first met Skipper when we both served on the Board of Directors of the Houston Branch of the Federal Reserve Bank of Dallas. I quickly realized that he was a conservative banker who had little in common with my liberal background. However, shortly thereafter, and increasingly over the last twenty years that I have known him, I found that we have a great deal in common, especially when it comes to values and particularly our respect for an individual's dignity. Skipper is a bridge builder between differing interests of people and business.

He is an acknowledged leader and someone whose views are respected not only by those in the board rooms, but also in the public arena because with his depth of knowledge, he often challenges normal ways of thinking. His recognized desire to do the right thing allows him liberties that others seldom grant. Skipper has achieved considerable success and has done so with complete integrity and without any sacrifice of character. He has been a real friend to the minority community. His willingness to risk friendships by honestly expressing what he feels to be right is equally balanced with his ability to truly listen to the views of others.

Skipper has built a sound reputation among his peers and a great deal can be learned from *The Wisdom of Generations*."

**—Milton Carroll, Chairman, CenterPoint Energy, Inc.,
and Chairman, Health Care Service Corporation**

"Hispanics, through music and the arts, which are an expression of the soul, will continue to define our rich culture. Our culture's character is defined by either conscience or convenience. Skipper, "The Texas prophet of conscience," wisely realizes that Hispanics will not allow politicians to identify who we are. *The Wisdom of Generations* eloquently articulates our values—God, family, and serving others."

—Little Joe y la Familia

"I have made numerous official visits to China leading trade delegations as Texas Secretary of State. I have also made visits as a tourist and in my law practice. However, the visits to China with Skipper Dippel and the Texas Lyceum were of an entirely different character because we not only met with high level officials, but we engaged with them on frank and serious discussions of culture, identity and perspective. The Central Party School's decision to publish Skipper's book, *The Language of Conscience*, was the foundation of some of the most remarkable conversations that have probably ever been held between China and the West. Discussions started on common cultural values, and then proceeded to common views of how cultural values lead to economic and political values. Skipper has described China as being like an apartment building where people look at themselves as part of a whole and look at the building security and rules as a benefit because of their long cultural perspective. In the West, we view ourselves more as individual houses with certain legal rights that provide boundaries with others, especially the government. Skipper's careful scholarship of ethics and values, and his analysis of Chinese and Western cultures, has enabled him to provide insight and explanation of the contemporary world in a way that is both startling and comforting at the same time. *The Wisdom of Generations* is a book that illuminates the similarities and differences of East and West in such a way that the opportunities are made manifestly clear. This book is valuable as a new way of thinking through the wisdom of values in the world, and, more importantly, it is a welcome cultural bridge in the modern world and the all-important China-US relationship."

—Geoff Connor, Former Secretary of State of Texas

"The many mansions of the Arts are found not only on the stages of the world. They are all found in the cultivated heart. Nowhere is this more fundamentally realized than in the Arts because that is where thought, practice and discipline are paramount. I have had the great pleasure to know and admire Skipper Dippel for over thirty years, a man of thoughtful intellect and decisive action. He is a consummate supporter of all the Arts and Humanities, down to his fingertips! His optimism, energy, positive attitude and stimulating writing embody the ancient Chinese proverb: 'Always keep a green tree in your heart – for one day, a singing bird will come.' This is the inspiration of the truly gifted! We are so fortunate to have Skipper's voice to hear and read."

**—James Dick, Concert Pianist, Founder,
Round Top Festival Institute**

PRIOR WORKS

The Language of Conscience Evolution

The New Legacy

21st CENTURY UPDATE

Tieman H. Dippel, Jr.

The First Book in the Language of Conscience Evolution

The New Legacy

Praised for authenticity and a fresh perspective on progress, Tieman H. Dippel Jr. began a thought process and a series of books that would forever lead our leaders with *The New Legacy*. This book focuses on the importance of family, its value and its applicability in the modern world. Dippel introduces the concept of Enlightened Conservatism—a code of behavior based on individual responsibility. The book, however insightful, avoids the intention of convincing the reader, and instead challenges the reader to ask the right questions to gain critical perspective into their own lives, the political powers that influence, and the economics of the modern world.

"Skipper Dippel has the amazing capacity to re-formulate traditional ideas and values to meet the exigencies of tomorrow. In writing this book, he has given us a map to the future."

—Ann W. Richards, former Governor of Texas

www.WisdomofGenerations.com/Legacy

The Language of Conscience

Using Enlightened Conservatism to Build Cooperative Capital and Character

With Case Studies of Private Sector, Nonprofit Leadership

By: Tieman H. Dippel, Jr.

The Second Book in the Language of Conscience Evolution

The Language of Conscience

Awarded "Book of the Year Finalist" by *Foreword Magazine*, *The Language of Conscience* has been applauded by global institutions, educators and world leaders as a framework for understanding the importance of character and morality in shaping individuals and the futures of nations.

Using case studies from the private sector, nonprofit leadership, politics, and history, Tieman H. Dippel Jr. focuses on character, asking the questions that allow the reader to comprehend the divide between conscience and convenience, and the impact each has and can have on our future.

The Language of Conscience has become a bridge with China on ethics, morality, and cultural values, and amongst their leaders, and institutions is providing insight for future leadership.

"If you believe the purpose of life is to matter—to have made a difference that you lived at all—then you'll treasure the character values and the understanding that comes from them in this insightful book."

—U.S. Congressman, Kevin Brady

www.WisdomofGenerations.com/Conscience

Instilling Values in Transcending Generations

Bringing Harmony to Cultures Through the Power of Conscience

Tieman H. Dippel, Jr.

The Third Book in the Language of Conscience Evolution

Instilling Values in Transcending Generations

Awarded a Clarion Five Star Review and a Book of the Year Award Finalist for both Philosophy and Political Science by *Foreword Magazine, Instilling Values in Transcending Generations* focuses on the power of morality and the need for having a common core of ideas, so that catalysts can be formed to effectively fight in a world dominated by the powers of convenience, corruption, and terrorism.

This book not only spotlights the role personal dignity plays within cultural context and the global spectrum but in it, Tieman H. Dippel Jr. reveals a philosophy of unification through a tool he calls, *The Triangles of Enlightened Conservatism.*

Widely regarded as one of the most important books in shaping our cultural future, *Instilling Values in Transcending Generations* is a hearty book for the hearty-intentioned leader.

"The world of the future must find some common values or civilization will disintegrate. Dippel argues for a culture of responsibility."

—Roger Ream, President, The Fund for American Studies

(. . .*from the Forward*)

TheWisdomofGenerations.com/Values

UNDERSTANDING ENLIGHTENED CONSERVATISM

Granting Others the Same Dignity and Rights You Expect Personally

(OBLIGATIONS OF CONSCIENCE)
CULTURE OF ETHICS (THE GOLDEN RULE)

MEASUREMENT STANDARDS
POLITICS (LEADERSHIP)
PERSONAL DIGNITY

CONSCIENCE
CHARACTER

ENLIGHTENMENT
ECONOMICS (SELF INTEREST)
ANALYSIS
(BASIC CODIFICATION OF COMMON RULES)
(RULE OF LAW)
DISCIPLINE WITHIN SOCIETY

CULTURAL VALUES
CULTURE (MEDIA)
TRENDS
CULTURE OF SERVICE
(NON-PROFIT STRUCTURE DEVELOPMENT)
(COMPASSIONS OF CONSCIENCE)

The Destiny of each generation is judged by how it uses its limited time to advance civilization

The Language of Conscience is not of words but of the heart and is the leveraged catalyst of society to bring the greatest good

Perspective of Character

Goals—To Achieve an Environment of Conscience

Arenas of Power—The Strategic Drivers of Society

Approaches to Understanding—The Methods of Analysis

Measurement Criteria for Enlightened Conservatism

Tieman H. Dippel, Jr.

The Fourth Book in the Language of Conscience Evolution

Understanding Enlightened Conservatism: Granting Others the Same Dignity and Rights You Expect Personally

This much anticipated ebook, was Tieman H. Dippel Jr.'s transitional work which helped organize existing materials and thought from the series in a philosophical and cultural presentation of *Enlightened Conservatism*. The book offers a dialectic for comparison with the Chinese Harmonious Society and refined concepts from the previous books.

The book includes many of the reports and summaries of efforts of groups, committees, and commissions to address key issues over a number of years, including: the work of the study group founding the Texas Economic Development Commission, the efforts and approach of Texans for Quality Education and for the Arts, sections on the Texas Commission on the Arts, and a spotlight on the Texas Cultural Trust. They are presented as a reference more than as a large compiled book. Catalytic efforts, such as the Texas Lyceum, represents a process within the book.

This ebook is must-have reference to the series.

TheWisdomofGenerations.com/Enlightened

ᴛʜᴇ **Essentials** of
The Language
of Conscience

A Summarization and Guide to
The Language of Conscience Series

Building a Modern Decision Matrix on Ethics
to Avoid Moral Hazard in Public Policy and
Create an "Educated Citizen" of Responsibility

Tieman H. Dippel, Jr.

The Fifth Book in the Language of Conscience Evolution

The Essentials of The Language of Conscience: **A Summarization and Guide to The Language of Conscience Evolution**

Awarded the Bronze Award Book of the Year in Philosophy and a finalist in Social Science by *Foreword Magazine*, *The Essentials of The Language of Conscience* focuses not only on providing a guide to the series of thought to date, but it also discussed building a Modern Decision Matrix on Ethics to Avoid Moral Hazard in Public Policy and Create an "Educated Citizen of Responsibility."

In the book, Tieman H. Dippel Jr. discusses *How* you think about something often dictates *What* you think about it. And, this book enables the reader to view a new perspective of their thought processes.

"The greatest need of character-based organizations is an umbrella thought that unifies perspective and is a catalyst for joint efforts. *The Language of Conscience* is the most strategic and powerful book I have seen to accomplish this end."

—Bill Redgate, Founder/Director,
The Center for Values Based Leadership

www.WisdomofGenerations.com/Essentials